MW00982377

PC Magazine Guide to Using Windows 3.1

PC Magazine
Guide to
Using
Windows 3.1

Gus Venditto

Ziff-Davis Press
Emeryville, California

Development Editors	Eric Stone and Gail Todd
Copy Editors	Deborah Craig and David Peal
Technical Reviewer	Richard Ozer
Project Coordinator	Sheila McGill
Proofreader	Pat Mannion
Cover Design	Tom Morgan/Blue Design
Book Design	Laura Lamar/MAX, San Francisco
Technical Illustration	Cherie Plumlee Computer Graphics & Illustration and Sidney Davenport
Word Processing	Howard Blechman and Kim Haglund
Page Layout	Adrian Severynen and Anna L. Marks
Indexer	Ted Laux

This book was produced on a Macintosh IIfx, with the following applications: FrameMaker®, Microsoft® Word, MacLink®*Plus*, Aldus® FreeHand™, Adobe Photoshop™, and Collage Plus™.

Ziff-Davis Press
5903 Christie Avenue
Emeryville, CA 94608

ISBN 1-56276-009-2
Manufactured in the United States of America
10 9 8 7 6 5 4 3 2 1

**To Doe and Jo,
may they
continue to
grow alike.**

CONTENTS AT A GLANCE

Introduction xix

1. A Guided Tour of Windows 1
2. Program Manager 31
3. File Manager 51
4. The Writing Tools 97
5. The Personal Information Tools 135
6. The Graphics Tools: Paintbrush 175
7. Terminal: The Windows Communications Tool 207
8. Saving Time with Recorder 235
9. Customizing Windows with Control Panel and SysEdit 249
10. Running More than One Program 301
11. Sharing Data among Programs 333
12. Controlling the Print Process 355
13. The Sound Tools 379
14. Maximum Performance 391
15. Planning for the Future 415

Appendix A: Troubleshooting 423
Appendix B: DOS Fundamentals for Beginners 427
Appendix C: A Guide to WIN.INI and SYSTEM.INI 432
Glossary 443
Index 455

TABLE OF CONTENTS

Introduction xix

How This Book Will Help xix

Is This Book for You? xix

Chapter by Chapter xx

How to Use This Book xxi

1. A Guided Tour of Windows 1

How to Start Windows 1

Mouse Handling: An Exact Science 1

The Heart of Windows: Boxes Inside of Boxes 3

   Minimizing Windows and Restoring Icons with the Mouse 3

   Minimizing Windows and Restoring Icons with a Menu 5

Moving and Sizing a Window 7

   Stretching One Side of a Window with the Mouse 7

   Stretching Two Sides of a Window with the Mouse 8

   Moving the Whole Window with the Mouse 9

   Moving and Sizing Windows with the Keyboard 9

The Scroll Bars 10

Document Windows versus Application Windows 12

   Active versus Inactive Windows 13

   Arranging Windows inside an Application 14

Running a Program 15

   The Menu Option Bar 15

   Dialog Boxes 17

Calling for Help 21

   The Logic behind Help 22

   The Help Menu Bar 22

   The Help Command Buttons 26

Closing Windows 28

2. Program Manager 31

Program Groups 31

   Working with Program Groups 32

   Running Programs 37

Program Items: Tools That Should Suit You 40

   Adding a Program Item 40

DOS Program Items 41
Deleting Program Items 45

Mixing Items to Form Your Own Groups 45
Moving Items between Groups 45
Copying Items between Groups 45
Creating a New Group 46
The Startup Group 47

Saving Your Changes 48

3. File Manager 51

Navigating through the Directory Windows 52
The Parts of the Directory Window 52
The Selection Cursors 54
Controlling the Directory Window 55
Activating a Selection 56
Working with Directories and Subdirectories 57
Choosing the Starting Directory 58
Working with More Than One Window 59

File Operations 63
Copying and Moving Files 63
Printing, Deleting, and Renaming Files 66
Searching for Lost Files 68
Creating New Directories and Subdirectories 69
Working with Groups of Files 70
File Properties 75

Disk Operations 76
Copy Disk 77
Label Disk 77
Format Disk 77
Network Commands 78

Controlling the File Manager Display 80
The Tree Commands 80
The View Commands 81
Confirmation Options 85
Window Options 87

Running Files from File Manager 88
    Associating Files with Programs 88
    Customizing WINFILE.INI 92
Using File Manager Instead of Program Manager 92

4. The Writing Tools 97

The Basics of Graphical Word Processing 97
Notepad: For Quick and Simple Jobs 98
    Creating a Notepad File 99
    Valid Notepad Files: ASCII Text 100
    Notepad's Tools 101
    Printing in Notepad 105
    Fitting Text in a Window 108
Write: A Full-Featured Graphical Word Processor 110
    Creating Write Documents 110
    Editing in Write 111
    Character Formats 114
    Choosing Fonts 116
    Formatting Paragraphs and Entire Documents 118
    Printing in Write 124
Exchanging Data with Clipboard 127
    Moving Text from Notepad to Write 127
    Inserting Graphics into Write Documents 128
Write Tips 129

5. The Personal Information Tools 135

Calculator 135
    Different Modes, Same Principles 136
    Basic Calculations 137
    Storing Numbers in Memory 140
    The Statistics Box 141
    Programmer's Options 142
    Engineer's Options 144
    Advanced Mathematics 144
    Using Calculator with Other Programs 146
    Keeping Calculator in Memory 147

Calendar 148
  Daily and Monthly Views 148
  Maintaining an Appointment Schedule 150
  Special Days 152
  Alarms and Early Warnings 152
  Printing Daily Appointments 154
  Sharing Calendars on a Network 155
  Loading the Right Calendar Automatically 155
  Creating Separate Icons for Separate Calendars 156
Cardfile 157
  Making a Card List 157
  Card View versus List View 159
  Moving from Card to Card 159
  Finding Information in a Card File 160
  Editing a Card 161
  Merging Cardfiles 164
  File Sharing 164
  Dialing Phone Numbers Automatically 164
  Printing Cardfiles 165
  Linking and Embedding Cardfile Objects 165
Clock 165
  Clock Options 166
A Strategy for Using the Personal Information Tools 167
  A Personal Information Folder 167
  Shortcut Keys 168

6. The Graphics Tools: Paintbrush 175

Paintbrush Basics 175
  Six Essential Steps to Create a Graphic Image 175
  Before Starting a New File 177
  Looking at a Sample File 177
Starting a Drawing 177
  Adjusting Your Workspace 177
  Tracking the Cursor Position 178
  Setting the Drawing Size 178
  Choosing Foreground and Background Colors 180
  Customizing Your Colors 180

The Drawing Tools 181
    Selecting a Tool 181
    Using the Airbrush 183
    The Paint Roller 183
    Freehand Drawing with the Paintbrush 184
    Creating Curved Lines 185
    Using the Straight Line Tool 187
    Making Boxes 187
    The Circle/Ellipse 188
    The Polygons 188
The Text Tool 189
Making Changes and Fixing Mistakes in a Drawing 189
    Using the Erasers to Cover Mistakes and Add Special Effects 190
    Selecting an Area of a Drawing with the Scissors and the Pick 191
    Moving and Duplicating Parts of a Drawing 192
    Creating Special Effects with the Pick Commands 192
    Fixing Mistakes 195
    Previewing and Fine-Tuning with the View Commands 196
Working with Graphic Files from Other Programs 197
    Pasting Images Displayed in Other Windows Programs 198
    Capturing Windows Screens 198
    Viewing Files in Unusual Formats 198
    Opening Graphic Files 199
    Saving Paintbrush Files 201
Converting Graphic Files 202
Printing Paintbrush Files 202

7. Terminal: The Windows Communications Tool 207

Making a Connection 207
    Settings that Establish a Connection 207
    Dialing the Phone 212
    Saving Your Settings 214
Working with On-line Data 214
    Scrolling through Incoming Text 214
    Printing Incoming Text 215
    Sending and Receiving Files 216
    Sharing Data with Other Windows Programs 221

Customizing Terminal 222
    Terminal Preferences 222
    Shortcuts with the Function Keys 226

A Strategy for Terminal Files 230
    Building a Library of Terminal Tools 230

8. Saving Time with Recorder 235

How Recorder Works 235
    Avoid Recording Mouse Movements 236
    When to Use Recorder 236
    Recording a Macro 237
    Playing a Macro 238
    Saving Macros 239
    Stopping a Macro 239
    Editing a Macro's Properties 239
    Recording Mouse Movements 241
    Storing Default Preferences 242
    Loading Programs with Macros 243

Managing Recorder Files 244
    Merging Files 244
    Nesting Macros 244

Keeping Recorder within Reach 245
    Loading Recorder at Startup 245
    Creating Unique Icons for Recorder Files 245

9. Customizing Windows with Control Panel and SysEdit 249

The Control Panel 249
    Control Panel's Unique Design 249
    Color 251
    Fonts 259
    TrueType Fonts and No Other 261
    Ports 262
    Mouse 263
    Desktop 265
    Printers 271
    International 276
    Keyboard 280

Date & Time 281
Sound 281
386 Enhanced Mode 284
Networks 288
Editing the INI Files 289
Word Processors and INI Files 289
SysEdit, the System Configuration Editor 290
SYSTEM.INI 292
WIN.INI 294

10. Running More than One Program 301
Making the Right Hardware Choices 301
Two Modes: Standard and 386 Enhanced 302
How Windows Uses RAM 304
Use the Task List to Stay Organized 306
Keep an Eye on Free Memory 308
A Strategy for Avoiding Disk Swapping 309
Running Several Windows Programs 310
Running DOS Programs 311
Program Information Files (PIFs) 311
Creating and Editing PIFs 313
Switching between DOS Programs and Windows Programs 324
Cycling through Open Programs: Alt-Esc 324
Cycling through Message Boards: Alt-Tab 325
Changing Settings of DOS Programs in 386 Mode 325
Switching Quickly from a Window to Full Screen 326
Closing Programs 326
Responding to Freeze-Ups 327
Speeding Up Sluggish DOS Programs 327
Making DOS Program Icons Stand Out 328
Customizing PIFs for a Large Group 328

11. Sharing Data among Programs 333
The Clipboard 333
The Basic Cut and Paste Operation 333
Exchanging Data with DOS Programs 336
The Clipboard Viewer 339

OLE: Object Linking and Embedding 339
    OLE Clients, Servers, and Objects 340
    Embedding Objects 340
    Linking Objects 343
    The Three Paste Commands 345
    The Object Packager 346
Dynamic Data Exchange 349
    Creating DDE Links 350

12. Controlling the Print Process 355

Understanding How Windows Prints 355
    Differences between Printers 355
    Device Independence 356
    Choosing Printer Settings 356
    When You Have More than One Printer 358
Controlling Fonts 359
    Font Characteristics 359
    The Font Dialog Box 360
    How Windows Generates Fonts 361
    How to Get Your Printed Page to Match Your Displayed Page 364
Getting the Most from Your Printer 367
    Choices for Graphics Printing 367
    Displaying Special Characters 368
    Common Mistakes 369
    Some Ways to Get Better Performance 371
Controlling Jobs Sent to the Printer 372
    Print Manager 372
    Dragging Files to the Printer in File Manager 375

13. The Sound Tools 379

What You'll Need 379
The Basic Techniques of Sound Recording 379
Sound Recorder 380
    Playing WAV Files 380
    Sound Controls 381
    Special Effects 382
    Cutting and Mixing Sound 383

Recording Sound 384
Embedding Sound in Other Programs 384
Media Player 386
Media Player Controls 386
Controlling Media Player 387
Two Scales 387

14. Maximum Performance 391

Setting Up Your Machine 391
The Different Types of Memory 391
Choosing between Expanded and Extended Memory 392
Make Sure You're Using High Memory 395
Make Sure a Cache Is Installed 397
Don't Waste Memory in DOS 401
Get More Memory 403
Make Your Swap File Permanent in 386 Enhanced Mode 403
Working Smarter 404
Create Program Groups for the Way You Work 404
Don't Open Program Group Windows If They're Not Needed 404
Let Windows Install DOS Icons 405
Create Icons for Often-Used Files 405
Keep Your Opening Desktop Familiar 406
Use File Manager for Drag-and-Drop Power 408
Reverting to the Original Windows Shell 409
Always Keep a Backup of WIN.INI and SYSTEM.INI 410
Keep More than One Configuration 410
Choose between Super-VGA Resolutions 411
Stay Current on Windows News 412
Secret WIN.INI Commands to Customize Your Desktop 412
Make Menus Align to the Right 412
Change the Fonts in Program Icons 413

15. Planning for the Future 415

Windows Applications Coming to Market 415
Making Applications Work Together 417
What You'll Need 417
Creating Your Own Windows Programs 418

Extensions Available Today 418
    Multimedia 419
    Pen Computing 420
Beyond the Horizon 422

Appendix A: Troubleshooting 423

Appendix B: DOS Fundamentals for Beginners 427

Appendix C: A Guide to WIN.INI and SYSTEM.INI 432

Glossary 443

Index 455

ACKNOWLEDGMENTS

PC Magazine would be nothing without a spirit that has informed its pages and inspired its writers.

That spirit comes directly from Bill Machrone, and I thank him for sharing it with me.

I also thank Eric Stone for guiding this book from faint outline to finished form.

And Cindy Hudson for having faith in a first-time author.

INTRODUCTION

I HEAR IT ALL THE TIME: "WINDOWS WAS SUPPOSED TO MAKE THINGS EASY." It's usually muttered through clenched teeth by my colleagues at *PC Magazine* as they click on the mouse again and again, peering at a computer display with all the intensity of detectives looking for clues at a crime scene. Far too often, they resolve the problem with a shortcut key that's not found in the Windows manual: the three-fingered reboot.

It's true that Windows was designed to make life easier for millions of PC users. And it can. But there's a paradox.

Your first encounter with Windows can be a liberating, heady experience. Windows puts all of the power of the computer within easy reach. The menu choices are in plain English, the mouse is responsive, and the colorful icons almost beg to be tried. You can begin to use Windows programs immediately.

Yet it's exactly because Windows puts all that power at their fingertips that many people have trouble. They open two, three, and four programs within seconds, and then they can't find them. They click on icons looking for help, but instead they just get more confusion.

Trying out Windows is like visiting a large city for the first time. Your pulse quickens as you take in the new sights. You want to explore but you don't know where to start. You wander from sight to sight for a while, but you spend most of your time lost, learning little.

What you need is a guide.

How This Book Will Help

This book is your guide to Windows 3.1. Its goal is to show you the highlights of the terrain, to take you to the places where the work gets done, and to steer you away from the traps with cautious warnings.

Is This Book for You?

This book is for people who have had some experience with a PC and want to make better use of Windows. It is intended to be a reference and an adviser for people with work to do. It doesn't waste your time showing you how to play games or draw pretty pictures. It's written for people who want to get more from their computer so they can get home earlier.

Even if you're a power user with long experience running Windows programs (like my colleagues at the magazine), I think you'll find dozens of valuable tips here. The table of contents, the section headings, and the index will help you find the clues you need.

If you're like many *PC Magazine* readers, your coworkers and friends may view you as a walking reference, able to answer any computing problem. This book is also intended to help you help them. I've paid special attention to the techniques that can prepare a PC for use by a novice. In fact, there's even a diagram of the menu structure of each program; you'll want to use it when you have to walk someone through a problem over the phone.

Chapter by Chapter

In Chapter 1, I give you an overview of the simple things, like the mouse techniques that can be very simple to master if they're explained correctly, and the concepts behind the most common Windows features, such as dialog boxes and menus. Even if you've used Windows for years, I urge you to skim through this elementary chapter and see if you can't fill in some gaps in your knowledge. (Like any good guidebook, this work is designed to be easy to skim through; I hope you'll browse around and look for ideas just as often as you use it to solve a problem.)

In Chapter 2, I show you the power behind the simple shell program that greets you when you first open Windows: the Program Manager. Building on the concepts learned in Chapter 1, this chapter demonstrates how to run several programs at once and keep track of them effortlessly.

The next few chapters explore the programs that come with Windows, grouping them in a way that's designed to provide insight into their possibilities.

In Chapter 3, you'll see how the File Manager program can be used for basic disk maintenance and a lot more.

Chapter 4 explores not just the word processors that come with Windows—Notepad and Write—but the concepts that are common to any graphical word processor. After reading this chapter, you'll be well on your way to using any word processing program in Windows or in any other graphical environment.

Chapter 5 looks at a group of utilities in the Accessories window (Calendar, Cardfile, Calculator, and Clock), showing how you can use them alone, or integrate them to form a personal-information management system.

In Chapter 6 you'll learn how to use Paintbrush and, in the process, become familiar with the drawing tools that appear in other graphics programs.

Chapter 7 guides you through the process of communicating with other computers and exchanging files.

In Chapter 8, we explore some techniques for reducing the amount of work you do in Windows by building macros with the Recorder program.

The next chapters look at some of the features that work in all Windows programs.

Chapter 9 shows you how to fine-tune Windows to your taste in two ways. First, it explains all of the options available in Control Panel (with special attention to the settings to avoid). Then it shows you how to get under the hood and adjust Windows's settings directly by editing the configuration files WIN.INI and SYSTEM.INI.

In Chapter 10 you'll master the intricacies of running several programs at once—both DOS and Windows programs—with a guide to creating and editing PIFs, the files that control how DOS programs run under Windows.

Chapter 11 focuses on sharing data among programs, using the cut-and-paste technique as well as the new Object Linking and Embedding (OLE) technique that was introduced in version 3.1 of Windows.

Chapter 12 is about printing, with special attention to font selection and other techniques for making your documents look better. Even if you've used Windows for years, I think you'll find the discussion of fonts and typefaces in this chapter to be very valuable.

Chapter 13 covers the sound tools available in Windows 3.1. You'll learn how to record, play, and manipulate sound files with the Sound Recorder and the Media Player.

In Chapter 14, we look at the tricks for making the best use of your PC. There's an explanation of Windows memory management and a checklist for items that are essential to getting maximum performance from Windows.

The last chapter, Chapter 15, looks ahead, helping you create a plan for growing with Windows, and explaining some of the new technologies that will make the time you spend learning Windows pay off for years to come.

Finally, there are a Glossary and three appendices. Appendix A, "Troubleshooting," is designed to help you solve common problems. Appendix B, "DOS Fundamentals for Beginners," will help the newcomer to navigate through the directory structure that DOS and Windows share. Appendix C, "A Guide to WIN.INI and SYSTEM.INI," is a reference to the settings in the WIN.INI and SYSTEM.INI files, which are described in Chapter 9.

How to Use This Book

This book guides you through Windows in the way that makes the most sense. Sometimes that means I'll start a chapter by showing you how to set a seemingly obscure option. If this seems unusual, trust me: This is an option that can undermine your work if you don't set it properly first.

This book is also designed so that you can skim through it. Any time the material is familiar, feel free to jump ahead to a topic that interests you. The book was written to save you time, not to bog you down.

At many points in the book, you'll find step-by-step instructions on using features and options. These are numbered and tell you exactly how to perform a task. They'll also tell you what to expect your PC to show in response. And when there's a common mistake, I point it out so you can avoid it.

Any time you're asked to enter keystrokes using common letter keys, they're printed in bold; keystrokes that involve a PC's control keys (Shift, Del, Alt, Spacebar, Tab) are printed in normal type. So you might see an instruction that says, "Type **win** and press Enter."

At the end of each chapter that demonstrates a specific Windows program, you'll find a diagram of the program's menus. They're reproduced exactly as you'd find them on the Windows menu, and I hope you'll use them any time a friend calls with a Windows question. You don't need to run that program just to see the menu structure; simply refer to the chapter.

And at any point where you find a term with which you're not familiar, check the Glossary.

1

A Guided Tour of Windows

How to Start Windows

Mouse Handling:
An Exact Science

The Heart of Windows:
Boxes Inside of Boxes

Moving and Sizing a
Window

The Scroll Bars

Document Windows
Versus Application
Windows

Running a Program

Calling for Help

Closing Windows

THE BEST WAY TO MASTER WINDOWS IS TO EXPERIMENT WITH IT. YOU'LL never feel comfortable with the program until you feel at home with the mouse and the mouse tools that are at the heart of Windows. In this chapter, you'll acquire these skills while trying out some of Windows's basic modules, including the Program Manager and the Help system. Most importantly, you'll become familiar with how Windows manages the screen and with the concepts behind the Windows desktop.

How to Start Windows

To start Windows, get to the DOS prompt, usually C:>, type **WIN** and press Enter. If this fails to start Windows and you see the message "Bad Command or File Name," you're not in the correct directory. Try changing to the Windows directory before entering **WIN**. If you're still having trouble, see Appendix A, "Troubleshooting." If you don't know how to get to the DOS prompt, see Appendix C, "DOS Fundamentals for Beginners."

As Windows takes a few moments to start, you'll see a brief title screen and then your screen will display an arrow and a box labeled Program Manager, as shown in Figure 1.1. This box is "command central" for Windows. It's a program whose sole purpose is to be a platform from which you can see all of the other programs that you can run from Windows.

Inside the Program Manager window is another window, titled Main, and several small icons. These represent executable programs and will be covered in depth in Chapter 2.

If your display looks different from Figure 1.1, it's probably because someone has already made changes. There might be several windows open, or more icons displayed than appear in the figure. These changes won't affect Windows performance or the principles that you will learn in this chapter. In fact, after reading this chapter and Chapter 2, you'll have the knowledge needed to make your opening screen appear the way you want it to.

Mouse Handling: An Exact Science

If you've never used a mouse before, half of the effort you expend to learn Windows will be in mastering the mouse. The first thing to know is that only one mouse button, the left one, is used for most work in Windows. Some programs use the right button (or even two other buttons, if you have a three-button mouse), but only for special commands. This book emphasizes the distinction on the rare occasions where the second button is used.

Figure 1.1
The Program
Manager window is
command central
for Windows; it's
the first program
you see after
installing Windows.
Each of the
pictures along the
bottom of the
Program Manager
window is an icon
that represents a
group of programs.

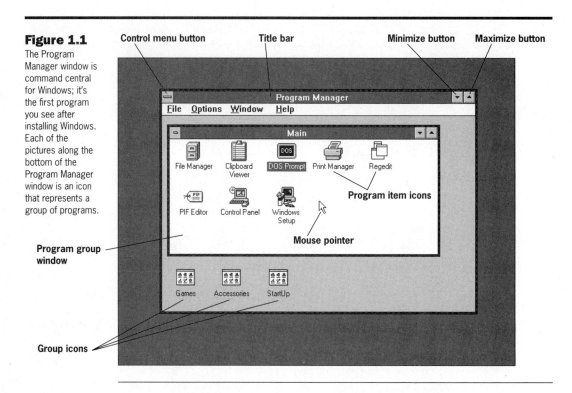

First, you need to understand the terms used for mouse handling:

Pointer is the arrow on the screen that shows the area now controlled by the mouse. As you slide your mouse across a desk, the pointer moves in that direction across the screen.

Click means to quickly press and release the mouse button. It usually has the same effect as pressing Enter.

Double-click means to press and release the mouse button twice in rapid succession.

Drag means to press and hold down the left mouse button, and then move the pointer. Dragging usually means carrying an object across the screen to a new location. When you've dragged your object to the correct spot, release the button. The object remains in its new location and your pointer is available for the next assignment.

If the pointer doesn't seem to move in the right direction, you may need to use a better surface. Most mice use a rubber ball that needs good traction; a highly polished desk can present a problem. The mouse pads sold in computer stores are usually the best solution; newspapers and cardboard work, too.

If you have an optical mouse, you must use the pad that came with the mouse because the mouse needs to read information from the pad in order to position the pointer in the right location.

If you want to make the right rather than the left mouse button the active one, see the section in Chapter 9 titled "Left-Handed Relief for Mouse-Clicking."

The Heart of Windows: Boxes Inside of Boxes

The central idea behind using Microsoft Windows is that you can manage your work better by keeping it inside a box—called a window—that you can control quickly and easily. Everything you see on the screen is called the *desktop*, and the windows are the parts of the desktop where work is done.

A window can take one of three forms:

- It can be only a part of the screen, as is Program Manager when you start.

- It can take up the entire screen, in which case it is considered *maximized*.

- It can be reduced to a small picture, called an icon. This kind of window is said to be *minimized*.

The next chapter explores Program Manager in more depth. In this chapter, you use the Program Manager to practice with mouse and keyboard control windows.

Refer to Figure 1.2 as you try each of the screen elements. At this point, it is most important to drop your inhibitions and give the mouse and the window in front of you a good workout. You're not going to work with valuable data, so this is the time to make your mistakes. If you make a mistake and get lost, reboot your system by pressing Ctrl-Alt-Del, reload Windows, and then pick up the session again.

Minimizing Windows and Restoring Icons with the Mouse

Let's start by conquering the worst problem you're likely to encounter: reducing the Program Manager to oblivion. The upper-right corner of the Program Manager window contains two arrows that sit side by side. These are called the Minimize and Maximize buttons.

1. Move your mouse until the pointer covers the left arrow (the one pointing down), the Minimize button. Be sure to pick the two arrows on the upper Program Manager bar rather than those on the Main bar.

Figure 1.2
Each of the labeled
areas represents a
control function for
the appearance of
your screen. Think
of the arrows as
buttons on electric
appliances and the
borders as handles.
Every Windows
program uses these
screen areas in the
same way.

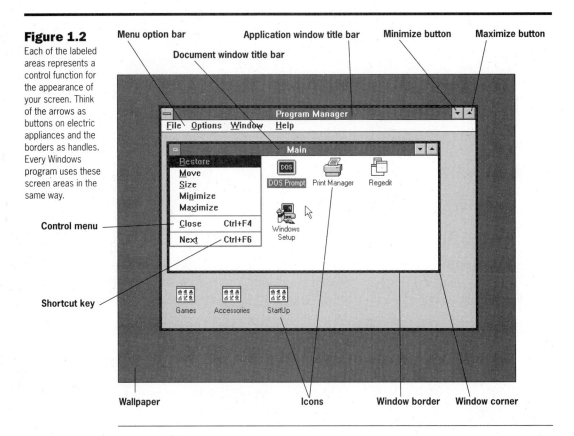

2. Click the left button on your mouse. Your Program Manager window will suddenly disappear. This is a moment that has thrown panic into countless new Windows users. However, don't worry. In the lower-left corner of your screen you'll see a picture of several boxes over the words "Program Manager." You've just reduced your Program Manager window to an icon, saving space on your desktop.

3. Move your mouse until the pointer rests on the Program Manager icon, and then double-click. The Program Manager will instantly return to its earlier status. You've just restored an icon.

There are always at least two ways to accomplish any job in Windows; let's look at the second way to turn Program Manager into an icon and then restore it.

Minimizing Windows and Restoring Icons with a Menu

You can minimize and restore the Program Manager window using the menu system.

1. Move your cursor to the upper-left corner of the screen. The large dash there represents the Control menu for the Program Manager.

2. Click the left mouse button to display a menu directly below the dash (be sure not to double-click this time). This menu gives you control over the appearance of your Program Manager window.

3. Take your hand off the mouse and press the Down Arrow key on your keyboard.

4. Gently press the Down Arrow key a few times and then try holding it down steadily. The different words in the list will be highlighted as your arrow key selects them. Notice how your cursor selects the choices in sequence and then starts at the top again after you reach the bottom. All of the menus in Windows operate in this way.

5. Press the Down Arrow key until you've selected Minimize and then press Enter.

You've just reduced Program Manager to an icon again. The method was different but the result was exactly the same as if you'd used the mouse to double-click the Minimize button.

To restore Program Manager, press the key combination Alt-spacebar or point and click with the mouse. The Control menu will pop up from the Program Manager icon. This time select Restore (either by moving the mouse pointer until it covers the option, or by pressing the Down Arrow key until you've selected the option). You can either press Enter or double-click the mouse and Program Manager will return to its old self.

The Control menu (also called the System menu in some manuals) offers slightly different choices, depending on whether your window is a program or a data file. However, you always use it to control your window's appearance.

To review, here are the three menu commands for controlling a window's size:

- **Minimize** Reduces a window to the status of an icon. The contents of the window remain intact and it still uses up system memory. Nevertheless, it's easier to keep track of a window that's been reduced to an icon, since windows can become hidden behind other windows as you work. The icon for a minimized program appears in the lower-left corner of the screen.

■ **Maximize** Enlarges a window until it fills the entire screen. This command gives you the most workspace in a window, but will obscure everything else on the desktop.

Restore button

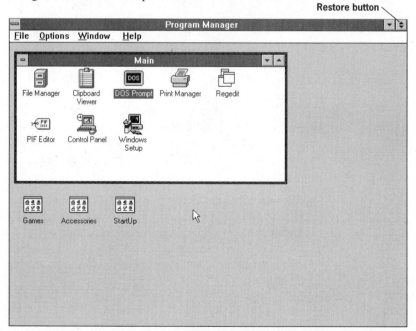

■ **Restore**   Returns the window to its previous size after either Minimize or Maximize has been invoked. To restore the screen, press Alt-spacebar and choose Restore, or click the Restore button (double arrows that appear on maximized windows where the Maximize button is usually found).

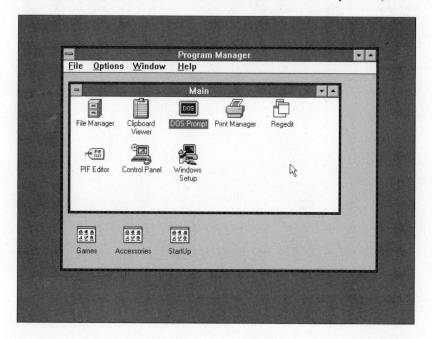

Moving and Sizing a Window

The Control menu includes choices for moving and sizing the window. You can experiment with these menu options, but it's more efficient to move and size windows directly with your mouse, since this way you don't have to open the Control menu.

Stretching One Side of a Window with the Mouse

Like most windows you've encountered, the Program Manager window has thick borders. If you run your mouse pointer slowly over these borders, it becomes a double arrow called a *sizing pointer*, as shown in Figure 1.3.

Place the mouse on the lower border of any window, moving it slowly so that you can see it become a double arrow and then change back to a single arrow as it crosses the border. Since the mouse is very sensitive to its exact position on the screen, you will do well to become familiar with this border zone.

Figure 1.3
When a mouse cursor crosses a window border, the pointer becomes a sizing pointer, indicating that the border can be moved. Vertical sizing pointers appear on top and bottom borders; horizontal sizing pointers appear on side borders; and diagonal sizing pointers appear in corners.

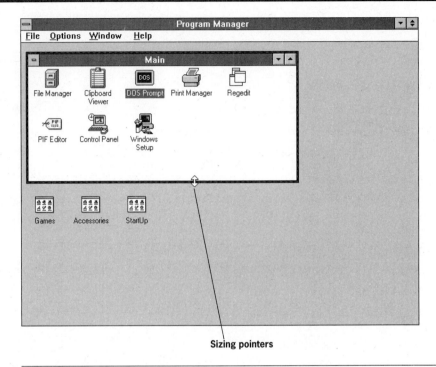

Sizing pointers

Move the mouse until the pointer becomes a sizing pointer (see Figure 1.3), and then press the mouse button and slide the mouse down. The border will move with the mouse, enlarging the window. When you release the mouse button, the border will stay in this new spot and you'll be left with a slightly larger Program Manager window.

This procedure is known as *clicking and dragging*. You'll be using it frequently in Windows to move objects other than window borders, so you may want to practice by trying to stretch all four sides of your Program Manager window. Very few click-and-drag operations are as delicate as moving a window border, so if you master this you'll be in complete control of the mouse.

It's common to miss the border, since the very act of pressing a mouse button may move the mouse out of the border zone. Don't be discouraged; it takes time to develop the hand-eye coordination needed to use a mouse.

Stretching Two Sides of a Window with the Mouse

Notice that the window border is marked off by short lines in the corners. As you move your mouse cursor over this area, it will become a sizing pointer that points diagonally. Position the sizing pointer on the window corner and drag; this time two sides of the window will move with your mouse. Dragging from the corners is the easiest way to dramatically enlarge or reduce a window.

Moving the Whole Window with the Mouse

The *title bar* is the band that runs along the top of the Program Manager window, as well as every other menu in Windows. This bar reports the name of the active program.

1. Move the mouse cursor until it touches any part of this bar. Then press the mouse button; the menu border will change colors. (The default color scheme shows a gray border changing to a lighter gray, but it's possible that the colors on your system will be different.)

2. With the button held down, drag the mouse a small distance in any direction. Notice that the new border moves away as though it were a shadow of the original, while the original border remains.

3. When the shadow is in an acceptable spot, release the mouse button. The original window will relocate to the new spot.

Moving and Sizing Windows with the Keyboard

If you prefer to use the keyboard, the Control menu also has Move and Size commands that let you use the arrow keys to change a window's appearance.

1. Press Alt-spacebar to open the Control menu.

2. Highlight the word Move—either by clicking on it with the mouse or by pressing arrow keys—and then press Enter. A diamond-shaped cross composed of four arrows appears (see Figure 1.4); this cross is called a *move pointer*.

3. Press any of your keyboard's arrow keys. The border will change to a different shade.

4. Press each of the arrow keys, one at a time, and observe how the new border moves a set distance in each direction.

5. Now move your mouse and note that you can use either the mouse or keyboard to move the window.

6. When the shadow-window is in an acceptable spot, press Enter.

You may want to try these steps with the Size command too. The procedures are the same, but you must expand the window in only one direction at a time if you use the arrow keys, while you can stretch two sides if you use the mouse in the window corners.

Figure 1.4

The cursor turns into a diamond-shaped cross when you select the Move or Size command from the Control menu. The move pointer lets you know that Windows is waiting for you to move or size a window with the arrow keys rather than with the mouse.

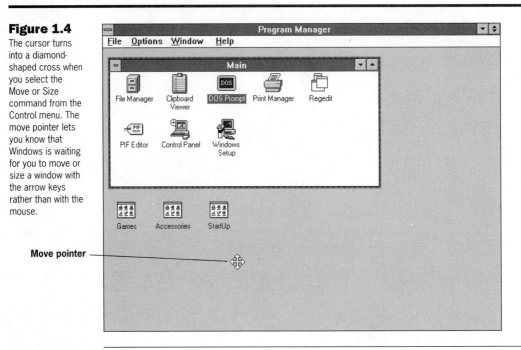

Move pointer

The Scroll Bars

The last set of arrows to master are part of the scroll bars running along the right and bottom edges of the Program Manager window. The *scroll bars* show your location within a window. Since a window can contain much more information than is visible at any time, this feature can be a lifesaver when you're working with large files.

When you first start Windows, every icon inside the Program Manager is visible. You've been changing the shape of this window, and now you'll make it smaller to see how a scroll bar works.

1. Move your mouse cursor to the lower-right corner of the Main window until it becomes a diagonal sizing pointer.

2. Use the mouse to drag the lower-right corner of the window toward the upper-left corner. Keep moving it until you can only see one whole icon and part of a second one; your screen should resemble Figure 1.5.

3. Release the mouse button.

Figure 1.5

When a window becomes too small to show all of the information it contains, you can use the scroll bars to bring everything into view a bit at a time.

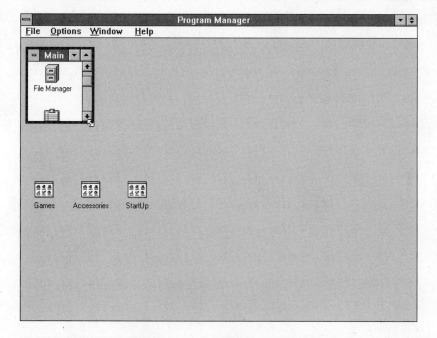

The icons aren't lost, they're simply out of the range of the current window. To bring them into view, click on the right arrow in the scroll bar that runs along the bottom of the window.

Notice that icons move into view from right to left as you press the arrow. At the same time, the white square or scroll box in the scroll bar moves from right to left. The *scroll box* indicates your position in the full document. When you have seen all of the icons, the scroll bar will be at the far right.

This principle works in any Windows screen, even if the program you're using fills the entire screen. Windows will always open a document at the upper-left corner, so your bottom scroll box will always start out in the extreme left and your right scroll box will always start out at the top.

You can also move the scroll box to change your view of the window contents. Try grabbing the bottom scroll box with the mouse and moving it from side to side; this will change your view of the window contents when you release the mouse button. In this small window, you don't have a great distance to travel, but when you work with large word processing documents or spreadsheets in a window, the scroll box will seem like the fastest little vehicle around.

After you click on and move the scroll box, you should see the box's outline move with your mouse. Don't be confused if the box outline disappears.

This simply means that you're moving it so fast that the screen cannot keep up. Move it more slowly and you will see the outline move with your mouse. There are three ways to control the screen display with the scroll bars:

- The **scroll arrows,** when clicked on with the mouse, move the window contents one line horizontally or one character vertically. If you hold down the mouse button, the contents scroll continuously.

- The **scroll box** can move the display dramatically through the entire document if it's dragged with a mouse. It also indicates the position of your current screen relative to the whole document.

- The **scroll bars,** when clicked on with the mouse at any point past the scroll box (that is, to the left or right of the bottom scroll box or above or below the side scroll box), will move the display by one screenful.

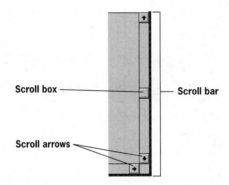

Scroll box ————   —— Scroll bar

Scroll arrows ——

Document Windows versus Application Windows

There are three basic window types: document windows, application windows, and dialog boxes. Dialog boxes are a special class of windows and will be discussed in the section "Dialog Boxes." Document windows and application windows are nearly identical. However, it's worth understanding the subtle differences between them for the times when you have several windows open on your desktop.

- **Application windows**   Contain the workspace for an active program. The name of the application, along with the name of the open file, appears in the center of the title bar above the menu option bar. Everything within this window is controlled by the active program. Your word processor and spreadsheet are examples of applications; smaller programs, like utilities, are also called applications, and their names will appear in the title bar.

■ **Document windows** Operate only inside an application window. They have their own set of scroll bars, borders, and sizing buttons. There can be several document windows inside an application window, and these windows can overlap, but you cannot move a document window outside the borders of its application window. Not every application has document windows; only programs that can juggle more than one file at a time use document windows. For example, Microsoft Excel spreadsheet files have their own document windows and the name of the file appears in each; Notepad files occupy the entire application window; there is no document window when you run Notepad.

The Program Manager is an application window, the Main window inside the Program Manager is a document window, and each of the icons on the bottom of the Program Manager window represents other document windows, even though these icons are used to launch programs.

Active versus Inactive Windows

As soon as you open more than one window, there is potential for confusion; with every additional window, this potential multiplies.

The key to keeping your bearings straight in Windows is to recognize which window is active. Only one window is active at a time, and the menu commands only work on the contents of the active window. To get the menu commands to work on an inactive window, you have to activate it.

The active window is always the one that has had the most recent activity; its title bar is brighter or a different color than the others.

The active window is usually the largest window on screen, and will appear in the foreground, perhaps covering parts of inactive windows. An active window becomes inactive when you open a new window, which then becomes the active window.

A dialog box is not considered an active window. Dialog boxes require immediate input and will cover the active window, but it's more accurate to think of them as extensions of a window.

The easiest way to activate an inactive window is to move the mouse pointer to any spot inside the borders of the window you want to activate and click. If there are so many open windows you can't see all of them, open the Window menu on the program's menu bar (press Alt-W). This menu will show a numbered list of all the open files; you can activate the desired window by typing that number at the keyboard.

If the active window is in a different program, press Alt-Esc. This key combination will move you to the program used last, and you can select the active window in this application by using its Window menu. If there are still more open programs with hidden windows, press Alt-Esc repeatedly until you find the buried window.

Arranging Windows inside an Application

Try to move the Main window outside the Program Manager window; you can't. Document windows can't exist outside of their application's workspace.

Let's see what happens when we open several document windows in the Program Manager.

1. Double-click on the Accessories icon in the lower-left corner of the screen; an Accessories document window will open. Note that its title bar is highlighted and the Main window's title bar becomes white, indicating that the Accessories window is now the active window.

2. Double-click on the Games icon. Note that its window appears on top of the other two and its title bar is highlighted.

3. Select the Window option from the Program Manager menu either by using the mouse or by pressing Alt-W.

4. Select Tile, either by using the mouse or by pressing T. The size of each window changes so that all three can fit on the screen at once. Windows that are adjacent to one another in this arrangement are called *tiled windows*. (The Cascade option, in contrast, arranges the windows so that they overlap—such windows are called *cascading windows*.) Your screen should look like Figure 1.6.

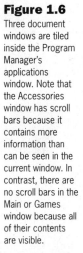

Figure 1.6

Three document windows are tiled inside the Program Manager's applications window. Note that the Accessories window has scroll bars because it contains more information than can be seen in the current window. In contrast, there are no scroll bars in the Main or Games window because all of their contents are visible.

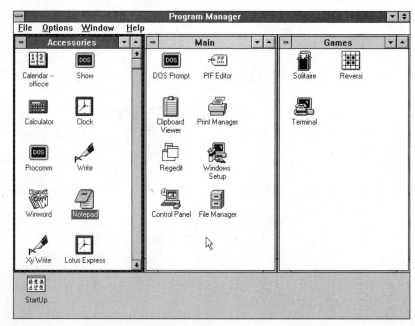

5. Click the mouse in the white area of each window in turn. Notice that when you choose each window as the active window, it has the same allotment of Minimize and Maximize buttons, scroll bars, and Control menu choices.

Running a Program

Now that you've learned how a window works, let's see how to use Windows to run a program.

The Menu Option Bar

Running across the top of every program window is the *menu option bar*—a list of different groupings of functions or program tools for that program. In every menu option bar, the File functions are at the extreme left and Help is at the extreme right.

```
File   Options   Window   Help
```

Using a Menu Option with the Mouse

In this section, you'll try using some of the menu options with the mouse.

1. Move your mouse until the cursor touches the File option.

2. Click the left mouse button once. A menu will drop down.

3. Move the mouse down until your cursor touches the Run option.

4. Click the left mouse button once. The Run window will appear on the screen. This kind of window is called a *dialog box* because it asks a question and expects a response. Dialog boxes pop up when you've selected a function that requires more details before it can be carried out. The thin blinking vertical line (the cursor)at the left end of the long rectangular Command Line box (see Figure 1.7) indicates that input is expected here.

5. Move your mouse and observe that as the mouse pointer enters the Command Line box, it changes from a pointer to a tall bar that resembles the letter "I." This *I-beam pointer* indicates that you're in an area of the screen where the program expects you to type in text from the keyboard.

6. Type the word **CALC** to indicate that you want to use the Calculator program.

7. Move the mouse cursor so it touches the OK button and click. The Calculator program will appear on the screen.

Figure 1.7

The Run dialog box prompts you for the name of a program to run. Notice the small line in the text box below the words Command Line. This line indicates that the program is expecting you to supply the name of the file you want to run.

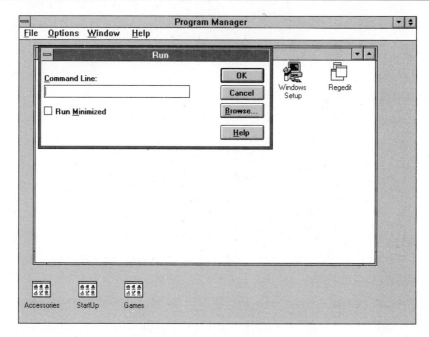

Notice that the Run dialog box disappeared because it had fulfilled its purpose. In addition, the shading in the Main window's borders changed from a dark color to white. This shows that it is no longer active now that the Calculator program is running.

All of the calculator functions are covered in Chapter 5. For now, press the Minimize button to clear the Calculator from the screen.

There are several other ways to load programs in Windows; the next method doesn't use the mouse at all.

Selecting a Menu Option with the Keyboard

Notice that each selection in the menu option bar has one underlined letter. This letter is a *shortcut key* that will help you make your choices with the keyboard. You can press the underlined letter in combination with the Alt key to make that selection.

1. Press Alt-F. The File menu will drop down.

2. Press R to bring up the Run dialog box.

3. Type **CALC** and press Enter. The Calculator will appear.

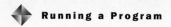

Menu Option Shortcut Keys

If you're a good typist, it's faster to use the keyboard to run a program. But since you can use both the mouse and the keyboard, you should feel free to combine the two methods. You can also press Alt to activate the menu option bar and then use the keyboard's right and left arrow keys to select the desired pull-down menu.

I usually keep my left hand on the keyboard and move my right hand from the keyboard to the mouse. Since it's easy to press Alt-F with the left hand, I'm more likely to use the keyboard to open files. If I have to pause to decide what I'm going to enter, my hand gravitates toward the mouse and I'll use the mouse for my next operation.

Open the File menu again. In this list, the first letters of Open and Run are underlined, but it's the "x" in Exit that is underlined as a shortcut key. The reason for this is that the letter "E" is used in almost every Windows program to select the Edit commands. Using it for Exit as well could cause confusion.

As you become familiar with Windows, you'll find yourself memorizing combinations like Alt-F-O (to open a file), and Alt-F-X (to close a file). You'll never be able to memorize all of the Windows shortcut combinations, but Alt-F-O works in every Windows program that keeps data files, so it will probably become second nature to use this shortcut.

Windows offers many other shortcut combinations for common tasks. Some of these are listed on menus. For instance, if you open the Window menu in Program Manager, you'll see that Cascade has the shortcut combination Shift-F5. Most of the shortcut combinations that don't use the Alt key plus a letter involve function keys.

There's a table which shows all the shortcut keys in each Windows program at the end of the chapter where the program is discussed, but it's not a good idea to set out to memorize them. If you use certain commands repeatedly, you'll find that they become committed to memory without any effort. At this point, you'll be better off learning the principles behind Windows than trying to memorize shortcuts.

There's one other important shortcut key that is not listed on any of the windows: Esc. When you're using the mouse or keyboard, Esc instantly cancels the current operation, closing the pull-down menu or dialog box. You can use the Cancel button if you're in a dialog box, but pressing Esc is quicker than positioning and clicking the mouse.

Dialog Boxes

The dialog box is a special type of window. Even though it looks a lot like the application windows we've just explored, it doesn't give you all of the same tools. For example, you can't stretch the window borders and you won't see Minimize or Maximize buttons.

You'll encounter a dialog box whenever you select a command that is followed by an ellipsis (three dots) on its menu listing.

Making Selections in a Dialog Box

1. Select the Run command from the File menu, using any of the methods in the previous sections.

2. Press the Tab key. Note that the blinking line disappears from the Command Line box and now the Run Minimized (or Maximized) option is highlighted. (Run Maximized and Run Minimized control whether the program appears in a full window or as an icon.)

3. Press the Tab key again. Now the OK key is highlighted instead of Run Minimized.

4. Press Tab once more. Now Cancel is highlighted rather than OK.

5. Hold down the Tab key and watch how each of the six boxes is highlighted and returns to normal very quickly. Each box is being selected in rapid succession.

Try the previous steps with Shift-Tab and you'll see that the four boxes are selected in the reverse order.

You use the Tab key to move around inside of dialog boxes because the arrow keys are needed for editing. Try typing **CALC** into the Command Line box and then editing the word by using the Left Arrow key. Notice that the arrow keys work only to move from selections that don't require typed words. When you're in a box that does require typed input, you must use the arrow keys to edit the words and the Tab key to switch to a new selection box.

Moving the Dialog Box

You may want to move a dialog box because it obscures a part of the screen that you need to see. The simplest method is to move the mouse pointer so that it touches any part of the dialog box's title bar, and then click and drag the box to a new location. If you prefer to use the keyboard, you open the dialog box's Control menu.

1. Select the Run command.

2. Open the Control menu, either by pressing Alt-spacebar or by selecting the Control menu dash with the mouse.

3. Select the Move command; the Control menu will be replaced by the move pointer.

4. Press your keyboard arrow keys and notice how a shadow dialog box moves in the direction in which you point.

5. Move the arrow keys until the shadow dialog box is in the desired location. Now press Enter or click the left mouse button; the dialog box will move into the new location.

Closing the Dialog Box

Try to select other areas of the screen while the dialog box is still open—you won't be able to. If you try to click on a Minimize button or select the File menu, the screen won't change and you'll hear a beep. Windows insists that you respond to the dialog box.

If you realize that you made a mistake when you selected the menu command and you don't want the dialog box to proceed with the command, you have three ways to close the box: You can press Esc, you can select the Cancel button, or you can select Close from the Control menu.

Dialog Boxes That Talk Back

If you give the dialog box the required answer, your program will carry out the requested function and the dialog box will disappear. If the job will take a while, an on-screen hourglass lets you know that Windows is at work.

Sometimes, your response to a dialog box will generate a message box that requires an acknowledgment. For example, if you supply an answer that the program can't understand, you'll see an Application Execution Error message box. This box lets you know that Windows is having a problem with your instructions.

For example, if you had misspelled **CALC** in the previous steps, Windows would not have found the program and would have displayed a message box with the title "Application Execution Error." It would include Windows' best guess as to why it couldn't carry out the error. It didn't know you misspelled the program name so it can't tell you exactly what to do next, but it will provide a suggestion, such as "check to ensure that path and filename are correct."

You can move the message box the same way you move other dialog boxes; in fact, you often need to move the box in order to make best use of the information it conveys, since the message box usually appears in front of the command that provoked it—exactly the information you need to inspect if you're going to correct the situation.

To acknowledge the message and make the message box disappear, you must press either Enter or Esc from the keyboard, or click the OK button with the mouse. In most cases, you'll then want to correct your mistake and try the command again.

Other times, these message boxes seek a confirmation that you want the system to carry out your orders. Some programs allow you to cancel a time-consuming job—like printing a file—this way. Many applications use these dialog boxes when you're quitting the program to ask if you want to save the open file. In such dialog boxes, you'll have the three choices—Yes, No, or Cancel.

Ways to Carry on a Dialog Box Conversation

Dialog boxes pop up in all kinds of situations within Windows, requesting every conceivable type of esoteric information. As a result, you'll encounter many dialog boxes. Every dialog box will contain some of the following elements:

■ **Command buttons** finalize the dialog box action. OK, Cancel, Yes, and No are the most common command buttons. You can use the Tab key to highlight the desired action and then press Enter, or simply click your mouse.

■ **List boxes** appear when your program has many choices for a command, installing a printer, for example. You can use the mouse or arrow keys to move through the list, or you can use the scroll bar that appears to the right of lists too long to fit inside the available space. The best way to move around a long list is to use the PgUp, PgDn, Home, and End keys, or click on the scroll bar arrows.

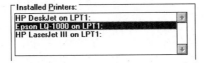

■ **Drop-down list boxes** function like list boxes, but you can only see the first item on the list when the dialog box opens. You select more items either by using the mouse to click on the arrow at the right of the box, or by pressing the Up and Down Arrow keys on your keyboard.

■ **Option buttons** are round buttons that present mutually exclusive options. One of the buttons is always selected as a default when the dialog box opens. You can use a mouse or the Tab key to highlight a different option.

■ **Text boxes** are contained within some dialog boxes. These dialog boxes usually ask for a file name, like the Run command. The mouse pointer becomes an I-beam when you're entering text in one of these boxes. You can use the Backspace and Delete keys to edit text in a text box, and you can use the Left Arrow and Right Arrow keys to help with editing.

Program Filename: [   ]

■ **Check boxes** are square boxes present in some dialog boxes. They offer options that you select either with a mouse or with a shortcut key (remember, the shortcut key is the underlined letter). Sometimes there's just one check box and sometimes there's a list. If the check box is empty, the option is not selected; if there's an X in the box, the option is in effect.

Reserve Shortcut Keys: ☒ Alt+Tab   ☐ Alt+Esc   ☐ Ctrl+Esc
                          ☐ PrtSc   ☒ Alt+PrtSc ☒ Alt+Space

Avoiding Mistakes in a Dialog Box

The design of a dialog box is a mixed blessing: It makes it very easy to make a lot of changes, but sometimes it makes it too easy to choose the wrong option.

Before you leave a dialog box, ensure that all of your desired options have been selected. Since programs always need to start with a default setting, you may not realize how many choices you can make in a dialog box. Just because the cursor is blinking on only one box does not mean that this is the only available choice—any option or check box can be changed.

If your program doesn't operate as expected, reopen the dialog box and try some other options. For example, a typical problem with Windows occurs when you set up the printer. You can almost always fix the problem by changing an option box or check box in the Printer Setup dialog box—there are so many options, it's easy to overlook two or three.

Calling for Help

"Dial" F1 for help. It's easy to remember and it almost always works. You won't get help if you have an open menu or dialog box, and you may encounter a Windows program that doesn't come with help. However, pressing F1 will generally bring up a help window, as shown in Figure 1.8.

If the program you're running does have help, you'll see the choice Help on the menu option bar. You can select this menu choice by clicking your mouse or by pressing the key combination Alt-H. Of course, you can also access help by pressing F1.

After you've asked for help, you'll probably have to work a bit more to find exactly the right information.

Figure 1.8

The Help option available for all Windows programs has the same appearance, but each Windows program has its own text. Every program has an index, or table of contents, that can help you move quickly to individual topics.

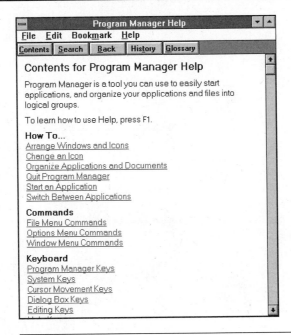

The Logic behind Help

Think of the Help system in Windows as a book. Each Windows program has a chapter within the book, and each of these chapters has its own table of contents. When you call Help in any program for the first time, you'll see the table of contents for the chapter. These chapters are broken down into individual sections, called "topics."

Each topic covered in a Help file is listed in green type. You can use the mouse or the Tab key to select a topic. Once you've selected a topic, either click again or press Enter, and the Help window will display an explanation of the topic.

Definitions are available for some of the terms that appear in the Help topics. These terms appear in green and are underlined with a dotted line. When you click on such a term, a window appears with a definition.

When you've opened a topic, you can use the scroll bars to move ahead or back in the text. But to see other topics, you'll need to use commands on the menu bar or the command buttons that appear at the top of the window.

The Help Menu Bar

The options in the Help program's menu bar enable you to deal with the individual chapters in the Help system. Here's a summary of each.

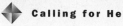
File

The text for each program's Help chapter is stored as its own file in your Windows directory. For example, the help for the Calculator program is stored in a file called CALC.HLP.

You can use the File menu's Open command to look at the help text for any program. With Help open, simply press Alt-F-O, and use the keyboard down arrow key to highlight the file you want, and press Enter. (Note: while these HLP files display text when run in Windows' Help system, the files are not text files that can be opened with a word processor.)

The File menu also has a Print Topic option. If no topic is selected, it will print the index of topics.

Let's put this together into a practical example. Let's say you wanted to print a copy of the help information available for the Calculator program.

1. Press F1; a Help window opens.

2. Press Alt-F-O; the File Open dialog box opens (see Figure 1.9).

Figure 1.9

The Help system's File menu lets you go directly to the information available for any Windows program that comes with a Help system—even if the program is not running at the time.

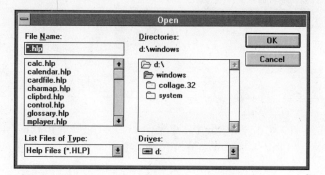

3. Press Tab and then press the Down Arrow key until CALC.HLP is highlighted. (It's highlighted when CALC.HLP appears in the Filename text box and when a bar appears on top of CALC.HLP in the Files list box.)

4. Press Enter or click on the OK button. The Help window's title changes to "Calculator" and the window contains the Calculator Help Index.

5. Select a topic by pressing the Tab key until you've highlighted something you're interested in learning more about. Press Enter, and the window now displays detailed information on that topic.

6. Press Alt-F-P; a message box appears letting you know that the topic has been sent to the printer.

Edit

The Edit menu provides a way to use help topics in another program (the Copy command) or to add your own comments to the topic (the Annotate command).

The Copy command lets you insert the text of any topic into another Windows program. For example, if you followed the example above and opened a topic in the Calculator help system, you can now copy the text in that topic to another program by following these steps:

1. Press Alt-E-C; the Copy dialog box opens (see Figure 1.10). Note that the contents of the Copy dialog box are the same as those that appear on the screen.

Figure 1.10

The Copy command on the Help system's Edit menu lets you insert text from a Help topic into another Windows program.

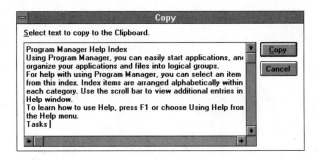

2. Press Alt-C or click on the Copy button; the text in this topic can now be inserted into any active Windows program with the shortcut key Ctrl-Ins.

The Annotate command lets you add a note to a Help topic. It's especially useful if you'd like to help someone who'll be learning on your system or if you'd like to prepare a Help file that you'll copy to someone else's system. (If your office has specific procedures everyone must follow, this is an ideal way to distribute instructions for the tasks.)

Here are the steps you'd take to annotate a Help topic:

1. With a Help topic open, press Alt-E-A; the Annotate dialog box opens (see Figure 1.11).

2. Enter your comments and press Save. The dialog box closes and a green, paper clip-like symbol appears next to the title of the topic.

3. Point the mouse at the paper clip; as the mouse pointer touches the paper clip, the arrow changes to a hand, indicating that you can "grab" it.

Figure 1.11
The Annotate option lets you store notes about any Help topic. The notes will be available whenever the Help topic is called again.

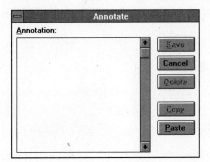

4. Click the mouse and the Annotate dialog box opens, with your comments displayed.

You can use the Paste option in the Annotate dialog box to add the text in a different topic. To use this option, you first need to copy the topic to the Clipboard. (You can also paste in any text that's currently stored in the Clipboard.)

Bookmark

The Help system has many topics, and you may sometimes want to refer back to one. The Bookmark command helps you go right to the topic by storing the topic title on the Bookmark menu.

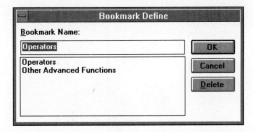

To store a Bookmark:

1. Press Alt-M; the Bookmark menu opens.

2. Select Define; the Bookmark Define dialog box opens. The title of the topic now open appears in the text box.

3. If you'd like to use a different name, type it in. When you're done, press Enter. The Bookmark Define dialog box closes.

4. Press Alt-M to open the Bookmark menu. You'll see this topic listed on the menu. You'll now be able to go right to that topic in the future by entering the number on the menu.

The Help Command Buttons

The command buttons that appear beneath the Help file menu enable you to quickly open a particular topic.

Contents

When you click on the Contents button (or press Alt-C), the index or table of contents for the open Help file will appear. Remember that each program has its own unique Help file and that you can see all of the topics by clicking on the phrases highlighted in green.

Search

The Search command button represents a fast way to find any topic that is listed in the index. Selecting Search brings up a dialog box (see Figure 1.12) that asks for the term you want explained and that lists all the available topics.

Figure 1.12

The Search command lets you look through an alphabetical listing of the topics in any Help file.

```
┌──────────────────────── Search ────────────────────────┐
│ Type a word, or select one from the list.    ┌─────────┐ │
│ Then choose Show Topics.                      │  Close  │ │
│ ┌──────────────────────────────────┐         └─────────┘ │
│ │ advanced functions               │         ┌─────────┐ │
│ └──────────────────────────────────┘         │Show Topics│ │
│ ┌──────────────────────────────────┐▲        └─────────┘ │
│ │ advanced functions               ││                   │
│ │ Advanced Statistical Functions   ││                   │
│ │ average                          ││                   │
│ │ base                             ││                   │
│ │ binary                           ││                   │
│ │ calculation                      │▼                   │
│ └──────────────────────────────────┘                    │
│ Select a topic, then choose Go To.            ┌─────────┐ │
│                                               │  Go To  │ │
│ ┌──────────────────────────────────┐         └─────────┘ │
│ │ Advanced Statistical Functions   │                     │
│ │ Other Advanced Functions         │                     │
│ │                                  │                     │
│ │                                  │                     │
│ └──────────────────────────────────┘                    │
└─────────────────────────────────────────────────────────┘
```

The Search dialog box will go to the topic that seems closest to the one you typed in. Caution: It may not find the right topic. Since it searches alphabetically on the topics that are included in the index, it will stop at the word that's spelled most like the term you're seeking, but it could have nothing to do with the topic you're looking for.

For example, if you're searching in the Calculator help system for an explanation of how the Calculator does addition, you would not find help by typing "addition" in the text box; that will only bring you to "advanced topics." The topic that will come closest to helping you with addition is "calculation," so you'll need to browse through the list of topics and choose "calculation."

To see the desired topic, first you must choose your topic by selecting the Show Topics command button (press Alt-S). Then, click on the Go To command button (or press Alt-G).

Back

When you click on this command button, you'll see the Help topic that you saw most recently. Click again and it will bring up the next most recent topic.

Help keeps a record of every topic you've seen since you started Windows, and Back will track your steps through all of them. For an idea of how many topics you can step back through, choose History (see the next section).

History

This command button opens a dialog box that lists every Help topic you've displayed since you opened Windows. The first time you use Help, the History dialog box will list just the topic you're now looking at. But as you open new topics, each will be recorded.

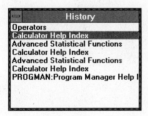

To go immediately to any of these topics, move the cursor until you highlight the desired topic and then press Enter.

Glossary

The Glossary command button opens a list of commonly used words and phrases within Help. Think of it as the dictionary for the Help system. When you use the Glossary, you see a list of terms like "application window" and "dialog box." You can select any of these terms to see a brief definition.

The descriptions you'll find in the Glossary are also available whenever you're using Help. These terms are underlined and if you double-click on the word, a definition will immediately appear.

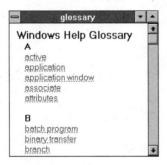

Closing Windows

Double-clicking on any Control menu will close that window, whether it's a dialog box, a data window, or a program window.

You can close every Windows program in one of four ways. You can select Exit from the File menu, you can select Close from the Control menu, you can double-click the Control menu button, or you can press Alt-F4. In each case, the window will disappear, the program's icon will reappear, and the memory used by the program will be freed.

Most Windows programs use data files, and when you close the application a dialog box will query you if you haven't saved your active file. You will always have one of three options: You can save the changes you've made to that file, you can let the current file go unsaved, or you can cancel the Quit procedure.

To leave Windows and return to DOS, you quit the Program Manager by any of the four methods.

CHAPTER

2

Program Manager

Program Groups

Program Items: Tools That Should Suit You

Mixing Items to Form Your Own Groups

Saving Your Changes

MICROSOFT WINDOWS ENABLES YOU TO WORK WITH MORE THAN ONE job at a time. With Windows, you can refer to a list of instructions while creating a spreadsheet, or write a letter to a client while referring to a price list. You can even move text from one application to another; for example, you can insert a spreadsheet price list into a letter.

In Microsoft Windows, there's virtually no limit to the number of files you can have open at once. The only restriction is the amount of memory in your computer. You can open more windows than you can see long before you run out of memory. You can also make a mess out of your screen with just a quick series of mouse clicks—but after you read this chapter, I don't think you will.

The Windows Program Manager helps you keep track of screen windows. It lets you start a program either by clicking on an icon or by typing the program name. It allows you to exit to DOS or move from one active Windows program to another. Finally, it enables you to arrange your files in groups that facilitate your work.

Program Groups

When Windows opens for the first time, the Program Manager's window occupies most of the screen, with the Main program group window inside it. You can identify each screen item by referring to Figure 2.1, a typical Program Manager desktop.

- **Program group windows** are boxes that hold program icons. These windows are represented by icons at the bottom of the Program Manager window if they have been minimized. The grouping of programs should be a logical collection, but you can combine any group of programs to create a group window. Although a program group window holds only icons for executable programs, it's considered a document window inside the Program Manager's application window.

- **Group icons** are rectangular pictures at the bottom of the Program Manager window that have short descriptions below. Their design suggests a file folder that's holding documents. If you click on a group icon once, Control menu will open; if you double-click, it will change to a program group window. Since the group icon is considered a document within the Program Manager, you can move it within the borders of the Program Manager, but not outside. In addition, you cannot place a group icon inside another open group window.

Figure 2.1

A typical Program Manager arrangement. In this window, the PIF Editor program item is selected. Note that the Accessories window has no scroll bar, indicating that all of the program items are visible. However, the Main program group window has scroll bars because some of its icons are hidden.

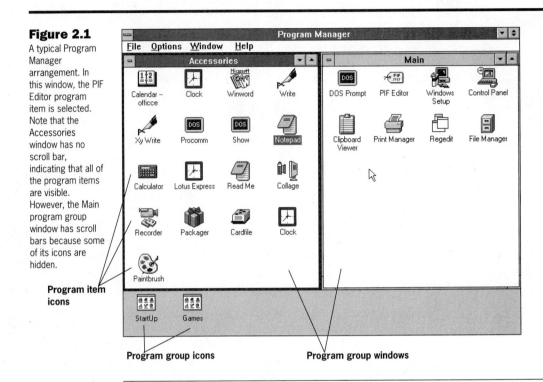

Program item icons

Program group icons   Program group windows

■ **Program items** are icons that represent executable programs and appear only inside the Program Manager's group windows. If you click on a program item once, it is highlighted, at which point you can edit its *properties*. (The properties are the description, program file name, document file name, and icon.) Double-click to activate the underlying program. Since the program item is just an icon and occupies very little disk space, you can create multiple instances of an application's icon, each perhaps dedicated to opening a different document. You can move a program item to a different group window, but you cannot move it outside of a group window.

Working with Program Groups

When Windows is installed, the Program Manager starts off with at least four group windows: Startup, Main, Accessories, and Games. (If you instructed the installation program to set up your disk for other applications, Windows will automatically add group icons for Windows applications and non-Windows applications.) There's nothing permanent about this arrangement; it's simply the way Microsoft started you off. You can add new groups for programs you work with often and remove the icons for program items that you don't use.

Moving from One Group Window to Another

In Chapter 1, you mastered the most basic Program Manager function: starting a program by double-clicking on its icon. To run programs in other groups, you simply double-click the program's icon to open the window, and then double-click the particular program. There are several ways to move among the windows and icons in the Program Manager.

The following exercises assume that you've opened Windows to its initial screen: The Program Manager will show a Main group window and three or more program group icons along the bottom border.

If you need help starting Windows, refer back to Chapter 1. If you do not see the Main window when Windows starts, you should see a Main icon at the bottom of the Program Manager window. To follow these exercises, close the open window by double-clicking on its Minimize button and then double-click the Main icon.

1. Move your mouse until it touches some part of the Accessories icon. Click the left mouse button once. The Accessories icon will be highlighted and a Control menu like the one in Figure 2.2 will pop up.

Figure 2.2
The icons that represent group windows each have their own Control menus. If you click the mouse when the pointer rests on blank space in the Program Manager window, the Control menu will disappear.

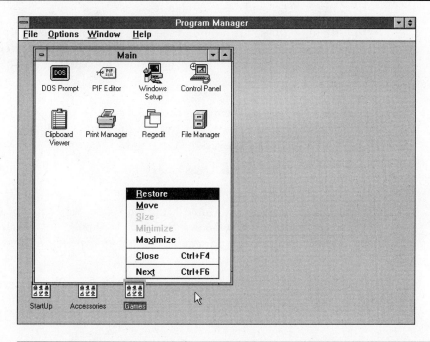

2. Without moving the mouse, click again. The Control menu disappears but the icon is still highlighted.

3. Click the mouse again and the Control menu pops back up; this time, press Esc to remove the menu.

4. Click the mouse yet again. After the Control menu pops up this time, move the mouse away from the icon until it's surrounded by blank space. Click and the Control menu disappears.

This exercise demonstrates how sensitive you must be to the mouse pointer's position. While the icon's Control menu was open, you could have unintentionally activated a different command if you had allowed the mouse pointer to stray. Careful pointing is one of the keys to success with Microsoft Windows.

There are always several keyboard procedures for accomplishing even the most elementary task in Windows, and you can use any combination of these techniques. For example, you can also move from icon to icon without the mouse.

1. Press Ctrl-Tab. The Accessories icon is no longer highlighted, but the next icon is highlighted.

2. Press Ctrl-Tab several times and note how the icons and open windows are selected and deselected in sequence.

It's easy to use the mouse to select an icon when your desktop is neat. When you start using a variety of programs, however, your screen can become cluttered with many open windows and Ctrl-Tab can help you find a hidden window or icon.

Managing Multiple Program Groups

Now that you know how to use some of the Program Manager's tools, it's time to roll up your sleeves and dirty up the desktop.

1. Double-click on the Accessories icon; the Accessories group window will appear.

2. Double-click on the Games icon; the Games window appears, obscuring parts of the other windows. Your screen should look something like Figure 2.3; the precise arrangement will vary depending on how these windows were last arranged.

3. Move the mouse to a blank part of the Main window, an area that isn't covered by another window (make sure the pointer doesn't touch a program icon). Click and the Main window will obscure the Games window.

Figure 2.3
When you have three windows open, some of them will be at least partially covered. In this figure, the Main program group window is partly hidden by the Games window. The Window menu lets you control which windows can be seen.

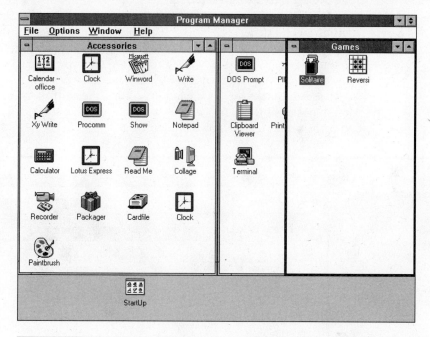

4. Select the Window menu from the Program Manager's menu bar, either by clicking on it with the mouse or by pressing Alt-W.

5. When the Window menu drops down, notice that it has a listing for the three windows and that a check appears next to the Main window. Select Games from the menu (either with the mouse or with the Down Arrow key). The Games window now moves in front of the Main window.

6. Press Ctrl-Tab; the Accessories window is highlighted and the Games window is obscured.

This is a good place to experiment. Notice what happens when you click in a visible window and how the Games window is covered and uncovered if you press the Ctrl-Tab keys repeatedly. Also try changing the size of the Main window to help find the hidden Games window.

It's worth spending some time now to learn how the different windows can hide each other. A common mistake many people make is to open the same file twice because the first file is hidden under a larger window. You might fear you've lost a letter you spent 30 minutes on, when you simply covered it with a different program. The Alt-W and Ctrl-Tab shortcut keys will save you in most cases.

Cascading and Tiling Windows

The Window menu on the Program Manager's menu bar has several tools for putting an end to desktop clutter. The Cascade and Tile selections enable you to size and move windows to rearrange your screen. You can select these options either by pressing Alt-W-C or Alt-W-T, or by clicking on the Window menu bar and selecting Cascade or Tile.

Cascade stacks the open windows so that their title bars are visible. This option positions the active window on the top of the stack and makes all windows the same size, as shown in Figure 2.4.

Figure 2.4

The Cascade option automatically sizes and moves the open windows so you can see each window's title bar and the contents of the window that's currently highlighted.

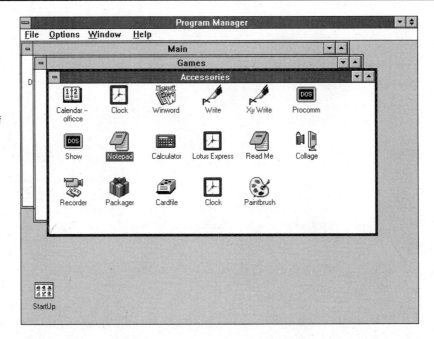

Tile rearranges the windows on the screen so that they each have an equal share of the real estate and are touching. Thus the more windows you tile the smaller each window becomes. The active window gets the spot in the upper-left corner, as shown in Figure 2.5.

First with Cascade selected and then with Tile selected, try using Ctrl-Tab to cycle through the windows. It's a good idea to practice now with just three windows; before long you may find you have six or seven group windows open.

Figure 2.5
The Tile option splits the spreadsheet into sections, one for each open window. The active window is placed in the left or upper-left corner of the screen.

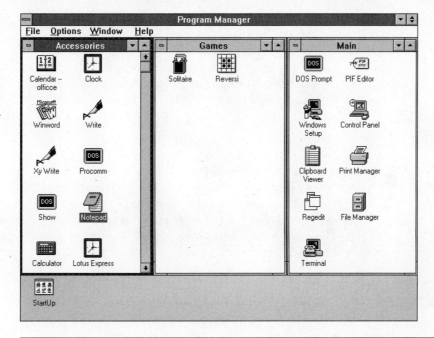

If you find yourself doing lots of window arrangements, you may want to memorize special shortcut keys. Shift-F5 will Cascade the open windows and Shift-F4 will invoke Tile; these commands work from anywhere in Program Manager, except when you're in the middle of a command (for instance, if you have an open dialog box or an open option menu). If you've got a good memory for small details, you may remember these shortcut keys. However, this book does not assume that you've committed any shortcut keys to memory. The menu bars will always be there, and you'll probably find the Alt-W selection much easier to use. I've been using Microsoft Windows for years and have memorized only a few key combinations.

Running Programs

Any icon in a program group window represents an executable program. If you want to run a program that isn't represented by an icon, you can use the File menu's Run command (covered in Chapter 1) as long as you know the name and path of the file. Running a program from its icon just involves double-clicking your mouse. However, finding the program can be a bit more challenging.

Let's see what happens when you start a program from Program Manager.

1. Move your mouse to the Accessories window and double-click on the Notepad icon. The Notepad program opens.

2. Move the mouse to an open area of any other Program Manager window and double-click. The Notepad disappears and the Program Manager windows are visible again.

You didn't close the Notepad, you just hid it. If you resize or minimize the Program Manager screen, the Notepad will still be running.

Finding Lost Programs with the Task List

There are many ways to bring a window back from obscurity. The simplest two methods involve either shrinking the largest window until you can see behind it, or moving the largest window off to the side by dragging its title bar.

There are a few useful shortcut keys that you may want to memorize for these tasks. Table 2.1 lists some key combinations worth remembering.

Table 2.1 **Key Combinations Worth Remembering**

Key Combination	Description
Ctrl-Tab	Moves from one program group to another in Program Manager
Alt-Esc	Moves through every open program in sequence, including icons inside the Program Manager and programs running outside of the Program Manager window. When you select an obscured window, that window moves to the front of the screen. This key combination is useful for uncovering hidden windows
Ctrl-Esc	Opens the Task List dialog box so you can choose any open program. This key combination is useful for getting a summary of the open programs

---

Ctrl-Esc pops up the Task List, which lets you select any of the open programs from a list (see Figure 2.6).

You can also call the Task List by selecting the Control menu for any open program and choosing Switch To. . . . Besides letting you switch to any open program, the Task List provides Tile and Cascade commands that work just like those in Program Manager. The Program Manager's group windows stay inside the Program Manager window, so your screen is organized to show only the open programs (see Figure 2.7).

Figure 2.6

The Task List is always available with the Ctrl-Esc key. It can be invaluable in finding your way to hidden windows. In this figure, you can see that both Program Manager and the Notepad are open, and that the Notepad is using a document called PRINTERS.TXT.

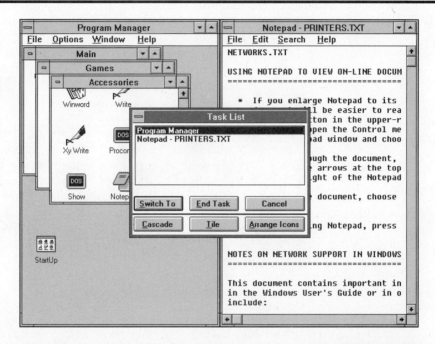

Figure 2.7

Using the Task List's Cascade command, you can put all of your programs into an easy-to-understand context. However, the Task List treats Program Manager like other applications. Even though Program Manager holds several group windows, it's still an application just like Notebook.

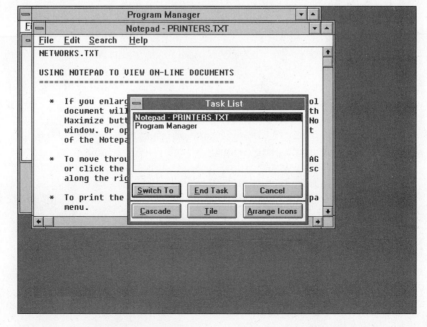

The Arrange Icons button will organize all of the program icons that appeared when active programs were minimized. You don't need to use Arrange Icons with the simple arrangement of applications developed so far, but with many programs open, your icons can become scattered over the screen and hidden behind open windows. Arrange Icons will move them all into the corner of the screen where you can see them.

Avoiding Lost Windows with Minimize on Use

One way to keep window clutter to a minimum is to use the Minimize on Use option on the Program Manager's Options menu. This is a check-list option; when you click on it, you'll see a check box confirming that it's on. Click again and the check disappears to indicate that the option is not in effect.

With Minimize on Use selected, the Program Manager itself will be reduced to an icon whenever you run a program. After you quit that program, you'll have to double-click the Program Manager icon to use it again, or call up the Task List with Ctrl-Esc.

Program Items: Tools That Should Suit You

A program group is nothing more than a convenience. You don't have to live with the way Microsoft has arranged program items into groups. You don't even have to look at the program items they give you. For example, if you rarely use the Paintbrush program or the games, they needn't be on your screen every morning. You can and should delete the icons for these programs.

When you remove a program item icon from a group, you are not removing it from your hard disk. You can start any Windows program with the File-Run command if it doesn't have an icon, so you can safely eliminate a little-used program from the Program Manager without losing it entirely.

As you add new programs, they'll be added to your Program Manager automatically by the installation routine that comes with the software. Nevertheless, you can organize your programs any way that seems right. You should create program groups that make sense for the way you work. More importantly, you need to create the right program items to put into groups.

You change program item icons with an option called Properties on the Program Manager's File menu. Selecting Properties while any particular icon is highlighted displays the name of the program that this icon represents.

Adding a Program Item

To learn how to add a program, let's duplicate one of the existing icons. Remember that an icon is just a graphical representation of a program, and not the program itself. You could theoretically have 30 icons for a single program.

1. Make Accessories the active group; if it's not open, press Alt-W and choose Accessories from the list.

2. Click once on the Notepad icon in the Accessories window; it will be highlighted.

3. Select Properties from the File menu (Alt-F-P from the keyboard). A dialog box will show the description printed below the Notepad, and the command line will show the name of the file Windows will run when you select this icon. Note that the name is NOTEPAD.EXE

4. Select OK.

5. Now select New from the File menu (Alt-F-N). A dialog box will ask you to choose between a new program item or program group. Make sure you're choosing Program Item and click on OK.

6. You'll now be confronted with a fresh Program Item Properties window. You're going to give it a new description—call it Notepad 2, testing, or anything you like—and the same command line that appeared in the Notepad properties: NOTEPAD.EXE.

7. Select OK and a second Notepad icon appears, with the name you selected underneath.

8. If you want, you can try changing the name by selecting Properties again and editing the description.

You can start to build a powerful collection of tools with this technique. Suppose that you generally use four or five standard documents during the course of a day. You can create a different program item for each document. After adding a description, simply use the program name of your word processor on the command line, followed by a space and the full path and name of the document. You can name this new program item anything you like. Because program items take up very little space on the disk, you can create as many as you like.

DOS Program Items

You'll probably need to add program items for DOS programs more than you will for Windows programs. Even though the Windows installation provides an automatic routine for creating program item icons for DOS programs, it rarely finds all programs.

And, you'll probably add DOS programs that you'll want to run from Windows. Most Windows programs automatically install an icon as part of their setup routine; DOS programs don't. Windows applications have icons built into their program code. When you created a second Notepad icon, for example, the Program Manager found the illustration for the icon inside the program.

Adding a DOS Program Item

To create a program item icon for any DOS program, you need to know two things: the command that is typed at the DOS prompt to run the program, and the directory where you want the program to look for files when it first runs.

You'll have two choices to make: whether you want to accept the DOS icon and whether you want to assign a shortcut key to run the application.

A shortcut key is the sequence Ctrl-Alt followed by a key you choose for this application. When you hold down these three keys, the program will run, even if the program item is not visible. It's a good idea to add a shortcut key to any DOS program you can.

DOS programs don't have unique icons. When you create a program item for a DOS program, Windows automatically assigns it the same generic icon that all DOS programs get: it looks like a computer monitor with "DOS" displayed. You can change this icon by selecting the Change Icon command button in the Program Item Properties dialog box.

Here's the procedure you'd follow to add an icon for WordPerfect 5.1, assuming that you keep your WordPerfect documents in a directory called \LETTERS. It will work for any other DOS program; simply make the appropriate substitutions.

1. With the Program Manager window open, press Alt-F-N; the New Program Object dialog box opens.

2. Make sure Program Item is selected, and press Enter; the Program Item Properties dialog box opens with the cursor active in the Description text box.

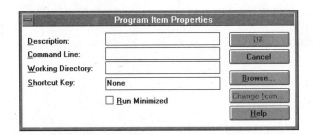

3. Type WordPerfect or whatever words you'd like to see displayed beneath the icon; press Tab and the cursor moves to the Command Line text box.

---

4. Type the exact path and program name used to load WordPerfect; you should include the full program name, not just the abbreviation used at the DOS command line. (Strictly speaking, the directory does not need to be listed if it is included in your DOS path, but it's a good idea to include it here.) For example, for WordPerfect, you'd probably to enter "C:\WP.EXE" or "C:\WP.BAT." (For more help, you may want to read Appendix C, "DOS Fundamentals for Beginners.") Then press Tab and the cursor moves to the Working Directory text box. If you're not sure of the exact path and program, click on the Browse command button to open the Browse dialog box. If you are sure of your program's name and the proper spelling, skip ahead to step 6.

5. The Browse dialog box has two parts: the File Name list and the Directories list. The first step in using this box is to make sure the correct drive is selected; if it's not, click on the arrow in the Drives list box and choose the right one from this list. Then, select the correct directory on this drive by clicking on the directory names in the Directories list box. Then, look through the list of files in the File Name list box. By default, the Browse dialog box will show you only valid Command Line files, such as EXE, PIF, COM, and BAT files. Double-click on the file you want to insert on the Command Line and it will be transferred, with the correct path; press Tab and the cursor moves to the Shortcut Key text box. Skip ahead to step 7.

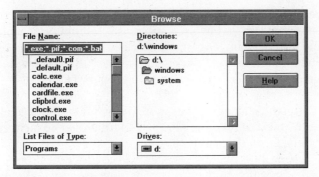

6. Type **C:\LETTERS** or the name of the directory where you keep your documents for this application; press Tab and the cursor moves to the Shortcut Key text box.

7. Here you have the option of creating a shortcut key for running Word-Perfect. You can enter only one character here; Windows will automatically assign the first two characters (Ctrl-Alt). Press W for WordPerfect; the sequence Ctrl-Alt-W will appear in the text box. Press Tab and the cursor moves to the Run Minimized box.

8. Press R only if you want WordPerfect to load as an icon so that it runs as a minimized program instead of as an active program. Whichever you choose, press Tab. The OK command button is highlighted.

9. If you want to use the standard DOS icon for WordPerfect, press Enter. If you want to try a different icon, press Tab three times. The Change Icon command button is highlighted.

10. Press Enter to select the Change Icon command. A message box appears to tell you that this program does not have its own icon but that Windows will let you assign an icon from the choices available for Program Manager.

11. Press Enter and the message box closes. The Change Icon dialog box opens.

12. Press the Right Arrow key or use your mouse to click on the Right Arrow. You'll see a range of icons that you can select.

13. When you've highlighted the icon taht you want to use, click on OK. The Change Icon dialog box closes and the Program Item Properties dialog box displays the icon you chose.

14. Press Enter; the Program Item Properties dialog box closes and the new program item appears in the current program group window.

Program Item Properties

A program item has five properties: the description that appears below its icon, the command line (the DOS name for the program that runs when you double-click the icon), the directory where the program looks for files, the icon that represents the program item, and whether the program runs in an active window or runs minimized.

You can change a program item icon's description at any time by highlighting the icon, choosing Properties from the File menu, and changing the wording in the description box.

The most common reason to use the Properties command on the Program Manager's File menu is to fine-tune program items. For example, you may want to change your shortcut key or change the working directory.

When you run the Properties command, you have access to the same Properties dialog box that opens when you create a new program item, so if you've followed the last two examples you're already familiar with the options available.

Deleting Program Items

The Delete option on the Files menu will remove the currently selected icon. You should delete program items carefully, making sure you have selected the correct one. However, don't be afraid to clear away unused icons since you can always create a new icon for the program if you use it frequently.

As with most delete operations in Windows, the Delete key on your keyboard provides a very simple shortcut key to remove the extra items:

1. Select the extra icon by clicking once with the mouse.

2. Press the Delete key. A dialog box will ask if you're sure you want to delete the icon.

3. Select Yes or press Enter. If you want to retain the icon, select No.

Mixing Items to Form Your Own Groups

When you installed Windows, it's unlikely that the main program group included the programs that you consider important. You should move program item icons into groups that are convenient for you.

Moving Items between Groups

Moving a program item from one group to another is one of the easiest tasks in all of computing.

1. Make sure the Main and Accessories program groups are open.

2. With your pointer touching the Print Manager, hold down the left mouse button and drag the icon until the pointer is in the Accessories window.

3. Release the mouse button. The Print Manager icon will now be a permanent part of the Accessories program group.

It's this easy to move any program item from one group to another. If you want to add a program item to a closed group, just move the program's icon over the group icon.

Copying Items between Groups

It's a good idea to keep a copy of frequently used program items in every program group. This way, you'll have fewer program group windows cluttering your screen and frequently used programs will always be within reach.

Copying a program item from one group to another is just like moving a program item, with one exception: when you copy, you hold down the Ctrl key throughout.

1. Click on a program item icon in the Main window that you plan to use often; File Manager is a good candidate.

2. Keep the pointer position over the program item icon as you press and hold down the Ctrl key.

3. Drag the item over to the Accessories window; as soon as it is inside the Accessories window border, release the mouse button and the Ctrl key. The File Manager item now appears in both windows.

To copy the item to a closed program group, follow steps 1 and 2, but this time drag the item until it touches one of the group icons at the bottom of the Program Manager window, and then release the mouse button and the Ctrl key. The program item will now be a part of that group, while remaining in the Main and Accessories groups.

You may want to experiment with the copy and move procedures at different locations on the screen. When you're dragging a program item, notice how the icon changes to a no symbol (a circle with a diagonal line) when you drag it over areas where there are no group windows or group icons. If you release the mouse button in any of these forbidden zones, the item will return to its original spot and no copy or move will be accomplished.

Creating a New Group

The Program Manager's File menu also enables you to create new program groups. The steps are similar to those in the section "Adding a Program Item," but you choose Program Group and give it a new name. Let's assume you've just been given a new task: You're going to organize training sessions at your company. A new program group can become the focal point for all of your work on the training sessions.

1. Select New from the File menu; the New Program Object dialog box appears.

2. Select Program Group; click the OK button. The Program Group Properties box appears.

3. Type **Training** in the Description box; press Enter. A group window titled Training appears. You can now fill the Training program group with program items for all of the programs that you'll use in this project.

You can fill your new group with program items by dragging them with the mouse from an old group. Alternately, you can use the Copy or Move command on the File menu to move or copy the currently selected icon to any existing program groups (see Figure 2.8).

Figure 2.8

The File menu's Move command lets you arrange program groups to suit your needs. You could accomplish the same thing by clicking on an icon with the mouse and dragging it to a new group.

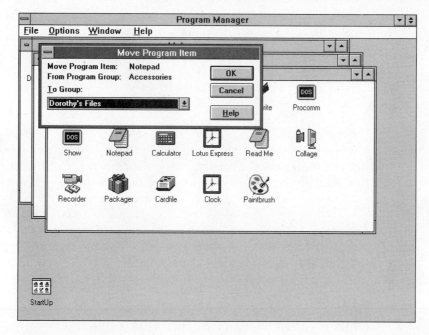

Your selection of program groups should change frequently. Any time you get a new project, a major new client, or a new interest, you should create a program group just for this work. Fill it with program items that will call up the applications and programs you use most often on these tasks. When you complete the project, delete the group and the items, clearing space for new work. Remember, program icons merely represent programs; the program is not deleted when an icon is deleted.

The Startup Group

One Program Manager group has a unique quality: any program represented within it is automatically loaded every time Windows starts.

For example, if you want Notepad to be open when Windows starts, simply copy the Notepad icon into the Startup group.

Since you can have more than one copy of any program item, you may want to have slightly different properties for the program items that are stored in the Startup group. For example, you may want the Notepad icon in the Startup group to run minimized so that it will be more readily available when you start work, but it won't occupy too much of the screen. In that case, you'd simply copy the Notepad icon from Accessories to Startup, and then edit the properties of the Notepad icon within the Startup group to indicate that it should run minimized.

Saving Your Changes

All of your changes to the Windows configuration are saved in files. If you look in your WINDOWS subdirectory, you'll find a MAIN.GRP, GAMES-.GRP, and GRP file for every group. The GRP files hold information about which programs are represented in a group, and the properties you've given them. Whenever you create a new group, move items between groups, or make changes to an item's properties, the information is saved in a GRP file and made permanent as soon as you execute the change.

When you leave Windows, you can save information about the way the Program Manager will look the next time your start Windows: which groups are open, where their windows are located, and which program item was last highlighted.

You can preserve the current appearance by checking Save Settings on Exit on the Options menu. If this option is checked on, the file PROGMAN-.INI will be updated with the exact position of each program group when you quit Windows. If this option is not checked, PROGMAN.INI will not change.

The next time Windows loads, it will read PROGMAN.INI before it positions the program groups on screen.

The best way to use Windows is to arrange your program groups so they suit your work habits. Then, press Alt-O and note if there's a check next to Save Settings on Exit; if not, press S. The menu closes immediately, so you may want to press Alt-O again to make sure you've got the option set correctly.

Then, quit Windows, either by pressing Alt-F4, by entering Alt-F-X, or by double-clicking on the Program Manager's Control menu. Now, start Windows again (type **WIN** at the DOS prompt) and press Alt-O-S to turn Save Settings off.

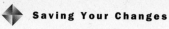

Program Manager Menus: A Complete List

File

New. . .	
Open	Enter
Move. . .	F7
Copy. . .	F8
Delete	Del
Properties. . .	Alt+Enter
Run. . .	
Exit Windows. . .	

Options

Auto Arrange
Minimize on Use
Save Settings on Exit

Windows

Cascade	Shift+F5
Tile	Shift+F4
Arrange Icons	
1. Main	
2. Startup	
3. Accessories	
4. Games	

Help

Contents
Search for Help on. . .
How to Use Help
Windows Tutorial
About Program Manager

CHAPTER

3

File Manager

Navigating through the Directory Windows

File Operations

Disk Operations

Controlling the File Manager Display

Running Programs from File Manager

Using File Manager Instead of Program Manager

THE HEART OF FILE MANAGER IS A GRAPHICAL VIEW OF YOUR FILES AND directories. With multiple windows and more than a dozen options for viewing these windows, File Manager presents a dazzling array of tools for managing your files. If you only have a handful of directories, there are probably more tools than you need in File Manager. This chapter discusses the most valuable features first and then explains the customization options that will only be of interest to users with complex directory structures.

In addition, File Manager's ability to link data files with programs can save you time in many of your daily chores. File Manager lets you drag files to programs for fast execution. For example, files that have to be printed can be "dropped" on the Print Manager for immediate printing.

As in all Windows programs, the simple jobs are easy to learn. To copy, move, or delete a file in File Manager you simply choose one of those commands from the File menu and then type in file names. However, if you rely only on the commands listed in File Manager's menus, you miss out on the very rich set of tools available for managing all the data on your system and for running programs simply by selecting their data files.

To become comfortable with this powerful set of tools, you must first learn how to manipulate the directories and file names that appear in the File Manager's document windows. With that knowledge, you'll be able to use the menu commands with great dexterity.

This chapter assumes that you have a basic understanding of the DOS file system (directories, subdirectories, and so forth); if you need an introduction to the techniques DOS provides for managing files, read Appendix B, "DOS Fundamentals for Beginners."

If you've used File Manager in Windows 3.0, you'll find that, aside from simple click-and-drag copying, almost everything in the program has changed in Windows 3.1.

Since I don't know the names of directories and files on your hard disk, I cannot give you detailed directions for file operations in File Manager. The rest of the chapter asks you to choose your own files and directories for the exercises. It points out when you're in danger of erasing or misplacing a file, so you can practice on just about any group of files that you want most of the time. Just be sure to use unimportant files if you are on unfamiliar or uncertain ground.

You start File Manager by double-clicking its icon in Program Manager's Main window or by typing **WINFILE** in the dialog box for Program Manager's Run command. (See Figure 3.1.)

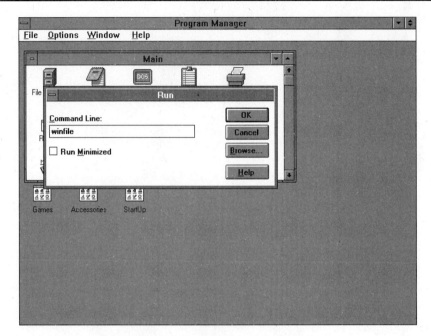

Figure 3.1
You start File Manager the same way you start any Windows program. You can double-click on its icon or type the name of its program file, WINFILE, in the dialog box for Program Manager's Run command.

Navigating through the Directory Windows

File Manager's initial screen presents a view of the directory of the active disk; this view is called the Directory window. Since it's a document window, it has a special set of tools you can use to control it, such as a Control menu and scroll bars. (These were explained in the Chapter 1 section "Document Windows Versus Applications Windows.") The Directory window gives you a complete picture of any single directory, including a perspective view of the other drives and directories on your system.

As you'll see in the upcoming sections, it's this graphical representation of all the files on your system that enables you to click on files for fast moving, copying, or deleting.

The Parts of the Directory Window

Each Directory window shows the path (or directory name) for the directory it displays in the title bar. (See Figure 3.2.) Directory windows are composed of three distinct parts.

- The disk drive icon bar runs along the top of the window and displays an icon for every drive that's available, including floppy disks, hard disks, RAM disks, and network drives.

Figure 3.2

When File Manager opens for the first time, it displays a Directory window with three parts: a bar that shows an icon for each disk drive, a Directory Tree window that shows the directories in the current drive, and a Directory Contents window that shows the files and subdirectories in the current directory.

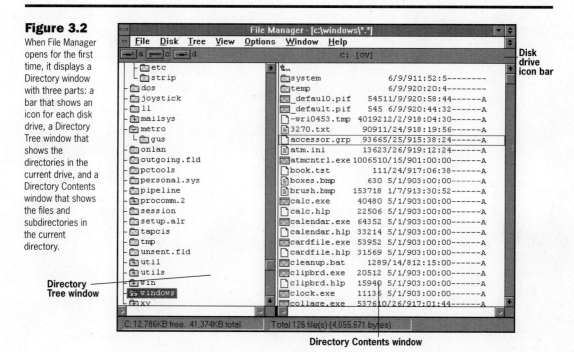

Disk drive icon bar

Directory Tree window

Directory Contents window

- The Directory Tree window occupies the left side of the Main window. It shows a diagram of the directories on the currently selected drive.

- The Directory Contents window occupies the right side of the Main window. It shows everything in the currently selected directory, including all files and subdirectories. This window may also show certain details about the files and subdirectories, including the date and time the file was last changed, the size of the file, and file attributes (such as the archive bit). This information is optional; it's turned on or off with commands on the View menu. You can also limit the types of files displayed with View commands. (These options are explained later in the chapter in the section, "The View Commands.")

The first time you open File Manager, the Directory window shows the contents of the current directory. That's usually the directory where your Windows files are stored. If there's a different directory or more than one directory window displayed, someone has probably used File Manager already and saved the settings used in his or her session.

There are four different icons that represent files and two that represent directories; see Table 3.1 for an example of each.

Table 3.1   **The Icons That Appear in Directory Windows**

Icon	Type of File	Double-Clicking
	Directories and subdirectories (when closed)	Displays the contents of the directory
	Directories and subdirectories (when open)	Closes the directory
	Data file with no associated program	Produces an error message
	Data file associated with a program	Runs the associated program with this data file open
	Program or batch files (that is, COM, EXE, PIF, and BAT files)	Runs the program or batch file
	System or hidden files	Produces an error message

The Selection Cursors

Within the Directory window, there are always two or three *selection cursors:* rectangles that surrounds the icon and name of the most recently selected disk drive, directory, subdirectory, or file. (See Figure 3.3.)

- In the disk drive icon bar, the selection cursor indicates which disk drive is current.

- In the Directory Tree window, the selection cursor shows which directory is active or current.

- In the Directory Contents window, the selection cursor shows which file will be used next *if* you execute a command.

Usually, all three selection cursors are visible. If the last selection was made in the disk drive icon bar or the Directory Tree window (with either a mouse click or the Enter key), there will be no selection cursor in the Directory Contents window; a cursor appears only after a selection has been made in the current Directory Contents window.

Only one of these selection cursors is active at any time, meaning that any actions taken (such as a File-Copy command) will affect the files or directories within this part of the screen. The other selection cursors are inactive; you activate them either by clicking on a selection in that part of the screen or by using the Tab key to activate that part of the screen.

When you choose a new part of the Directory window, the color of the selection cursor in that area changes. The boldest colors are used to show the active cursor. When the selection cursor is inactive, it's a thin rectangular line. (The exact colors differ from one system to another. Chapter 9 explains how to change the colors throughout Windows.) In Figure 3.3, the active cursor is on the file CALENDAR.EXE in the Directory Contents window.

Figure 3.3

Each of the three parts of the Directory window has its own selection cursor. Only one of these three selection cursors is active at any given time.

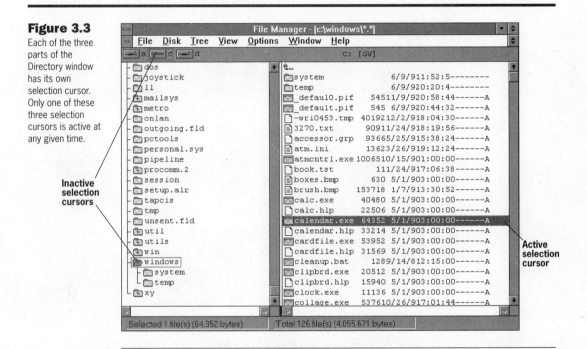

It's important to pay attention to the location of your active selection cursor. This selection is the directory or file that File Manager will attempt to change when you choose any of the commands on the File menu (such as Copy, Move, or Delete). Most mistakes in File Manager happen when you execute a command without realizing which file or directory was highlighted with the selection cursor. The following section explains several techniques for highlighting the right parts of a Directory window.

Controlling the Directory Window

To choose any icon or name in the three areas of the screen, simply move the mouse until the mouse pointer rests on the desired area, and then click. If the icon or name is not visible, click on one of the scroll bar arrows to see more of the window.

However, you can work much faster—and with more accuracy—if you use the keyboard some of the time. There are just a handful of keys that you need to use, and learning to control the Directory window with them is also a good way to become familiar with the logic that governs File Manager.

- Tab moves the selection cursor between the three Directory window sections: from the Directory Tree window, to the Directory Contents window, to the drive icons, and then back to the Directory Tree window. Shift-Tab does the same thing in the reverse order. It's a good idea to press the Tab key rapidly several times to get a feel for the process.

- The arrow keys move you up or down within the active Directory Tree window or Directory Contents window and when the disk icons are the active selection.

- PgUp and PgDn move the contents of the windows up or down by a single "window-length." For example, if all the files in a list have letters as names, pressing PgDn when "A" to "E" are visible will display "E" to "I," pressing PgDn again will display "I" to "M," and so forth.

- End displays the last item in a list.

- Home displays the first item in a list, which is always the root directory.

- Finally, pressing a single letter moves the selection cursor to the next item in the list that begins with that letter. If you have a file or directory named WYOMING, and you press W, the selection cursor will highlight the next file that begins with "W"; you may have to press the key several times before you find the file WYOMING.

In the Directory Tree window, you can use a few more shortcut keys to handle directories that contain subdirectories. Table 3.2 lists these shortcut keys. These keys will be useful only if you have dozens of directories and subdirectories; otherwise, the arrow keys and scroll bars are probably all the navigation help you'll need.

Activating a Selection

Double-clicking or pressing Enter activates a selection. That means something different in each of the three areas:

- When a disk icon is active, double-clicking or pressing Enter changes the directory and Directory Contents window to show the contents of this disk.

- When the Directory Tree window is active, double-clicking or pressing Enter changes the Directory Contents window to show the contents of the highlighted directory.

- When the Directory Contents window is active, double-clicking or pressing Enter may activate the file: If the "file" is a subdirectory, the Directory

Contents window changes to a list of the subdirectory's contents; if the "file" is a program, File Manager runs it.

Table 3.2 **Shortcuts for Navigating through Directory Trees**

Key	Moves Selection Cursor To
Up Arrow	Directory above the current directory
Down Arrow	Directory below the current directory
Right Arrow	First subdirectory of the current directory (works only when one exists and is displayed)
Left Arrow	Parent directory of the current subdirectory (works only when a subdirectory is selected)
\ (Backslash)	Root directory

However, most files cannot be activated: they're data files for programs that File Manager doesn't understand. The types of files that File Manager can activate include Windows programs, PIF files that will activate DOS programs under Windows, and data files that have been associated with a program. (File Associations will be explained in detail later in this chapter in the section "Associating Files with Programs.")

If you activate a data file that's associated with a program, both the program and the data file will be loaded into memory. (Note in Table 3.1 that data files have different icons, depending on whether or not they have an association with a program.) For example, files with the extension TXT are associated with the Windows Notepad (a word processor). If you press Enter when a file with the name README.TXT is highlighted, Notepad will run with README.TXT displayed.

Working with Directories and Subdirectories

Much of the power in file manager comes from its ability to give you control over groups of files (directories and subdirectories) with single commands. But it's important to distinguish between those directories that contain subdirectories and those that contain only files. There's an option on the View menu, called Indicate Expandable Branches, that will display a marker on directory icons to let you know whether the directory contains subdirectories or only files.

When Indicate Expandable Branches is selected, the folder icon of any directory that has subdirectories beneath it is marked with a plus sign (+) in the Directory Tree window. When you highlight one of these directories, the

Directory Contents window includes the names of the subdirectories and all of the files in the root directory of that directory.

When you activate one of these directories (by pressing Enter or by double-clicking), the Directory Tree window shows a diagram (or tree) of all the subdirectories, and instead of a plus sign the directory's folder is marked with a minus sign (–). When you press Enter or double-click on a directory folder with a minus sign, the subdirectories disappear and the plus sign returns.

The icons for subdirectories that have their own subdirectories behave in the same way.

Changing Directories

When File Manager first opens, the cursor controls the directory tree. Press the Down Arrow key and the selection cursor moves to the directory below, while the list on the right side of the window (in the Directory Contents window) changes to show the names of the files in the new directory. Also, the folder icon of the previous directory is now closed and the icon of the new directory is open.

You've just changed active directories.

Navigating through Subdirectories

Folder icons representing subdirectories appear in both the Directory Tree and Directory Contents windows. In the Directory Tree window, File Manager presents a diagram of subdirectory relationships; in the Directory Contents window, it merely lists all subdirectories that exist within the current directory, although it always puts them at the top of the list, no matter how you've chosen to sort the files (using options on the View menu).

In order to see the files within a subdirectory, you must activate the subdirectory in one of two ways in the Directory Tree:

- Select the subdirectory—meaning that the selection cursor highlights the name and folder icon.

- Click once on the subdirectory name or folder icon. (The selection cursor doesn't need to be highlighting this file at the time.)

Once the subdirectory is the current directory, all of the files and subdirectories within it will be listed in the Directory Contents window.

Choosing the Starting Directory

In future sessions, File Manager will open with a display of the directory that was active the last time you left File Manager. For example, if during a File Manager session you change directories to a directory called C:\LETTERS, the next time you open File Manager you'll see the contents of the C:\LETTERS directory.

This happens because of an optional setting—Save Settings on Exit on the Options menu—that stores your current choices when you leave File Manager. By default, this setting is on, which means that every change you make to File Manager's settings is stored to a file called WINFILE.INI at the time you leave File Manager. The next time File Manager is opened, the system reads the contents of WINFILE.INI and sets all settings according to the notations in this file. If you turn off Save Settings on Exit, File Manager no longer updates the contents of WINFILE.INI; it will continue to open with the settings that were saved in the file.

For example, if you open three directory windows, with the directories C:\LETTERS, C:\123\CONTRACTS, and C:\DOS, and then exit while Save Settings on Exit is on, the next time you run File Manager, all three directories will be displayed. If you then close the last two directory windows, turn off the Save Settings on Exit option, and quit, all three directories will still be displayed the next time you run File Manager, because the WINFILE.INI file was not changed.

Your work style will determine whether you want to keep Save Settings on Exit active. If you work with the same two or three directories constantly, you will probably want to open these directories, save the settings, quit File Manager, and then open it again and turn off the Save Settings on Exit option. This way, you'll always see the directories you want, even if your work takes you into less familiar territory.

If you're comfortable editing configuration files, you can open the WIN-FILE.INI file with any word processor that generates pure ASCII text and enter the directories you want to see in the Directory window. Just be careful to retain the exact format of the file. (See Figure 3.4.)

Working with More Than One Window

You can perform most file operations by selecting commands from the File menu. But you can perform almost every operation with the mouse alone—provided that you have more than one Directory Tree window or Directory Contents window open.

There are a number of ways to open another window, as explained in the upcoming sections.

Opening a Duplicate Directory Window

To open another Directory window, make sure the selection cursor in the Directory Tree window is highlighting the desired directory; press Alt-W-N or open the Window menu and select New Window. A second Directory window opens. (See Figure 3.5.)

Figure 3.4

The file WINFILE.INI stores the directory that will open when you first start File Manager. In this version of the file, the directory C:\WINDOWS will open the next time File Manager runs.

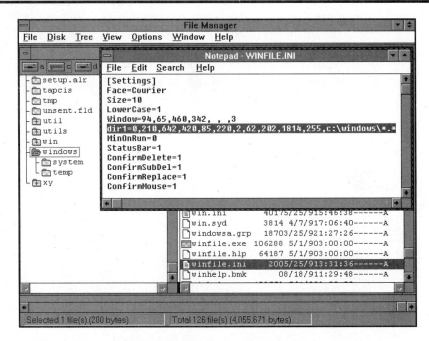

Figure 3.5

When a second Directory window is opened, it will overlap the first Directory window; you can resize the window using the mouse or you can use the Tile command on the Window menu.

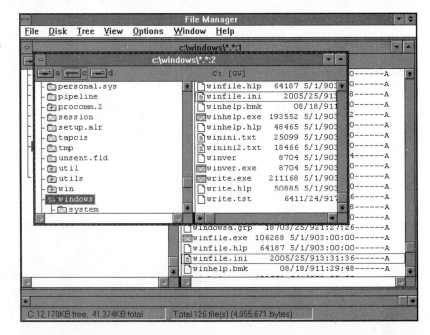

After you've opened the second directory, you'll need to rearrange the two windows, since the second will obscure the first. You can use the Size command on the window's Control menu, press Alt-W-T, or select Window from the main menu and choose Tile. The two Directory windows will be arranged neatly, one above the other.

Opening a Fresh Directory Window

You can open a Directory window for a different drive by double-clicking on a disk drive icon. To use the keyboard, press the Tab key to select the disk drive icon bar, use the arrow keys to select the desired icon, and press Enter.

This method opens a Directory window that displays the root directory of this disk; the result looks like the screen in Figure 3.5. In most cases, you'll still have to navigate through subdirectories to open the directory you want, but even if you're working on the same disk, this is probably the easiest way to gain access to a new set of files when you're doing lots of file management.

Duplicating a Directory Contents Window

For simple file operations like copy and delete, you don't need to see an entire directory tree. You can open a smaller version of the Directory window: a window that's composed only of a Directory Contents window. To do so, move the active selection cursor to a directory or subdirectory. (It can be in either the Directory Tree or Directory Contents window.) Press Shift-Enter and a second Directory Contents window will open.

You can change this window into a standard Directory window by pressing Alt-V-R, which selects the Tree and Directory option from the View menu.

Keeping Track of Multiple Windows

Note that the title bar of any Directory window or Directory Contents window in File Manager contains the name of the disk drive and directory that are being displayed. When you create duplicates of any directory, numbers appear after the directory information. The original window is window number 1, the second is number 2, and so on. You can continue to create more copies, and File Manager numbers them accordingly.

After you have more than one window, opening the Window menu (by pressing Alt-W) displays a list of all the open windows, as shown in Figure 3.6.

As new windows open, they cover earlier windows, and you need to select either the Cascade or Tile commands on the Window menu to establish a sense of order. You probably want to choose Tile, which gives you a partial view of each window. (Tile and Cascade were covered in Chapter 2 under "Cascading and Tiling Windows.")

There are several ways to move from one Directory window to another. The simplest method is to use the mouse to click on the Directory window you want to move to. However, this isn't always practical, since the directory name isn't always visible. Another way to switch Directory windows is to open the Control menu for the Directory window that's active (press Ctrl-hyphen) and select Next. Or you can press Ctrl-Tab repeatedly until you find the desired window. Frequently, the most practical solution is to open the Window menu and choose the desired window from the list that appears.

Figure 3.6
As File Manager opens new windows, it overlaps earlier windows but numbers each new window. You can see a list of the windows by opening the Window menu.

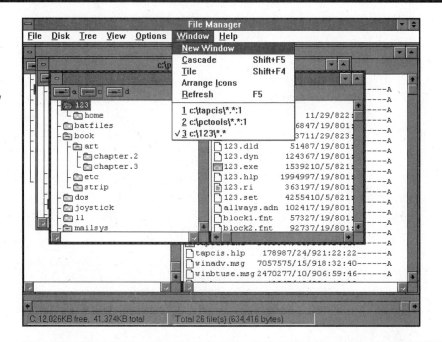

Minimizing Directory Windows
You can minimize any Directory window by clicking on the Minimize button or using the Minimize command on the window's Control menu. Minimized Directory windows are represented by icons that appear in the lower-left corner of the File Manager screen. (See Figure 3.7.) If another Directory window is maximized in the File Manager window, these icons are hidden behind the active Directory window. You can find these icons by pressing Ctrl-Tab to select the next window or icon. If you've opened several windows, press Ctrl-Tab several times.

The Window menu also lists every directory that's open, including icons.

Closing a Directory Window
When you're done with a Directory window, you can close it by using one of the following three methods that are available for closing any document window in any Windows program.

- Double-click on the Control menu icon (the dash in the upper-left corner of the screen).

- Make it the active window by clicking somewhere within it. Then open the Control menu (press Alt-hyphen) and select Close.

- Make it the active window by clicking somewhere within it, and then press Ctrl-F4.

Figure 3.7

Icons for minimized Directory windows are automatically placed in the lower-left corner, but they can be hidden by newly opened Directory windows. You can find them by pressing Ctrl-Tab.

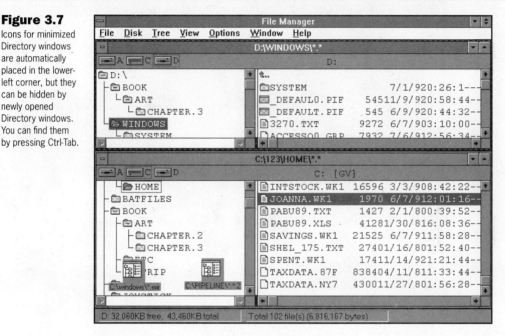

File Operations

The File Manager has seven menus, offering a wide range of commands that affect the way you work with files in Directory windows.

Any work that you need to do on a file is performed with the commands on the File menu. The Disk menu is used for dealing with entire disks. All the other menus are supporting tools that make your file and disk operations more efficient by helping you get different views of your directory structure.

Copying and Moving Files

The File menu includes two of the most commonly used commands: Copy and Move. These two commands are quite similar.

- **Copy**   Creates a duplicate of the file on another disk or in another subdirectory. It leaves the original intact.

- **Move**   Places a new version of the file on another disk or in another subdirectory and removes the first version of the file.

Copying and Moving with the Mouse

It's easiest to copy and move files with the mouse—as long as you have a Directory window open for both the source directory and the destination. Both windows don't have to be fully visible on screen, as long some part of the destination directory window is visible.

1. Click on a file name; the selection cursor will highlight the file name. If it was already highlighted, there's no confirmation that you've selected the file until you move the mouse.

2. Drag the file to its new location. As soon as you move the mouse, a file icon replaces the mouse pointer.

3. Release the mouse button when the file icon rests on the correct window, directory name, or disk drive icon.

File Manager makes an intelligent guess as to whether this click-and-drag operation should move or copy the file, depending on where the file was first stored (the source) and where it will end up (the destination).

- If the click-and-drag operation involves directories on the same disk, File Manager will move the files.

- If the click and drag involves directories on different disks, File Manager will copy the files.

You can generally just click and drag whenever you want to either copy or move files. Before the action is completed, File Manager displays a dialog box that gives you an opportunity to confirm or cancel the action.

When you need to make a duplicate on the same disk or move a file off one disk, these are the rules:

- When you're copying files from one directory to another on the same disk, press Ctrl before you click, and then hold down Ctrl throughout the drag operation.

- When you're moving files from one disk to another, press Alt before you click, and then hold down Alt throughout the drag operation.

Note that the dialog box confirming a Move or Copy operation is an optional feature; it's active when you install Windows but you can turn it off. All of the options are covered in the section "Confirmation Options" later in this chapter.

Copying and Moving with the Keyboard

To either Copy or Move a file by using the menus, you simply:

1. Press Alt-F-C (for Copy) or Alt-F-M (for Move). The From text box will display the name of the currently selected file.

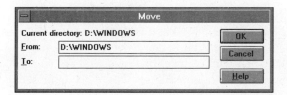

2. If this is the right file, press Tab to select the To text box; otherwise, you can either edit the file name or cancel the operation. Then select the right file from the Directory window and return to step 1.

3. Enter the destination disk or directory in the To text box; if you wish to change the name of the moved or copied version of the file, type the new name after the disk and directory.

4. Press Enter or click on the OK button to execute the command.

A Shortcut for Copying to a Different Disk

If you want to copy a file to a new disk's root directory, you don't need to open a Directory window. Instead, you can drag the highlighted file to the icon for the disk drive. When you release it on top of the disk icon, File Manager copies it to that drive, if possible. This is the best technique for copying files to a floppy disk.

Copying Files to the Clipboard

Some Windows programs can make use of files stored on the Windows Clipboard. These are programs that can embed one file in another or that support object-linking; the documentation for such programs will say that they support the OLE (object linking and embedding) standard.

To use this feature from File Manager, you copy a file to the Clipboard by clicking on the Copy to Clipboard option button. You don't need to enter a destination in the To text box.

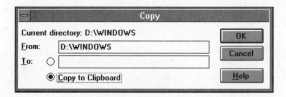

Embedding files and linking objects will be discussed in several places in the book. In Chapter 4, for example, the section "Exchanging Data with Clipboard" explains how to use files that are on the Clipboard. A full discussion of file sharing and linking appears in Chapter 11.

Printing, Deleting, and Renaming Files

Printing, deleting and renaming files works much like copying and moving. You select the file you want to print, delete, or rename, and then choose Print, Delete, or Rename from the File menu. Seasoned PC users are accustomed to selecting a command first and the file name second; File Manager reverses that order.

If you inadvertently select the wrong files, you can still correct the file names before the command is executed since File Manager lets you edit the dialog box that opens before executing the operation.

Printing

Even though there's a Print command on the File menu, File Manager does not have its own printing feature. It does, however, let you use the printing capability of other programs.

When File Manager tries to print a file, it first checks to see if a program is associated with the file. If not, File Manager reports the error, "Unable to Execute File." If it finds an associated program, File Manager runs the program, prints the file, and then closes the program.

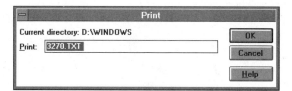

You can associate any file with a Windows program by using the Associate command on the File menu. The process of associating files with programs is covered later in this chapter in the section, "Associating Files with Programs."

Deleting

In general, this book doesn't advocate that you memorize too many shortcut keys. However, you already know the shortcut key for deleting files: it's the Delete key. Pressing Delete on the keyboard is just like pressing the key combination Alt-F-D. In both cases, File Manager opens the Delete dialog box before it deletes the file, letting you verify that you've selected the correct file. From this dialog box, you can edit the name of the file, cancel the operation, or proceed with the erasure.

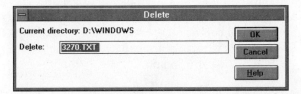

In addition, a Confirm File Delete box pops up after you click on the OK button, giving you a second chance to prevent an accidental deletion. You can turn off this dialog box using the Confirmation command on the Options menu. When File Manager is installed on your system, however, the default setting for Confirm File Delete is on. (This topic is covered in detail later in the chapter under "Confirmation Options.")

Renaming

The Rename dialog box picks up the file highlighted by the selection cursor as the file to be renamed and prompts you for the new name. Once you've confirmed that the correct file is about to be renamed, type the new name in the To text box. If you've selected the wrong file, you can edit the name in the From box.

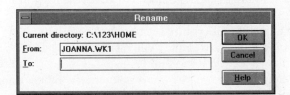

If you wish to rename a directory, you must type in the full path of the new directory name, including the disk drive.

Searching for Lost Files

When you need to work with a specific file, you can navigate through directories and subdirectories until you find it, or you can simply execute the Search command. Use Search before you waste too much time looking through subdirectories. The Search command shows you the directory where you've stored any file. It works with wildcards, so even if you do not know the exact name of a file, you can usually find it.

The Starting Point for a Search

If a file is currently selected in the Directory Contents window, File Manager uses the file extension of that file as the default Search For file when you open the Search dialog box. If you want to find other files with this extension, you can simply run the Search command at this point. (For example, if you were highlighting a file named SMITH.INV, Search would be prepared to search for all *.INV files.)

Also, Search looks down through a disk's directory structure starting from your currently active directory. You must override the default directory in the Search dialog box to make sure you're looking at a large enough portion of the disk.

Using Search

1. Open the File menu and select Search either by clicking the mouse or by pressing Alt-F-H. The Search dialog box appears, with *.* as the default file name.

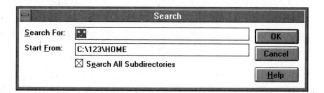

2. Type the name of a file you're seeking in the Search For text box. You can use wildcards; for example, type ***.EXE** to find all of the executable files on the disk or ***.WK1** to find Lotus 1-2-3 files. (If you're unfamiliar with the concept of wildcards, see Appendix B, "DOS Fundamentals for Beginners.") Press Tab to move to the next text box.

3. Type **C:** in the Start From text box, or use another letter for a different disk on your system.

4. Make sure that the Search All Subdirectories checkbox is checked.

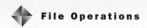
5. Click the OK box. An hourglass icon indicates that Search is working. In a few moments a "Search Results" message box appears, listing the directory and name of each file on the disk that meets your Search For entry. (See Figure 3.8.)

Figure 3.8

When File Manager finishes searching for the file you described, it lists all of the files that match the description in a Search Results window.

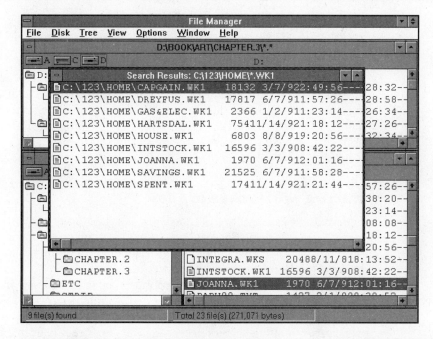

The Search All Subdirectories option should be turned off only when you're certain that a file is in a particular directory. Network users in particular can save a lot of time by turning the option off. When you're working on your own hard disk, you'll probably want it on most of the time.

Similarly, you will generally want to search an entire disk most of the time by using the root directory as the starting point—except when working on a network drive.

Creating New Directories and Subdirectories

To create a new directory or subdirectory, use the Create Directory command on the File menu. When the dialog box opens, it is prepared to create a subdirectory below the current directory. For example, if the current directory is \123, typing \HOME will create the subdirectory \123\HOME.

You can create a subdirectory for any directory—not just the current directory—simply by typing the full path name, including the disk drive. For example, if your current directory is \WIN, you can create a subdirectory named \OLD on the C:\LETTERS directory by typing C:\LETTERS\OLD in the dialog box. Your new directory will appear immediately in the directory tree.

Working with Groups of Files

File Manager can save lots of time if you learn how to work with more than one file in a directory. For example, instead of copying several files by typing the Copy command over and over, you can define a group of files and then perform the Copy command just once.

In DOS, to use multiple files, you must type in a file name that uses wildcards (* and ?) to select a group of files. This strategy only works, however, if the files have similar names. File Manager lets you create groups of files using wildcards, but also lets you select groups in a few other convenient ways.

The only restriction on a group is that all the files must be in the same directory. You can create more than one group if more than one Directory window is open, but you can only use file commands like Copy and Move on the group in the active directory. The group that has been selected in an inactive directory will stay inactive until you select that Directory window, either by clicking on the window or by selecting it from the Window menu.

Selecting More Than One File in Dialog Boxes

Dialog boxes that work with most of the File menu commands will prompt you for file names. They always open with the name of the file highlighted in the Directory window, but you can change it or add to it. Here are a few ways to increase the number of files you're changing at any one time:

- The DOS wildcard character * can be used in dialog boxes that ask for a file name. It's used to include all files in the subdirectory, and can be used as either as a suffix (extension) or a prefix in the name. For example, if you wanted to copy all the files created by a spreadsheet, you could enter

*.WKS in the Copy command's From text box. If you use *.*, you'll select every file in the subdirectory.

■ The DOS wildcard ? can be used in dialog boxes as a wildcard for a single character. If you label files numerically, you might use ? to include all numbers in a series. For example, SALES?.WKS would include the files SALES1.WKS, SALES2.WKS, SALES3.WKS, and so on. It would not include SALES10.WKS, since ? includes only single characters in the file name. In that case, you would use SALES??.WKS

■ You can also type more names in the dialog box, leaving a space after each file name to create a list of files. The box will accommodate long lists and it will keep scrolling the file names as you add to the list. You can use arrow keys or the mouse to move back through the list if you need to edit the names.

Selecting More Than One File

As you know, you can select any file in a directory window by moving the cursor to its name or by clicking once with the mouse. There are several ways to extend the selection to multiple files with mouse clicks.

You can select a sequential list of files from a directory window by holding down the Shift key and pressing the Up Arrow or Down Arrow key until all desired files are highlighted (see Figure 3.9). Release the Shift key after the last file is selected. You can accomplish the same thing with the mouse if you select the first file and then hold down Shift while you select the last file in your group with a mouse click; every file between the two will be selected.

You can select a *nonsequential* group of files from a directory contents window by holding down Ctrl while you click on each item. If you want to remove a file from the group, hold down Ctrl and click on the highlighted name a second time. Figure 3.10 shows a nonsequential group of files that has been selected.

You can select files in this way even if they are not initially visible on screen. Make your first selections among the files that are in view, and then press the scroll arrows to bring other files into view, selecting new files from the files that are now displayed. (Remember to hold down Ctrl before you select the new files.)

You can select several lists of files by combining these last two methods. After one list of files is selected, continue to add files to the list by holding down the Ctrl key as you click on individual file names. To add more sequential lists after one list of files is already selected, you must hold down the Ctrl key when the first file in the new list is selected, and then hold down both Ctrl and Shift while you click on the last name in the list.

Deselect a group of files by clicking once on any file name without holding down Shift or Ctrl or by clicking on a new directory in the directory tree.

Figure 3.9

A sequential list of files will be selected if you press the Shift key as you click on the first and last names of a list.

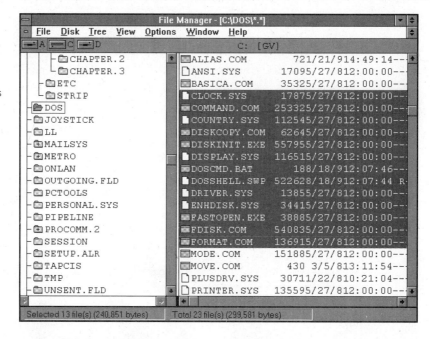

Figure 3.10

This nonsequential group of files was selected by holding Ctrl down as the mouse was clicked on each file name.

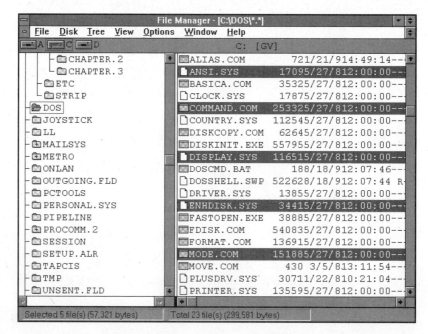

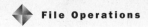

Selecting Multiple File Groups

Here's some practice in selecting a varied group of files, using the techniques just described. When you're done, your group of files will look something like Figure 3.11.

Figure 3.11

This group of files was selected using a mixture of the Shift- and Ctrl-key techniques for selecting groups of files.

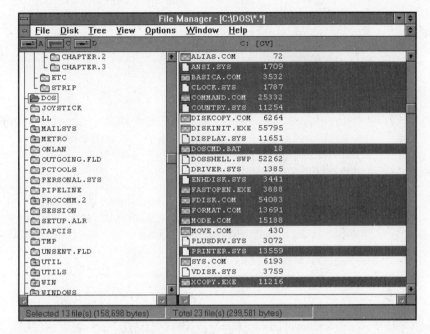

1. Open a Directory window on a large group of files.

2. Click the Maximize button so you can see as many files as possible.

3. Select a file, either by clicking on its name or by pressing arrow keys until it's highlighted.

4. Hold down the Shift key while you click on a file that's four or five names below. Release the Shift key and every file between the first and last files is selected.

5. Hold down the Ctrl key and click on another file name. It will be selected while the first group remains selected.

6. Repeat step 5 several times. The next two steps will add a second list to the group.

7. Hold down the Ctrl key while you click on a file name. Release the Ctrl key. The file is selected.

8. Choose a file that will represent the end of the second list. Then hold down Ctrl-Shift while you click on that file. Every file between the first file and the last is selected.

9. Repeat steps 7 and 8 if you wish.

10. At this point, you can open the File menu and choose Print, Copy, or Move. A dialog box will open with the names of every file you've selected. Press Esc or click on Cancel.

11. Deselect all files by clicking on any individual file or directory name without holding down the Shift or Ctrl key.

The Select Files Command

If you want to work with a group of files whose names have similarities, select them by using the Select Files option on the File menu. This option lets you specify letters in the spelling of a file name as a group selection criterion, and then select that group from the same dialog box.

To use Select Files, first enter the file name, using wildcards (* and ?) freely. Then click on Select Files. For example, if you use the file extension .INV in all of your invoices, you might want to use *.INV as a Set Selection. In Figure 3.12 a set selection of *.XLS was used to highlight all of the worksheet files with the .XLS extension in the active directory.

Figure 3.12

The Select Files command highlights files that match a spelling you specify, including wildcards.

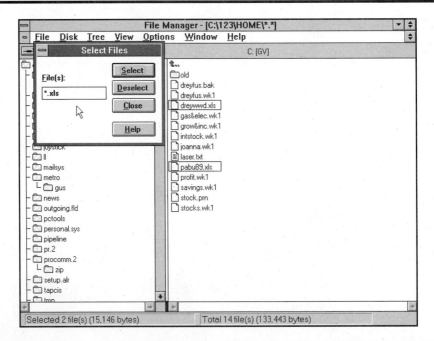

Once you've selected Files, you can use the Copy, Move, Delete, Print, Rename, and Search commands on the files in this group. If you do not intend to use another File command on this group, click on Deselect before you close the dialog box.

You can combine groups of files. You do this by selecting one group, replacing the file name in the File text box and choosing the Select command button again. For example, if you had selected a group of files with the name *.WK1, and then selected the group *.XLS, all files with both extensions would be selected. If you deselect a group, only those files with that name are removed from the selection.

File Properties

File Manager includes two things in its definition of file properties:

- The basic statistics displayed in a DOS directory display (size, and the date and time of the last modification of the file)

- DOS file attributes (the hidden bits that establish a file as either hidden, read-only, system, or archived)

The basic file statistics are useful to know, but you cannot change them from this dialog box. If you've selected All File Details in the View command, you already see the same information on screen. The file attributes, on the other hand, can be altered in the Properties dialog box.

If you're not familiar with file attributes, you should handle them with extreme care. Misusing them can accidentally hide a file that you'll need. If you are familiar with file attributes, the easy access File Manager gives you to these optional settings will provide a terrific way to customize your system. With so many destructive viruses being circulated, you'll want to protect your system by establishing important program files as read-only, and if other people use your system, you'll want to make it more secure by hiding sensitive data.

Displaying File Properties

You can see the properties of any highlighted file by pressing Alt-Enter or Alt-F-T.

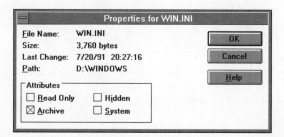

A dialog box pops up with all of the information that both DOS and Windows use to manage a file:

- The file name

- The file size in bytes

- The date and time the file was last changed

- The directory in which the file is stored

- The status of four attributes: Read Only, Archive, Hidden, and System

Changing File Attributes

An *attribute* for any file is a single bit that is stored along with the file name in a disk's directory structure. Each of these bits controls key features about how the file will behave under certain circumstances:

- Archive is a record of whether a backup program was used to save this file. When a backup program makes a copy of a file, it sets the archive bit on, so that when the backup program is run again, it knows that a copy of this file has already been made. An incorrect setting can interfere with the way a backup program is keeping archives on your disk.

- The Read Only option prevents a file from being changed. Some people use this attribute to protect files, especially if other people use their PC. If you change a frequently used file to read-only, any work performed on that file cannot be saved. Generally, only program files and system files should be stored as read-only.

- Hidden files are not seen in a normal directory listing. Programmers will hide files that shouldn't be changed by users. In DOS, for example, two files essential to a PC's booting are hidden to prevent accidental erasure, among other things. In File Manager, you can display hidden files by using the View menu's By File Type dialog box.

- System files are used to properly set up the computer when it's turned on. Generally, system files are also hidden, but in File Manager they can be displayed by using the View menu's By File Type dialog box.

Disk Operations

File Manager's Disk menu has a few straightforward commands for managing hard and floppy disks. There are four commands for working with disks connected directly to your PC, and two commands for working with network drives.

Copy Disk

Copy Disk is equivalent to the DOS DISKCOPY command. It's not a replacement for the Copy commands on the File menu: Copy Disk works only with two floppy disks of the same type, so you can't use it to copy files from a floppy disk onto a hard-disk directory.

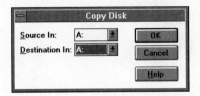

Be careful: Like the DISKCOPY command in DOS, Copy Disk first formats and then duplicates the contents of the first floppy disk onto the second floppy disk. If there's valuable data on the receiving disk, do not run Copy Disk because the data will be lost during the format. You should use Copy Disk mainly for creating backup copies.

Label Disk

The Label Disk command is used to change the name of a disk, sometimes called the *volume name*. The label is the text that appears before the list of file names whenever you type **DIR** at the DOS prompt.

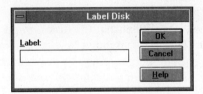

Label Disk works on either floppy disks or hard disks. It won't work on directory names; you must use the Rename command on the File menu for that.

Format Disk

The Format Disk command prepares a disk so that DOS and Windows can use it; don't experiment with Format if you are not sure what it is for. Brand new disks need to be formatted; floppy disks that already hold data will lose that data if they're reformatted.

File Manager gives you several formatting options:

■ The Capacity option allows you to choose between high and low capacity formatting if you have a high-density floppy-disk drive. The high-density format is the default; press Alt-C or click on the Capacity drop-down list box to choose a low-density format. If the disk drive you're using for the format is a low-density drive, you won't have an option.

■ The Make System Disk option will transfer DOS files to a floppy disk so that it can boot a PC. Because the DOS files take up space, you don't want to click on this option unless you plan to use the disk as a startup disk.

■ The Quick Format option can reduce the time for formatting a disk from several minutes to several seconds. It is faster than a normal format because it does a simple erasure of a disk's file allocation table and root directory, but it does not scan a disk, looking for problem areas. Use this command only when you're confident that the disk is in good condition. Do not use it with new disks because it may cause you to lose data; that's because there is a fairly good possibility that any new disk you're formatting will contain bad sectors. A normal format will find these areas and prevent you from storing data there.

■ Label is text that will appear when you display the directory of a disk. You can later change the label on a disk using the Label Disk command as described previously.

Network Commands

The Network Connection's Connect Net Drive and Disconnect Net Drive options appear only if Windows detects a network connection in your system. (Your system's link at the NETBIOS or IPX level must be established when you begin Windows.) The Connect Net Drive command lets you log on to a network drive. If you already logged on to the network before you started Windows, you won't need to connect again but you may want to use this command to log on to additional network drives. You'll know when a network connection is active because disk icons appear for every recognized network drive in a Directory Tree window.

Once a network connection is established, you can use the files on network directories the same way you use your own hard disk, with one exception: The network administrator decides which directories you can open and change.

Use Disconnect Net Drive when you're finished using a network drive. This makes more memory available and helps the network perform better for the other users.

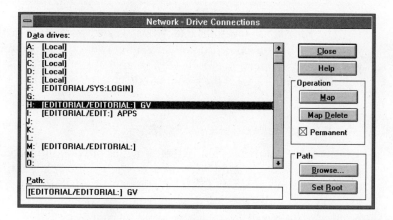

The specific features available with this command will vary from one system to another, because it relies on software written specifically for a particular network operating system (such as Novell NetWare, Microsoft LAN Manager, or Banyan VINES). On Novell NetWare systems, you'll see the above dialog box when you select the Network Drive Connections command; it summarizes the disk drives available to you through the network.

In the dialog box's Data drives list box, the letters that are followed by a description represent drives that can be mapped or browsed. To do either, first select the drive and then choose the Map or Browse command button; in most cases, letters with no description cannot be used, since the network administrator has not given you access. You can use this dialog box to change the mapping of your network connection only if your network administrator has made this option available to you.

The following dialog box appears when you select Browse after selecting a valid driver.

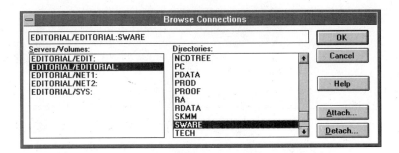

The Browse Connections dialog box also lets you attach new servers to your network connection, but only if your network administrator has given you access to the servers. You'll need to have a password for the new server before you can use the Attach command.

Controlling the File Manager Display

The Tree, View, Options, and Window menus provide supporting tools that help you use the File and Disk commands better. These tools affect what you see during your work with File Manager. Mostly, that means controlling the files and directories that are displayed, but it also includes determining whether certain warning messages are displayed as well as the typeface used to display information.

The Tree Commands

Most of the commands in the Tree menu provide a way to look at subdirectories. It's generally easier to use a mouse instead of most the Tree commands, but if you prefer using a keyboard, you'll want to learn about the Tree commands. The Expand All command can be especially useful to help you get a perspective on your disk.

Following is a summary of each Tree command:

- Expand One Level is the equivalent of double-clicking on a directory that has a plus sign in its icon. It opens a folder.

- Expand Branch is the equivalent of double-clicking on a directory that has a plus sign and then double-clicking on every successive subdirectory below that has a plus sign. It opens all folders.

- Expand All is the equivalent of double-clicking on every directory and every branch in a Directory Tree window.

- Collapse Branch closes the highlighted directory. Unfortunately, there's no way to collapse all the directories at once. You want to avoid collapsing a branch when the root directory (usually C:\) is highlighted; all of your directories will disappear. If this happens, click once on the root directory's plus sign or choose any of the Tree menu's Expand commands.

- Indicate Expandable Branches displays a plus sign in the icon of every directory that contains subdirectories, and displays a minus sign in the folder if the subdirectories are being displayed. The default for this setting is on. If this option is selected, you can click on it to deselect it, and the plus and minus indicators will no longer appear inside folder icons.

The View Commands

The View menu presents options that determine which files will be displayed in a Directory window and what details you'll see about each file. There are five different sections on the View menu and they arrange the 12 View commands into logical groups. Following is a discussion of each group and its commands.

Choosing the Parts of a Directory Window

The first three View commands let you change the composition of a Directory window. Instead of displaying all three parts of a Directory window, you can select just two. Figure 3.13 illustrates the three options.

Figure 3.13

The same directory displayed using the View commands for Tree and Directory (top), Tree Only (middle), and Directory Only (below).

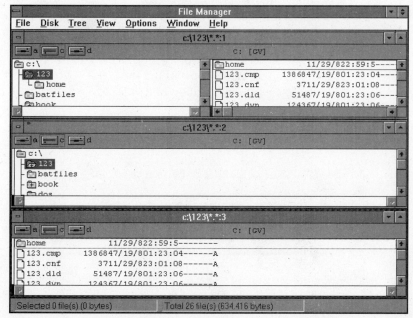

- Tree and Directory is the default setting. Both the Directory Tree window and Directory Contents window are open.

- If you click on the Tree Only setting, the Directory Contents window disappears and the Directory window will consist of just the disk drive icons and a Directory Tree window.

- If you click on the Directory Only setting, the Directory Tree window disappears and the Directory window will consist of just the disk drive icons and a Directory Contents window. (This produces the same effect as pressing Shift-Enter with the selection cursor in the Directory Tree window.)

Splitting a Directory Window

You can achieve a very similar effect by using the Split command. Split lets you move the line that divides the window between the tree and the directory contents.

When you select Split, the scroll bar that divides a directory window becomes a solid line that you can move with the mouse or with the arrow keys (right or left). You can also move this scroll bar at any time in the same way that you can change any document window border: Move the mouse slowly across the scroll bar until it becomes a sizing pointer. You can now reposition the border the same way you could when the Split command was active. (This technique was explained in Chapter 1 under "Moving and Sizing a Window.")

Choosing the File Details You See

The choices Name, File Details, and Other are mutually exclusive: You can choose only one of the three. A check mark appears next to the active choice.

- If Name is active, directory windows list no information about the file other than its name. Most of the time, this is probably the option you want selected, since it allows File Manager to display the greatest number of files.

- If All File Details is active, you receive details about each file, in four categories:

  - The size, or number of bytes it occupies

  - The date it was created or last changed

  - The time of day it was created or last changed

  - The status of file attributes

  You probably want to use this option only rarely since the time of day a file was changed and the file attributes are not something you need to see often. You would generally want to see all file details only when doing disk housekeeping chores.

■ The Partial Details option allows a great degree of customization. You can turn on or off any of the categories in the All File Details section.

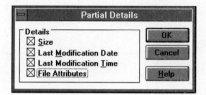

If you're unsure of which choices to select, try Partial Details with Size and Last Modification Date. This will probably provide you with the most useful file information.

Choosing How Files Are Sorted

The View menu's Sort options control the way files in a Directory Contents window are listed.

■ Sort by Name is an alphabetical listing of file names. Files that begin with numbers will appear before the first file that begins with a letter.

■ Sort by Type is also an alphabetical listing but it alphabetizes by a file's extension first. When more than one file has the same extension, it alphabetizes the files by name. For example, the file WIN.COM appears before the file EXCEL.EXE, while the file EXCEL.COM comes before WIN.COM.

■ Sort by Size lists files in descending size. This command works even if you are not viewing the number of bytes.

■ Sort by Date lists the most recently created files first.

Limiting File Listings to Special Types

When you first run File Manager, the Directory Contents window displays every file in the selected directory (except hidden files). The By File Type command enables you to suppress the listing for some files, which can make it easier for you to find the files you need.

You gain the greatest amount of control over file types by entering a file type in the Name text box. For example, to view only spreadsheets with the extension .WKS, you would type *.WKS here. Any text entered here will override the categories. Generally, you would enter a file type in the Name option only temporarily, to find a very specific type of file. Or you might set up a system for novices, only letting them see the specific type of documents they should be working with.

There are five different file categories. By default, the first four are on; to remove these types of files, click on the appropriate box to deselect it.

For the categories to work properly, make sure that *.* appears in the Name text box. (If you delete the text in the Name text box, File Manager inserts *.* automatically.)

- The Directories option displays subdirectories within a Directory Contents window. This will not affect the directories that appear in the Directory Tree window.

- The Programs option displays files that have one of the four file extensions that Windows recognizes as a program: .BAT, .COM, .EXE, and .PIF. Such files will be executed if you double-click on them. By the way, just because a file has these letters as its extension does not mean it is really a program. If you name a document with one of these extensions, it will still be listed with the View by File Type Programs option, even though it is not a program.

- The Documents option displays all files that are associated with an application program. By default, all files with the extension .TXT are displayed when this category is selected, because Windows is installed with an association between these files and the Notepad program. Any file type that you associate with a program will be included in this list. (A full discussion of associating programs appears in the section, "Associating Files with Programs.")

- The Other Files option lets you see all files that do not fall into the above categories.

- The Show Hidden/System Files option lets you see files that have a DOS file attribute of hidden or system (such as the hidden files required to run DOS). By default, this option is off, since changing or deleting these files can interfere with a PC's normal operation. If you do choose to show these files, they'll be affected by the earlier file type limitations (that is, hidden

.COM files will be visible only if Programs is selected). For an explanation of hidden and system file attributes, see the section "File Properties," earlier in this chapter.

Confirmation Options

On the Options menu, the Confirmation command provides five types of warning messages that you can choose to turn off. These messages normally appear as you're about to perform an activity that's a potential source of problems.

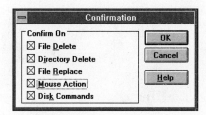

- File Delete lets you turn off the warning message that appears after you've selected OK on the Delete dialog box to delete a file. A good rule of thumb is, if you don't own an unerase program, make sure this and the next box are checked.

- Directory Delete lets you turn off the warning message that appears after you've selected OK on the Delete dialog box when a directory or subdirectory is about to be deleted.

- File Replace lets you turn off the warning message that appears after you've selected a copy command that will replace a file (that is, copy a file onto an existing file). It's good to keep this message on, since it's very easy to accidentally overwrite a file, and undelete programs can not repair this type of damage.

- Mouse Action confirms that you're performing the correct action when you use a mouse to copy or move files. Novice Windows users will want this option on, but after you've become proficient, you may want to turn it off.

- Disk Commands turns off the warning message that appears before you format a floppy disk or copy a file to a floppy disk. Turn off this warning only when you're about to format a large group of disks; otherwise, keep it on.

Font Options

The Font options give you control over the typeface that File Manager uses in showing directory and file names. See Figure 3.14.

Figure 3.14

The directory and file names in this screen are displayed in Courier 12 point bold. Arial 20 point bold italic is displayed in the Font dialog box. If you select OK in this dialog box, the directories and file names will switch from Courier 12 point bold to Arial 20 point bold italic.

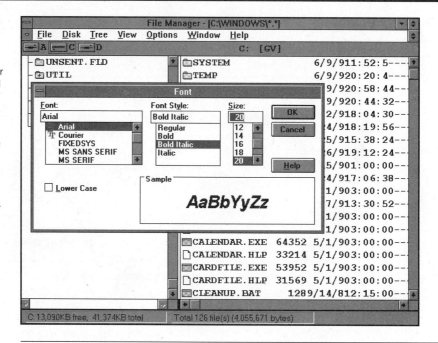

This option works in the same fashion as other Windows programs for font selection.

1. Choose a font from the Font list box; the Font Style and Size list boxes change to show the options available for this style, and the Sample box displays several letters in this font.

2. Choose a style from the Font Style list. (Most fonts have four styles: regular, italic, bold, and bold italic, although some have a different range of choices.) The Sample box displays the font in this style.

3. Choose a size; the Sample box displays the font in this size.

4. Click the Lower Case box if you wish to change between lowercase and uppercase.

5. Click OK. The display changes to reflect your font choice.

Status Bar

The Status Bar option, when turned on (checked), gives you handy information at the bottom of the screen. You can see the status bar at the bottom of Figure 3.14. When the Directory Tree window is active, it tells you the number of bytes available on the current disk, and the total amount that the disk can hold. In addition, it shows the number of files in the active Directory Contents window and the number of bytes these files occupy.

You would only turn off the status bar if you needed to see more lines of the screen. As a rule, you should keep it on.

Minimize on Use

If the Minimize on Use option is selected, File Manager will be minimized (reduced to an icon) when you activate a program. For example, if you double-click on a file with the extension .TXT, Notepad will open to display the file. With Minimize on Use selected, File Manager will become an icon when the Notepad opens.

Minimize on Use reduces screen clutter, but it does not save memory, since File Manager remains loaded in memory. It also requires that you restore File Manager to its original size when you intend to return to it.

Save Settings on Exit

When the Save Settings on Exit option is selected, File Manager stores the current options, including the directories displayed in Directory windows, in a file called WINFILE.INI. This file exists before you ever run File Manager, and if you do not choose Save Settings on Exit, File manager always uses the original File Manager settings.

You may want to use File Manager by opening the directories you use most often, choosing the options you are most comfortable with, choosing Save Settings on Exit, and then closing File Manager. If you immediately open File Manager and turn Save Settings off, you will then start File Manager with the settings you want to see, not with the end result of a busy day's work.

Earlier in the chapter, the section "Choosing the Starting Directories" explained how to use this option or edit the file WINFILE.INI.

Window Options

Like Program Manager, File Manager has a Window menu that lets you arrange every open window in either a tile or cascade arrangement. The Window menu can be especially valuable when you have three or more Directory windows open, since it lists each directory by number. You can activate a directory window by selecting its number.

You already learned how to use the Window command to choose among directories and to arrange directories on screen ("Keeping Track of Multiple Windows"), and in Chapter 2 you learned how to use the Window menu commands ("Cascading and Tiling Windows"). There's one additional Window menu command that's unique to File Manager: Refresh. If you change files in the active directory with a program other than File Manager, your Directory window will reflect the old information. It won't show the change in file size or a deletion until you choose Refresh. You'll generally want to use Refresh any time you believe activity took place on a disk since the last time you opened a Directory window.

Network users will need to use Refresh periodically since someone may change the files in a network directory after File Manager has taken its first look at the server.

Running Programs from File Manager

Most of File Manager's menu commands are devoted to helping you manage your files. But File Manager can also be used as a platform for all of your work in Windows. While Program Manager simplifies the task of starting programs, File Manager gives you more powerful tools, since it lets you focus your attention on data files, loading programs based on which data you want to use.

The Associate command on the File menu establishes a link between a program and a type of data file, so that File Manager can take over the job of loading programs when you double-click on a data file.

Associating Files with Programs

All computer programs understand only certain types of files. Word processors understand the document files they create, and spreadsheet programs understand the worksheets they create. In Windows, this relationship is called an *association*. It expands the relationship between programs and their data files so you can click on a program that has a particular type of name and Windows can open it automatically.

For example, files with the extension .TXT are usually text files. When you click on a file that has the extension .TXT in File Manager, the word processor Notepad opens with this text file open. That's because Windows comes with a built-in association between .TXT files and the Notepad program. You can establish associations between programs and any file extension, as long as the program will understand the data. If you name some of your text files with the extension .LTR, for example, you can establish an association between a word processor and the extension .LTR. This way, any time you try to activate a file with the extension .LTR, that word processor will open and will display the file.

Windows automatically creates associations between some kinds of files and programs. The WIN.INI file in the main Windows directory provides details about which defaults will be used to establish associations every time

Windows is loaded into memory. A section in WIN.INI called "extensions" is where associations are stored.

Most Windows applications give their files unique extensions. For instance, the Calendar calls its files .CAL and the Notepad calls its files .TXT. When these programs were installed, Windows added new lines to the extensions section in WIN.INI, and as a result, if you click on a file with the extension .TXT in File Manager, the Notepad will run and will open the .TXT file that you selected. (You can do the same thing with the Open command in the File menu.)

You can add as many new associations to WIN.INI as you like. You can do it yourself with a word processor, but it's a lot easier to use the Associate command in the File menu.

Creating Associations between Files and Programs

To establish an association between a data file and a program, you use the Associate command on the File menu.

1. Open a Directory window and move the selection cursor to a file that has the extension you want to associate with a program.

2. Press Alt-F-A to open the Associate command on the File menu. The extension of your highlighted file will appear in the dialog box. (See Figure 3.15.)

Figure 3.15

The Associate dialog box lets you establish connections between data files and programs.

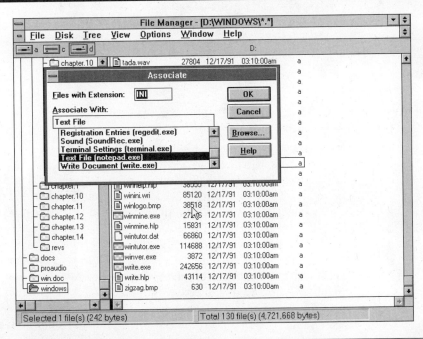

3. You can choose a program from the list box, but it will show you only Windows programs that are already associated with data files. To associate the data file with a new program, click on the Browse command button. The Browse dialog box opens with only valid programs currently displayed.

4. Select any program, including DOS programs (though you should only use DOS programs that are run with a PIF file; see Chapter 10 for more information about PIF files). You can look through any disk drive or directory on your system with this dialog box. When you've found the desired program, click on OK. The dialog box closes and the program is inserted into the Associate dialog box.

5. Click on OK when you've selected the desired program to be associated with this type of data file.

The Browse Dialog Box

If you've encountered the Browse dialog box for the first time by using the steps above, it's a good idea to spend a little time with it because this is one of the most common dialog boxes that appears in many Windows programs. (see Figure 3.16).

Figure 3.16

The Browse dialog box that helps you find programs for the Associate command is the same as the one used by the Program Manager's Run command.

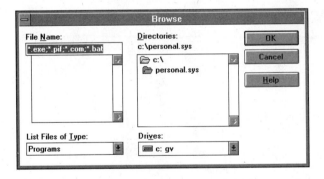

The Browse dialog box has two main parts: the File Name list and the Directories list. When using this box, you should first make sure the correct drive is selected. If not, click on the arrow in the Drives list box and choose the right one from this list. Then, select the correct directory on this drive by double-clicking on the directory names in the Directories list box. (If you see only subdirectories, click on the .. listing, such as C:\..: to display the directory above.) Next, look through the list of files in the File Name list box. By default, the Browse dialog box displays only valid Command Line files, such as .EXE, .PIF, .COM, and .BAT files. Double-click on the file you want to insert on the Command Line and it will be transferred, with the correct path, to the Program Name text box in the Associate dialog box.

Running or Viewing Files

If you want to run a Windows application not visible in the active Directory window, use the Run command on the File menu. Simply enter the name of the Windows program or .PIF file (if it's a DOS program) and press Enter. The program will run, without closing File Manager. If you want to start a program and work on a document that's not associated with it, you can enter both the program name and the document you want to start working on.

You can use the Run command to overcome one of File Manager's greatest weaknesses: the lack of a function for viewing a text file, like the TYPE command in DOS. In order to view the contents of a file, highlight the file name, select Run, and insert "notepad" before the file name. File Manager will then run Notepad with this text file open.

Check the "run minimized" box only if you want the program to appear as an icon instead of as a full-featured program.

Embedding Files

You may want to run File Manager even when you're not performing file management chores because of the ease with which it lets you *embed* one file within another. Embedding a file means that when the receiving program (called a *client*) runs the data file that has an embedded file within it, the embedded file will perform actions according to the way the original program (called the *server*) specified.

For example, if you embed a Write document within a Calendar program, when you open the Calendar document, you'll be able to see the contents of the Write document. (Windows will run Write with the document loaded automatically if you click on the embedded file.) Normally, Calendar would not understand a Write document, and you would not be able to link a word processing document with an appointment book.

Embedding makes the process of sharing files between different Windows programs as easy as clicking on a data file from one application and dragging it to the data file of a different application. You can see the programs that accept another program's data files by running the Registration Database, which manages file associations; to do so, type **REGEDIT** at the Run command on the File menu.

You can embed the data files of some Windows programs into the data files of programs that conform to the Object Linking and Embedding specification (OLE). A full discussion of file embedding and associations appears in Chapter 11.

Checking System Memory

The Help menu includes an option called About File Manager. As in Program Manager, this option shows you the amount of free memory. It's a good idea to check this box from time to time so you have a sense of how many programs you can run at once (see Figure 3.17). If you try to run programs without several hundred kilobytes of free memory, your computer will run slowly. Close some of the open windows to free up more memory.

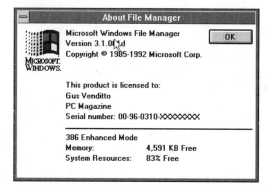

Figure 3.17
You can check the amount of memory available by selecting the About File Manager option in the Help system.

Customizing WINFILE.INI

If you like to tinker, you may want to examine and edit the contents of WIN-FILE.INI, a file stored in the main Windows directory. It maintains the settings for all of File Manager's options, as shown in Table 3.3.

The WINFILE.INI file is merely a list of parameters. Every time File Manager is loaded, these parameters are used to set up File Manager. You must edit this file with extreme care, since changes to the spelling of a parameter could prevent WINFILE.INI from loading properly.

The file uses 0 to indicate that an option is off, and 1 to show that it's on. For instance, the phrase "MinOnRun=0" in the file means that the Minimize on Run option is off. If you replace the 0 with a 1, the next time File Manager is loaded, the Minimize on Run option will be set on.

Because Windows comes with an association between .INI files and the Notepad, you can edit WINFILE.INI by double-clicking on the file name in an active Directory Contents window. Be careful if you do decide to edit WINFILE.INI. File Manager won't be able to run properly if you delete essential lines or if you move it to the wrong directory. Before you edit the file, be sure to make a backup in a separate directory or on a floppy disk.

Using File Manager Instead of Program Manager

By now, you may be hooked on File Manager. It will spare you from arcane DOS commands, cut down dramatically on the amount of typing you have to do to manage your files, and maybe make it easier to run programs than the Program Manager.

Table 3.3 **A Guide to WINFILE.INI Settings**

Parameter	Option Controlled
Face	Font
Size	Font size
LowerCase	0 for uppercase; 1 for lowercase
MinOnRun	0 for Minimize on Use on; 1 for off
StatusBar	0 for Status Bar off; 1 for on
ConfirmDelete	0 for File Delete off; 1 for on
ConfirmSubDel	0 for Subtree Delete Confirmation off; 1 for on
ConfirmReplace	0 for File Replace Confirmation off; 1 for on
ConfirmMouse	0 for Mouse Action Confirmation off; 1 for on
ConfirmFormat	0 for Diskette Commands off; 1 for on
Save Settings	0 for Save Settings on Exit off; 1 for on
dir	The screen coordinates where each Directory window is displayed and the path of the active directory

If you're happy enough with File Manager that you want to use it instead of Program Manager, here's how:

1. Display Program Manager. If you're within File Manager, press Ctrl-Esc to bring up the task list and double-click on the listing for Program Manager.

2. Open the Main group window, if it's not visible. If you need help finding it, press Alt-W to open the Window menu and then choose the number listed for the Main window.

3. Find the Startup group icon. If it's not visible, press Ctrl-Tab repeatedly until the Startup icon is highlighted. (You could also use the Window menu, as in step 2.)

4. Click on the File Manager icon in the Main group window and hold down the mouse button.

5. Drag the File Manager icon until it's resting on the Startup window or icon.

6. Release the icon. The next time you open Windows, File Manager will be running.

File Manager's Menus: A Complete List

File	
Open	Enter
Move. . .	F7
Copy. . .	F8
Delete. . .	Del
Rename. . .	
Properties	Alt+Enter
Run. . .	
Print. . .	
Associate. . .	
Create Directory. . .	
Search. . .	
Select Files	
Exit	

Edit

Copy Disk. . .
Label Disk. . .
Format Disk. . .
Make System Disk. . .
Select Drive. . .

Tree	
Expand One Level	+
Expand Branch	*
Expand All	Ctrl+*
Collapse Branch	
Indicate Expandable Branch	

View

Tree and Directory
Tree Only
Directory Only
Split
Name
All File Details
Partial Details. . .
Sort by Name
Sort by Type
Sort by Size
Sort by Date
By File Type. . .

File Manager's Menus: A Complete List (continued)

Options

Confirmation. . .
Font. . .
Status Bar. . .
Minimize on Use
Save Settings on Exit

Window

New Window
Cascade   Shift+F5
Tile   Shift+F4
Arrange Icons
Refresh   F5

Help

Contents
Search for Help on. . .
How to Use Help. . .
About File Manager

4

The Writing Tools

The Basics of Graphical Word Processing

Notepad: For Quick and Simple Jobs

Write: A Full-Featured Graphical Word Processor

Exchanging Data with Clipboard

Write Tips

WINDOWS PROVIDES TWO PROGRAMS FOR WRITING TEXT AND reading text files: Notepad and Write. Both were installed in the Accessories group when you ran the setup program. If you're currently using DisplayWrite, MultiMate, Microsoft Word, WordPerfect, XyWrite, or another DOS word processor, you'll probably want to keep using your own word processor. Neither Notepad nor Write has enough features to merit the switch. However, these two programs can be very helpful even if you continue to use your original word processor for most writing chores.

Notepad is useful for jotting down notes or for taking a quick look at text files, whether they're documentation for Windows or documents that you created with another word processor. Notepad lets you change the words in these text files but gives you no text-formatting options. It loads quickly and uses very little memory (about 15k), while your current word processor probably requires about 200 or 300k of RAM and may require that you clear Windows programs from memory before it will fit into RAM. (Chapter 10 discusses the issues to consider when running DOS programs with Windows.)

Write is valuable for taking advantage of Windows' graphical tools. You can use it to create letters and other short documents that you want to look good. Write lets you quickly print text in any of the fonts supported by your system, format your page with a few mouse clicks, and place graphic images within a text document. It may not have as many features as your daily word processor, but it only takes about 65k of RAM.

Write may be most useful as an introduction to graphical word processing. If you're debating whether to replace your current DOS-based word processor with a Windows word processor like Lotus' Ami, Microsoft Word for Windows, or WordPerfect for Windows, you'll be able to get hands-on experience with the techniques that make these programs special. Write does not have the advanced features of these programs—features like spell checking, style sheets, and multiple windows—but it provides a good preview of graphical word processing.

The Basics of Graphical Word Processing

There are two new features in graphical word processing that will seem unfamiliar if you've only edited DOS programs. These features are common to most Windows programs that allow you to process text, even if the program is not a word processor. The first feature is that the position at which characters are inserted into the document—the *insertion point*—is controlled by the keyboard but can be changed by the mouse. As a result, you'll find two separate cursors. The insertion point is the spot that the keyboard controls; it's a tall, thin blinking line that you can move with the keyboard's arrow keys.

The second cursor is controlled by the mouse; when the mouse moves into the document editing window, it becomes an I-beam pointer. When you click the I-beam pointer at a position in the document, the insertion point moves to this spot.

The second feature is that any block of text can be changed once it has been highlighted. This allows you to move the text, delete it, or change its font. You define a block with the mouse by clicking at one point in the text and holding down the mouse button as you drag the mouse to cover the entire area you want to change. When you release the mouse button, the area is highlighted, as shown in Figure 4.1. When an area is highlighted, you choose a command from the Edit menu or use a shortcut key to make a change.

Figure 4.1

Highlighting text is one of the most basic techniques in graphical word processing. Once you've highlighted a block, you can move it, delete it, change its font, or use another of the formatting options on the pull-down menu.

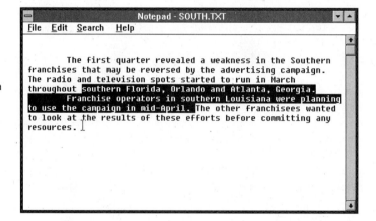

Once you've become familiar with these concepts, you'll be able to start using any graphical word processor, whether it's running under Windows, OS/2, or another operating system.

Notepad: For Quick and Simple Jobs

Because Notepad has few functions, it's easy to use it to open a new file, add a few words, and then quickly close it. Such simplicity makes Notepad ideal for jotting down notes while you're in the middle of other work. Even more useful is Notepad's ability to open text files created by more powerful word processing programs. You can quickly check a fact or add a few more words to these text files, without disturbing your other work.

Creating a Notepad File

The basic note-taking procedure is to open Notepad, write down your thoughts, and then save the file. If you're likely to add more words, don't bother to close Notepad, since it uses up so little memory.

Here's a step-by-step guide to creating a note:

1. Open Notepad by double-clicking on its icon in the Program Manager's Accessories group. You can also use the Run command in the Program Manager's File menu; in the Run dialog box's command-line prompt, type **NOTEPAD**. When another program is active, you can find Notepad by pressing Ctrl-Esc to activate the task list, selecting Program Manager, and opening the Accessories window.

2. When the Notepad window opens, you can immediately begin typing a new note.

3. When you're done typing, press Alt-F-S. The Save As dialog box opens, as shown in Figure 4.2.

Figure 4.2

You can start to jot down thoughts in the Notepad window as soon as it opens. When you're finished writing, save the note by calling the Save command under the Notepad's File menu; this dialog box will appear the first time the document is saved. When you save the file again, there's no confirmation.

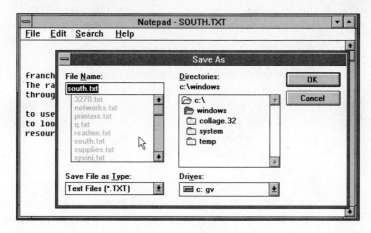

4. Type a name for your Notepad file in the Filename text box.

5. Press Enter; the dialog box closes and the Notepad title bar includes your new file name.

After the note is saved, the Notepad window remains open with the contents of the note. You'll probably want to switch to a new task without closing the Notepad since you may want to work on the note later. You can clear the window out of the way while keeping the contents of this note active by clicking on the Notepad window's Minimize button.

If you save a subsequent version of this file and then choose File-Save, the Save As dialog box won't open and the file will be saved immediately. Save As appears only when the active file was not previously saved.

If you wish to change the name of an open file, choose Save As from the File menu. The Save As dialog box will open and you can follow steps 4 and 5 above to store this file with a different name. The original file on disk will not be affected. This feature allows you to keep several versions of a file on disk.

To close Notepad, you can either double-click on the Notepad control menu, press Alt-F-X, or press Alt-F4. If you change the note after you save it, before it closes Notepad will open a dialog box that gives you a chance to save the changes.

Valid Notepad Files: ASCII Text

Notepad takes advantage of one of the most prevalent standards in all of computing: ASCII text, the format that defines how software should store the characters in the number system and the alphabet. ASCII, an acronym for American Standard Code for Information Interchange, defines each character as a number. For instance, an uppercase "A" is ASCII character 65, an uppercase "B" is character 66, and so on.

Most word processing programs give you the option of using ASCII characters to store documents, although they may add special formatting characters to control the way that the document is printed and displayed on screen. You can use Notepad to open any document that is stored in ASCII format. In addition, you can open a Notepad file with any word processor.

Programs such as spreadsheets and database managers don't use ASCII text at all, or use it in a limited way. These programs insert a "header" of binary data at the beginning of their data files to classify the file as being stored in a special format. When Notepad attempts to open a file, it looks for a binary header. If you try to open one of these non-ASCII text documents, Notepad will see this header, and instead of displaying the file it will report that the file "is not a valid Notepad file."

If you open a file that was created by another word processor, Notepad may display the file if the first few characters are standard text characters rather than formatting commands. Within such a document you'll probably see strange characters like @, >, and ^ before some of the words, as in Figure 4.3. These are the formatting commands used to change the fonts of words or set the margins of a page. You can edit formatted documents in Notepad and then edit them again in the original word processor, as long as you don't change any of these formatting characters.

Figure 4.3

This document was created in the XyWrite word processor and includes formatting characters that XyWrite uses to set margins and typefaces. The document can be edited in Notepad and still be read by XyWrite, as long as the formatting characters aren't changed.

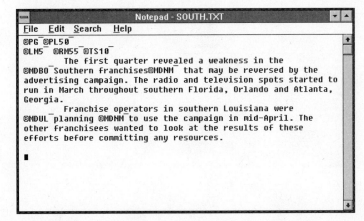

If Notepad won't open a document that you're certain contains ASCII text, the first few characters may be formatting characters, which causes Notepad to interpret this as a non-ASCII file. You might be able to trick Notepad into opening the file by using the original word processor to insert a carriage return at the very beginning of the document, in front of the formatting characters.

Notepad does not add any special formatting characters of its own, so it's an ideal program for making minor changes to large word processing documents or writing DOS batch files.

Notepad's Tools

Notepad is most commonly used for looking at a text file stored on disk. Since Windows installs several help files in the main Windows directory, you can use these to explore the tools on Notepad's main menu. If you prefer, you can use any other text file in these exercises.

The File Open Dialog Box

You'll need to employ all of the techniques you learned in Chapter 1 under "Dialog Boxes" to use the File Open command in Notepad. It's worth spending some time becoming familiar with the Open dialog box (see Figure 4.4), since almost every Windows program has one just like it.

If the file you want is in the current directory, just type the desired file name in the Filename text box. When you don't remember the name of the file, you'll need to search through the files in the directory and sometimes in other directories. Press the Tab key once to move the cursor to the Files list. There may be more files than will fit in the window. To bring these files into view, press the Down Arrow key.

Figure 4.4
The Open dialog box has a default setting to show TXT files.

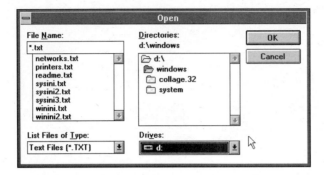

Instead of using the Tab key to select a name in the Files list, you can click once on any name and then use the Down Arrow key to bring others into view. Note that as you move the cursor down, the highlighted file appears in the Files text box. To open a file in the list, double-click on the name or press Enter when the right name is highlighted.

At first, the file list will display only files that have the extension .TXT (such as README.TXT). You can edit the Filename to find files with other extensions, or type *.* in order to see every file in that directory. Below the file list is a drop-down list that lets you choose between seeing only TXT files or all files in the directory.

If you need to find a file in a different directory, you use a similar procedure with the Directories list box. If you double-click on any directory name or press Enter while a directory name is highlighted, the list of files changes to include only the files in that directory.

You find files in subdirectories by double-clicking on closed folders, thereby opening them. It works very much like the Directory Tree in File Manager (see Chapter 3). When a folder icon is open, that means either its subdirectories or its files are being displayed. When a folder icon is closed, you can double-click to see its contents.

To change disk drives, double-click anywhere on the Drives drop-down box (either on the Down Arrow key or in the text box) and then select the correct disk from the list. To use the keyboard, enter Alt-D-Down Arrow to open the drives list, select the drive with an arrow key, and press Enter. Both the directories and the files listed will change to reflect the new drive.

Editing, Deleting, and Undoing in Notepad

Remember, you'll see two distinct cursors when you open a document with any Windows word processor: one controlled by the mouse and one controlled by the keyboard. Let's walk through the basic editing process and see how these cursors work together.

1. Open Notepad. (See the earlier section "Creating a Notepad File" if you need help.) The Notepad window opens.

2. Press Alt-F-O or select the Open command in the File menu with your mouse. An Open dialog box opens; it should include several files in the Files list.

3. Double-click on any of these files.

4. Move the mouse pointer around the screen; notice that it changes from an arrow pointer to an I-beam when it enters the Notepad window, indicating that you can edit text in this area. If you move the pointer to the scroll bar or menu bar, it will become the familiar arrow pointer, indicating that you can select the menus or scroll bar movements. (See Figure 4.5.)

Figure 4.5
The insertion point and I-beam pointer are common to all Windows word processing programs. The insertion point is controlled with the keyboard arrow keys and shows where text can be added or deleted; the I-beam pointer is controlled with the mouse.

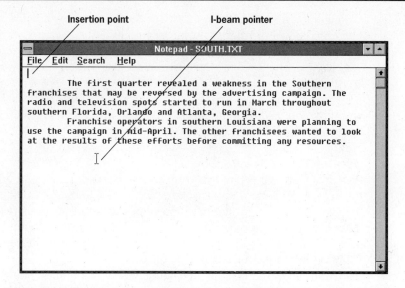

5. Press the Down Arrow key and notice that a tall blinking line moves from the upper-left corner of the screen, moving in concert with the arrow key. This line is called the insertion point. If you enter a letter from the keyboard, it is inserted at the cursor location.

6. Move the mouse pointer to the right of any line and click. Notice that the insertion point moves to this spot. Any time you click the mouse, the insertion point moves to the place in the text nearest to the mouse.

7. Hold down the Shift key while you press the Right Arrow key until you've come to the beginning of the line; the text is highlighted as the insertion point passes over. Release both keys.

8. Open the Edit menu and select Cut; the highlighted text disappears.

9. Open the Edit menu and select Paste; the highlighted text reappears.

In Notepad, you change highlighted text only with the Edit menu command. Write gives you the ability to format text with various fonts, and more powerful word processors add still more features.

Because highlighting a block and then making a change is so fundamental to graphical word processing, experiment with the previous steps until you feel comfortable. You won't change any data if you don't save the file.

Highlighting Text

To highlight text with the mouse, click to create a new insertion point and then hold down the mouse button as you drag the I-beam over the desired text. When you've highlighted the right words, release the mouse button. If you want to highlight just one word, place the pointer on the word and double-click.

You can quickly highlight a long block of text that follows the insertion point by holding down the Shift key when you click; this selects all of the text between the insertion point and the I-beam pointer.

Placing Text in the Clipboard

When you cut a block of text from a Notepad document, that text is placed in an area of memory known as the Windows Clipboard. You can review the text by opening the program called Clipboard in the Accessories group. However, you don't need to look at Clipboard to use its contents; when you used Paste in step 9 in the last section, you were pasting the contents of the Clipboard into the document.

Since all of the Edit menu commands are common to many Windows programs, we'll cover them in depth later in this chapter in the section "Exchanging Data with Clipboard."

Searching in Notepad

The Search menu lets you find any word or phrase in the open file. If the specified word or phrase is in the document, Notepad highlights it and moves the insertion point to the end of the word or phrase.

1. Click to the left of the first word in the file to make sure your search covers the entire document.

2. Open the Search menu and select Find. The Find dialog box opens.

3. Type a phrase that you see in the document into the Find What text box and select OK. The phrase "continue with Setup" will quickly be highlighted in the document.

The Find command has three options: It can execute the search forward or backward in the document; it can make the search case sensitive or not (that is, it will look for matches based on your use of capitalization); and it will match whole words or not. (For example, if you want to find a short word like "see," you would select the option to match whole words, so search would not stop at words like "seem," and "foresee.")

After Find highlights a match in the document, you can continue the search by using the Find Next choice in the Search menu to look for the next occurrence of the phrase.

Printing in Notepad

Notepad has few print options. However, you can set the margins or insert headers and footers on the page. You make these enhancements by selecting the Page Setup option under the File menu, and editing the text boxes within the dialog box.

Page Setup

You can select Page Setup at any time while you work in Notepad, but its function is to control two basic factors in the appearance of the printed document: the margins (on all four sides) and the headers or footers that will appear on each page. (Typical headers and footers are the title of a report or the page number.) See Figure 4.6.

Figure 4.6
Notepad's Page Setup option has a default setting for all four margins and both the header and the footer.

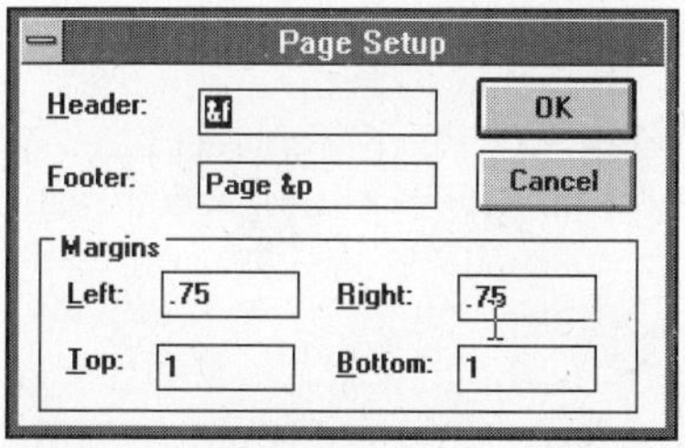

Page Setup	
Header: &f	OK
Footer: Page &p	Cancel
Margins	
Left: .75	Right: .75
Top: 1	Bottom: 1

The default setting for the header is "&f," which will print the name of the file. Of course, you can edit this to be the title of your report or anything else you want to print on each page, like "For Internal Use Only."

The default setting for the footer is "page &p," which will print the word *page* followed by the page number on each page printed.

There are four codes that insert text into a header or footer:

&f   Prints the filename

&p   Prints the page number

&d   Prints the date that the document is printed

&t   Prints the time that the document is printed

There are three codes that format the text in a header or footer line:

&l   Left-aligns the words after the code

&r   Right-aligns the words after the code

&c   Centers the words after the code

The margins establish how much of a border space your document will have. The default settings are .75 inch on the left and right sides, and 1 inch on the top and bottom. This creates a very full page. You may want to double these.

Recording the Date in a Document

There's a handy way to insert the date into the body of a document using the Time/Date command under Notepad's Edit menu. Either select Time/Date from the Edit menu, press Alt-E-D, or press F5, and the current date will appear in the document at the insertion point.

You can change the format of the date by running the control panel program in the Main windows group and selecting the International icon. You can choose either a month-day-year, day-month-year, or year-month-day format. You can also control whether leading zeros are used (whether January is represented as 1 or 01 for instance). If your system time is not set correctly, use the control panel's Date/Time module to enter the correct time. You'll probably need to set the time after the switch between standard and daylight savings times. (Chapter 9 gives detailed instructions on changing the time and date.)

Notepad also lets you date-stamp a text file. If you type **.LOG** (uppercase only) at the far left margin on the first line in a file, Notepad adds the time and date to the end of the file every time you open it. If you open the file several times a day, Notepad adds the time and date each time.

For example, if you have many clients you can keep a date-stamped Notepad file that records your dealings with each client. After every conversation, you can quickly jot down comments and save the file. The date-stamp will automatically insert today's time and date after every comment. Figure 4.7 shows a date-stamped file used to track service requests.

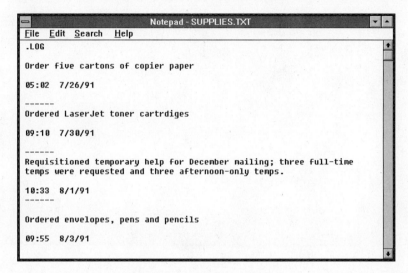

In fact, if you like to keep to-do lists, you can use Notepad to create activity logs for regular chores with the date-stamp feature. Every time you open such a file, Notepad adds the date and you'll have a running history of your activities. To create the log, first set up a Notepad file with the .LOG option. Then change the Windows settings so that it opens at the beginning of each Windows session. You do this by editing your WIN.INI file with Notepad.

1. Open Notepad, type **.LOG** (uppercase only) on the first line, and then enter your list of to-do items on subsequent lines. Save the File as TODOLIST.TXT.

2. Press Alt-F-O; the File Open dialog box opens.

3. Type **WIN.INI** in the Filename text box and press Enter. The File Open dialog box closes and the WIN.INI file opens in Notepad. (The WIN.INI file is stored in the main Windows directory. If Notepad can't find it, someone altered the path in your system from the Windows default. See Appendix A for help.)

4. The third line of the WIN.INI file reads run=; type **TODOLIST.TXT** there so that the line reads run=TODOLIST.TXT, as shown in Figure 4.8.

5. Press Alt-F-S to save the file.

6. Press Alt-F-X to close Notepad.

Figure 4.8
You can use
Notepad to start
every Windows
session with a
reminder of your
chores by editing
the WIN.INI file's
RUN command
to equal
TODOLIST.TXT.
You can include a
.LOG date-stamp at
the front of your
TODOLIST.TXT file
to create an
historical record of
your to-do lists.

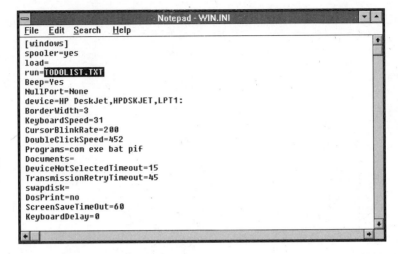

```
Notepad - WIN.INI
File  Edit  Search  Help
[windows]
spooler=yes
load=
run=TODOLIST.TXT
Beep=Yes
NullPort=None
device=HP DeskJet,HPDSKJET,LPT1:
BorderWidth=3
KeyboardSpeed=31
CursorBlinkRate=200
DoubleClickSpeed=452
Programs=com exe bat pif
Documents=
DeviceNotSelectedTimeout=15
TransmissionRetryTimeout=45
swapdisk=
DosPrint=no
ScreenSaveTimeOut=60
KeyboardDelay=0
```

The next time you begin a Windows session, the .LOG File will open automatically. You can use any file that has the extension .TXT in step 4 and Notepad will load it. You don't need to include the program name after run= in the WIN.INI file because the WIN.INI file has an association between Notepad and files with .TXT extensions: When you tell Windows to run a .TXT file, it already knows that you want Notepad to do the running. (Refer back to Chapter 3.)

If you want to use a file that does not have the .TXT extension, simply enter **NOTEPAD** *filename* in step 4. If you want your TODOLIST.TXT file to be available as an icon instead of an open window whenever you start Windows, insert the file name after the second line (load=) in the WIN.INI file. When you load a file it becomes an icon; when you run a file it appears as the active window.

Fitting Text in a Window

While Notepad is a quite limited program, it does have two important options that help you manage text in a window. Both are located in the Edit menu.

- **Select All**   Highlights every word in the file; this option is useful for cutting the entire text to place it in the Clipboard.

- **Word Wrap**   A toggle command; if it's checked, Notepad makes each line fit within the window. If it's not checked, text continues on a single line until a carriage return is inserted in the line.

For example, if Word Wrap is off, the lines you type will get so long that they won't fit inside the window. Notepad then scrolls the document to the left, and the first part of the line won't show on the screen. If Word Wrap is on, Notepad wraps each line as it reaches the end of the window so that you can see the complete text on each line (see Figure 4.9). In general, you'll want to keep Word Wrap on; when Notepad starts, the default setting is off.

Figure 4.9

The same text file in separate Notepad windows illustrates the Word Wrap option. On the left, Word Wrap is on and you can see full sentences. On the right, Word Wrap is off and the sentences are so long that they're not displayed in full.

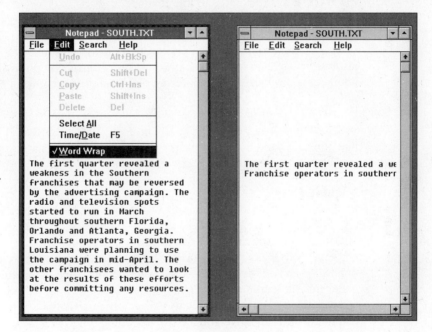

You should turn Word Wrap off to work on large files. On many systems, the Word Wrap option cannot work with files larger than about 20k, but if you have several megabytes of free memory available in Windows, you may be able to word wrap files as large as 22k.

Notepad needs the Word Wrap feature since it cannot limit the length of a line. Write and other word processors control line length with margin settings and other page format options. Word Wrap is the most important setting to adjust in Notepad; keep it on so that you'll be able to see your documents as you work with them.

Write: A Full-Featured Graphical Word Processor

With the exception of time- and date-stamping and Select All, Write can do everything that Notepad does. And it can do a lot more.

Creating Write Documents

You open Write by double-clicking on its icon from Program Manager's Accessories window or by using Program Manager's Run command and typing **WRITE** at the command line text box.

When Write opens, the blinking insertion point is on the top line and next to it is a four-pointed box called the *end mark*. You can begin to type your document immediately. As you do, the end mark moves so that it's always the last character in the document. The insertion point also moves, but it remains where you're entering text. The document will be untitled until you give it a name with the Save command.

When you save a document, Write gives it the extension .WRI unless you add your own. For example, if you save a file as REPORT, Write automatically adds the .WRI extension. When you open your REPORT file later, you'll need to open the file REPORT.WRI.

Opening Files

In Write, you can use any document saved in ASCII text format. When you try to open a file created by a different word processor, Write gives you the option of converting it to Write's own format.

However, Write won't translate your formatting so that it appears in the same style as your original file. For example, this conversion will not change italics that appeared in the original word processor into Write's italics. Instead, the conversion will try to strip out the original word processor's format commands and give you a clean text file. Sometimes it will not be able to strip out the formatting command and you'll end up with unusual characters that appear where formatting commands had been. You'll have to delete these yourself, and add new formatting to replace the old one.

Choose the No Conversion option when you want to look at a file in Write that you know you'll want to use again in the original word processor; this way, you won't have the messy job of trying to replace the formatting characters.

When you use Write's File Open command, the dialog box only displays files with Write's unique .WRI extension in the current directory. You can use the mouse to change the default setting in the list box that appears in the lower-left corner so that it displays all types of files; there's also an option for displaying only Microsoft Word files (those with a .DOC extension). Refer back to Figure 4.4 to see this dialog box; the File Open dialog box in Write works the same way it works in Notepad. If you know the name of the file you're looking for, you can type it in the File Name text box (using the full path if it's in a different directory), or you can type the wildcard *.* in the File Name text box to see a list of all files in that directory. To look for files in a different directory, click on the names in the Directories list. Click on a closed folder icon to move up to a parent directory.

Saving Files

When you're ready to save the document, you have the option of keeping it in Write's format (.WRI) or storing it as a standard text file (with a .TXT extension). In a standard text file, the formatting you do in Write will be lost, but you'll be better able to use the file in other word processors.

You can also save the document in the format used by Microsoft Word, which is useful if you use Microsoft Word in either DOS or Windows.

If you have a heavily formatted document in Write and you want to use it in a different word processor (like WordPerfect or MultiMate), you can store in Microsoft Word format, and then use a word processing format-translator program (such as Word for Word) to convert it from Microsoft Word format to the format used by your word processor.

Editing in Write

The techniques for editing with a mouse in Write are identical to those used in Notepad: Highlight a block of text and use Cut and Paste in the Edit menu. (See the earlier section, "Editing, Deleting, and Undoing in Notepad.") Write adds another technique: you can highlight a single line by clicking the mouse just to the left of the line in the left margin.

Write also offers a small set of keyboard editing techniques. See Table 4.1 for a summary of key combinations that move the position of the insertion point. Note that Write uses the 5 key on the numeric keypad as GoTo (the Num Lock key must be off). These commands work best if you place your hand over the numeric keypad with your middle finger resting on the number 5 (GoTo). If your computer has a 101-key keyboard (with a separate arrow keypad), it's probably easier to use the numeric keypad (with Num Lock off) instead of the arrow keypad.

Most of the individual keys—such as Tab, PgUp, PgDn, Del, Shift, and Caps Lock—work as they do in other programs. The Home and End keys bring you to the beginning and end of a single line, respectively.

You can select blocks of text as explained earlier for Notepad (see "Highlighting Text"); Table 4.2 shows some mouse techniques for highlighting text that are unique to Write. The white space to the left of your document in the Write window is used for highlighting large blocks of text. It may take some practice to find this area, which is between the leftmost character and the window border.

Table 4.1 **Shortcut Keys for Moving the Insertion Point**

Key Combination	Action
Ctrl-Right Arrow	Moves the insertion point to the next word
Ctrl-Left Arrow	Moves the insertion point to the previous word
GoTo (the 5 Key on the numeric keypad)	Used in combination with other keys
GoTo-Right Arrow	Moves the insertion point to the next sentence, but stops at carriage returns and periods
GoTo-Left Arrow	Moves the insertion point to the previous sentence, but also stops at carriage returns, periods, and tabs
Home	Moves the insertion point to the beginning of a line
End	Moves the insertion point to the end of a line
GoTo-Up Arrow and GoTo-Down Arrow	Move the insertion point to the paragraph or carriage return above or below, respectively
GoTo-PgUp and GoTo-PgDn	Move the insertion point to the next and previous pages, respectively. New documents or files that weren't created in Write don't have page breaks yet. You must use the Repaginate command (on the Print menu) first to establish page numbers, which appear in the lower-left corner of the Write window
Ctrl-Home and Ctrl-End	Move the insertion point to the beginning and end of the document, respectively

Table 4.2 **Mouse Tricks for Highlighting Text**

To Highlight	Action
A line	Move the mouse pointer to the white area to the left of a line. Click once to highlight the entire line. Hold the mouse button down and drag the mouse up or down to select more than one line.
A paragraph	Double-click with the mouse pointer next to any line in the paragraph. For multiple paragraphs, hold the mouse button down after the second click and drag the mouse. Release the mouse button when you're done.
A large block	Highlight a line or paragraph using the techniques above and release the mouse button. Now hold down the Shift key and move the mouse pointer to the left of a new line. Click the mouse button to highlight all of the material between this point and the earlier highlighted material.
An entire document	Move to the left of any line, hold down Ctrl, and click the mouse.

Deleting and Inserting Text

There's one major difference between Write and other word processors. In Write, you're always inserting: You can never turn insertion off with the Ins key. In most word processors, you can turn Ins off and overwrite text, but in Write you must first delete text (as explained earlier under "Editing, Deleting, and Undoing in Notepad") and then type in the new words.

Searching for Text

Write has several commands for finding text within an open document and for replacing text. To search for a word or phrase (any string up to 255 characters), select the Find menu. Use the Find command if you only want to see the phrase. Use the Replace command if you want to replace the phrase with new text.

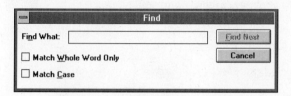

Searching in Write is similar to Searching in Notepad, but Write provides a few more options. When you use Find, you'll see these two choices:

- Match Whole Word Only is good when searching for short words. It finds only entire words, not strings that appear within words. For example, if you are searching for the word "man" and don't check the Match Whole Word Only option, the Search will stop at the word "command."

- Match Case helps restrict the search so that you find only words with the exact capitalization that you want.

After you fill out the menu, click the Find Next box and Find will stop at the first occurrence of the word. You can look for the next occurrence by pressing the F3 key or selecting Repeat Last Find. Find always starts its search from the beginning of the document.

If no words have been found, a message box will appear to let you know.

One caveat: The Find dialog box may hide the word after it's been found. If you select Find Next and nothing changes on the screen, Write is highlighting the word behind the dialog box. You must move the dialog box—either by clicking on the title bar and dragging it to a new location, or by using the Move command on the dialog box's Control menu.

Replacing Text

The Replace command enables you to replace one word or phrase through-out a document. You provide a word or phrase of up to 255 characters that you want the program to find, and then enter the replacement text.

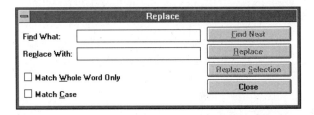

The Replace command provides several options that give you a high level of control over searching and replacing.

- Find Next continues the search after it has found the desired text, but doesn't replace this occurrence of text.

- Replace makes the change and then moves on to the next occurrence.

- Replace automates the search and replace operation, replacing all occur-rences of the desired text without delay.

The Replace command has the same problem that Find has: The dialog box may hide the work that it's done. This can be a problem when you're using the Find Next and Replace options; if you execute a Find Next or Replace and nothing seems to happen, move the dialog box so you can see the highlighted text.

Going to a Page

The Go to Page command on the Find menu lets you quickly move the inser-tion point to a different page in the file. The command works properly only if you have already used the Repaginate command on the File menu. If you use the Go to Page command on a file that has not been repaginated, the insertion point will move to the top of the file, no matter which page you had entered in the Go to Page dialog box.

Character Formats

The Character commands let you select fonts in the following two ways:

- You can change the font for the characters that you are about to type.

- You can change the font for characters already displayed.

To format characters before you type them, follow these steps:

1. Open Write by double-clicking on its icon or by typing **WRITE** at the Program Manager's Run command. The Write window opens.

2. Select Character with the mouse or by pressing Alt-C. The Character menu drops down. It shows that the Regular style of the default font will be used.

3. Press Esc to clear the Character menu and type a few words. They appear in the default font.

4. To select a different style, open the Character menu and press B. Press Esc and type a few new words.

5. Repeat step 5 with other styles, selecting italic, underline, and so on. Your screen should resemble the screen in Figure 4.10.

Figure 4.10

You can change fonts "on the fly" by selecting options from the Character menu. Each choice is a toggle; if you turn one option on without turning off the previous option, both choices will be in effect.

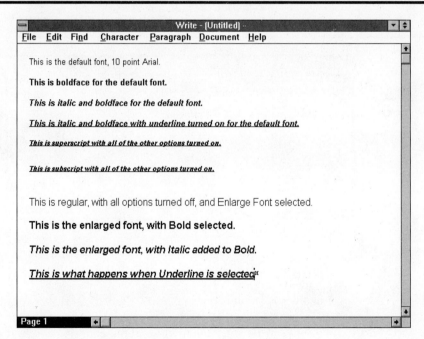

To change a font after the text is displayed, use the mouse to highlight the words you want to change, open the Character menu, and select a new font. As soon as you've made your font selection, the Character menu will close and the text will change to the new font.

As you selected new styles for the font, the previous selections stayed in effect most of the time (the exceptions are superscript and subscript, which cancel each other). Most of the time, you'll need to turn off one option as you select a new one.

The list of styles on the Character menu is provided as a convenience for making minor changes to the current font; to make a major change to the current font you should use the Font at the bottom of the Character menu.

Choosing Fonts

You can control every aspect of the characters in your documents with the Fonts dialog box. To open it, select Fonts on the Character menu. This dialog box appears in almost every Windows program that lets you control the fonts used in your documents.

The basic procedure for using this dialog box (shown in Figure 4.11) is to start by choosing a font from the list box. As you highlight a new font, a sample is displayed in the lower-right corner.

Figure 4.11
The character pull-down menu lets you choose a font in several ways.

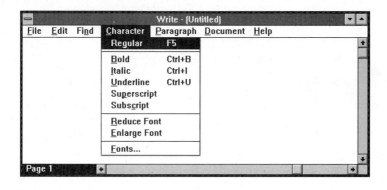

Then, choose the Font Style from the list and note that the Sample display changes.

Finally, you should choose the size; the Sample display changes once again.

This may be all you need to know about choosing a font. If you want to have precise control over the way your documents work, read the following section "A Word About Fonts"; otherwise, skip ahead to "Formatting Paragraphs and Documents."

A Word about Fonts

The subject of fonts in Windows could fill an entire book; in fact, Chapter 12 is devoted entirely to printing in Windows. That chapter covers fonts in depth, but as you begin to work with Windows, a brief summary of your font choices will be helpful.

A *font* is a typeface in a specific size and style. For example, Courier is a typeface; 10-point Courier italic is a font. Points are a measure of the character's height; one point equals $1/72$ of an inch. A *typestyle* is a variation on the typeface's basic appearance. Regular, bold, italic, and bold italic are the choices generally offered in a typeface.

Each printer's hardware provides a selection of several fonts. Windows learns about this selection when the printer is installed. These fonts are called *printer fonts* or *hardware fonts*, and they're stored in ROM (read-only memory) chips within the printer itself or on a cartridge that plugs into the printer. Printer fonts are indicated with a small printer icon in the Font dialog box. When you select a printer font, only specific styles and sizes will be available. (See Figure 4.12.)

Figure 4.12
The Fonts menu lets you see a sample of the font before you select it.

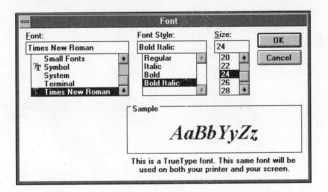

Printer fonts produce excellent quality when printed but the font you see on screen will usually not match the font that prints. Windows does not have enough fonts in a display format to match all of the possible printer fonts.

Windows comes with two other types of fonts that are stored in software files. The first of the software fonts are the Windows system fonts. Some of them are used by Windows programs to display menus and dialog boxes; others are provided mainly to provide compatibility with programs written for earlier versions of Windows. These are the least desirable fonts to use, since they'll produce the least attractive output. These fonts have no icon identifying them in the Fonts dialog box.

The second type of software font available is the one you'll want to use most often, especially when you want to create truly handsome documents. These are the TrueType fonts, recognizable in the Fonts dialog box because there's a TT logo to the left of each.

These fonts were created by Microsoft specially for Windows, and they're one of the big advances in technology that Windows 3.1 provides. There are four typefaces (Arial, Courier, Times New Roman, and Symbol), and they can be both printed and displayed in a wide variety of sizes and in the four basic styles (regular, bold, italic, and bold italic).

The TrueType fonts are said to be *scalable* because the program code that describes every character within a typeface's many sizes is stored in a single Windows file. When Windows programs display or print the file, they scale the characters to the needed size. This system cuts down dramatically on the amount of disk space needed for storing the font, making it practical to have lots of fonts available within a budget.

Formatting Paragraphs and Entire Documents

The commands that control the arrangement of words on a page are under Write's Paragraph and Document menus.

Paragraph Formats

If you select Paragraph commands at the beginning of a document, the settings will remain in effect for the rest of the file. If you want to change the appearance of an individual paragraph, simply select one of the Paragraph commands when the insertion point is inside that paragraph; the new setting will take effect immediately.

Here are the settings controlled via the Paragraph menu:

- Text Alignment aligns text to the left, right, or center, or makes it justified, as shown in Figure 4.13. Note that the justified option sometimes looks like left aligned on screen. When printed, however, justified text will be both left and right aligned.

- Line spacing sets the space between lines. Single spacing puts little spacing between lines, one-and-a-half spacing puts an extra half-line's space between lines, and double-spacing adds a full extra line's worth of space between every two lines, as shown in Figure 4.14. The line spacing on screen is very much like the spacing for printed text.

Figure 4.13

Left aligned text has a straight left margin and is ragged on the right. Center aligned text is ragged on both sides. Right aligned text has a straight right margin and is ragged on the left. Justified text has a straight margin on both sides when printed.

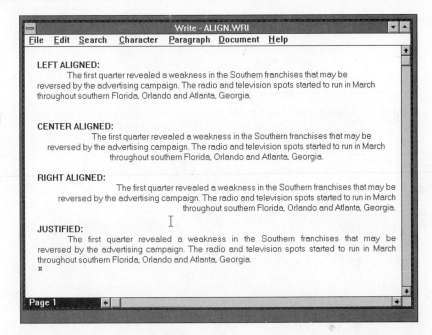

Figure 4.14

These three paragraphs are all left aligned and illustrate three different paragraph spacing styles possible with Write.

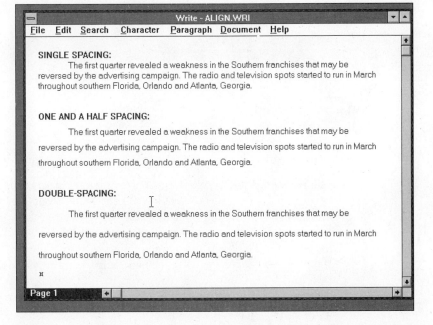

■ The Indents selection indents text from the margins, using inches or fractions of an inch as the measurement. You can set an indent for an entire paragraph or just for the first line in the paragraph. You can achieve a special effect called a *hanging indent* by setting the indent for the first line to a negative value, as shown in Figure 4.15.

Figure 4.15

The Paragraph menu's Indent command is useful for making individual paragraphs look special. You can create the hanging indent shown here by setting the indent for the first line to a negative value.

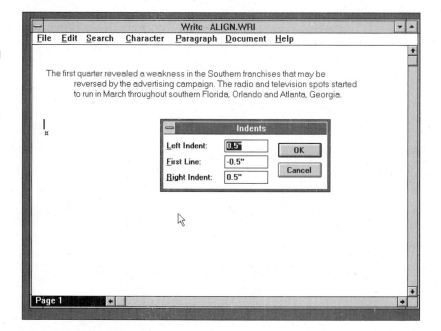

Document Formats

In Windows programs, it's fairly common for most menus to be logical groupings and one or two to seem like a catchall for miscellaneous functions. In Write, the Document menu is the catchall that contains the following options:

■ The Headers and Footers options bring up a fresh screen for entering the header or footer text with a dialog box for special options. For example, in Figure 4.16 the title bar indicates that a footer rather than a document is being edited. Your header or footer can be as long as you wish, and can have the benefit of Write's character and paragraph formatting commands. If you choose Insert Page #, each page will be numbered; the page number will print at the point where you insert it. You also have the option of not printing your headers and footers on the front page (where you may plan to use a special heading). When you've finished writing and formatting the text, select Return to Document. The header or footer will be cleared from the screen and will be printed with the document. You won't be able to see it on the display, however.

Figure 4.16

Selecting either Header or Footer from the Documents menu brings up a fresh window for writing, editing, and formatting the header or footer. Write displays the word "(page)" where you choose to insert the page number. When you print the document, Write prints the number here, not the word "(page)."

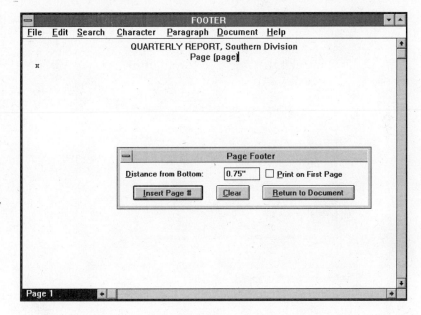

■ The Tabs option changes the tab settings. Write spaces tabs at every half-inch by default. You can use the Tabs command to set up to 12 tabs precisely. To set tabs, enter numbers that represent inches or centimeters from the left margin (the next paragraph explains how to choose between inches and centimeters). You don't need to set all 12 tabs; set only the ones you're going to use. You can also set decimal tabs, to align the numbers on the decimal point. Check the decimal tab box to use this option, which is extremely valuable if you print columns of numbers in your documents.

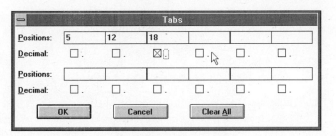

■ The Page Layout option changes the margin settings. Write uses a default 1¼-inch margin on the right and left, and a 1-inch margin on the top and bottom of your printed page. You can change these settings in the Page Layout dialog box. This is also where you can choose between inches or centimeters as your measurement throughout the document. In addition, you can choose to start numbering your document several pages after it has begun. This is useful when your document has cover sheets that you don't want numbered. When you change the Start Page Number entry, you'll see an adjustment in the lower-left corner's page status display.

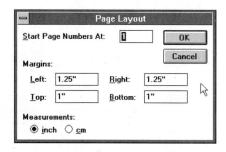

The Ruler: A Formatting Shortcut

The Document menu includes a very useful tool for setting paragraph formats without using the Paragraph menu commands. The Ruler is a graphic summary of the paragraph settings and a few more settings. It includes numbers that represent the columns running horizontally across the document, markers that represent the indents and tabs, and icons for changing paragraph formats (see Figure 4.17).

You turn the Ruler on by selecting it from the Document menu. It operates like a toggle switch: Choose it once to turn it on and it remains on the screen; choose it again from the Document menu and it disappears.

It's a good idea to keep the Ruler displayed as you work, since it lets you get quickly to some of Write's settings without the extra step of choosing the menus. The only reason to not display the Ruler is if you want to use every bit of the document window to see what you're writing.

When you use the Ruler for formatting, you must first select the paragraph or group of paragraphs that you want to format. Then, click on the setting you want to change. If the setting affects margins (such as indents and tabs), you must drag the marker to the desired margin.

■ The indent markers set the indent settings, and are represented by arrows at either end of the Ruler, left and right. To change a margin, first highlight the text, click on the arrow for the margin you want to change, and drag the marker to the new position. The left arrow marker covers a small circular marker that represents the first-line indent. It's difficult to distinguish the two, so look carefully to make sure you're dragging the correct marker. You'll need to drag both markers separately to set a hanging indent properly.

- The tab icons set the tabs, which is much easier with the Ruler than with the menu command. You set a tab by first clicking on the Tab icon and then clicking on a spot within the Ruler. After the tab marker appears within the ruler, you can drag it to a new location. To remove a tab, drag it to the far left of the margin. The left tab icon is for standard left-aligning tabs; the right tab icon is for decimal tabs.

- The line spacing icons regulate the space between lines. Click on the icon for single, one-and-a-half, and double-spacing when the insertion point is in the desired paragraph.

- The text alignment icons align your text. Click on the icon for left, center, right, or justified text when the insertion point is in the desired paragraph.

Figure 4.17

The Ruler is useful for viewing and changing the current settings for paragraph and tab formats. Note the small size of the marker for the first-line indent; when it and the left-indent marker are both set at zero, it's difficult to distinguish them.

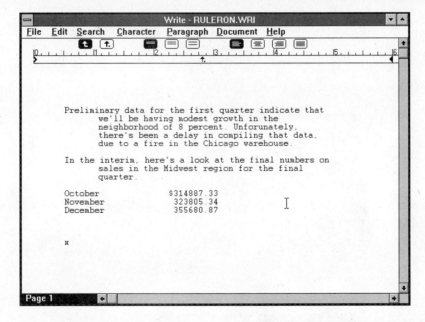

Printing in Write

Before printing your document, you need to run the Repaginate command. When your document is ready for printing, follow these steps:

1. Press Alt-F-E to select Repaginate in the File menu. A Repaginate Document dialog box appears.

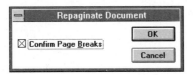

2. You have the option of confirming page breaks. It's a good idea to select this option because it can help enhance the appearance of your document. Confirming page breaks lets you check that the end of the page does not contain the very beginning of an important section that you want to begin on a new page.

3. Select OK. The dialog box closes and repagination begins.

4. A Repaginating Document dialog box will appear so that you can confirm whether the highlighted line is a good page break; a double arrow will appear to the left of the first line on the next page. You can choose Up or Down to make the page end on a different line. Choose Confirm when the page break is in a good spot.

5. A new Repaginating Document dialog box will appear for every page. When the entire document is paginated, the insertion point will be at the last line, with a double arrow pointing to the last line. The page number for the last page will be displayed in the lower-left corner of the window. You're now ready to print the document.

Printing Options

After a document has been repaginated, you can select Print on the File menu. This command opens a dialog box that's used by many Windows programs for printing; see Figure 4.18.

Figure 4.18

The Print dialog box controls options ranging from which printer is currently active to the quality of the printed copy.

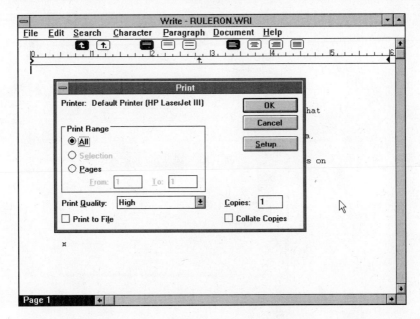

There are several choices to make in this dialog box. The following list is a guide to the entire Print dialog box.

Setup   Click on this command button if you want to select one of your printer's optional settings. These settings can include the paper tray (if you have more than one); whether the document prints in portrait mode (like a standard letter) or landscape mode (sideways); and the size of the paper.

The dialog box that opens when you click on the Setup command button is the same box that opens if you choose Printer Setup from the File menu. It has a second dialog box, which opens if you click on the Options command button.

This dialog box is unique for every printer. Figure 4.19 shows the dialog box that opens when an Epson LQ-1000 printer is active.

The first time you print a document, you should explore all of the settings. Follow this sequence:

1. Select the Print command from the File menu. The Print dialog box opens.

2. Select the Setup command button on the Print menu. The Print Setup dialog box opens.

Figure 4.19

These dialog boxes are available when you select either the Printer Setup command on the File menu or the Setup option on the Print dialog box. In both cases, the Print Setup dialog box (top) opens first; the second dialog box (More) opens if you choose the Options button.

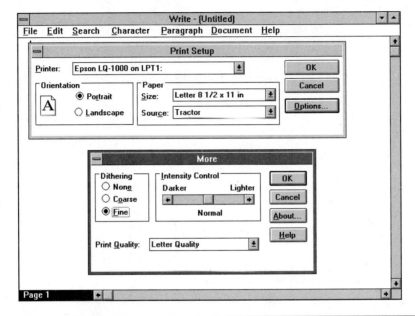

3. Selection the Options command button. Your printer's unique dialog box opens.

The settings in this dialog box have the greatest control over your printed document. In general, you'll want to decide whether to use the printer for speed or for high-quality output. Most printer settings are designed to give you a choice between letter quality (which looks better but takes longer to print) and draft quality (the fastest but least attractive output setting). Some printers provide a variety of ways to fine-tune the options, such as choosing between fine and coarse dithering or darker and lighter intensity. You may need to refer back to your printer manual for help in getting the most out of your printer.

Printer   Check the name of the printer listed at the top of the dialog box as your default printer. If it's not correct, you'll need to install the correct printer using the Control Panel. Chapter 9 covers this topic.

Print Range   This box offers three choices: All, Selection, or Pages. Select the All option to print the entire document. Selection is dimmed to indicate that it's not available. (This dialog box is shared among Write and other Windows applications, and Write does not take advantage of the feature.) The Pages option lets you choose only certain pages within the entire document;

enter both a starting page number and the last page number to print if you click on this setting.

Print Quality   This is another way to choose among best quality (slowest printing) and draft quality (fastest printing).

Copies   You can generate multiple copies of any document (or the portion you selected in Print Range). If you choose more than one copy, you probably want to click on Collate Copies, so the finished pages will be arranged sequentially.

Print to File   This option stores the option as a file on disk instead of generating printed output. It's used most often by people who use the PostScript page description language. Typically, you would print to disk if you wanted to get printed copy from a printer of higher quality than the one attached to your system; this way you could copy the file over to that computer to be printed later.

Exchanging Data with Clipboard

The Clipboard is the secret behind much of Windows' power. When you use the Edit menu commands to cut or copy any block, you're using the Clipboard. In effect, the Clipboard program is always active in Windows. Whenever you select Cut or Copy from a Windows Edit menu, the block is moved into the Clipboard. When you Paste the block into a document, you insert a copy of the data from the Clipboard into your document.

The difference between Cut and Copy is simple: Cut removes the material from the original document as it is transferred to the Clipboard. Copy leaves the original document unchanged as the material is transferred to the Clipboard.

You can see the contents of the Clipboard at any point by double-clicking its icon in Program Manager. Generally, however, you don't need to run Clipboard to experience its benefits.

Moving Text from Notepad to Write

The Clipboard will exchange data between any two Windows programs. Here's how to exchange a block of text between a Notepad file and a Write file:

1. Open Notepad by double-clicking on its icon in Main, and open the file README.TXT.

2. Minimize the Notepad window.

3. Open Write by double-clicking on its icon in Program Manager.

4. Restore the Notepad window.

5. Highlight any block of text and select Cut from the Edit menu (or press Shift-Del). The block of text disappears.

6. Press Alt-F4 to close Notepad; do not save the changes to READ-ME.TXT.

7. The Write window should be the active window; if not, use Program Manager's Task List (press Ctrl-Esc) to return to Write. Open Write's Edit menu and select Paste. The block of text now appears in the Write document. Select Paste and the block of text appears again.

Data in the Clipboard remains there until a new block of data is cut from a document, so you can continue to paste the block again and again. If you highlight a section of the text and select either Cut or Copy from the Edit menu, Paste will insert this new block.

Inserting Graphics into Write Documents

You can use the Clipboard to insert graphic elements into your document. For instance, a letter about a new product could contain a scanned image of the product or a drawing created in Windows' Paintbrush program.

First you need to get the graphic into the Clipboard. In most cases, this means using either Paintbrush or another Windows program to display the image, and then using Cut or Copy to put it in the Clipboard.

Since you can also put the image of an entire display into the Clipboard, we'll try placing a screen image in a Write document.

1. Open Write. You can try this with an untitled document or with a file that you don't mind losing.

2. Press the Print Screen key to place the screen image in the Clipboard. (This may not work, depending on the keyboard or software drivers installed in your system. If the screen image is not transferred to Clipboard, repeat this step with the key combination Alt-PrtSc or Shift-PrtSc.) There's no way of knowing if the screen was successfully captured until you try step 3.

3. Select Paste from Write's Edit menu. The hourglass icon will appear if step 2 was successful. In a few seconds, a small graphic image of the screen will appear. If it doesn't, repeat step 2 with a different key combination.

4. You can position the graphic by using the mouse button or arrow keys. When it's in the right place, press Enter.

Problems with Graphics

Windows requires lots of memory to work at full efficiency. If your system has less than 2Mb or if you have several programs loaded into memory when you try the operation, you may not be able to insert screen images into a Write document.

Since you'll rarely need to save a screen image, don't be too concerned if you can't do it. You'll still be able to insert graphics that were created in programs like Paintbrush. Simply open those programs, cut the image, close the program, and open Write.

Sizing and Moving Graphics

The Edit menu has two commands for editing graphics: Move and Size. They work in a similar fashion. First, you click on the graphic to select it. Then choose either Move Picture or Size Picture. A square cursor appears, indicating that you're editing the graphic.

To move the graphic, position the square cursor in the new location and then press Enter. To align it properly, select one of the Paragraph menu's align commands before you press Enter.

To change the graphic's size, choose a direction while the square cursor is displayed. Click on the top, lower-right, or left side of the image and then drag the side until it's the desired size.

Linking Objects

The Edit menu lets you share files between Write and certain other Windows programs through the process of *linking*. This technique makes the sharing of files more efficient than cutting and pasting, since when you link files, your original file simply refers back to the linked file. That linked file doesn't get copied or changed in any way.

When you click on the linked file from the original file, you can use the linked file in the application that created it.

You can link files only among Windows programs that, like Write, conform to the OLE (object linking and embedding) specification that Microsoft introduced to Windows in version 3.1.

A full discussion of linking, embedding, and sophisticated data-exchange techniques is in Chapter 11.

Write Tips

If you use a DOS word processor, you'll find that you will use Write mainly when you want to take advantage of its fonts and graphics features. Use Write as an introduction to graphical word processing. The tools it provides for formatting and editing are elementary, and unless you have very limited word processing needs, you shouldn't invest much time mastering the program.

Write can be a terrific complement to a DOS word processor. You'll want to use Write for fancier documents like resumes, invitations, and bulletins that would be difficult to create in another word processor.

If you own a more powerful Windows word processor, like Ami, WordPerfect for Windows, or Word for Windows, you'll never have much use for Write.

Notepad's Menus: A Complete List

File

New
Open. . .
Save
Save As. . .
Print
Page Setup. . .
Print Setup. . .
Exit

Edit

Undo   Ctrl+Z
Cut   Ctrl+X
Copy   Ctrl+C
Paste   Ctrl+V
Delete   Del
Select All
Time/Date   F5
Word Wrap

Search

Find. . .
Find Next   F3

Help

Contents
Search for Help on. . .
How to Use Help
About Notepad

Write's Menus: A Complete List

File

New
Open. . .
Save
Save As. . .
Print
Printer Setup. . .
Repaginate. . .
Exit

Edit

Undo	Ctrl+Z
Cut	Ctrl+X
Copy	Ctrl+C
Paste	Ctrl+V

Paste Special
Paste Link. . .
Links. . .
Object
Insert Object. . .
Move Picture
Size Picture

Find

Find. . .	
Repeat Last Find	F3
Replace. . .	
Go To Page. . .	F4

Character

Regular	F5
Bold	Ctrl+B
Italic	Ctrl+I
Underline	Ctrl+U

Superscript
Subscript
Reduce Font
Enlarge Font
Fonts. . .

Paragraph

Normal
Left
Centered
Right
Justified
Single Space
1½ Space
Double Space
Indents. . .

Document

Header. . .
Footer. . .
Ruler On
Tabs. . .
Page Layout. . .

Help

Contents
Search for Help on. . .
How to Use Help
About Write. . .

5

The Personal
Information Tools

Calculator

Calendar

Cardfile

Clock

*A Strategy for
Using the Personal
Information Tools*

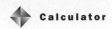

T HE ACCESSORIES GROUP IS A COLLECTION OF UTILITIES THAT CAN increase your productivity in a variety of ways. This chapter is about four utilities that can help you stay organized: Calculator, Calendar, Cardfile and Clock. These Accessories, shown in Figure 5.1, are usually found in separate DOS applications called *personal information managers*, or PIMs.

Figure 5.1
The Accessories group has several utilities to help you do common chores. The four utilities discussed in this chapter— Calculator, Calendar, Cardfile, and Clock—are commonly called personal information managers, or PIMs.

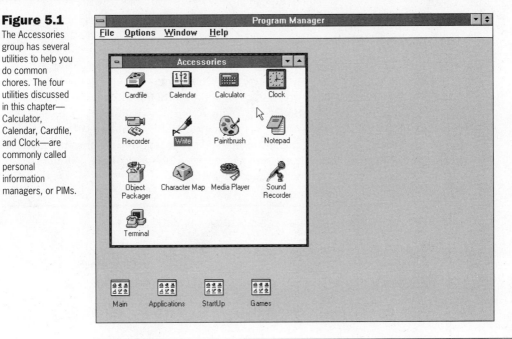

Because you can keep these programs loaded in memory while you work on a word processor or spreadsheet, they may become the programs you use most frequently. In this chapter, I'll show you how to make the most of each. They're simple programs with a limited range of features, so I'll also be pointing out limitations to spare you the trouble of doing things that the programs weren't designed to handle.

Calculator

In its Standard mode, Calculator operates like a hand-held calculator. To solve complex equations, Calculator offers a Scientific mode that provides more than 30 advanced mathematical functions. These functions will be familiar if you're experienced with scientific calculators. If, like most people, you forgot logarithms and cube roots the day you received your diploma, you can still make good use of some of the options in the Scientific calculator. For instance, you may want to use the Statistics Box, even if you never analyze statistics, because it lets you add numbers using a running tally, similar to the way an adding machine's paper tape lists all of the numbers entered.

Earlier sections of the book haven't mentioned every shortcut key, since keystroke equivalents are plainly visible on menus. This section mentions all of the shortcut keys, since the Calculator menus do not show them.

Different Modes, Same Principles

You open Calculator by double-clicking on its icon in the Accessories window (see Figure 5.1) or by typing **Calc** at the Run command in the Program Manager's File menu. You can use the View menu to switch between Calculator's Standard and Scientific modes. The Scientific calculator is a superset of the Standard calculator; it has every function on the Standard calculator in almost the same layout, plus more than 30 programming, number-base, statistical, and trigonometric functions. Figure 5.2 shows Calculator's Standard mode, and Figure 5.3 shows its Scientific mode.

Figure 5.2

The Calculator's Standard mode has a numeric keypad at the center. Buttons for saving a number in memory, and retrieving it, run down the left side, while the basic arithmetic operators appear on the right. Below the display are keys for editing the display: C, CE, and Back.

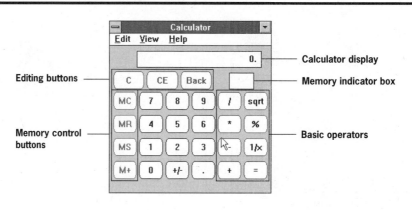

Calculator is unique among Windows programs in a couple of ways. First, the Calculator window is not a standard application window. You can move it, but you can't change its size. It has no border and no scroll bars. Second, it has no data files. As a result, it lacks a File menu and Exit command. When you want to clear it from memory, you must select the Close command from the Control menu, double-click on the Control button, or press Alt-F4.

Figure 5.3

The Calculator's Scientific mode is a superset of the Standard mode. Groups of advanced functions surround the buttons that appear in the Standard mode.

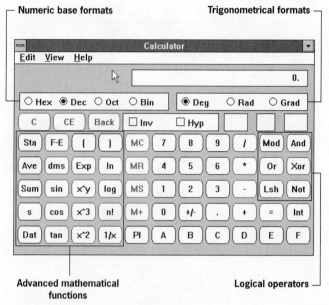

Numeric base formats

Trigonometrical formats

Advanced mathematical functions

Logical operators

Basic Calculations

The technique for using Calculator in either mode is the same. Click on the MC button to make sure the Calculator memory is clear, and then enter a calculation. Enter numbers by clicking on buttons with the mouse or typing from your keyboard.

Here's how to enter a basic calculation in either Standard or Scientific mode. You can follow these steps using any of the mathematical operations summarized in Table 5.1.

1. Click on the MC button to clear Calculator's memory. The MC button is briefly highlighted. This step is not needed the first time you use Calculator during a Windows session, but it's a good habit to adopt.

2. Click on C or press Esc to clear Calculator's display, (This is *not* the same as typing *C* on the keyboard.)

3. Enter a number, using the mouse or the keyboard. Each number you select is briefly highlighted on Calculator's keypad before appearing in Calculator's display.

4. Enter a numeric operator with either the mouse or the keyboard. The operator is briefly highlighted on Calculator's keypad.

Table 5.1 **The Basic Calculator Operators**

Button	Keystroke	Operation
/	/	Division
*	*	Multiplication
–	–	Subtraction
+	+	Addition
+/–	F9	Change sign
1/x	r	Reciprocal
=	= or Enter	Calculate

5. Enter another number.

6. Press Enter or click on the = button. The result is displayed.

Check Memory Early and Often

Clearing memory and clearing Calculator's display, which you did in steps 1 and 2 in the previous section, help you ensure the integrity of your data. If you ever get unexpected results in a calculation, it's very likely that you didn't clear the remnants of an old calculation (by pressing C or Esc) or clear the entry in stored memory (by pressing MS).

When a number is stored in memory, an M appears in the Memory Indicator box, which is located below the Calculator display, as shown in Figure 5.2. If the box is empty, you don't need to clear memory.

There's no indicator to show whether a calculation has been partly entered. When the Calculator displays zero, it's usually clear. But not always: If a calculation was started and then a zero was entered, the first part of the calculation would still be active. To be safe, always press Esc (or click on C) before starting a new calculation.

How Calculator Updates the Display

If you're entering a long calculation, the display shows a running total whenever you enter a new operator or whenever the keystrokes entered thus far generate a new number. For example, as you enter the minus sign in

10 + 9 - 8

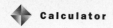
the display shows the total of the operation thus far, 19. As you enter 8, the 19 is replaced with 8. Press the Enter key or click on the equal sign (=) to complete the calculation and display the result, 11.

It's good practice to press Enter or click on the equal sign to complete a calculation instead of relying on Calculator's running total, since Calculator displays partial results until the equation is complete.

Deleting Calculator Entries

You can delete or clear numeric entries in the Calculator display using the buttons and keystrokes summarized in Table 5.2. You can't use the mouse for editing numeric Calculator entries, but you can use it to clear the display.

Table 5.2   **Clearing the Calculator Display**

Button	Shortcut	Description
C (clear)	Esc	Erases all numbers and operators in the current sequence of calculator entries; does not affect numbers stored in memory.
CE (clear entry)	Del	Erases the current number being entered; does not affect earlier numbers or operators. For example, if you typed 2*100, pressing CE clears only the 100; Calculator is still expecting a number to multiply by two.
Back (backspace)	Backspace or ←	Deletes numeric entry one character at a time.

Repeating the Last Operation

Calculator lets you repeat the last operation in any calculation. Press Enter after the equation is completed to apply the last operation performed to the number displayed. This works even with simple calculations. If you enter

    10 * 3 =

pressing Enter a second time applies *3 to (10*3) and changes 30 to 90. Pressing it a third time changes 90 to 270. You can continue until you reach Calculator's upper limit.

The Upper Limit

If you're calculating large numbers and suddenly see a figure like 1.e+013, you've encountered a number too large to be displayed. In Standard mode, Calculator displays numbers up to 10 trillion. Above 9,999,999,999,999 it automatically switches to scientific notation for displaying numbers. (Use the

Exp button to convert any number, even a small or negative number, to scientific notation.) In this type of display, a number is expressed as an integer multiplied by 10 to a certain power. The number ten trillion is displayed as 1.e+013, which means the number ten raised to the 13th power (ten multiplied by ten thirteen times, or one followed by 13 zeros).

Calculator can continue to work with numbers above ten trillion, but it displays them only in scientific notation. The upper limit for calculations is the number 10 followed by 308 zeroes, or 2.0e+307. The range for the Scientific calculator's alternative base number systems—hexadecimal, octal, and binary—is $-2^{31}-1$ to $2^{31}-1$.

Storing Numbers in Memory

You can store a number in Calculator's memory and use it in any calculation. Only one number can be stored at a time. Numbers are stored in memory only when you click on the MS or M+ buttons, shown in Table 5.3. When you've stored a value in Memory, an *M* appears in the Memory Indicator box.

Table 5.3   **Memory Keys**

Button	Shortcut	Description
MC (Memory Clear)	Ctrl-C	Sets memory to zero
MR (Memory Recall)	Ctrl-R	Displays number in memory
MS (Memory Store)	Ctrl-M	Places number in memory, deleting any number already stored
M+ (Memory Plus)	Ctrl-P	Adds number displayed to number already in memory

Let's assume you want to calculate the amount of a sale, where the amount of goods sold is $297, and the sales tax is 6%. If you store 297 in memory, you can use it in two separate calculations: first to compute the sales tax due on $297; then to add the tax to $297.

1. Check the Memory Indicator box. If an *M* is displayed, click on the MC button or press Ctrl-C. The *M* in the Memory Indicator box disappears.

2. Click on C or press Esc to make sure the entry is clear. Clicking on C is *not* the same as typing *C* on the keyboard.

3. Enter **297**. Click on MS. An *M* appears in the Memory Indicator box.

4. Enter ***6**, and click on the **%** key to calculate 6% of 297. The number 17.82 appears.

5. Click on **M+** to add 17.82 to the number stored in memory, 297. The Calculator display does not change.

6. Click on **MR** to display the number in memory. The total, 314.82, appears in the Calculator display.

One thing to remember: if you want to store the result of addition, press Enter or = at the end of the sum. Normally, adding numbers with the + key works fine; but if you're going to store the sum, you must signal the end of the computation.

The Statistics Box

The Statistics Box in Calculator's Scientific mode has a terrific feature you'll want to use when working with a long series of numbers: It displays a running tally, like an adding machine's paper tape, as shown in Figure 5.4.

Figure 5.4
The Scientific mode's Statistics Box is a separate window that can be positioned anywhere. However, it's impossible to place it in a spot where you can see it together with all of the Calculator, so you may need to move it occasionally.

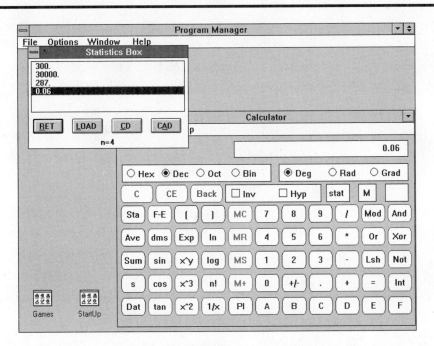

Since the Statistics Box operates more like a special type of memory, it can be used for many functions unrelated to statistics. For example, you can copy several numbers from the Scientific calculator display to put together a running list in the Statistics Box. You can then find the sum, average, or standard deviation of the numbers in the list.

Unfortunately, there's no way to copy a list in the Statistics Box to another program; only the results of a calculation can be used by other programs, via the Windows Clipboard.

To use the Statistics Box, first display the Scientific calculator by opening the View menu and selecting Scientific. Then, click on the Sta button to open the Statistics Box. Like any window, this one can be moved to another place in the display by clicking on the title bar and dragging. With the Statistics Box open, you can still use any of the Scientific calculator's functions but first you must press Enter or click on the Ret button.

To transfer a number to the Statistics Box, press the Insert or Ins key on your keyboard or click on the Dat key on the Calculator display. When you have copied the desired list of numbers, click on one of the three statistical functions which appear below the Sta button:

- **Ave** computes the average of the numbers in the list.

- **Sum** calculates the sum of the values in the list.

- **s** calculates the standard deviation, using a population parameter of n–1. To use a population parameter of n, select Inv before pressing s.

At the bottom of the Statistics Box, you always see the total number of items that have been entered. Before you enter numbers, you'll see *n=0*. As numbers are added, n increases.

The four buttons in the Statistics Box help you to insert and delete entries and to control interaction with the Calculator.

- **RET**   Switches you to the calculator without closing the Statistics Box. To return, click on the Calculator's Sta button or click on the Statistics Box to make it the active window.

- **LOAD**   Inserts the highlighted number from the Statistics Box into the Calculator's display.

- **CD**   Deletes the highlighted (selected) number in the box.

- **CAD**   Deletes all numbers in the box.

Programmer's Options

In Scientific mode, Calculator lets you display a number in one of four different base systems: Hex (hexadecimal); Dec (decimal); Oct (octal); and Bin (binary). You select the number base by clicking the appropriate button just below and to the left of the display.

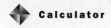

In hexadecimal, octal, or binary, you display either the full number or its shortened form, using the following options: Dword, Word, and Byte. See Table 5.4 for a description of these options. If the display of a number is shortened to appear as a word or byte, the *value* of the number is not affected; any calculations performed use the full value, not the shortened form.

Calculator prevents you from entering an invalid number for the number system selected; for example, if you've selected binary, you can enter only 0 or 1. The letters on the bottom row of the Calculator, A through F, are used for entering the hexadecimal representation of the numbers 10 through 15.

The functions useful to programmers are listed in Table 5.4.

Table 5.4   **Programmer's Operators in Calculator**

Button	Keystroke	Operation
Decimal Operators		
Int	;	Changes displayed number to its integer value, truncating decimals. When Inv is selected, it truncates the integer, leaving only the decimal value; it does not round numbers
Mod	%	Displays the modulus (remainder) of x/y. Works in other base systems also
Binary Operators		
And	&	Calculates bitwise AND
Lsh	<	Shifts binary numbers left; with Inv on, binary numbers shift right
Not	~	Calculates a bitwise inverse
Or	|	Calculates a bitwise OR
Xor	^	Calculates a bitwise exclusive OR
Non-Decimal Operators		
Dword	F2	Shows full 32-bit number
Word	F3	Shows lower 16 bits of number
Byte	F4	Shows lower 8 bits of number

Engineer's Options

In Scientific mode, with the decimal system selected, you can enter numbers in a specific trigonometric format by selecting one of these buttons:

- **Deg** Computes in degrees. For example, to find the sine of 40°, make sure the number system is decimal and Deg is selected; then enter 40, and click on sin.

- **Rad** Computes in radians.

- **Grad** Computes in gradients.

Advanced Mathematics

Most of the Scientific mode buttons perform trigonometric and other mathematical functions. In most cases, the calculation is automatic: Enter a number, click on the function, and the result is displayed. Two check boxes change the way many of these functions operate:

- **Inv** Turns on the Inverse function for sin, cos, tan, PI, $x^{\wedge}y$, $x^{\wedge}2$, $x^{\wedge}3$, In, log, Ave, Sum, and s. When the function is completed, Inv turns off automatically.

- **Hyp** Sets the hyperbolic function for sin, cos, and tan. When the function is completed, Hyp turns off automatically.

   Table 5.5 summarizes the advanced mathematical operators.

Using Parentheses

For complex calculations, the Scientific calculator has open and closed parentheses that can be positioned appropriately within the calculation. You can type parentheses from the keyboard or click on the buttons that appear above the Exp and In buttons respectively. Statements in parentheses are calculated first, starting with the innermost parentheses. For example, the parentheses in the statement

```
25 + (5 * 7)
```

mean "Multiply seven by five, and add the product to twenty-five." A display box, the Open Parentheses indicator, is located to the right side of the Memory Indicator box and monitors the use of parentheses. This indicator displays (=1 for the initial parenthesis and the number of every nested parenthesis, up to 25. (See Figure 5.5.) The display appears for parentheses opened by either clicking on the display or by using the keyboard's parentheses (the round ones above the number 8, not the square brackets). When the parenthetical phrase is closed, the display box clears.

Table 5.5   Advanced Mathematical Operators

Button	Keystroke	Operation
cos	o	Computes cosine. With Inv selected, calculates arc cosine.
dms	m	Converts numbers to degree-minute-second format. With Inv selected, calculates degrees only.
Exp	x	Changes display to exponential mode.
F-E	v	Switches displayed number between scientific and normal notation.
ln	n	Calculates natural or base logarithm.
log	l	Calculates natural or base 10 logarithm. With Inv selected, calculates 10 raised to the xth power.
n!	!	Calculates factorial of displayed number.
PI	p	Displays pi. With Inv selected, displays 2*pi.
sin	s	Calculates sine; with Inv selected, calculates arc sine; with Hyp selected, calculates hyperbolic sine; with Inv *and* Hyp selected, calculates arc hyperbolic sine.
tan	t	Calculates tangents; with Inv selected, calculates arc tangent; with Hyp selected, calculates hyperbolic tangent; with Inv and Hyp selected, calculates arc hyperbolic tangent.
x^y	y	Computes x raised to the yth power (X^y). With Inv selected, calculates the y root of x.
x^2	@	Squares the displayed number. With Inv selected, calculates a square root.
x^3	#	Cubes the displayed number. With Inv selected, calculates the cube root.

Use the Open Parentheses indicator to keep track of complex, nested parenthetical statements. For example, in the following calculation, the Open Parentheses indicator displays *(=2* as you enter 4*2:

```
500 * ( (4*2) + 5)
```

Figure 5.5

When a parenthetical phrase is being used in an operation, the Scientific calculator displays the Open Parentheses indicator. When the phrase is closed, the indicator disappears.

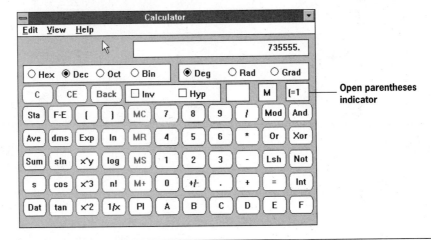

Open parentheses indicator

Using Calculator with Other Programs

You can paste Calculator results into another program. You can also paste calculations from another application into Calculator via Clipboard, and solve them.

For example, in Notepad you might compose a letter that needs some figure totals. As you write your letter, you type the formula followed by an equal sign. You then copy both formula and equal sign to the Calculator via the Clipboard, get the result, and paste it back in the Notepad document via the Clipboard.

Here's a step-by-step description:

1. Open a Notepad document and type in the formula you need to solve, followed by an equal sign (=).

2. Highlight the formula, including the equal sign, with the mouse. Make sure the block includes only characters that are part of the arithmetic statement.

3. Press Ctrl-Ins or select Copy from the Edit menu. The calculation is copied to the Clipboard.

4. Open Calculator. (If the icon is not visible, press Ctrl-Esc to bring up the Task List; if Calculator is on the list, select it; if it's not on the list, select Program Manager and load Calculator.)

5. When Calculator appears, press Shift-Ins. The numbers in the calculation are inserted into the Calculator, and the answer appears in the Calculator display, as shown in Figure 5.6.

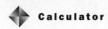

Figure 5.6

You can paste calculations from a document into Calculator, and then paste the answer back into the original document. Here, the last line in the Notepad document (the statement, *12 + 685 + 287 =*) is inserted into Calculator, and the result 984 is displayed.

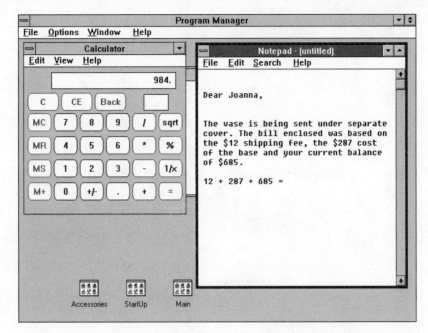

6. Select Copy from the Edit menu, or press Ctrl-Ins.

7. Click on the place in the original document where you want to insert the result. Select Paste from the Edit menu or press Shift-Ins. The result appears in the original document.

Keeping Calculator in Memory

Since Calculator uses only 25k of memory, you may want to keep it running all the time. If you use numbers frequently in your work, you will probably want to move the Calculator icon to the Startup group, so that it will load every time you start Windows.

Calculator stays in memory when you switch to another program. Because it's small when run in Standard mode it's easy to lose track of the Calculator display. To find it, press Ctrl-Esc to bring up the Program Manager's Task List. If Calculator is still in memory, it will be listed here. Double-click on its listing to make it the active window. It's a good idea to get into the habit of looking at the Task List before opening Calculator. Otherwise, you'll find yourself running three or four Calculators, each using precious memory.

Calendar

The Calendar accessory combines an appointment book and an alarm clock. Calendar lets you see appointments for a day at 15-, 30-, or 60-minute intervals. It also lets you see a monthly calendar on which you can mark special dates like holidays and deadlines. You can even have Calendar give you an audible and visual warning several minutes before an appointment is due to start.

You open Calendar by double-clicking on its icon in the Accessories window or by typing **Calendar** at the Run command in the Program Manager's File menu.

Daily and Monthly Views

When the Calendar window opens, it displays the *Daily view*, a list of time slots for today, as shown in Figure 5.7. You can start to record your appointments as soon as the Daily view is displayed.

Since the time used by Windows is based on the system clock in your PC, the wrong date is displayed if your system clock is incorrect. You can correct the date in your system by running the Date/Time module in the Control Panel (see Chapter 9 for detailed instructions on doing this), the DOS DATE function, or by using the setup program that came with your computer.

Figure 5.7

Calendar opens to a list of daily appointments that you have recorded. Move to new dates by using the arrow keys to the left of the date or by selecting the appropriate commands from the Show menu.

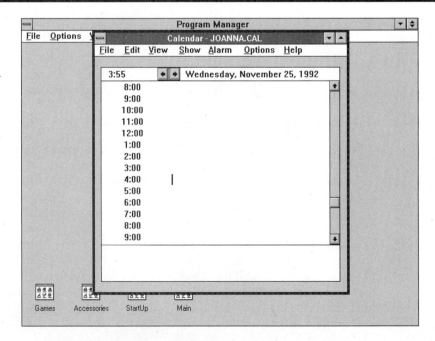

To change the display to the Monthly view, as seen in Figure 5.8, double-click on the date. To switch back, double-click again. If you prefer menus, you can use the View menu to switch. For shortcuts, use the function keys F8 and F9.

Figure 5.8

The Monthly view displays a standard calendar. A scratch pad at the bottom can be used for making notes about the entire month, while the arrow keys to the left of the date move you forward and backward a month at a time.

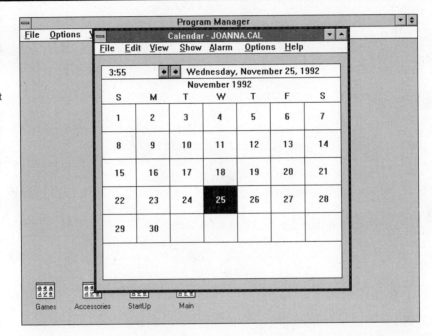

The Daily and Monthly views share a common design. The top line always shows today's time and date and provides arrow buttons for moving ahead and behind a day or month at a time. You can also move forward and backward with the Previous and Next commands on the Show menu. At the bottom of both views, there's a scratch pad: an area to enter text that you want to appear whenever a particular day or month is displayed.

Calendar can display any date between January 1, 1980 and December 31, 2099. To display any date within that range, use the Show menu's Date command. The Date command expects you to enter a date in numerals, separated either by hyphens or slashes. For example, to see appointments for January 2, 1999, enter **1-2-99** or **1/2/99**. Assuming you selected United States as the date format during installation, Windows set the default for date handling to the American style (month-day-year). If you prefer a European style (day-month-year or year-month-day), you can change Windows's date format by running the International module in the Control Panel (see Chapter 9 for detailed instructions).

The Date command accepts two-digit abbreviations for years up to 1999, but it requires that the full four-digit year be entered for dates in the 21st century. For example, you must enter **1-2-2001** or **1/2/2001** to see appointments for January 2, 2001; it will not accept 1-2-01.

The Show menu's Today command returns you to the correct date.

Maintaining an Appointment Schedule

In the Daily view, maintaining a schedule is as simple as moving the insertion point to a time period and typing a description of your appointment. You can move the insertion point with the keyboard's arrow keys or with the mouse.

Each time slot can hold a description of up to 80 characters. Calendar scrolls your entry to the left when you type in more than the 33 characters that fit within the Daily view. After you've typed an appointment, hit the return key to indicate that it should be saved.

Although you can change the size of the entire Calendar window, the Daily and Monthly views do not have the same properties as other document windows, and there's no way to change the sizes of their displays.

Changing the Appointment Intervals

Calendar uses a default of 60-minute intervals for appointments. Keeping the settings at a 60-minute interval helps you see as many of your scheduled appointments as possible. However, you can adjust intervals with the Option menu's Day Settings command to 15, 30, or 60 minutes. You can also use this dialog box to choose between a 12-hour (American) or 24-hour (international) clock display and to choose the hour the Daily view starts.

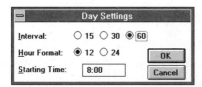

Appointments at Special Times

In Calendar you are not limited to the Daily view's hourly, half-hourly, or quarter-hourly appointment times. You can use the Special Time command on the Options menu to create an appointment that's exact to the minute.

After you enter an appointment, Calendar positions it between the closest default intervals, as shown in Figure 5.9.

Figure 5.9
You can create any time slot you need. This Daily view was set for 60-minute intervals, but a special time, 4:35, was set using the Options menu's Special Time command.

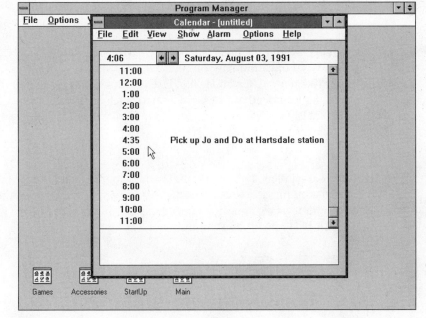

Saving a Schedule

The entries you make in Calendar must be stored if you want to use them again. When you're finished entering appointments, save the file by selecting Save on the File menu. The File Save As dialog box that opens is the same used by other Windows programs, except that it uses the default file name extension, CAL.

If you share your system with others and want to keep your personal Calendar hidden from prying eyes, then it's a good idea to give your Calendar a file with an extension other than CAL. Be aware, however, that in doing so you run the risk of losing the file. When you try to open the file, Calendar by default shows only files with the extension of CAL. If you've used a different file name, it will appear only if you change the selection in the Open dialog box's List Files of Type list box to display all files. You can also enter *.* at the File Name text box.

Maintaining Multiple Schedules

Calendar could be used to maintain separate schedules for personal and business appointments, or could help a doctor's receptionist track appointments for each doctor in the office. To accomplish this, Calendar lets you save different sets of appointments as separate files. If you want to create a special version of your calendar, open your main calendar and make your changes. Then choose the Save As command on the File menu and enter a new name. Your original calendar file does not change, and you'll have two separate calendars.

A word of caution: if you're using Calendar for yourself, you'll find it easier to keep one Calendar file. Use multiple files only if you must track schedules that need not be coordinated, such as the schedules of different individuals.

Special Days

Calendar can flag a day so that it is underlined, boxed, marked with an *x* or *o*, or placed in parentheses. First select the particular day (in either the Daily or Monthly view), and then choose the Option menu's Mark command. You can combine any of the symbols.

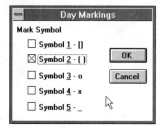

The idea is that you'll use certain symbols or combinations of symbols to mark different types of days—boxes for paydays, x's for holidays, and so on. Figure 5.10 shows a Monthly view with each type of mark and a couple of combinations.

Alarms and Early Warnings

The Calendar's Alarm menu lets you use your PC as a sort of early warning system. You can add an alarm to any appointment and choose to have the PC beep and display a dialog box as early as ten minutes or as late as one minute before your appointment. It's a helpful way to get to meetings on time.

You turn on an alarm in the Daily view by positioning the cursor in the correct time slot and selecting the Set option from the Alarm menu. Set works like a toggle switch: When you select Set, a check mark appears by its menu listing, and a small alarm bell is inserted into the current display. Figure 5.11 shows the alarm bell to the left of the 4:45 appointment.

Figure 5.10

The *special day* markers on this Monthly view were added by selecting the Mark command from the Options menu and selecting symbols from the Day Markings box.

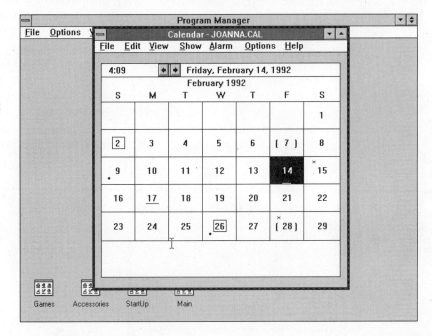

Figure 5.11

When an alarm is set for a particular appointment or meeting, a bell appears to the left of the time. You can make the alarm sound earlier than the appointment by using the Alarm Controls command.

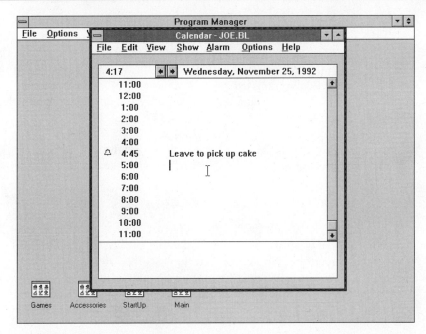

By default, the alarm sounds right at the appointment time. You can make the alarm sound earlier than the appointment time by using the Alarm menu's Controls command. For example, to set the alarm for a 4:45 appointment to sound at 4:40, select Controls from the Alarm menu and enter 5 as the Early Ring in the Alarm Controls dialog box. If you want a beep to sound, make sure there's an X in the Sound check box (by default, sound is on).

When the alarm goes off, a dialog box appears with the message *Please remember...*, followed by the description of your appointment, as shown in Figure 5.12. If Sound was selected in the Alarm Controls dialog box, you'll also hear a series of beeps.

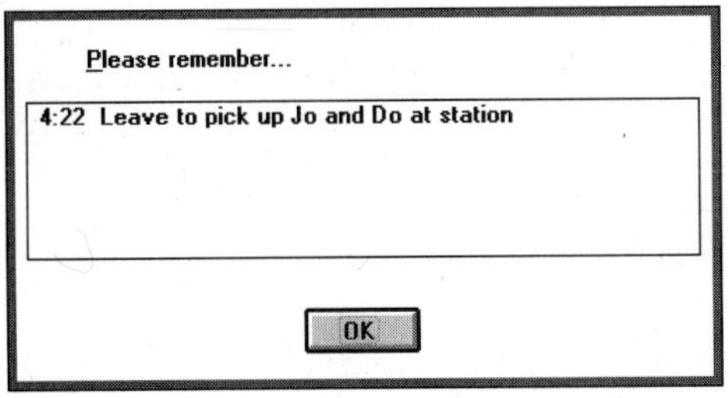

Figure 5.12

Whenever an alarm is set for an appointment, the Please Remember... box pops up and describes the appointment.

The alarm works only if Calendar is active and running the file that has an alarm. If you have not run Calendar since you loaded Windows and an alarm is due to go off, you won't be warned at the right time. The next time Calendar loads with the file that has the alarm, Calendar posts any reminder boxes that you missed.

If Calendar is loaded but *minimized* to an icon when an alarm is scheduled, the Calendar icon flashes and beeps at the specified time. When you click once on the flashing Calendar icon, the Please Remember... box displays a description of the scheduled appointment. If Calendar is open but its Window is *inactive*, the Calendar title bar flashes and beeps at alarm time.

Printing Daily Appointments

The File menu's Print command provides an easy way to get a printed version of your daily schedule. Calendar prints only the appointments that have been entered; it does not waste paper by printing blank time slots.

When you select Print, you are given the option of printing a range of dates. You can also add headers and footers to your printed list by choosing the Page Setup command from the File menu. As in most Windows programs, the headers or footers can be formatted with codes. Here's a summary of formatting codes:

&d   Inserts the date that the printout is being made
&p   Inserts the page number
&f   Inserts the Calendar file name
&l   Left-aligns text
&r   Right-aligns text
&c   Centers text (the default setting)
&t   Inserts the printing time

Chapter 4 contains detailed information on headers and footers.

Sharing Calendars on a Network

Calendar has one option designed to help network users share appointment books. When Calendar is opened, you can choose the Read Only option. By choosing this option, you'll be able to read a coworker's appointment book and not be concerned about making accidental changes.

In an office where files are shared over a network, it's possible to maintain a group-meetings file on a network directory. Everyone who has access to the group's Calendar should be instructed to use the Read Only option when opening the file. Calendar does not give you any way to protect a Calendar from being changed if a user does not select the Read Only option.

The best way to share Calendars on a network is to post them in subdirectories that have security rights controlled by a network administrator. This way, the network operating system enforces read-only privileges based on each user's name, and changes can be made only by authorized users.

Loading the Right Calendar Automatically

You can make sure the Calendar icon loads during every Windows session by clicking on its icon in the Accessories window and dragging it to the Startup group icon. You can also use either the Copy command on the Program Manager's File menu or the Move command if you want to retain a copy in the Accessories window.

That will only load a blank Calendar, however. Follow these steps to make sure that the correct Calendar loads with the correct appointment book:

1. Open the Accessories window in Program Manager.

2. Click once on the Calendar icon.

3. Press Alt-Enter. The Program Item Properties dialog box opens (see Figure 5.13).

Figure 5.13

You can use the Properties command in Program Manager to specify which Calendar file opens when you double-click the Calendar icon.

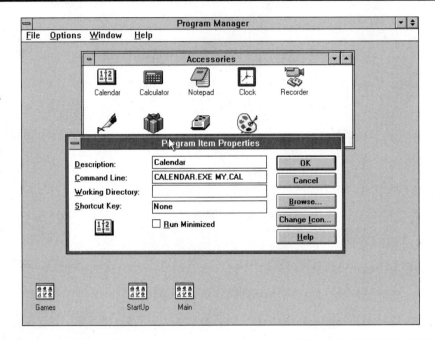

4. Click on the Command Line text box. An insertion pointer appears within the text box.

5. Press → until the pointer rests on the space after *CALENDAR.EXE.*

6. Press the spacebar once, and then type in the name of your personal Calendar file. If you've named your Calendar file MY.CAL, the Command Line box should read *CALENDAR.EXE MY.CAL* (see Figure 5.13).

7. Click on the OK button or press Enter to close the dialog box and save the change.

Now, when you click on Calendar, it will open with the correct Calendar file.

Creating Separate Icons for Separate Calendars

If you maintain several Calendars, you can create a new icon for each one by using the New command on the Program Manager's File menu. Select Program Item (not Program Group) to open a dialog box identical to the

Program Item Properties box in Figure 5.13, except with blank text boxes. In the Command Line box, type **CALENDAR.EXE** followed by the name of your Calendar file. You should give this icon a name different from the original Calendar icon.

If you keep this file in a directory other than the Windows directory or in a directory that is not in your DOS path, enter the disk drive and directory name in the Working Directory text box. This is especially important for files shared on a network.

You may want to use a different graphic for this icon, to help distinguish it from your initial Calendar. Click on the Change Icon command button to see the choices.

Cardfile

If you keep simple lists, Cardfile is a good place to create and view them. Cardfile is similar to a database manager, but it lacks many of the features found in even the simplest stand-alone applications, such as Symantec's Q&A, Professional File, or PC File. It has a search command for quickly displaying one of the cards in the list, but it has none of the sorting, filtering, or reporting features found in a database manager. Even a simple database task like printing a mailing list, either on envelopes or labels, is not possible with Cardfile.

In an office, Cardfile is best suited to managing lists of phone numbers, since you can dial any phone number displayed if you have a modem connected to your system. Because of Cardfile's limited features, don't use it for storing valuable or complex information that you'll want to manipulate or use extensively.

You open Cardfile by either double-clicking on its icon in the Accessories window or typing **Cardfile** at the Run command in the Program Manager's File menu.

Making a Card List

When Cardfile opens, it displays a box that resembles an index card. The top line, or *index line*, is separated by a double-underline from the body of the card (see Figure 5.14). Since, as you will see, Cardfile uses the index line as a tool for managing the cards, you should use it to describe the information on the body of the card. You can enter up to 40 characters on the index line.

To begin your stack of cards, you can enter text in the body of the first card if you wish, but it's better to complete the index line first. You cannot simply move the cursor to the index line, however. You must either choose the Add command on the Card menu or double-click on an index line.

Figure 5.14
On the Cardfile status line there are arrows for moving to the previous and next cards in your stack. The top line of the card is called the index line. It can be used to describe what's in the body of the card.

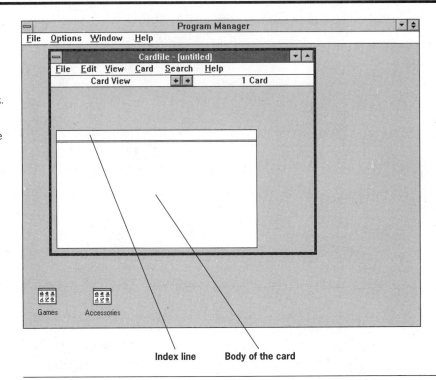

Index line   Body of the card

Either technique opens a dialog box that lets you enter an index line. When you double-click on an existing index line, you'll see an Index dialog box, which lets you edit the current line.

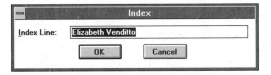

When you choose the Add command, you'll see an Add dialog box that lets you create a new index line.

Before deciding on the text you want to use on the index line, remember that Cardfile stores cards alphabetically, according to the first letter of their index lines. If you're maintaining a list of names and phone numbers, you'll probably want to enter the last name first on the index line.

Here's a quick guide to creating a stack of cards:

1. Press Alt-C, A. The Add dialog box opens.

2. Enter a last name or description for your first card, and press Enter. The new index line appears on a card.

3. Enter the body of the card's text, if any. The body of the card can hold up to ten lines, with 40 characters on each line, and can contain graphics copied from the Clipboard.

4. To add more cards, repeat steps 1 through 3.

5. Press Alt-F, S. The File Save As dialog box opens.

6. Enter a name for your new file, and press Enter. The dialog box closes and your file is saved.

If you have a modem connected to your system, it's a good idea to insert any phone numbers at the beginning of the body of the card. This will help when you use the Autodial command, as explained below in "Dialing Phone Numbers Automatically."

Card View versus List View

Card view displays your information a card at a time. *List view* displays a summary of cards. You'll see how important it is to use index lines that are descriptive when you switch from Card view to List view. You can switch between views by choosing the List option from the View menu. Figure 5.15 shows the two views.

You'll probably want to do most of your work in Card view, since many of the commands do not work fully in List view. For example, if you add a card while in List view, you'll be able to add only the index line. You'll have to switch back to Card view to add the body of the card. And you can't edit body text on a card while in List view.

List view is especially helpful with long card files, since you can see more in a window. List view gives you an overview of your card file, but Card view is the mode you should use for most of your work.

Moving from Card to Card

In Card view, press PageDown to move to the next card and PageUp to move to the previous card. In List view, you can use ↑ and ↓. If the list is longer than the window, a scroll bar appears to help you navigate. You can also use the mouse in either view to move to a card. Double-click on any card to highlight it or move it to the front of the stack.

Figure 5.15
Cardfile's Card and List views can be seen here, with two copies of Cardfile running. Card view shows both the index line and body of a card, while List view shows the index line of all your cards.

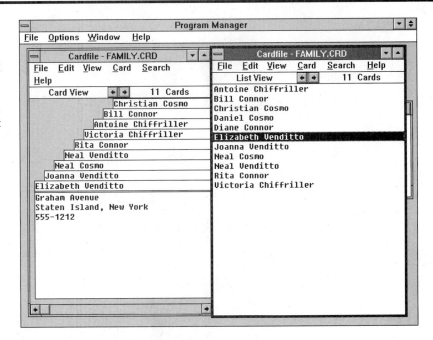

Finding Information in a Card File

Cardfile has two commands for searching through files, Go To and Search. In Card view, these commands bring the requested card to the front of the stack. In List view, they highlight the requested card.

- **Go To** Searches for a card whose *index line* contains a series of characters you specify in the Go To text box. This command is not case-sensitive, nor does it require you to type in the entire index line. It simply brings you to the first card whose index line contains the series of characters you enter. For example, if you type *will* in the Go To dialog box, it goes to a card whose index line is *John Williams*.

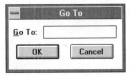

- **Find** Locates any word or phrase that appears in the *body* of a card. You type the word or phrase in the Find What text box. Find offers three options. First, you can choose to match only the whole word. For example, if you were looking for the word *man* with this option on, Find would not stop at words like *command*. Second, you can also choose to have Find stop only at words that match the case of the word, letter for letter. For example, by searching for *Man* with Match Case turned on, Find would not stop at the word *man*. And finally, with the Direction option, you can specify the direction in which the Find command will search through the stack before stopping on the first card containing the word or phrase you entered.

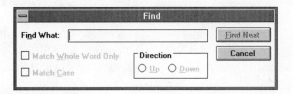

Editing a Card

You can edit the text on a card's main body by bringing it to the front of the display and making changes in the same way you'd edit a text file. See Chapter 4 for detailed instructions on editing text in Windows.

To edit an index line, double-click on the index line in either Card view or List view. A dialog box appears, and you can make any changes. Alternatively, select the Edit menu's Index command to bring up the same dialog box.

The Card menu also has a Delete command if you want to erase both the index line and the body of the card.

Undoing Mistakes and Restoring Cards

The Edit menu has an Undo command that you can use to undo typing or editing commands. Undo is limited to the single, previous editing action, and it does not work for menu commands.

If you've made extensive changes to a card, you can use the Restore command to change the text back to the way it was. Restore only works on a card that has been displayed continuously since it was edited; if you change the display to a new card or switch to List view, you can't use Restore on a card you changed earlier.

It's worth taking a moment to consider the technical differences between Undo and Restore.

■ **Undo**   Common to many Windows programs. It uses a small area of temporary memory called a buffer. As you type into the computer, the Undo buffer keeps a copy of the keystrokes entered since you last used a command. By selecting Undo, you use a copy of this buffer to reverse your last action. Since the buffer is not large, you can only reverse one action.

■ **Restore**   Unique to Cardfile. It reverses any changes made to a card since it was last indexed. Whenever you change your Cardfile display, either by switching between List and Card views or by using the Search command, Cardfile indexes, or re-alphabetizes, your cards. When Cardfile indexes your cards, it flushes the previous version of the cards from memory and places this new version in memory. Restore can only work on cards not flushed from memory.

If you've made unwanted changes to several cards and Restore does not work, you can go back to the original file still stored on disk, as long as you have not used the Save command since you made the changes. To do this, choose the Open command on the File menu. When Cardfile displays a dialog box asking if you want to save the current file, click on No.

If you do want to save parts of the current file without losing the original, save the current version with a new name by using the Save As command. You'll end up with two different versions of the same Cardfile file, but you can eventually use the Merge command on the File menu to combine the two versions and delete the cards you want to remove. See "Merging Cardfiles" below for details.

Cutting and Pasting

Like most Windows programs, Cardfile lets you cut and paste text. The basic procedure is as follows:

1. Highlight a block of text, either by clicking and dragging with the mouse or by holding down the Shift key as you press the keyboard arrow keys.

2. Either cut or copy the block. Choose Cut or Copy from the Edit menu, or use a shortcut: Ctrl-X to cut, Ctrl-C to copy. Cut text when you want to delete it from the current card; copy text when you want to keep it in its original location.

3. Move to the new card, and select Paste (or press Ctrl-V) to insert the block of text.

For more details on cutting and pasting in Windows, see "Editing, Deleting, and Undoing Notepad" in Chapter 4.

Pasting Graphics

Any graphic file that can be displayed in a Windows program can be copied to the Cardfile. To paste a graphic, you must first place a copy of it on the Clipboard. The procedure is similar to the one explained in the Chapter 4 section, "Inserting Graphics into Write." In Chapter 6, you'll learn how to create original graphics and place them on the Clipboard.

Before you choose an image, make sure that it's small enough to fit on your card. It will be added to the card exactly as copied to the Clipboard, and cannot be resized. If it's larger than the card, part of it will be lost. You can use Paintbrush (see Chapter 6) to edit a large image so that it fits.

Once you've copied an image to the Clipboard, follow these steps:

1. Bring the desired card to the front of the display.

2. Press Alt-E, E to select Picture on the Edit menu. You are now in Picture mode and cannot add or change text.

3. Press Ctrl-V to paste the graphic into the card. The picture will appear in the upper left corner of the card.

4. Move the mouse and notice that the picture is framed by a thin line, which follows your mouse movements. Drag the picture to the desired spot in the card. As long as you're still in Picture mode you can continue to move the card until you've placed it where you want.

5. Press Alt-E, X to select Text from the Edit menu. Leaving Picture mode locks the graphic into place on the card. You can now add or edit the text on the card.

The result will be similar to the card in Figure 5.16.

Figure 5.16

The map on this card was created in Paintbrush, then copied to the Clipboard. Using the Picture command on Cardfile's Edit menu, it was inserted into the active card.

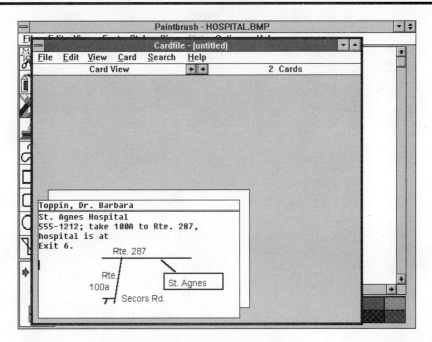

Duplicating Cards

It's common for cards to share information. For example, you may want to add a card for a person who works at the same office as someone already listed. Rather than reenter the existing information on a new card, you can save time by using the Card menu's Duplicate command. After you've duplicated the card, change the index line on one of the cards (see "Making a Card List" above) to show the new person's name.

Merging Cardfiles

The Merge command on the File menu is very straightforward. You specify a file name, and it adds a copy of every card in the specified file into the current file and displays a newly alphabetized file. If cards with the same index line exist in both files, they will be duplicated. The file that is merged into the open file remains unchanged on disk.

File Sharing

Cardfile has very limited options for sharing files with other programs. You can't import or export lists for use by other programs, other than the version of Cardfile in Windows 3.0. As you've seen, though, you can import text and graphics and paste them onto the active card via Clipboard.

Dialing Phone Numbers Automatically

If you have a Hayes-compatible modem properly installed in your system, Cardfile's Autodial command will dial a phone number entered on the active card. To use Autodial, you must have a telephone connected to the modem.

To have Cardfile dial a number, select the Autodial command on the Card menu. The Autodial command searches the body of the active card and selects the first group of numbers it finds that resembles a phone number.

It's a good idea to make a phone number come first on the body of a card, because Cardfile will attempt to dial the first number with four or more digits, even a zip code if it appears before a phone number. The only way to make Cardfile dial a subsequent phone number is to highlight that number before selecting the Autodial command. Either use the mouse or press the arrow keys while pressing Shift to highlight the numbers.

If your office requires a 9 or some other code before the phone connects to an outside line, click on the Use Prefix check box, and enter the correct prefix in the Prefix text box.

Click on the Setup command button if you need to select modem speed, the modem's communications (COM) port, or a communications parameter like tone dialing. These parameters are usually set at installation and don't need to be fiddled with.

Printing Cardfiles

Cardfile's File menu has two print commands that begin a print job:

- **Print**   Sends the first card displayed to the printer.

- **Print All**   Sends the entire active file to the printer.

  To control the way cards are printed, there are two more commands:

- **Page Setup**   Controls the headers and footers on the page; you can't control the formatting of the cards themselves. The options are identical to those used by Calendar; for a summary, see "Printing Daily Appointments" earlier in this chapter.

- **Print Setup**   Allows you to choose the printer and any printer options, such as paper trays and draft quality. The choices are the same as those explained under "Printing Options" in Chapter 4. For a full discussion of printing in Windows, see Chapter 12.

Linking and Embedding Cardfile Objects

The Edit menu has five commands for sharing Cardfile data with other Windows programs that conform to the object-linking and embedding specification (OLE). When you link a card with another program, an icon appears on the card. When the icon is double-clicked, the linked program runs. Linking and embedding objects requires more than one OLE-aware program, a topic discussed in depth in Chapter 11.

Clock

The Clock is the simplest utility in Windows. It has but one job: to tell you the time in either analog form (two hands moving around a clock face) or digital form (numbers representing hours, minutes, and seconds, like a digital watch). Clock uses only a very small amount of memory (18k), so you probably won't affect your system's performance by running it all day. Figures 5.17 and 5.18 show the two modes.

Figure 5.17

There are two settings for the Clock; this is the digital setting.

Figure 5.18

This is the Clock's analog setting.

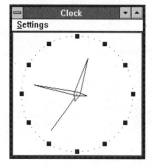

Open Clock by double-clicking on its icon in the Accessories window or entering **Clock** at the Run command in the Program Manager's File menu. Switch between analog and digital modes using the Settings menu.

To make the best use of Clock, tuck it in a place unused by your other programs, like a corner. If you want to use it regularly, copy the Clock icon from the Accessories folder into the Startup folder so that it will load every time you run Windows.

Clock Options

The Clock's Settings menu lets you expand the display so that seconds and the date are seen with the hours and minutes. And, when you've selected the digital display, it lets you choose the font to be used.

Clock also lets you remove the title bar, giving you the most efficient use of its display space. Watch out: While you can turn off the title bar from the menu, once it's gone you can't use the menu to make it return. When the title bar and menu are off, you can make them return by pressing either Esc or double-clicking anywhere in the Clock window. In fact, you can turn the title bar off by double-clicking anywhere in the Clock window too.

A Strategy for Using the Personal Information Tools

Like all tools, the four utilities in this chapter—Calculator, Calendar, Card-file, and Clock—can help you stay organized and be more productive only if you get into the habit of using them.

Aside from having each tool load at Windows startup, as was explained earlier in the chapter, there are two things you can do to make this happen:

- Create a folder in Program Manager for all the utilities you want to use regularly, so you can find them faster.

- Assign a shortcut key to each one.

The following sections show you how.

A Personal Information Folder

Here's the way to create a new folder to store program icons for your personal information tools:

1. Select New from the Program Manager's File menu. The New Program Object dialog box opens.

2. Select Program Group. The Program Group Properties dialog box opens.

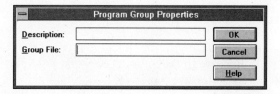

3. In the Description text box, type the name of the folder you want to use (e.g., *Get Organized*). Leave the Group File text box blank. Select OK. A new program group window opens, with the text you entered in the description box appearing as the title.

4. Open the Accessories group window. If your screen is getting cluttered, use the Tile command on the Program Manager's Window menu to arrange the windows so you can see more than one window at a time.

5. Click on the first program icon you want to move. If you want to keep a copy of the icon in the original folder, hold down Ctrl and drag the icon to the new folder. If you want to move the icon without retaining a copy, drag the icon without holding down Ctrl.

6. Repeat step 5 for every icon you want to move into this new folder.

Shortcut Keys

Every program icon that you see in Program Manager has certain properties, including the file that is loaded when you double-click the icon and the name that appears below the icon. Both of these properties were established by Windows when it was installed on your system.

A third property you can add is a shortcut key combination: a series of keys that, when pressed simultaneously, open a program as if its icon were double-clicked. For example, a shortcut key for the Clock would let you see the time while running any Windows program. The first two keys of the shortcut must be Ctrl-Alt.

Here's how to create a shortcut key:

1. Highlight the icon for Clock (or whichever program icon you prefer).

2. Press Alt-Enter. The Program Item Properties dialog box opens.

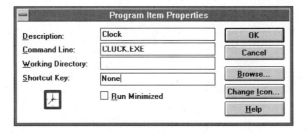

3. The first text box, Description, is highlighted; press Tab three times or press Alt-S to move to the Shortcut Key text box. The blinking insertion pointer appears after the word *None*. (If anything other than *None* appears here, someone has already assigned a shortcut key to this icon; you can change it with the following steps.)

4. Enter **C**. Windows inserts *Ctrl + Alt + C* to indicate that the shortcut consists of all three keys.

5. Click on the OK button. The dialog box closes.

6. Press Ctrl-Alt-C. The Clock opens.

Remember that all shortcut keys must begin with Ctrl and Alt. You can choose any letter or number on the keyboard, either alone or with the Shift key. Windows automatically inserts both Ctrl and Alt. You can use only the white keys, not the gray ones (Insert, Delete, Backspace, and so on).

Calendar's Menus: A Complete List

File

New
Open. . .
Save
Save As. . .
Print. . .
Page Setup. . .
Print Setup. . .
Exit

Edit

Cut   Ctrl+X
Copy   Ctrl+C
Paste   Ctrl+V
Remove. . .

View

Day   F8
Month   F9

Show

Today
Previous   Ctrl+PageUp
Next   Ctrl+PageDown
Date. . .   F4

Alarm

Set   F5
Controls. . .

Options

Mark	F6
Special Time	F7
Day Settings...	

Help

Contents
Search for Help On...
How to Use Help
About Calendar

Calculator's Menus: A Complete List

Edit

| Copy | Ctrl+C |
| Paste | Ctrl+V |

View

Scientific
Standard

Help

Contents
Search for Help On...
How to Use Help
About Calculator

Cardfile's Menus: A Complete List

File

New
Open. . .
Save
Save As. . .
Print. . .
Print All
Page Setup. . .
Print Setup. . .
Merge
Exit

Edit

Undo	Ctrl+Z
Cut	Ctrl+X
Copy	Ctrl+C
Paste	Ctrl+V
Paste Link	
Paste Special	
Index. . .	F6
Restore	
Text	
Picture	
Link	
Object	
Insert Object...	

View

Card
List

Card

Add. . .	F7
Delete	
Duplicate	
Autodial. . .	F5

Search

Go To. . .   F4
Find. . .
Find Next   F3

Help

Contents
Search for Help On...
How to Use Help
About Cardfile

Clock's Menus: A Complete List

Settings

Analog
Digital
Set Font
No Title
Seconds
Date
About Clock

6

The
Graphics Tools:
Paintbrush

Paintbrush Basics

Starting a Drawing

The Drawing Tools

The Text Tool

*Making Changes
and Fixing Mistakes
in a Drawing*

*Working with
Graphic Files from
Other Programs*

Converting Graphic Files

Printing Paintbrush Files

ALTHOUGH PAINTBRUSH MAY SOUND LIKE A TOOL FOR ARTISTS AND people who like to doodle, you can use it to create illustrations needed in business every day. For example, you can use it to construct simple maps and diagrams, even if you've never been able to draw. Paintbrush is also a valuable tool for editing images that were created with a scanner or by another program.

Today, not all Windows programs can accept graphic images. But virtually every Windows program will eventually add features for incorporating graphics into its files. Word processors, spreadsheets, and databases will add the ability to display illustrations, enabling you to display your company's logo in a document or paste the image of a part into a letter confirming a sale.

Paintbrush provides a basic set of tools for working with graphics images. If you've used drawing programs before, you'll feel right at home in Paintbrush. At the same time, Paintbrush is an excellent program to learn if you're new to graphics editing since it uses tools that are common to virtually every Windows paint and design program. The time you spend learning Paintbrush will pay off down the road as you encounter other programs that use a similar approach to graphics editing.

Paintbrush Basics

You open Paintbrush by double-clicking on its icon in the Accessories window or by entering **pbrush** at the Run command in the Program Manager's File menu. The Paintbrush window is like a workshop. It includes a menu bar across the top, tools stacked along the left side, color choices arranged along the bottom, line-width choices in the lower-left corner, and a large workspace that's called the drawing area (see Figure 6.1).

You create and edit images by selecting a tool and using the mouse to click on the drawing area where you want the tool to work. Every tool requires a different series of mouse clicks and drags, depending on the function it performs.

You should save often because a drawing can go wrong with just one or two editing steps. For elaborate work, you should use the Save As command to create several copies of the work, each of them at a different stage. This technique is used by professionals; it provides a library of reusable images that can function as building blocks for subsequent drawings.

Six Essential Steps to Create a Graphic Image

You can begin to use the drawing tools as soon as you've loaded Paintbrush. However, you should first make sure the defaults for size and color are set correctly. You cannot correct the wrong drawing size, wrong choice of color versus black-and-white, or wrong background color after you've started drawing. These defaults are explained under "Starting a Drawing."

Figure 6.1

The Paintbrush screen has a menu bar with commands for controlling the way objects are drawn. However, the most important part of the screen is the tool bar on the left, which provides the editing commands and object shapes needed to work with a graphic image. The palette, linesize box, and menu bar commands provide functions that supplement the tool bar objects.

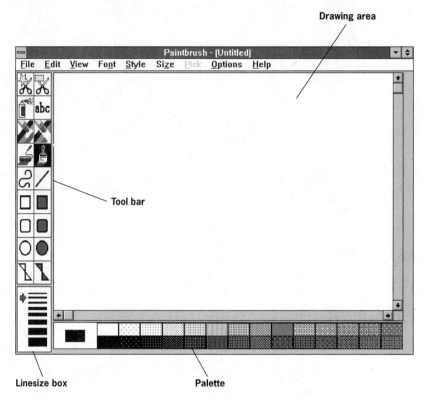

Drawing area

Tool bar

Linesize box

Palette

If you're just experimenting, however, feel free to jump ahead to "The Drawing Tools" section, so you can get your feet wet, but be sure to learn about Paintbrush's default settings before you begin important drawings.

To get the most out of Paintbrush, you should observe these steps when creating a drawing:

1. Select the correct drawing area and palette by choosing Image Attributes from the Options menu.

2. Use the drawing tools to create an image.

3. Use the editing tools to rearrange the image.

4. Save the file as soon as you've created something worthwhile.

5. Repeat steps 2, 3, and 4 until you're satisfied with your work.

6. Transfer the image into another program or print it.

If you're editing a file that was created by someone else, you'll start with step 3.

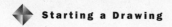
Before Starting a New File

When you load Paintbrush, your screen displays a new, untitled default file. You're now ready to create a new drawing or open a file on disk.

After you've started work on a file, you may decide you want to start fresh. To clear the screen, select New from the File menu or double-click on the Eraser tool (the icon directly below "abc"). When you choose New or double-click the eraser, Paintbrush lets you save your work to a file before it clears the screen. You can only work on one file at a time with Paintbrush.

To switch to a different file, select Open from the File menu; Paintbrush will give you the option of saving your current work before it opens another file.

Looking at a Sample File

You don't have to create a drawing to learn Paintbrush. Windows comes with several graphic files that you can use to experiment; they're the wallpaper files that were copied to your Windows default directory during installation.

Here's how to open one of these files:

1. Select Open from the File menu. The File Open dialog box will open, listing several files with the extension .BMP.

2. Double-click on one of these files; the file will appear on the screen. (If no files are listed, make sure the .BMP option is selected and that your directory is the Windows main directory. If .BMP is selected, you're logged to the Windows directory, and files still don't appear, someone has deleted the wallpaper files from your hard disk. If you need help navigating through the file choices, refer to "The File Open Dialog Box" in Chapter 4.)

Starting a Drawing

Paintbrush has default parameters that affect your workspace and the drawing. The workspace settings, under the View menu, control which tools will be available: the tool bar, palette, linesize box, and cursor tracking window. The drawing settings, under the Options menu, control whether color or black-and-white is used, which colors are available, and the size of the drawing.

Adjusting Your Workspace

When Paintbrush first loads into memory, the display includes the tool bar, linesize selector, and palette. You can remove these through the View menu. If a check appears in front of the Tools and Linesize option or the Palette option, these areas will be displayed. If you click on the menu choice, the check will disappear and the drawing area will be extended to replace those parts of the screen. Since the tool bar contains essential drawing commands, you'll probably want to keep it displayed. Unless your drawing requires lots of color mixing, however, you should turn the palette display off. When working with large images, you may want to turn the tool bar and palette on and off as you switch between working with a tool and viewing your work.

Tracking the Cursor Position

Paintbrush will monitor the position of your cursor if you click on the Cursor Position option in the View menu. This option introduces a small window in the upper-right corner of the screen that constantly displays the coordinates of your cursor when it's within the drawing area.

The left number or x coordinate indicates the distance from the drawing area's left margin, the right number or y coordinate reports the distance down from the top margin. Cursor Position uses pixels or pels (picture elements) as its measurement. This reading is valuable when you're trying to draw precise shapes or connect lines. And it can also give you a feeling for how much of the entire drawing is being displayed.

You can move the Cursor Position box, but only to positions that are outside the drawing area, such as on top of the scroll bars.

Setting the Drawing Size

When Windows was installed on your computer, information about the video card in your system was stored in a Windows configuration file (SYSTEM-.INI). Paintbrush uses that information to give your files a default drawing size that gives you the best balance of drawing detail and computer performance. For example, if you have a VGA display, the default drawing is 6.67 inches wide and 5.00 inches high; on an EGA display, the width is also 6.67 inches but the height is 4.86 inches.

If you want to create a larger drawing, select the Image Attributes command in the Options menu. You'll see the display shown in Figure 6.2, and you can enter a width and height for your drawing. Don't select a size that is larger than the area you need: Paintbrush's performance will deteriorate significantly with increases that are greater than an inch or two.

You don't need to reduce the drawing area to create an image that is smaller than the default. Nevertheless, it's a good idea to limit the drawing area so that it will fit only the objects you want to print; this way you won't have to scroll to see the hidden parts of the drawing. If you plan to transfer images to other applications through Clipboard, a tight drawing size is even more important, since you'll probably use a very small area of the screen for the graphic in the target application.

Figure 6.2

Settings in the Image Attributes dialog box cannot be changed once work has begun on a drawing.

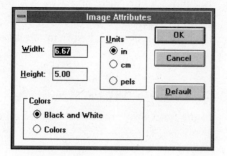

You must establish the drawing area before you begin work on an image; you must select New from the File menu to change the current drawing area to the selections you've made in the Image Attributes box. You cannot change a drawing size after any work has begun on an image. If you need to change the size of a drawing, you can use either the Scissors or Pick tool to cut the image, open a new file with the correct drawing size, and then paste the image into this file. These processes will be explained later in this chapter.

Selecting Color or Black and White

Paintbrush's default setting is color, except on monochrome systems where Paintbrush uses shades of amber or gray. If you're primarily using Paintbrush to create illustrations that will be transferred to other Windows applications or that will be printed on a color printer or plotter, you should keep the default setting of a color palette. If you're creating images that will be printed on a black-and-white printer, you should change the Image Attributes setting to Black and White. This will give you a choice of 28 different gray patterns instead of 28 colors to use in a drawing. If you select the Black and White option, you will know how the gray patterns look before your image is printed; moreover, you'll be choosing the patterns accurately right from the start.

When you print a color drawing on a black-and-white printer, Paintbrush uses a technique called *dithering* to simulate the color tones in shades of gray. The result may be an unpleasant surprise: Lines that seemed to provide a good contrast when displayed in color may seem to be too similar after they've been converted to shades of gray.

You can't switch from a color to a black-and-white palette after you start an image. If you switch from color to black and white (or visa versa) while a drawing is open, Paintbrush will give you the option of closing the current drawing and starting a new one. In order to make the switch, you have to close the current drawing and open a new one.

Although you can use the Pick tool to cut an image out of a color drawing and paste it into a file that has a black-and-white palette, Paintbrush does a poor job of converting colors to gray patterns. In short, you get the best results when you choose the right palette before starting to create your images.

Choosing Foreground and Background Colors

Before you begin your drawing, you should check the selected color or pattern in the palette.

Background color (right mouse button)

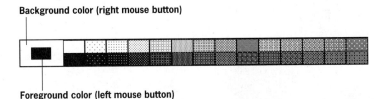

Foreground color (left mouse button)

The leftmost rectangle shows the current foreground and background selections. The color or pattern in the center of the rectangle shows how the foreground will appear; the surrounding area indicates the background. You select a background color by clicking inside any of the 28 color boxes with the *right* mouse button; you choose the foreground color by clicking inside a color box with the *left* mouse button.

Most objects created with the drawing tools are drawn in the foreground color. The filled-shape drawing tools draw objects with the foreground color as the inside shade and the background color as the outside border.

Customizing Your Colors

Whether you work in black and white or in color, Paintbrush enables you to create a custom palette by using the Edit Colors command in the Options menu. With the Edit Colors dialog box open, as shown in Figure 6.3, click on the color or gray pattern you want to change. The dialog box shows you the intensity level used to create this color out of the computer's three basic colors (red, green, and blue).

By making changes to the intensity level of red, green, or blue in the color you've selected, you can create a new color blend. Notice that as you add or subtract color, you're not creating a pure color.

Unless you have an expensive 24-bit color adapter in your computer, your graphics display system cannot provide 255 levels of intensity for each of the three basic colors, so Windows uses dithering, which creates a pattern with a symmetrical arrangement of different color pixels to simulate subtle shades of color.

Figure 6.3

The Edit Colors dialog box is used to create a custom palette.

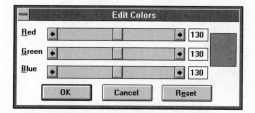

In blending colors, remember that an intensity of zero for all colors is black because there's no color being displayed. If all three colors are fully displayed, the result is white. If red is at its peak, and both blue and green are at zero, you have a pure red. If you then gradually increase blue, you'll see that blue pixels appear in the field of red in a geometric pattern; this is dithering. If you increase blue to its maximum intensity, you'll have a pure purple.

If you're working in black and white, you can change only the intensity level of a gray pattern; Paintbrush keeps the red, green, and blue indicators moving in lockstep. That's because blacks and whites are produced by having either all colors off or all colors on, respectively.

After you've blended a new color, you may want to save it so you can use the exact same proportions again. Paintbrush doesn't save individual colors, it saves entire palettes. When your color blends are just the way you want them, select Save Colors from the Options menu. Paintbrush will store them in a file with the extension of PAL. At later Paintbrush sessions, you can switch from the default colors to your personal mix by choosing the Get Colors option. Make sure you select the palette before you begin work on your file.

The Drawing Tools

The tool bar that runs down the left side of the Paintbrush display uses icons that are very much like icons in other paint and design programs. In Paintbrush, you must use these icons to draw and edit; there are no menu command equivalents for the tools. As shown in Figure 6.4, there are 13 tools for drawing, 2 for editing with color, 2 for cutting areas, and 1 that adds text.

Selecting a Tool

To use the drawing tools, you click on the tool's icon and then move the mouse pointer into the drawing area. The mouse pointer changes from the familiar arrow pointer to one of five new shapes, depending on the tool you've selected (see Table 6.1), indicating that Paintbrush is ready to begin drawing the object.

Figure 6.4

The tool bar consists of 18 individual tools. At the top are editing tools (scissors and pick); below them are the text tool and color editing tools (airbrush, the erasers, paint roller, and paintbrush). The bottom ten tools are used for drawing shapes. When a tool is being used, its icon is highlighted.

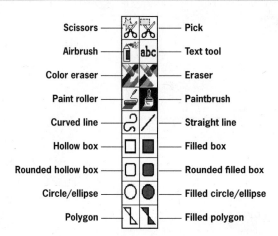

Scissors —
Airbrush —
Color eraser —
Paint roller —
Curved line —
Hollow box —
Rounded hollow box —
Circle/ellipse —
Polygon —

— Pick
— Text tool
— Eraser
— Paintbrush
— Straight line
— Filled box
— Rounded filled box
— Filled circle/ellipse
— Filled polygon

Table 6.1   Different Cursors for Different Tools

Tool	Cursor Style
Pick	Crosshairs
Airbrush	Crosshairs
Text	Insertion point
Erasers	Square
Paint roller	Point roller icon
Paintbrush	A tiny dot
Curved line	Crosshairs
Straight line	Crosshairs
Squares	Crosshairs
Circles	Crosshairs
Polygons	Crosshairs

Each drawing tool can create a new shape in any color available in the current palette. (You can work either in colors or in gray patterns; from here on, discussions about changing colors apply to gray patterns too.) Some of the tools create filled shapes, and use both a foreground and a background color.

Using the Airbrush

The airbrush creates a smudge effect in the foreground color, just like the spray spewing out of the can in the airbrush icon. It's often used to provide texture or to soften sharp edges in a drawing. If you're creating a landscape, the airbrush is perfect for drawing the clouds.

To use the airbrush, click on its icon and then, while holding down the mouse button, drag the crosshairs cursor to create the pattern. As long as you hold down the mouse button and move the mouse, the airbrush will leave a trail of dots.

The airbrush sprays its dots in the foreground color. Try selecting a new foreground color before using the airbrush and then spraying over a solid area. Notice that there's a blend of the colors, creating a smudged or sub-dued tone where the airbrush passed.

The Paint Roller

Think of the paint roller tool as a bucket of paint that you pour over your work. It changes the color of an area to the currently selected foreground color. To use this tool, select the foreground color, click on the paint roller, and then position it so that the lower-left tip of the icon is inside the object you want to paint. (Be sure you've got the tip in the right place!)

The paint roller changes the color of every part of the surface until it reaches a border. For example, if you use the roller inside a square, only the square's color changes. If you use paint roller in a complex drawing, every surface enclosed within a border is affected. For example, in Figure 6.5, adding a shade to the map will require several uses of the paint roller.

Also, the paint roller will change the background color only up to the edges of the visible part of the drawing. You'll need to scroll the window to change the color outside the window if you want a uniform color on the entire background. This is another good reason to make sure your drawing area is only as large as you need it to be.

Be especially careful to reselect the paint roller icon regularly so that if you need to use the Undo key, you won't undo more than you want to. The paint roller often produces surprising results since the color may leak into an area that looks as if it is fully enclosed by a border but that actually has gaps.

You can experiment with color selections by choosing various new fore-ground colors, but there may be some problems with this. Because of dithering, you may not be able to change certain colors. This happens because the dither-ing pattern has created minute objects that are "trapping" the new color; in real-ity, the paint roller is still working but it's only creating dots with the new color instead of a broad color change. To be on the safe side, save a backup copy of your drawing if you plan to change colors more than two or three times. This way, you'll be able revert to a backup if you create an unfortunate color combi-nation that you can't change.

Figure 6.5

After the lines were drawn in this map, the paint roller tool was used to add shading to the background. The roller was used outside the center object ("Hammond County") several times and, since the center object has a continuous border, shading did not enter it.

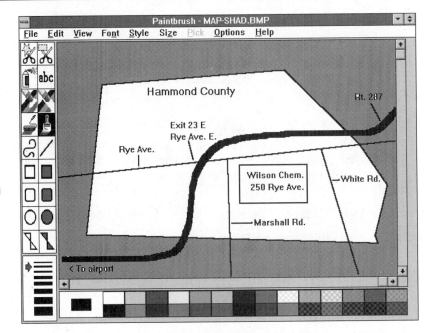

Freehand Drawing with the Paintbrush

You use the paintbrush for freehand drawing. It's especially valuable for cre-ating maps or diagrams since you can use it to define any irregular shape. The thick line in Figure 6.5 was created with the paintbrush.

To use the paintbrush:

1. Choose a foreground color and a line width.

2. Click on the paintbrush tool.

3. Move the cursor to the point where the line should begin and hold down the left mouse button as you move the tiny paintbrush dot cursor to cre-ate the line.

4. When you've completed the line you need, release the mouse button.

5. You can draw more lines now by repeating steps 3 and 4.

The paintbrush tool has a choice of six tips for drawing various shapes. You select these tips from the Options menu; the default is a square. Figure 6.6 shows the six choices and the lines that are produced with each.

Figure 6.6

The drawing area shows lines created with the paintbrush tool using each of the six tips, corresponding to the dialog box choices from left to right. Notice how the effect of the individual tips is most noticeable when you dab by clicking on the mouse button instead of dragging to create an unbroken line.

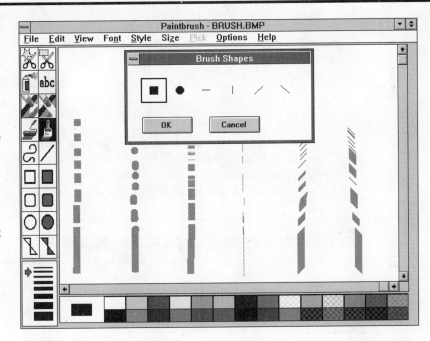

Generally, you need to change brush tips only if you're working with thick lines. The different tips look the same when working with thin lines. If you're using the brush to create small spots by dabbing it (single mouse clicks) you may appreciate the special effects that you can get by changing the tip. For example, you can use the slanted-line tips for calligraphy if you have selected a wide line size.

Creating Curved Lines

You can create well-proportioned lines with the curved line tool, but it takes some practice to perfect the technique. This tool lets you create a line with two arcs, although you can also use it to create a line with one arc.

Here's the technique:

1. Select the curved line tool.

2. Move the cursor to the point where the line should begin.

3. Click and drag the crosshairs cursor to where the line should end. Release the mouse button.

4. Move the cursor to a spot some distance from the line and press down the mouse button; the line will curve in the direction of this spot. Drag the mouse until the line is curved in the right way. Release the mouse button.

5. Move the mouse to another spot and press the mouse button; the line curves a second time in the new direction. Drag the mouse until your second curve is just right. Release the button.

If you double-click after defining the straight line and without moving the mouse cursor, the line will not curve. If you move the mouse only once to a new position and then double-click; the line will curve in only one direction. Figure 6.7 shows examples of these three uses of the curved line.

Figure 6.7

The curved line tool created these three lines. In the top line, the mouse was double-clicked after a straight line was created. The curve below was created by double-clicking the mouse in a new position after a line was defined. The bottom line was created by defining a line and then clicking in two new spots.

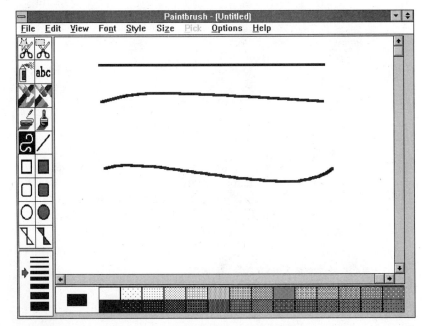

Unfortunately, the curved line is not a very precise tool. The curve does not extend to the point where you click; it pulls the line about half of the distance from the initial line to the cursor.

Using the Straight Line Tool

The straight line tool is easy to use: Simply click and drag to define the beginning and end of a line. You may want to change the line width before you draw the straight line. If you want your line to be perfectly vertical, horizontal, or diagonal (an exact 45-degree angle), hold down the Shift key while you draw the line.

Don't waste time using the straight line to create enclosed forms such as buildings or the county on the map in Figure 6.5. The polygon tool is much better suited to creating these shapes. In Figure 6.5, the straight line tool was used to create most of the roads.

Making Boxes

Paintbrush has four variations of the box tool. There's a hollow box with square corners, a filled box with square corners, a hollow box with rounded corners, and a filled box with rounded corners. (The icons for the hollow tools have black borders with white interiors; those for the filled tools have black borders with gray interiors.) The technique for using any of the four is the same.

1. Choose your colors and line size: For a hollow box, you just need to select a foreground color; for a filled box, choose the foreground color to define the interior and a background color to define the border.

2. Select one of the four box tool icons.

3. Hold down the left mouse button to define a corner. Then drag the mouse until the cursor is where the opposite corner should appear. Release the mouse button and the box is drawn.

All four of the box tools create rectangles that are perfectly straight on the horizontal and vertical plane. To create a square, hold down the Shift key as you define one of the boxes. In fact, you can use the Shift key to achieve neater results with most of the Paintbrush tools. Table 6.2 outlines which tools yield what results. When you hold down the Shift key while using the tools in the left column, the resulting shape is a perfectly rendered version of the shape on the right. Diagonal lines are always drawn at a 45-degree angle.

Table 6.2   **Creating Perfect Shapes with the Shift Key**

Tool	Result with Shift Key
Line	Straight vertical, horizontal, or diagonal lines
Paintbrush	Straight vertical or horizontal lines
Color eraser	Straight vertical or horizontal lines
Eraser	Straight vertical or horizontal lines
Boxes	Squares
Ellipse	Circles
Polygon	Straight vertical, horizontal, or diagonal lines

The Circle/Ellipse

There are two tools for creating circles or ellipses: one for hollow circles and ellipses, the other for filled circles and ellipses. You can create these shapes using the same technique described for boxes. To create a perfect circle, hold down the Shift key the entire time you are defining the shape. You can create both hollow and filled circles, depending on which tool you select.

The Polygons

The polygon tool is the most flexible of all the tools. As with the boxes and circle/ellipse tools, you can use it to create a hollow or filled shape. However, there's no limit on the final shape of the object you create with Polygon. Your object can have virtually any number of sides. It can be as simple as a triangle or can have as many sides as a complex map (in Figure 6.5, Hammond County was created with the polygon tool).

1. As with other tools, start by selecting a line size and colors. In hollow polygons, the borders use the foreground color. In filled polygons, the interior uses the foreground color and the border uses the background color.

2. Click on the polygon tool.

3. Position the crosshairs cursor where the first corner of the polygon should appear.

4. Click and drag to define the first side of the polygon. Release the mouse button when the line looks right.

5. Move the cursor to where the next line in the polygon should end and click. Paintbrush will connect the two lines.

6. Move to the spot where the third line should end and click again. The third line will be drawn.

7. Repeat step 6 for the remaining lines until you've outlined the polygon's shape.

8. Double-click. A line will be drawn connecting the last line with the beginning of the first line.

The Text Tool

abc
When you select the abc icon, you switch from a drawing mode to a writing mode. The cursor becomes an I-beam pointer that you can position anywhere; when you click the mouse, an insertion point appears at that spot and you can begin to add text.

Paintbrush provides the same font selection available in other Windows programs. Courier, Times Roman, and Arial will give the best appearance and provide the most flexibility since they can be scaled to virtually any size. (They're part of the new TrueType family.) Symbol is offered only for special characters, such as the Greek letters used in scientific notation. The other fonts are bitmapped system fonts that are provided for compatibility with earlier Windows programs; they provide the least flexibility and generally have a poor appearance. (A full discussion of fonts and printing is in Chapter 12.)

You can select your text formats either before you begin to type or as you're typing the text. However, unlike other Windows applications, Paintbrush will not let you change the font, style, or size of a text area after you paste it down by selecting a new tool or command.

Paintbrush has very crude text editing features. Just about the only way to edit is to delete the last letters typed using the Backspace key. And once you've selected a new tool or command, you have, in effect, pasted down the text, and there's no way to edit it again. If a text entry needs extensive editing, you'll need to delete the entire area using the pick tool or the eraser and then retype the text from the beginning.

Making Changes and Fixing Mistakes in a Drawing

There are four tools for making changes to a drawing, and several other ways to fix mistakes. The techniques you use with the editing tools can affect any area of the drawing you want to define; they can change an object, part of an object, or just the background. The other methods for fixing mistakes involve reversing an action.

Using the Erasers to Cover Mistakes and Add Special Effects

The two icons on the third row of the tool bar are used to cut a swath through anything in the drawing area, whether it's a hollow object, a filled shape, text, or background. The right icon is called the eraser and the left icon is called the color eraser. If you're working with black and white, both perform identically. When you're working with color, you can create startling special effects with the color eraser.

The Eraser

The eraser's main purpose is to cover a small mistake, since it changes the color of an area to the currently selected background. If you've drawn a line that's slightly too long, the eraser may be the easiest way to correct the error.

You use the eraser by selecting its icon. A square eraser icon appears, showing the area it will affect. Hold the left mouse button down as you move the square over the desired area; everything in the eraser's path will be changed to the current background color. The width of the eraser's swath is controlled by your choice in the linesize box. To erase in a perfectly horizontal, vertical, or diagonal path, hold down Shift as you drag the eraser square.

You can create interesting special effects by changing the background color before selecting the eraser. This permits you to use the eraser like the paintbrush to draw freehand lines. The eraser covers a much wider area than the paintbrush, so at times the eraser may be the better choice for line drawing.

The Color Eraser

You use the color eraser to change one color to another. Select the color you want to remove as the foreground color and the color you want to add as the background color. Then hold down the left mouse button as you drag the mouse over the desired area. The color eraser will change the color only in those areas where the color matches the current foreground color. In contrast, the regular eraser will change every color that it passes to the chosen foreground color.

You can also use the color eraser to change to a new color every occurrence of a certain color in the drawing. To do this, change the active foreground color to the color you want removed and change the active background color to the color you want to add. Double-click on the color eraser and the two colors will be switched in every part of the visible drawing area.

Selecting an Area of a Drawing with the Scissors and the Pick

You use the two icons at the top of the tool bar, the scissors and the pick, to select any area in the drawing. Once you've cut an area with the tools, you can delete it entirely, move it elsewhere, or change its appearance with one of the special effects on the Pick menu. When you select an area with one of these tools, it is copied to the Clipboard and can be inserted into another program.

You use the scissors like this to define an irregularly shaped area:

1. Click on the scissors icon.

2. Position the mouse at the spot you want to select.

3. Click and drag as you define the area you want to cut. A line will follow the pointer as you define the area.

4. After the entire area is enclosed, release the mouse button. The solid line will become a dotted line to show the selected area. You don't need to complete the line; Paintbrush will automatically complete the line you're drawing if you release the mouse button at a distance from the beginning of the selection.

You use the pick to define a rectangular area; the technique is similar to the scissors.

1. Click on the pick icon.

2. Position the mouse in the upper-left corner of the area you want selected.

3. Click and drag to define a rectangle; a dotted line will outline the area that you're enclosing.

4. After the entire area is enclosed, release the mouse button. The dotted line will blink.

Cutting and Pasting

When you have successfully chosen the area with either scissors or pick, you can do any of the following:

■ Cut the area by pressing Ctrl-X or selecting Cut from the Edit menu. This removes the area from the drawing and transfers it to the Clipboard. You can then switch to a different application and paste the graphic into that application, paste it into a different part of the current drawing, or simply leave it there. The Cut command is one of the quickest ways to delete an object from a drawing if Undo is not effective.

- Copy the area by pressing Ctrl-C or selecting Copy from the Edit menu. This copies the selected area to the Clipboard without changing the current drawing.

- Copy to another file by selecting the Copy To command from the Edit menu. This creates a new file consisting of the enclosed area without changing the current drawing.

- Insert a graphic file into the current drawing using Paste From.

Moving and Duplicating Parts of a Drawing

You can easily move an area selected with the scissors or pick without going through the extra step of cutting and copying. Simply place the pointer within the outlined area, and then click and drag the outline to a new position. If you hold down the Shift key during the click-and-drag operation, you'll duplicate the object.

Creating Special Effects with the Pick Commands

When you select an area of the drawing with either the scissors or pick tool, the Pick menu is activated, providing access to five special effects tools. To demonstrate each one, we'll show its effect on this electrical plug, drawn completely within Paintbrush using the drawing tools (see Figure 6.8).

Figure 6.8

A drawing of an electrical plug as it appears before using the Pick menu's special effects.

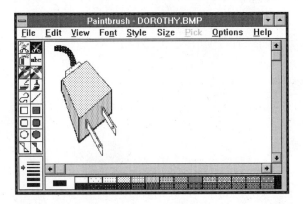

To use these special effects, first select an object with either pick or scissors. The object will be outlined with the dotted line these tools use to confirm a selection. Use these tools with care, since you cannot undo the first three Pick options. Only the Tilt and Shrink & Grow commands can be reversed with the Undo command.

The Flip Horizontal option rotates the object as though it were turned from left to right (see Figure 6.9).

Figure 6.9

The original electrical plug in Figure 6.8 after the Flip Horizontal command is used

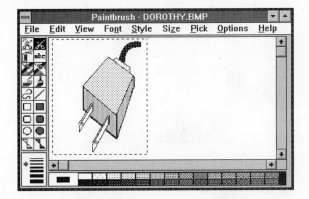

The Flip Vertical option rotates the object as though it were turned from top to bottom (see Figure 6.10).

Figure 6.10

The electrical plug after the Flip Vertical command is used

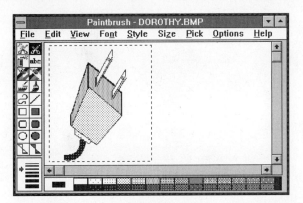

The Inverse option reverses colors so that black becomes white and white becomes black (see Figure 6.11). All of the colors are changed to the opposite number according to their position on the red-green-blue color wheel model used to generate colors on a computer display. Because dithered colors are re-created with each of the component colors reversed, it's almost impossible to predict how the Inverse command will affect a very colorful drawing.

Figure 6.11
The electrical plug after the Inverse command changes the colors.

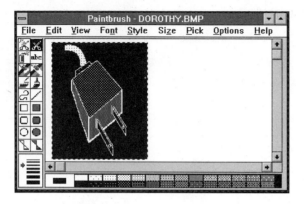

The Shrink & Grow option lets you reduce or enlarge the object (see Figure 6.12). After you've highlighted a drawing area and selected the Shrink & Grow command, you outline a box to indicate the new size. Hold down Shift as you define the new box if you want to retain the same proportions.

Figure 6.12
The electrical plug after the Shrink & Grow command was used to reduce the plug's size. Clear was not active during the operation so the plug was duplicated.

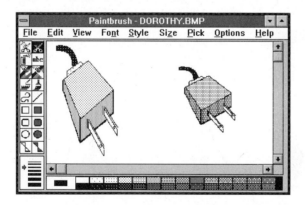

The Tilt option lets you slant the object. To tilt an object, select it, choose Tilt, and then click and drag (see Figure 6.13).

As soon as you press down the mouse button, a box will appear to indicate the outlines of the new area; your pointer represents the upper-left corner of the new area. As you move the pointer, you indicate how far the outline of the new box should shift. Moving one inch to the left will shift the lower-left corner of the new area one inch to the left. An object can be tilted only within a 45-degree range. In Figure 6.13, the pointer was moved a short amount to the right.

Figure 6.13

The electrical plug after the Tilt command was used to slant it. Here, the drawing area was shifted to the right. Clear was not active during the operation so the plug was duplicated.

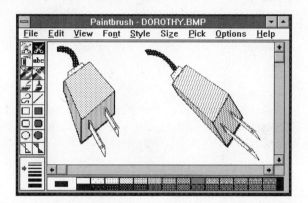

The optional setting called Clear works only with Shrink & Grow and Tilt. Clear removes the original object from the drawing after the change takes effect. When Clear is off, the Pick commands duplicate the original object. In the preceding figures, the Clear command was off. Select Clear before you begin a Shrink & Grow or Tilt operation.

Fixing Mistakes

With a computer drawing program, you can fix your mistakes cleanly to produce a drawing with no erasing and no smudge marks. There are three basic techniques for reversing an action as soon as it has happened. You can undo an object after you've drawn it, undo an object while you are drawing it, or fine-tune your drawing with the Backspace key. You can also delete whole areas of a drawing at any time with the Cut command on the Edit menu, which was explained in the section, "Cutting and Pasting."

Erasing with Undo

After you've drawn an object, you can erase it with Undo. When you select Undo or press Ctrl-Z, all of the objects drawn since you began working with this tool will be removed. For example, if you are working on an elaborate drawing, and then select the line tool to add three separate lines, when you select Undo you'll remove only those three lines.

You'll get the most help from Undo if you reselect drawing tools after you're satisfied with your work, even if you continue to use the same tool. This way, you'll be able to undo only those changes that you consider questionable.

Any of these actions will reset Undo: selecting a new tool, using a menu command (except Cursor Position), and scrolling or changing the way Paintbrush displays the drawing in any way (such as using the View commands or switching applications).

Erasing with the Mouse

To delete an object while you're drawing it, simply click the right mouse button. When drawing objects that require you to hold down the left mouse button until you're done, you can click the right mouse button while you're still holding down the left button.

Erasing with the Backspace Key

After you've drawn an object, press the Backspace key to turn the cursor into a special eraser that you can click and drag over the drawing. It will delete any part of the object you've just drawn but will not affect other parts of the drawing.

This eraser is most valuable for shortening lines in a complex drawing where objects are very close.

Previewing and Fine-Tuning with the View Commands

As a drawing takes shape, you'll want to see it as it will print (without the menus and scroll bars). The View Picture command on the View menu displays the entire drawing area, with nothing in the way. When you're in View Picture mode, no tools are available. You must press any key to return to the normal screen.

You can get a slightly different perspective by selecting Zoom Out on the View menu. Instead of displaying just the drawing, it fits the entire drawing area within the active window. You can only use the scissors and pick tools when zoomed out. This mode is useful for moving objects around on screen, since it lets you see the entire drawing area. To return to the normal drawing screen, select Zoom In. It's a good idea to use Zoom Out just before printing to get a last look at the entire drawing area.

There's a second level of zooming in that's very valuable for fine-tuning a drawing. When you're in the normal drawing display, select Zoom In to magnify the drawing so that each pixel (picture element) can be edited, as shown in Figure 6.14. This kind of tool is called a *fat-bit editor* because it turns each tiny pixel into a large block for editing.

Among other things, Zoom In lets you examine the areas where two lines meet. For example, colors may be leaking through when you use the paint roller. By zooming in, you can find and close the gap. Or, you may have ragged and sloppy edges, which you can clean up when you zoom in.

When a drawing is zoomed, only the paint roller and the paintbrush are available. The paintbrush comes on as the default tool.

Here's how to edit the pixels on a drawing with Zoom In:

1. Select Zoom In from the View menu. The cursor changes to a rectangle that indicates which area of the drawing will be magnified.

2. Move the cursor until it surrounds the area you want to view or edit.

Figure 6.14

The Zoom In command lets you fine-tune every pixel within a drawing with the paint roller and paintbrush. Pixel editing is especially useful for cleaning up a messy area in a drawing or for connecting lines.

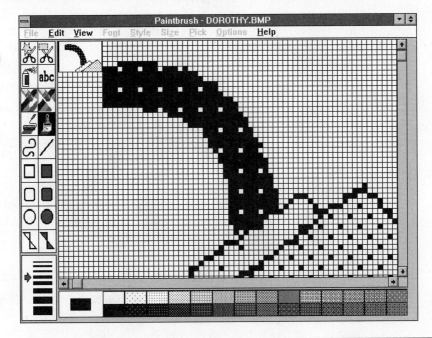

3. Click the mouse. The display changes to a grid representing each pixel within the area you selected. In the upper-left corner there's a view of the rectangular area you selected.

4. Choose a square to be changed and click on the square. Use the left mouse button to change the square to the current foreground color; use the right mouse button to change it to the current background color. You can change colors in the palette at any time. The squares in the grid will change to reflect your color choices and the rectangle in the upper-left corner will show how your changes are affecting the drawing in normal size. You can use the paint roller to change colors, just as you would in normal viewing.

Working with Graphic Files from Other Programs

Paintbrush can display graphic files that come from other sources. For example, Windows uses files with the extension BMP (bit-map) as the wallpaper or background display behind active windows. These BMP files are installed during setup in the Windows directory. You can use Paintbrush to display and edit these files, or to create a new BMP file to be used as wallpaper.

In addition, other software programs produce graphic files that you can display and edit. For example, PCX graphic files are common in business; many scanners and fax boards generate PCX files. If you've used Microsoft Paint, you can also import that program's MSP format.

Pasting Images Displayed in Other Windows Programs

Any type of image that can be displayed in Windows can be opened in Paintbrush thanks to the Clipboard feature. After an area of the screen has been cut in another Windows application, it's placed in the Windows Clipboard, a program that is always available for transferring information. If Paintbrush is open while that image remains in the Clipboard, you can insert the graphic into the active Paintbrush drawing by choosing Paste from the Edit menu or pressing Ctrl-V or Shift-Ins. Because the Clipboard can hold only one cut object at a time, it's a good idea to place an object in the desired spot as soon as you cut it.

Capturing Windows Screens

The Clipboard also allows you to capture the entire Windows desktop in most Windows programs. If you press PrtSc or Alt-PrtSc in a Windows program, a copy of the entire screen display should be placed in the Clipboard. You can then paste that image into Paintbrush so you can edit it and save it to disk. This option does not work with all keyboards. If it doesn't work for you, try Shift-PrtSc.

Viewing Files in Unusual Formats

You can view just about any type of graphic image that's stored in a bit-mapped format, thanks to the wide availability of format conversion programs. (Bit-mapped images are stored as a finite set of pixels, rather than as a set of instructions for drawing an image.) If a graphic image can be converted to either BMP, PCX, or MPS format, you can open it and edit it from Paintbrush. Or, if another Windows program can display it, you can transfer it into Paintbrush using the Paste command.

Paintbrush can be valuable for preparing images from outside sources to be used in your other documents, such as word processing files or databases. For example, there are a number of public on-line services that distribute graphic images. CompuServe has hundreds of images available, including reproductions of famous paintings and copies of photographs taken by NASA probes like Voyager and the lunar explorers.

The image displayed in Figure 6.15 was downloaded from an on-line service in Portland, Oregon called Events Horizons. It was scanned from photographs distributed by NASA and stored in a format called GIF (graphic image format). I converted it to BMP format using a conversion program also distributed by the bulletin board, and was able to open it with Paintbrush.

Figure 6.15

This image of an astronaut walking in space was released by NASA, scanned into a PC, and posted on a public bulletin board. The conversion from GIF to Windows's BMP format resulted in a slight loss of resolution. However, now that it's open in Paintbrush, you can enhance it with any of the drawing or edit tools. Copyright ©1990 Events Horizons.

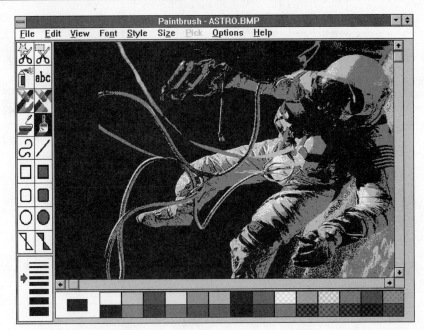

The ability to manipulate just about any image that can be photographed and then scanned into a PC is one of Windows's most exciting potentials. It's also one of the least understood and exploited capabilities. In coming years, encyclopedias, atlases, and clip-art programs will provide thousands of images that you can open in Paintbrush, edit, and then use in other programs.

Opening Graphic Files

Because Paintbrush can read files in three different formats, the Open command in the File menu works a bit differently from other Windows programs. When the File Open dialog box opens, it displays a list of files in the current directory that are in the format currently highlighted in the drop-down list of file types for the three formats (BMP, MPS, or PCX), as shown in Figure 6.16.

To view files in other formats, you need to select the format's file extension here. To view files in other directories, double-click on [..] in the Directories window and the listings will switch to files stored in the parent directory. You may need to click on the directory several times to choose the right parent and then the right subdirectory before you select the desired directory. (If you need help navigating through the file choices, see "The File Open Dialog Box" in Chapter 4.)

Figure 6.16

The File Open Dialog box is displaying a list of files in BMP format.

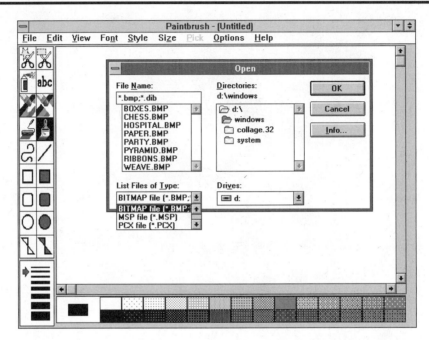

Looking at Wallpaper

Since Paintbrush opens in the Windows main directory, you'll probably find a number of BMP files when you select File Open. These are the files used for the wallpaper that appears when there's display space behind the active window. These files can be good samples to use in exploring Paintbrush's tools. As long as you don't save them, you won't do any damage.

If you want to use your own artwork as Windows wallpaper, you can make the change in the Desktop module within the Control Panel program, as described in Chapter 9.

Info about Paintbrush Files

The File Open dialog box has an option for learning some general details about a file before you open it. To access the feature, select the file and then select Info. A message box will display the size (in pixels) of the file, the number of colors used within it, and the number of planes.

Picture Information	
Width: 123	OK
Height: 160	
Colors: 16	
Planes: 1	

You can control the size of newly created files via Paintbrush's Image Attributes option. When you open files that were created by other programs, this information can help prepare you for problems. If the image is very large, you may want to free up some memory by closing another open application.

The Info box can alert you to potential problems with an image. Files that have more colors or a higher resolution than your system can display will appear distorted. For example, if you are using a VGA system, it can display only 16 colors; when you open a file that has 256 colors, the colors in the image will be muddy, since Paintbrush attempts to display similar colors for all those which it cannot display. By the way, just because an image is listed as having 16 colors does not mean it is actually using all 16 colors; when the Info box lists 16 colors for an image, it's referring to a file format specification. The most common formats for color images are 16, 256, 16-bit, and 24-bit.

Saving Paintbrush Files

Like other Windows programs, Paintbrush has two choices for saving files: Save and Save As. With new files, choose Save. When you have made changes to a file that is already stored on disk, you may want to choose the Save As option to create a second copy of the file. This way, you'll have before and after versions of the edited file.

If you choose Save with a new file, or Save As with an existing file, you have five options for controlling the file format. Paintbrush automatically selects the BMP option that is most appropriate for your drawing (most drawings will automatically be saved as a 16-color bitmap). At times, however, you might want to change the default.

- PCX is probably the most common format for graphic images. Hundreds of graphics programs and hardware devices (fax boards, scanners, and so on) store files in PCX. Choose this format if you plan to use the file in a PCX-compatible program. You must select the PCX option for the file to be saved as PCX.

- Monochrome bitmap will convert a color file to a gray-scaled BMP format. If you've selected Black and White as your palette, this will be the default.

- 16-color bitmap is the standard color setting for EGA and VGA personal computers.

- 256-color bitmap expands the file size to allow for the addition of more color when chosen on an EGA or VGA system. Select this option only if you are working with high-end graphics adapters or plan to give your image to someone who will. It will result in a much larger file size for images that use only 16 colors.

- 24-bit bitmap is similar to 256-color bitmap and is not appropriate for standard EGA and VGA systems.

Converting Graphic Files

The Save As command, when used with the options described in the previous section, presents an easy way to convert files. If, for example, you want to incorporate the wallpaper files that come with Windows into a program that reads only PCX, simply open the BMP file in Paintbrush and then save the file as a PCX file.

Printing Paintbrush Files

The Page Setup and Printer Setup options for Paintbrush are similar to those found in other Windows applications. You can add a header or footer to a Paintbrush document, change the margins from the default, or make changes to the options available on your printer. Generally, you won't need to change any of these, other than to add a header or footer.

The Print option on the File menu has settings that can save you a great deal of time. This can be valuable, since a printer can take several minutes to process Paintbrush images.

If your printer has a draft mode, you can save printing time by choosing Draft when you only need a rough idea of how an image will look. Choose Proof when you want the best results; it takes longer but produces a result with higher resolution.

You can also save time by printing a partial area of the drawing. When you choose this option, Paintbrush displays a crosshairs cursor that works like the pick tool. Choose two corners for the area you want to print and Paintbrush will send only that portion of the drawing to the printer. The smaller the area you select to print, the more time you'll save.

Generally, you should choose the Printer Resolution option to get better results, but the results depend on both the quality of your display and the quality of your printer. When Paintbrush prints, it attempts to print at screen resolution. If you have a high-resolution display (VGA) and low-resolution printer (dot matrix), you shouldn't choose the Use Printer Resolution option.

With an EGA display and a laser printer, you will probably want to choose Printer Resolution to get the sharpest quality. But, if you want the most faithful representation of the screen display, don't select this option. In order to adjust the drawing to printer resolution, the shapes of objects may change. For example, a perfect square may become a rectangle.

Paintbrush also lets you increase or decrease the size of the printout via the Scaling option. You can improve a grainy image by choosing a value of less than 100, and you can improve an image that's too small by choosing a value above 100.

Paintbrush's Menus: A Complete List

File

New. . .
Open. . .
Save   Ctrl+S
Save As. . .
Page Setup. . .
Print. . .
Print Setup. . .
Exit

Edit

Undo   Ctrl+Z
Cut   Ctrl+X
Copy   Ctrl+C
Paste   Ctrl+V
Copy To
Paste From

View

Zoom In   Ctrl+N
Zoom Out   Ctrl+O
View Picture   Ctrl+P
Tools and Linesize
Palette
Cursor Position

Text

Regular	
Bold	Ctrl+B
Italic	Ctrl+I
Underline	Ctrl+U
Outline	
Shadow	
Fonts...	

Pick *

Flip Horizontal
Flip Vertical
Inverse
Shrink & Grow
Tilt
Clear

Options

Image Attributes...
Brush Shapes...
Edit Colors...
Get Colors...
Save Colors...
Omit Picture Format

Help

Contents
Search for Help On...
How to Use Help
About Paintbrush...

* The Pick commands appear only after a part of the current drawing has been selected with the Pick tool.

7

Terminal: The Windows Communications Tool

Making a Connection

Working with
On-line Data

Customizing Terminal

A Strategy for
Terminal Files

UNTIL VERSION 3.0, WINDOWS'S SLOW SCREEN DISPLAY WAS SUCH A SIG-
nificant drawback that it was more efficient to leave Windows and
run communications programs under DOS. With version 3.0, the
display speed got better, and with the performance improvements
made in version 3.1, Windows is now an excellent platform for communicating with other computers.

Terminal is a simple communications program but it provides ready
access to the benefits of communicating under Windows, including the ability
to view incoming text that has scrolled out of range and to place incoming
text on the Clipboard for transfer to another program. Windows's graphical
display can be a boon to productivity thanks to the wonderful control it provides in an on-line session. To run Terminal, you must have either a Hayes,
Hayes-compatible, MultiTech, or Trailblazer modem properly installed on
your system.

Making a Connection

You open Terminal by double-clicking on its icon in the Accessories window
or by entering **terminal** at the Run command in the Program Manager's File
menu. The initial Terminal screen contains a menu bar and a blank display.
Although you can type text into this display, you can't edit the text. This display is used to send and receive text only after you have established a connection with another computer.

If a Terminal message box asks you to assign your modem to a port the
first time you run the program, you did not yet install a modem; most people
will have made this selection while installing Windows. If you get this message, select a modem port and make sure you choose a modem type that's
listed in the "Communications" section on the following pages. If you're not
sure which port to select, it's okay to guess; if necessary, you can change the
selection later with the Communications option on the Settings menu.

Settings that Establish a Connection

Before you can make a connection with another computer, you must tell Terminal certain facts about your modem, choose the protocols to be used in
communicating with the other computer, and type in the phone number you
want to call.

You establish these settings with commands in Terminal's Settings menu.
You can also store your settings for repeat performances using the File Save
command.

The key to using any communications program is to match the modem
settings and communications protocols of the remote computer to be used
for a particular session. This section details the menu choices you need to

make before linking up with a remote computer, and the section "Working with On-line Data" explains the data transfer features needed when you are connected.

Here's a general guide to the steps you'll perform in establishing any communications session. If your modem is correctly installed, you won't need to make any choices in steps 1 and 2, but you should open these menus to check that the right selections are stored.

1. Select Modem Commands from the Settings menu and choose your modem from the Modem Defaults check box. Choose Hayes if you have a Hayes-compatible modem. Select OK.

2. Select Communications from the Settings menu and choose the port to which your computer's modem is connected from the Connector list.

3. With the Communications selection still open, choose the Baud Rate, Data Bits, Parity, and Stop Bits specified by the remote computer as the correct protocol. Then select OK.

4. Select Phone Number from the Settings menu and enter the phone number of the remote computer. Select OK.

5. Select Dial from the Phone menu. Terminal will immediately call the remote computer. (The section "Dialing the Phone" lists possible problems that may prevent you from connecting with the remote computer, and also includes some remedies.)

6. When the connection is made, text from the remote computer will appear in the Terminal window (see Figure 7.1). When you're through exchanging information with the remote computer, choose Hangup from the Phone menu.

7. Select Save from the File menu and give these settings a name to remind you of the remote computer you're currently connected with. Select OK.

Modem Commands

If your phone line uses tone dialing, you only need to select the appropriate modem from the Modem Commands menu (see Figure 7.2) before dialing the phone. The default setting is Hayes, and if you use a Hayes-compatible modem you don't need to choose Modem Commands from the Settings menu.

If your phone line uses pulse dialing, you must change the text in the Dial text box to read **ATDP**. (You have pulse dialing if you hear clicks rather than tones when you dial your phone.)

The other settings in the Modem Commands dialog box contain codes for controlling communications; these codes are specific to the type of modem selected. The default settings will be fine for typical on-line sessions. If you're familiar with the command set used by your modem, you can customize the settings here by editing the text boxes. For example, if your phone system requires that a 9 be dialed in order to get an outside line, you can enter 9 in the Dial setting after ATDT. This way, all Terminal calls will dial 9 first and you won't need to add the 9 to every phone number.

Figure 7.1

The Terminal window is used to display text being received from a remote computer via modem. This screen shows the opening text received after connecting with *PC Magazine*'s on-line service, PC MagNet. After you choose your settings, it's a good idea to call up the remote computer to check the settings before you store them in a Terminal file.

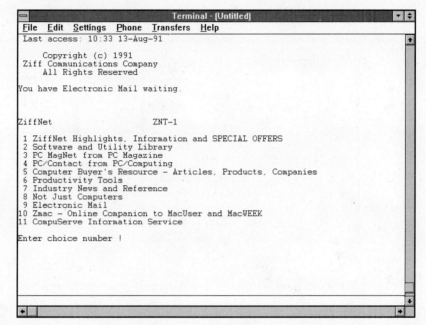

Figure 7.2

The Modem Commands dialog box offers settings through which you control the operation of your modem.

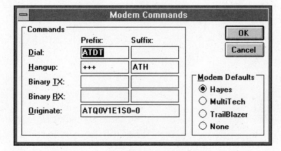

All of the command codes that will work with your particular modem should be listed in your modem manual.

Communications

The next option that you must choose from the Settings menu before starting an on-line session is Communications (see Figure 7.3). The correct choice of settings is crucial to linking successfully with another computer. Before attempting to dial a remote computer, you should ask the people who maintain the computer for the correct baud rate, data bits, parity, and stop bits. As a group, these settings are often called the *communications protocols*.

Figure 7.3

The Communications dialog box contains the settings that enable your computer to communicate properly with another computer.

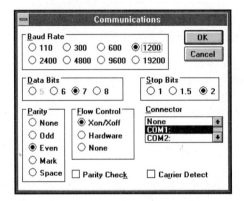

- **Baud Rate** Reflects the speed at which your computer will transmit and receive bits. If you're uncertain of the correct setting for a particular session, choose the highest speed rated for your modem.

- **Data Bits** Indicates the number of bits that will be contained in each word sent or received. The most common settings for on-line services are 7 and 8. Generally, you hear this setting expressed in the short phrase "set your modem to 7E2" or "N81."

- **Parity** Indicates the type of bit-counting that will be used to guarantee accuracy between the two modems. The most common settings for on-line services are None and Even. Parity is the letter used in the expression "7E2" or "N81."

- **Stop Bits** Indicates the number of bits used as separators between words. The most common settings are 1 and 2. Stop bits is the last number in the expression "7E2" or "N81."

- **Connector** Tells Terminal the port on your own computer that is connected to the modem. If you're unsure, select COM1. If the modem won't dial, try COM2 next.

The following commands are less important when establishing connections with another computer. In most cases, you won't need to set these before you begin an on-line session. However, you may need to alter these settings if you are having problems maintaining a connection.

■ **Flow Control**   A method for controlling the amount of text transmitted between two computers; it's often called software *handshaking.* The default setting is Xon/Xoff, and you shouldn't change this default unless you know that the remote computer uses a hardware flow control method (in which case, you must be using a modem that also supports this method) or requires that no flow control is used. Flow control ensures that your computer's text buffer will not get overwhelmed by incoming text.

■ **Parity Check**   Shows a question mark whenever a parity error is encountered. It works only when the on-line session uses a parity setting other than None. If you don't select parity check, when parity errors are encountered, the suspicious character will be deleted.

■ **Carrier Detect**   Switches from Terminal's normal method of detecting whether a connection was established to checking your hardware's carrier detect signal. Don't turn this setting on unless Terminal is disconnecting after you've established communications.

Terminal Emulation

Some communications programs emulate the software on mainframe computers. If you know that the remote computer you're calling requires a specific terminal emulation, select Terminal Emulation from the Settings menu.

You have three choices: TTY, DEC VT-100 (ANSI), or DEC VT-52. Most on-line services and bulletin boards will work fine with the default setting, DEC-VT-100 (ANSI). If you've been told to use an emulation that's not in this group, try each of the three; one of them is likely to work. If not, you'll have to obtain a different communications program, such as CrossTalk or ProComm, to connect with that computer.

Phone Number

The Phone Number dialog box lets you specify the number you're dialing and allows you to choose whether or not Terminal should try again if the remote computer doesn't answer.

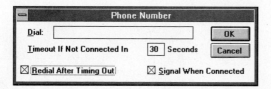

Enter the phone number you're calling in the Dial box. It's a good idea to insert a space between the various parts of your phone number (area code, prefix, and suffix) as you type it in so that it's easier to check the phone number for accuracy. These spaces won't affect the way Terminal dials the number. You can use the Phone Number text box to send command codes (such as 9 for an outside line) to the modem, but it's better to use the Modem Commands option for sending command codes.

There are three other choices in the Phone Number dialog box:

- **Timeout If Not Connected In**   Establishes the number of seconds that Terminal will wait for the other computer to answer the phone. Terminal begins counting after it starts to dial the call. If it reaches zero before the other computer answers the phone and transmits a signal, Terminal issues a "hangup" command to the modem. The default setting is 30, which is also the minimum that Terminal will accept. Generally, 30 seconds is plenty of time, but if you're calling overseas or have erratic phone service in your area, you may want to increase this setting to 45 or 60.

- **Redial After Timing Out**   Tells Terminal to dial again if the first attempt was unsuccessful. Terminal will continue to dial until the remote computer sends a signal that you are connected.

- **Signal When Connected**   Tells Terminal to beep when the correct answer signal is received. You should check this item unless you really dislike beeps, because Terminal will beep even if you've switched to another application. This can make your life easier when you try to connect with a bulletin board that's often busy, since it lets you do other work while Terminal attempts to place the call.

Dialing the Phone

After you've made all the selections described so far, you're ready to call the remote computer. Just select Dial from the Phone menu. Terminal immediately begins the call, using the phone number and protocols you established in the Settings menu.

If Terminal can dial the phone number, the above dialog box appears, showing the phone number that Terminal is calling and counting down the number of seconds specified in the Phone Number dialog box. The active

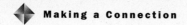

window also displays the command codes that Terminal sent to the modem in order to place the call.

If the connection is successfully established, Terminal displays the word "connect" followed by the baud rate of the connection. You'll then start to receive characters transmitted by the remote computer. (Some on-line services require that a carriage return or a key combination be sent at this point to stimulate the log-in sequence.) In most cases, the remote computer will send you instructions or will prompt you to identify yourself before you can continue.

You can hang up the phone by pressing Esc or selecting Cancel before the remote computer answers. After the remote computer answers, you can hang up by choosing Hangup from the Phone menu.

Troubleshooting

If you cannot make the connection, review the section "Settings that Establish a Connection," and make sure your computer has the correct settings needed to communicate with the remote computer.

Here are some general guidelines for diagnosing connection problems:

- If the modem doesn't dial, check the Modem Commands dialog box and make sure that you've selected the right modem and that the Dial box is properly set for tone or pulse dialing. If these settings are correct and the modem still doesn't dial, make sure you've chosen the right serial port in the Connector dialog box. Also, check that the modem is connected to an active phone line.

- If the remote computer answers but doesn't send information, press Enter several times after Terminal issues its "connect" message; this may prompt a response from the remote computer. If that doesn't work, check the Baud Rate setting in Communications. You may need to select a different baud rate.

- If the remote computer answers but you receive gibberish, check the settings for Data Bits, Stop Bits, and Parity to make sure you have the correct value in each. You can correct these settings while the connection is still established with the remote computer. Press Enter after you've changed one of these settings and closed the dialog box to prompt a response from the remote computer.

- If text is being received but part of it is cut off, you've probably scrolled the display area to the right. Click the left arrow along the bottom scroll bar until you can see all of the incoming text.

Hanging Up

When you're finished exchanging information with the remote computer, you'll usually be able to sign off by selecting a remote command. This may be enough to disconnect you from the remote service, but it's not enough to clear the line at your end.

You should always select the Hangup command on the Phone menu when you've concluded a remote session. This command sends the proper reset commands to the modem. Otherwise, the next time you try to dial the phone with the modem, it may not respond.

Saving Your Settings

Once you know that you have the correct settings, select the Save command from the File menu. Name the setting file and include a description of this type of connection. Terminal will add the extension .TRM to the file name.

When you want to communicate with another computer that has similar settings, you can open this file, make changes to the phone number and any other settings that are different, and then dial the phone. If the connection works successfully, store the new settings with the Save As command.

If you call a large number of bulletin boards and on-line services, you may want to create a basic setting file where you can save your choice of modem and other preferences.

Working with On-line Data

Once you establish a connection, you have a variety of options for printing and storing incoming data. These options are similar to the features in DOS communications programs. However, Terminal's unique advantage is that it lets you view incoming text.

Scrolling through Incoming Text

When you're connected with an on-line service that displays a steady stream of incoming text, such as a news service on CompuServe or PC MagNet's discussion forums, Terminal stores the last 100 lines received in a buffer.

You can scroll back through this buffer at any time during the on-line session without interfering with the exchange of data. Simply use the vertical scroll bars on the right side of the display. You can increase the size of the buffer to up to 399 lines. To make this change, choose Terminal References from the Settings menu and edit the Buffer Lines setting.

After scrolling, be sure that you've returned the display so that the most recent incoming text is visible. There will usually be a blinking cursor where the remote computer issued its last prompt.

Viewing Larger Characters

Most on-line services transmit text at a maximum width of 80 characters per line because most computers display 80 characters on each line. However, Windows lets you alter the display so that you can view characters in virtually any size.

When displaying incoming text of an uncommonly large size, you may not be able to see some of the incoming characters unless you scroll to the right using the scroll bar along the bottom of the display. In Figure 7.4, for example, the text in a CompuServe menu is too large for the display; the only way to see the characters at the extreme right is to scroll to the right. You can remedy this problem by choosing a font in a smaller size from the Terminal Preferences dialog box.

Figure 7.4

You can use Terminal's ability to change type sizes to keep an eye on the news being sent from an on-line service while you work on another program. You can use the scroll bars to display characters that don't fit within the current window.

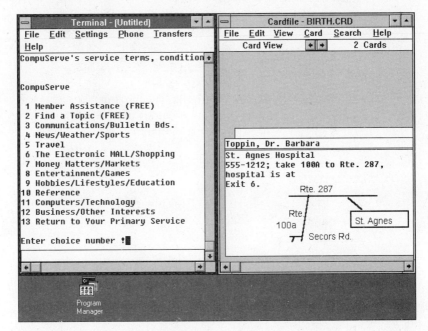

Printing Incoming Text

Terminal lets you print text just seconds after it appears on the display. You use this feature by selecting Printer Echo on the Settings menu. A check mark appears next to the Printer Echo menu listing when the printer is active.

Terminal prints the page after it has received enough incoming text to fill the page. If only a small amount of text is received on the display, the printed page will not appear until you press the printer's form feed switch. You stop incoming text from being printed by clicking on Printer Echo a second time to toggle this feature off.

The text is printed in the default font or the most recently used font on your printer, not in the font that you've selected for the Terminal display.

If you need to change the installed printer or select a printer option (like the paper tray to be used), use the Print Setup command on the File menu. But you do not have the printing options available in other Windows programs, such as font selection and page headers.

Sending and Receiving Files

The Transfers menu contains options for transferring both binary and text files. Any file can be sent or received in binary form; only files that can be displayed as text characters can be transferred as text files.

As soon as the two computers have begun to exchange data, an information bar appears at the bottom of the Terminal display.

| Stop | Pause | ▮▮▮▮│▮│▮│▮ | Sending: OUTLINE.6 |

When Terminal sends (uploads) a file, this bar displays a gauge that indicates the file's progress. In the previous illustration, the uploading of file OUTLINE.6 is nearly half completed.

| Stop | Pause | Bytes: 4096K | Receiving: CALC.TXT |

When Terminal receives (downloads) a file, the information bar displays the number of bytes received so far in kilobytes, rather than a gauge. (Since Terminal doesn't know the size of the file it's receiving, it can't estimate how long the download will take.)

When a text file transfer begins in Terminal, the information bar provides the choices Stop or Pause. You can abort the transfer by clicking on this Stop button, or by choosing Stop on the Transfers menu. If you choose Pause on either the information bar or the Transfers menu, you suspend the transfer and can continue the transfer by choosing Resume whenever you wish.

| Stop | | Bytes: 17664 | Receiving: WINCOLOR.EXE | Retries: 0 |

When a binary file transfer begins in Terminal, an information bar appears at the bottom of the display with a Stop button but no Pause button: Binary file transfers cannot be paused.

The following sections explain your options and the procedures you'll follow to send and receive files. The exact steps you'll need to take depend on the instructions that the remote computer sends, since file exchanges always require coordination. In Figure 7.5, note that the remote computer guided the user through the steps needed to transfer a file.

Figure 7.5

Every file transfer—whether you're sending or receiving—requires coordination. Most computers expect file transfers to begin within a minute of when they issue a go-ahead. That's plenty of time, as long as you've already selected the correct transfer protocol.

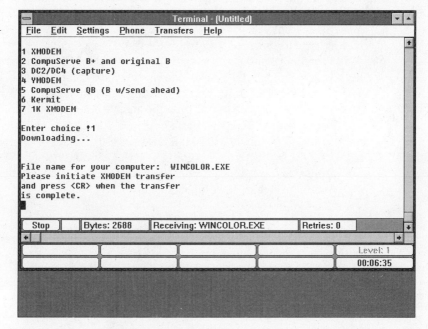

Preparing a Text File Transfer

The Text Transfers dialog box in the Settings menu (see Figure 7.6) controls the timing method that your computer and the remote computer use to coordinate when text should be received and when the computers should pause.

Figure 7.6

The Text Transfers dialog box controls the timing of text transmission between your computer and the remote computer.

In most cases, you'll want to use Standard Flow Control, which allows Terminal to maintain a text buffer that you can scroll through and allows the remote computer to send as much data as possible to your computer.

There are two choices for limiting the amount of text that's sent. You should only use the Character at a Time and Line at a Time choices when they are absolutely required by the remote computer's limitations. You're most likely to use these two settings for communicating with a mainframe that has very rudimentary software for transferring data.

If you find that data is being lost with Standard Flow Control, first switch to Line at a Time; if data losses persist, switch to Character at a Time.

Word Wrap Outgoing Text at Column is used when the receiving computer has a line length shorter than the standard length of 80 characters per line. For example, MCI Mail has a limit of 60 characters per line; if the text file you wish to send via MCI Mail has lines longer than 60 characters, you would set the Word Wrap Outgoing Text at Column setting to 60 or less. Only after you have selected the Word Wrap option can you enter the maximum number of characters on each line.

Sending Text Files

You send a text file to the remote computer by selecting the Send Text File option from the Transfers menu (see Figure 7.7).

Figure 7.7
Use the Send Text File dialog box to establish how text is sent from your computer to the remote computer.

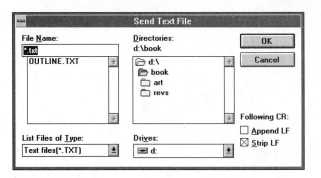

You don't need to coordinate a text upload; you can upload a text file while using a remote computer's message creation option, for example.

The Send Text File dialog box will display files in your Windows directory that end with the extension .TXT; you can send any file in ASCII text format by typing the full directory and file name in the Filename window. Click on the All Files choice in the List Files by Type box to see all files in this directory.

With File Send, you can have the carriage returns in the outgoing file interpreted in one of three ways:

- **Append LF**   Adds a line feed to your file where carriage returns appear. Typically, this will cause a text file that appears single-spaced on your machine to appear double-spaced on the remote computer.

- **Strip LF**   Removes line feeds from your file where carriage returns appear. This is useful when your file has carriage returns at the end of each line and you want the remote computer to receive the file as word wrapped text, without carriage returns.

- If neither option is checked, Terminal makes no effort to translate your carriage returns, which is probably what you would prefer.

Viewing Text Files for Easier Uploads

The View Text File command on the Transfers menu lets you insert the contents of any text file into a Terminal session. This is an easier way to transfer information than sending a text file, especially when you are creating messages in an Email service.

For example, if you wish to include a document stored on disk in a message you are composing on-line, use View Text File when you've reached the appropriate spot in your message. The file will be inserted into your message.

Use Text Send instead of View Text File if the outgoing file's carriage returns need conversion.

Receiving Text Files

You store incoming text to a file by selecting the Receive Text File option from the Transfers menu (see Figure 7.8) when the remote computer is prepared to transmit the file.

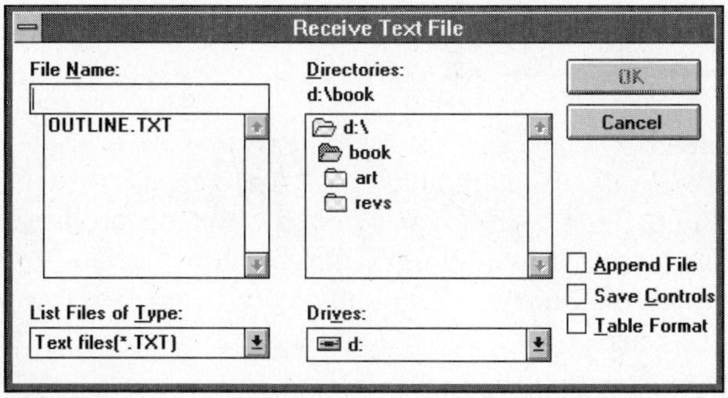

Figure 7.8
The Receive Text File dialog box lets you state where and how to store an incoming text file.

When the dialog box opens, click on the directory in which you wish to store the text file (double-click on [..] to switch to a parent directory). Then type in a file name.

You don't need to coordinate a text download with the remote computer. Receiving a text file can be a way of capturing as a file the words that the remote computer is sending. For example, if you connect to Dow Jones News Retrieval, when the service displays stock-transfer details that you request, you can store the incoming text to a file as you read it on the screen.

Three options control the way the incoming text is stored:

- **Append File**   Lets you add text to an existing file. This is useful when you're downloading information from an on-line service and the information is stored in several areas; you can build one long file instead of creating many small files.

- **Save Controls**   Enables you to include the formatting characters used in the remote computer's display. Generally, you won't want to select this option, since the formatting characters usually will not be understood by the software that you plan to use later to display the text file.

- **Table Format**   Interprets a series of incoming blank spaces as a tab so that material displayed on the remote computer as a table can be easily re-created as a table on your system.

Preparing to Transfer Binary Files

Before you send a binary file, you may need to change the default error-checking protocol that Terminal uses for binary file transfers. XModem/CRC is the default setting. You can change to the Kermit protocol by choosing the Binary Transfers option from the Settings menu.

XModem/CRC and Kermit are systems that govern the way bits are processed between the two computers in order to ensure that the files are transferred without error; each has an error-checking procedure. XModem is older and less sophisticated but it's used by more systems. Kermit is more flexible in adapting to problems in phone lines and can transfer files more quickly. You must choose the protocol that the remote computer is using. If you can use either method, use Kermit.

Sending Binary Files

You can send a binary file only when the remote computer is prepared to receive it. Once the remote computer gives you a go-ahead and you've ensured that the same transfer protocol will be used, choose Send Binary File from the Transfers menu.

You can select the file you want to upload by choosing the directory and then the file from the Send Binary File dialog box menu (see Figure 7.9), or by typing the name of the path and file in the Filename text box.

Figure 7.9
Use the Send Binary File dialog box to state the name and location of the file that's about to be uploaded.

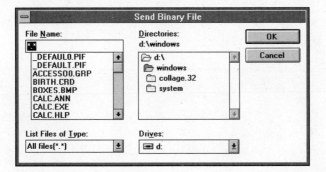

Receiving Binary Files

The procedures for receiving a binary file are similar to those for sending a binary file: First make sure you will use the same transfer protocol as the sending computer.

You can receive a binary file only when the remote computer is prepared to send it. Once the remote computer gives you a go-ahead and you've ensured that the remote computer will use the same transfer protocol you've chosen via the Settings menu's Binary Transfer option, choose Receive Binary File from the Transfers menu (see Figure 7.10). You can choose a directory in which to store the new file in the directories box, or simply type the full path and file name in the Filename text box.

Terminal uses the transfer protocol that you last selected through the Settings menu's Binary Transfer option, even if you made that selection to send a file.

Sharing Data with Other Windows Programs

You don't need to store a file if you just want to capture a small bit of data displayed during a Terminal session. You can highlight any area of the screen with the mouse by clicking and dragging. Then you can select Copy from the Edit menu (or press Ctrl-C) to transfer the highlighted area to the Windows

Clipboard. If you wish to copy everything in the current buffer to the Clipboard, choose Select All from the Edit menu and then choose Copy.

Figure 7.10

When you're about to receive a binary file from a remote computer, use the Receive Binary File dialog box to determine where to store the file.

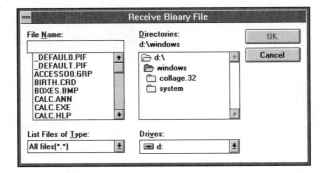

To use the data that you've stored in the Clipboard, open a word processing application by switching to the Program Manager (press the Ctrl-Esc key combination to open the Program Manager's Task List) and then double-click on the program item. Or, you can switch to another program by holding down the Alt key and pressing Tab repeatedly; a message box will display the name of each program running. When you see the program you want to use, release the Alt key. When the target application is open, you can paste the data into that program's data file. Figure 7.11 shows text cut from a Terminal on-line session and pasted into a Microsoft Word for Windows document.

In a Terminal session, you can also paste in data that was copied from another application. For example, you might keep a word processor open as you use an Email service. After you've used the word processor's editing functions to perfect your message, cut it from the word processor and paste it into the Terminal session.

Customizing Terminal

So far, this chapter has explained what you need to know to connect and exchange data with a remote computer. The rest of this chapter discusses two ways to customize Terminal: by tailoring Terminal's display to your taste and by using Terminal's shortcut keys to reduce typing.

Terminal Preferences

You access the Terminal Preferences dialog box (Figure 7.12) via the Settings menu. Until now, we've seen uses for two of its features: the ability to change fonts and to increase the buffer size. This section explains all of the options in this dialog box.

Figure 7.11

You can cut any text displayed during a Terminal session and paste it into another program. Here, the listing of an article found by searching the on-line service Computer Database Plus (top window) was cut and then pasted into a document open in Microsoft Word for Windows (bottom window).

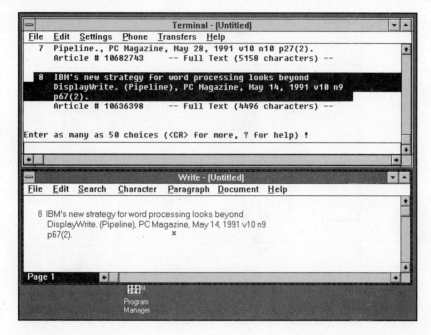

Columns

You have a choice of 132 or 80 columns (characters displayed on a line) but, unless the remote computer sends text at 132 columns, don't change the default setting of 80. Most communications software displays text at 80 columns, because almost all modern displays have 80 characters per line. With graphic displays, it's possible to display almost any number of characters per line, but there's no reason for you to select 132. In fact, the setting of 132 columns can make it more difficult to read incoming text, since incoming lines that do not have carriage returns will be too wide to be seen in their entirety. None of Terminal's fonts enable you to view 132 columns at once. Choose 132 only if the remote computer is sending data that would be lost with an 80-column width.

Terminal Modes

The three check boxes under Terminal Modes control widely disparate functions:

- **Line Wrap** Should be set on (the default). If you turn line wrap off, you will not receive text that is wider than the column setting of 80 or 132. Of course, if you set the column width to 132, this may not be a problem. For most people, however, using line wrap with a column width of 80 columns will be the most practical way to display incoming text.

Figure 7.12

The Terminal Preferences dialog box contains options that can make operation of the Windows Terminal more convenient.

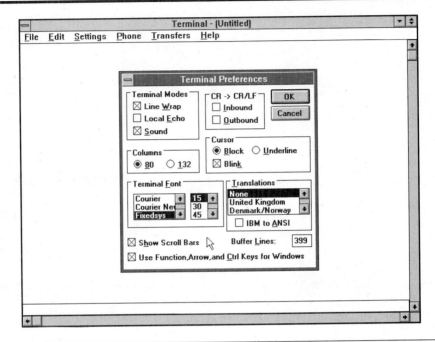

- **Local Echo** Should be off (the default) when you connect to most on-line services. When local echo is on, the characters that you type when on-line are displayed by your system. Most on-line services are sending these characters back to you automatically and, with local echo selected, you'll see two characters for each character you type. If you've connected to a computer that does not display your input, turn local echo on.

- **Sound** Is probably best kept on. When it's on (the default), you'll be able to hear beeps from the remote computer. Many on-line services beep when you're in danger of being disconnected for inactivity.

Terminal Font

Two list boxes control the font that Terminal uses to display incoming and outgoing text. You select a typeface from the left and select a type size from the right.

When you select a new font, Terminal will change the characters in the entire display. Not all changes will result in a new display, however. The list of fonts and sizes is misleading. Terminal does not always display the size you choose.

Terminal's selection of fonts is limited to the fixed-pitch fonts installed in Windows. To ensure compatibility with the mainframe computers that operate most on-line services, Terminal must use only typefaces that display each character in the same amount of space (also called monospace fonts). Many of the font choices available in the rest of Windows are proportional fonts (each character is a different width, depending on its shape) and Terminal cannot display these fonts.

For example, Arial is a proportional font. When you choose it from the Terminal Font list box, Terminal displays it in a monospace style. The result is often difficult to read.

The best choices on the Terminal Font list are System and FixedSys. These two choices are actually the same font. They were designed for clarity in the monospace display that Terminal provides. While they offer only three sizes, starting at 15, they can usually display more characters in a window than just about any of the other fonts, since their design produces a very thin character. As a result, size 15 System font displays more characters in a window than size 10 Arial. And it's much easier to read.

Buffer Lines

Terminal keeps the most recently received lines of text in memory until it reaches the number of lines entered under Buffer Lines. The default is 100, but you can have as many as 399 or as few as 25 lines of text in the buffer. Unless your system has very limited memory, choose 399; this may help you read a vital piece of information that would have otherwise disappeared. By keeping the Buffer Line setting at 399, you use 4k of memory more than you'd use by establishing a setting of 25 lines.

CR to CR/LF

The CR to CR/LF choice exists because early computers needed to be told to do a line feed and to return the carriage in separate instructions. On-line services conform to the way a PC works: A carriage return and a line feed are considered as the same. You may, however, need to select CR to CR/LF when connected to a mainframe or another computer if the incoming text is disappearing because succeeding lines are overwriting it.

If you like to see incoming text displayed as double-spaced instead of single-spaced (the default), select Inbound and the incoming carriage returns will get a double line feed.

Show Scroll Bars

With scroll bars on, you'll be able to view text that's too wide for the display or that has scrolled back through the buffer. Turn the scroll bars off if the remote computer is sending text that can't be seen behind the scroll bars.

Use Function, Arrow, and Ctrl Keys for Windows

This setting lets you decide whether special keys pressed while you're on-line will be used by your computer or by the remote computer. The default setting is on, so that function keys, arrow keys, and Ctrl keys pressed while you're on-line are not sent to the remote computer, but are processed by Windows on your PC.

For example, CompuServe uses certain Ctrl key combinations. When you're connected to CompuServe , Ctrl-S will suspend the incoming display of text. If you have this option checked (the default), you will not be able to issue the Ctrl-S command to CompuServe. The most popular on-line services generally do not use the same Ctrl and function key commands that Windows uses, so it's generally a good idea to turn this option off.

When you're connected to a remote computer, if you find that a function, arrow, or Ctrl key is not working the way you expect, then change this setting.

By the way, this setting does not affect Function Key shortcuts (explained later in this chapter); they work whether this option is on or off.

Translation

Terminal can attempt to interpret incoming text in the characters used in each of 11 countries (the United Kingdom, Denmark, Norway, Finland, France, French-Canada, Germany, Italy, Spain, Sweden, or Switzerland). Of course, this does not mean that Terminal can translate the words. It simply means that Terminal will attempt to display the accent marks and punctuation of the chosen language correctly. This option is provided for times when the incoming text is written in a language other than your Windows default language.

Cursor

Terminal lets you decide whether the cursor will appear as a solid block or a thin underline. You can also have either shape blink or not.

Shortcuts with the Function Keys

Most on-line sessions require that you type in a personal identification number (PIN) or a secret password every time you connect. Terminal enables you to type in your PIN or password once and play it back when needed. You do this by attaching the key sequence to a function key, creating a macro that is invoked by the function key.

Creating Function Key Shortcuts

You can have up to 32 function key shortcuts in each Terminal file. You can assign a series of keystrokes (a macro) to the first eight function keys (F1 to F8). In fact, each function key has four levels, so it can have four different macros assigned to it.

You assign keystrokes to the function keys using a command on the Settings menu.

1. Press Alt-S-K to open the Function Keys dialog box (see Figure 7.13).

2. Enter a name for the keystroke you want to record in the first box to the right of F1.

3. In the longer text box, enter the keystrokes that you want played back. You can enter up to 41 characters.

4. Click on the Keys Visible option so that an X appears in the check box.

5. Select OK. The dialog box closes and function key assignments appear at the bottom of the screen. The name given to F1 appears in the box at the left corner.

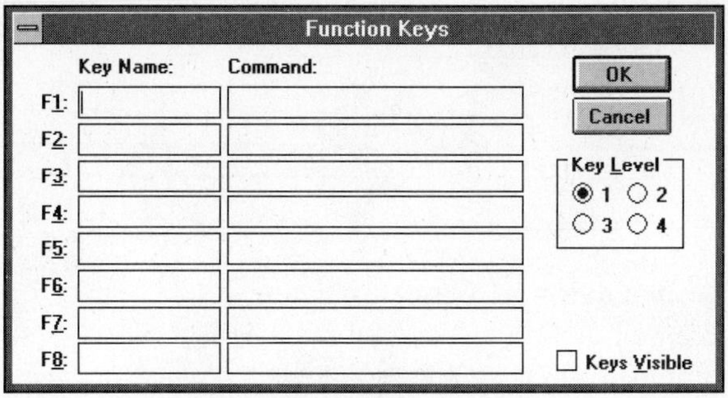

Figure 7.13
With the Function Keys dialog box, you can assign a series of frequently used keystrokes to a single function key.

Using Function Key Shortcuts

The text assigned to any function key will be played back when you click on the box for the desired function key with the function key menu displayed. You can turn the function key display on either by selecting the Keys Visible option in step 4 above or by choosing the Show Function Keys option from the Settings menu.

Terminal displays the function keys at the bottom of the active window in two rows; the far left box on the top represents F1, below it is F2, and so on. Figure 7.14 shows a sample of function key assignments and how they're displayed.

You can also play back the text at any time by pressing Ctrl-Alt followed by the function key, whether or not the function key display is visible. (For example, Ctrl-Alt-F1 would select F1.)

Figure 7.14

The function keys are displayed along the bottom of the Terminal display. The function key assignments used here provide a few login sequences for on-line services, but they don't include the passwords since that could create a security problem.

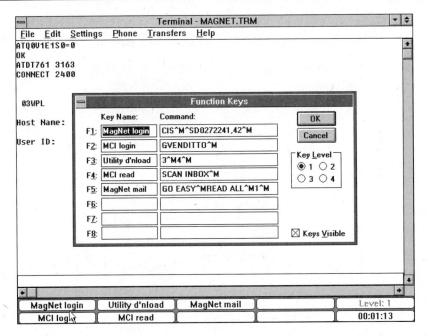

Using the Four Levels of Function Keys

When you create function key assignments, you choose one of four levels for those assignments. When the function keys are displayed, the level number is shown in a box at the right. As you can see in Figure 7.14, key level 1 is checked. To move up to a higher level, click on the desired level in the Key Level box; the function keys assigned at this level will be displayed and choosing any function key now (either by clicking or with a Ctrl-Alt combination) will choose the shortcut assigned at this level only. If you don't plan to use more than eight function key shortcuts in a file, keep all of them on level one.

When you select a function key with Ctrl-Alt-function key combinations, you choose the level that was made active most recently. If you plan to use many function keys, it's a good idea to give one of the function keys the job of switching from one level to another, so that you can use the Ctrl-Alt combination to switch levels.

Function Key Control Codes

You'll need to store more than ordinary letters and numbers on function keys. You'll need to store the Enter key, control codes that are understood by an on-line service, and command codes that are understood by your modem. Table 7.1 lists the available codes.

Table 7.1   **Control Codes for Function Key Shortcuts**

Control Code	Action
^A to ^Z	Send Ctrl followed by that letter
^D*nn*	Delays for *nn* seconds; must be a two-digit number
^M	Sends carriage return on most on-line services
^$B	Sends a break code of 117 milliseconds
^$C	Dials phone using number stored in Phone Number selection
^$H	Hangs up the phone
^$L1	Switches to level one function keys
^$L2	Switches to level two function keys
^$L3	Switches to level three function keys
^$L4	Switches to level four function keys

To use these codes, you use the ^ character, which appears on the number 6 key; to insert ^, press Shift-6 (use the number 6 key that appears above the keyboard letters, not the one on the numeric keypad).

One of the most important control codes is ^M, which is used by many on-line services for a carriage return. For example, if Jane Smith wanted to assign her name to a function key, she would type **Jane Smith^M** in the Command dialog box so that Terminal would send an Enter key after it sent the name. Control codes can also be embedded in the text sent by the function key. For example, "^MJane Smith^M" sends a carriage return before and after "Jane Smith." In Figure 7.14, note the extensive use of ^M after commands and sign-on information.

If you use a function key shortcut to send login information to a remote computer, you should omit your secret password.

Timer Mode

When the function keys are displayed, Terminal keeps track of the amount of time elapsed since you made the connection with a remote computer. You turn the timer on by choosing Timer Mode from the Settings menu. When the timer is on, a check mark appears next to the menu entry and the function menu slot in the lower-right portion of the screen stops displaying the current time and starts counting from zero in seconds.

Every time you establish a connection with a remote computer, the timer resets to zero. When you hang up the phone, the timer switches its display to the current time.

A Strategy for Terminal Files

To get the most out of Terminal, you should create a library of files, each of which sets up a special configuration. Even if you communicate with only one remote computer, there may be a number of different tasks that require different settings. For example, during some sessions you may be looking at numbers in tabular form (stock results or airline schedules, for example), which will be easier to read in a larger font. In other sessions, you may want to use a smaller font. You can save time and effort by creating a second version of your settings file with just the fonts changed.

Building a Library of Terminal Tools

When building a library of Terminal files, the best strategy is to start at the lowest level of communications options and add more details in later files.

Here's a general guide:

1. Select New from the File menu.

2. Select Modem Commands from the Settings menu. Make sure you have selected the right choices for tone or pulse dialing and the right modem type.

3. Select Communications from the Settings menu. Make sure you have chosen the right connector and the highest baud rate that your modem can achieve.

4. Select Save from the File menu and name your file something like BASIC.

Whenever you want to communicate with a remote computer you can now open the BASIC file, select the options needed for the session, and save the new settings under a different file name.

After you're satisfied that the settings for this remote computer work, you can save several versions of the Terminal settings that reflect different types of work: One that displays larger fonts, one that displays function keys, and one that uses a different phone number for the same computer.

Terminal's Menus: A Complete List

File

New
Open. . .
Save
Save As. . .
Print Setup. . .
Exit

Edit

Copy	Ctrl+C
Paste	Ctrl+V
Send	Ctrl+Shift+Ins
Select All	
Clear Buffer	

Settings

Phone Number. . .
Terminal Emulation. . .
Terminal Preferences. . .
Function Keys. . .
Text Transfers. . .
Binary Transfers. . .
Communications. ..
Modem Commands. . .
Printer Echo
Timer Mode
Show Function Keys

Phone

Dial
Hangup

Transfers

Send Text File. . .
Receive Text File. . .
View Text File. . .
Send Binary File. . .
Receive Binary File. . .
Pause
Resume
Stop

Help

Contents
Search for Help On. . .
How to Use Help
About Terminal

8

Saving Time with Recorder

How Recorder Works

Managing Recorder Files

Keeping Recorder
within Reach

WINDOWS'S RECORDER UTILITY IS A MACRO PROGRAM: IT LETS YOU assign many keystrokes to a single key combination, eliminating the drudgery of repetitive tasks and reducing the chances for error. Recorder can also be used to create presentations, since you can use it to display files in much the same way a slide projector displays images.

It's easy to create simple macros with Recorder: Turn the recording mechanism on, perform the keystrokes you want the program to remember, and then turn recording off. Whenever you want, Recorder plays back the keystroke session exactly as you stored it.

How Recorder Works

Recorder has few menu choices, because it does only two jobs: (1) capture activities (keys pressed at the keyboard or mouse movements) within Windows or Windows applications, and (2) play them back exactly as they happened. When you first open Recorder, the Recorder window is empty. As you create macros or open a Recorder file, the individual macros are listed here, available for playback, as shown in Figure 8.1. Every Recorder file can hold as many macros as fit in a 64k file. This design is ideal for creating customized suites of spreadsheet, word processing, and database macros.

Figure 8.1
This Recorder window shows the contents of FIRST.REC, a file that contains six separate macros. If you double-click on one of the listed macros, Windows plays it back. The last three also have shortcut keys.

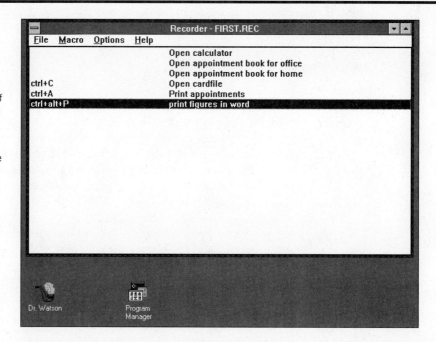

Recorder is very easy to use, but it does have some pitfalls. For example, Recorder plays back clicks and drags (mouse movements) in exactly the way you originally performed them; but when you play back the macro, your display may start out looking significantly different. Although your macro will exactly repeat your actions, it may not produce them in the right place or with the desired result. This chapter will guide you through Recorder to help you reap the greatest benefit and the fewest unpleasant surprises.

Avoid Recording Mouse Movements

Recorder plays back mouse movements by exactly capturing the screen location where they originally happened. It can attempt to adjust for a change in window size and location, but you're on thin ice if you try to create macros to change a window's appearance. When the macro attempts to drag a window that isn't sitting where it was when it was recorded, it stops and displays an error message.

You can avoid problems by using the keystroke equivalent of each mouse movement. If the macro you plan to record incorporates mouse movements, try to replace them with as many keyboard equivalents as you can. This is especially important if you plan to share macros with co-workers. Because mouse movements are defined by screen location, macros recorded on one type of display (VGA, for example) will be unpredictable if played back on systems that use a different type (EGA or XGA video, for example). If you must record mouse movements, see "Recording Mouse Movements" later in this chapter for some tips.

When to Use Recorder

Recorder is easy to learn and to use, but it makes sense to use it only if you perform the same task repeatedly. If you can't think of a task that you perform several times a week in exactly the same fashion, don't bother setting up a macro for it. If you work in a program that has its own macro utility (Microsoft Excel, for example), it will have features better tailored to the program. And Recorder is not as sophisticated as other macro programs, like ProKey; it does not pause to accept user input and does not allow branching into conditional actions.

It makes the most sense to record routine chores that use exactly the same series of keystrokes. Typical Windows chores include switching printers, sending often-used files to the printer, and opening often-used files.

Once you've created your macros, you'll need to load Recorder with the right file open to gain any benefit. At the end of the chapter, I'll show how you can keep Recorder at your fingertips with very little effort.

Recording a Macro

This section walks you through the process of creating a very simple macro. In later sections, I'll explain all of the options in greater depth and show examples of more powerful macros.

Here's how to build a macro that minimizes any window that has a Control menu. The macro plays back when you press Ctrl-N. This macro is useful if you like to work with the keyboard, because it reduces the keystrokes Ctrl-Spacebar-N to Ctrl-N.

Before you begin, make sure there's an active window displayed. Any Windows program other than Recorder will do.

1. Open Recorder by double-clicking on its icon in the Accessories window or entering **recorder** at the Run command in the Program Manager's File menu.

2. Press Alt-M-C to select Record... from the Macro menu and open the Record Macro dialog box, as shown in Figure 8.2.

Figure 8.2

The Record Macro dialog box controls most options that affect how individual macros will run.

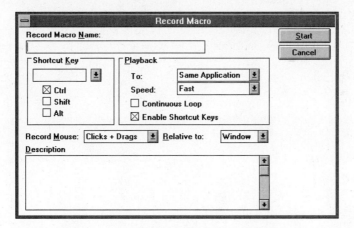

3. Type a name in the Record Macro Name text box. The name can be up to 40 characters. We'll call this macro **MINIMIZE**. (If you want to describe the macro, press Alt-D to enter text in the Description box.)

4. In the Shortcut Key (Alt-K) box, type **N**. Below it, leave the Ctrl box checked, making Ctrl-N the shortcut key for this macro.

5. In the Playback To: drop-down list box, click on the down arrow and select Any Application, to have the macro work with any Windows application. (The default is Same Application.) All of the other options are fine for this macro, so we can start recording.

6. Click on Start. The Record Macro dialog box and the Recorder window disappear. If you can see the Recorder icon, it is blinking, indicating that a recording session is in progress. (The icon may be obscured by active windows, depending on the way your windows are displayed.)

7. Press Alt-Spacebar to bring up the Control menu for an active window.

8. Press N to minimize the active window.

9. Press Ctrl-Break to stop recording. The Recorder dialog box opens (see below). Select Save Macro to end recording and store the keystrokes, and click on OK.

10. Double-click on the Recorder icon at the bottom of the screen. The Recorder window opens with the shortcut key, *Ctrl-N*, and the macro name, *Minimize*, displayed.

11. Press Alt-F-S to save the file. The Save As dialog box opens. Give the new file a name and press Enter.

Playing a Macro

After Recorder is loaded into memory and a Recorder file is opened, you can play any macro in that file at any time; you don't need to see the Recorder icon or window.

To run the macro we just created, use our shortcut key, Ctrl-N, to close the active window. (If you've just minimized your Recorder window, double-click on its icon to restore it.) The value of this macro is greatest if you have many windows open; by pressing Ctrl-N repeatedly you can quickly close each one.

If you prefer, you can run a macro from the Recorder window in one of two ways: by double-clicking on the macro name; or by selecting Run from the Macro menu. Had we not given our macro a shortcut key, we would have been forced to do it this way—a real inconvenience when Recorder is minimized.

Saving Macros

Although Recorder stores the macro that you're working on in active memory and displays it in the active window, it will not store the macro to a disk file until you select Save from the File menu. That's why it's important to save the Recorder file soon after you record and to test it by selecting Save on the File menu (or Save As if you want to create a new file with an existing macro). If you attempt to close Recorder before a newly recorded macro is saved, Recorder prompts you to save the file. If you turn off the system without closing Recorder, you'll lose the macro.

It's easy to forget to save a macro. When you work in Recorder, you'll frequently switch to other programs to test your macros, and once you've started working in a different window, you may forget about the work you've started in Recorder.

Stopping a Macro

You can suspend the recording of a macro—whether it's being recorded or being played—by pressing Ctrl-Break. When you suspend a macro during recording, the Recorder icon begins to blink and the Recorder dialog box shown earlier appears, giving you the option of saving the macro, resuming recording, or cancelling recording.

Save Macro   Choose this option after you've performed all the
                      keystrokes you want to assign to this macro.

Resume Recording   Choose this option if you suspended the macro
                      recording because you were interrupted.

Cancel Recording   Choose this option if you decide not to complete
                      the macro.

You can stop recording at any time by double-clicking on the blinking Recorder icon, but try to avoid the practice. If you're going to save the active macro, the apparently simple mouse movement of double-clicking on the icon could ruin the macro. Any mouse movement during a macro is a source of potential problems, even if it appears at the end of the macro. You're much better off pressing Ctrl-Break.

Editing a Macro's Properties

It sometimes requires a bit of tinkering to get a macro working just right. To adjust any options you saw in the Record Macro dialog box, choose the Properties command on the Macro menu (see Figure 8.3). The following sections explain your options when editing macro properties.

Figure 8.3

The Macro
Properties dialog
box is similar to the
Record Macro
dialog box, but it's
designed to let you
change your mind
about most of the
options you chose
initially for the
macro.

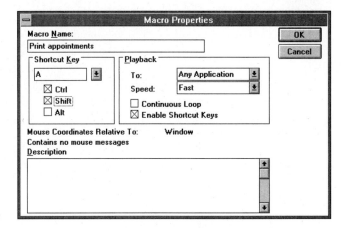

Shortcut Key

There are two parts to a shortcut key. The first part is one or more control keys—Ctrl, Alt, or Shift—which you choose with a check box. The second part is an alphanumeric key or a special key. Standard alphanumeric keys can be typed in the text box; special keys such as function, arrow, and tab keys must be chosen from the drop-down list.

It's a good idea, but not a requirement, to use a control key as part of the shortcut key. If you enter a single character without a control key, every time you press that character with the macro file open, the macro executes. (If you had used *N* without a control key in the "Recording a Macro" example, the active window would be minimized every time you pressed *N*!) If you use a special key without a control key, you may interfere with the operation of the program. (If you use F1 alone, for example, you'll disable Help.)

Avoid using Shift as the control key, since you might invoke macros whenever you want to type certain uppercase letters. It's also a good idea to avoid the Alt control key when you create shortcut keys, since Windows uses Alt in so many menu choices. If you happen to select a shortcut key that is used by an active program, your macro takes priority; if this particular key combination is the only way to perform a function in the active program, that function is unavailable until you clear the macro from memory.

It's a good idea to use two (or even all three) control keys together in creating a single shortcut key. When executing the macro, first hold down the control keys in any sequence, and then press the other key. Remember, however, that programs can have shortcut keys that load them into memory; it's a property of each program icon in Program Manager. These shortcut keys always include both Ctrl and Alt, so you may want to avoid that key combination in your Recorder macros.

Playback Options

The shortcut key initiates a macro; the Playback section of the Macro Properties dialog box controls how the macro performs.

Same or Any Application	The first and most important choice affecting a macro's performance is whether it works only in the application where you initially recorded it or in any Windows program. In the Minimize macro we created earlier in this chapter, we clearly wanted the macro to work in *any* application. Same Application is valuable for times when you have several Windows programs active at once. Recorder performs the macro in the *same* program in which it was created, even if it's buried in several layers.
Speed	The speed option is offered for times when your macro will be used as a demonstration (in a tutorial or a sales presentation, for example). Choose Recorded Speed to perform the actions slowly enough for observers to follow. If you keep the speed at Fast, the default, Windows, races through the actions as fast as your system allows, and interim macro steps zip by in a blur.
Continuous Loop	This option is also provided for demonstrations. When Continuous Loop is checked, the macro restarts itself when it reaches the conclusion. The only way to stop a macro in a continuous loop is to press Ctrl-Break or shut the system down. There may be times when you want a demonstration to be impervious to a Ctrl-Break. (Perhaps you want a system to run in an unsupervised exhibition area and don't want anyone to be able to stop it.) You can disable Ctrl-Break by selecting Control-Break Checking from the Options menu in Recorder so that there is no check mark.
Enable Shortcut Keys	This option lets you determine whether a macro can be started with shortcut keys or from the main Recorder window. The default setting enables shortcut keys.

Recording Mouse Movements

You're probably asking for trouble if you attempt to capture mouse movements with Recorder, because apparently identical mouse actions like clicking and dragging have different effects, depending on where the action takes place on a window, how big the window is, and the window's position relative to your monitor. If you must record mouse actions, here's what you need to know.

You must select two settings in the Record Macro dialog box (see Figure 8.2) before you start recording. You can also establish these settings as the defaults by using the Preference command on the Options menu, so that you won't need need to make as many choices each time you begin to record a macro.

- **Record Mouse.** This choice tells Recorder whether it should attempt to record mouse movements.

  - If you plan to follow my advice, choose Ignore Mouse and concentrate on keyboard actions.

  - If you select Clicks and Drags, Recorder ignores most mouse movement, recording mouse position only when the mouse button is pressed.

  - Select Everything if you truly want Recorder to position the mouse pointer in particular screen locations.

- **Relative to.** You must make a choice in this list box if you select either Clicks and Drags or Everything. This option establishes whether your macro captures mouse movements relative to the entire screen or relative to an individual window.

  You'll have the least amount of difficulty in recording mouse movements if you choose Window in the Relative option; Recorder can then translate mouse actions to screen objects. For example, instead of recording that a mouse click occurred at pixel 209,183, Recorder translates the action to "click on upper border." It's not a perfect science, so you may encounter a quirk or two, but the Relative option can make your mouse macros almost predictable.

Storing Default Preferences

You can establish the defaults for several of the options just described using the Options menu. If your macros perform the same type of task, you'll want to set your preferences to reflect your style of work.

The defaults can save you some time, but don't let them lull you into complacency. If you ignore all the choices in the Record Macro dialog box, you'll end up spending more time debugging the macros than you saved by customizing your preferences.

If you're taking my advice to avoid recording mouse actions, you may want to choose Ignore Mouse in the Record Mouse option.

Loading Programs with Macros

One useful type of macro loads a Windows application and performs a function, like printing a file. There's one trick to loading a program with a macro: You must press Alt-Tab repeatedly so that the macro can find Program Manager; then, select Run on the File menu. Avoid telling the macro to load programs with the mouse, since your macro may not be able to find the correct icon.

As an example, here's how to build a macro that loads Calendar and prints an appointment book when you press Ctrl-A. It assumes that you'll always be printing today's appointment book.

1. Press Alt-M-C to start macro recording. The Record Macro dialog box opens (see Figure 8.2).

2. Name the macro **PRINTCAL**, and enter **A** as the shortcut key, with Ctrl selected.

3. Make sure the preferences are set for playback of Any Application at Fast speed, the shortcut keys are enabled, and Record Mouse is set to Ignore Mouse.

4. Click on Start. The dialog box and Recorder application window disappear. The macro is now recording every keystroke.

5. Press Alt-Tab at least four times, until you have selected the Program Manager main menu. The active window changes with each Alt-Tab.

6. Press Alt-F-R to open the Run dialog box.

7. Type **calendar** and press Enter. The Calendar program opens.

8. Press Alt-F-P to open the Print dialog box, with today's date. Press OK. The file is sent to the printer and a Calendar message box displays the message that today's calendar is printing.

9. After the Calendar message box disappears, press Alt-F-X to close the Calendar application window.

10. Press Ctrl-Break to suspend recording. When the Macro Recording Suspended dialog box opens, select Save Macro and press Enter.

11. Press Ctrl-A to test your macro. Calendar reloads and prints a file with today's appointments.

12. Return to Recorder after the macro finishes executing and select Save on the File menu.

If you want this macro to print your calendar every time you load Windows, use the technique described later in this chapter in the section, "Creating Unique Icons for Recorder Files."

Managing Recorder Files

Since you can only use macros within the open Recorder file, you should try to manage your macros effectively. For example, when writing documents, you'll want all your word-processing macros in one file.

But you don't want to restrict yourself. If you have only a few macros for all your applications, keep them all in a single file. With a maximum size of 64k per file and with a collection of a dozen simple macros using only about 3k each, you have a lot of leeway.

The drawback to keeping all of your macros in a single file is that you may be wasting memory. On a system with 1 or 2 Mb of RAM, you should probably avoid using a Recorder file with more than two dozen macros. Instead, divide your macros into smaller files devoted to specific tasks. On a system that has more than 2 Mb, you can probably afford to let your macro file grow to include three or four dozen macros.

You'll get more from your macros if you create multiple Recorder icons, each one associated with a particular macro file. You can create these file-specific Recorder icons by using the technique described in Chapter 2 under "Adding a Program Item."

Merging Files

There's only one way to move macros from one Recorder file to another: merge all the macros in one file into a second file using the Merge command on the File menu. To trim this ungainly file down to size, remove each macro that you don't want duplicated, using the Delete command on the Macro menu.

Nesting Macros

One way to make the best use of Recorder is to *nest* macros, which means to call a macro from within another macro. Let's say you want to create a macro that prints files and minimizes the active window. You have already created a Minimize macro, so instead of re-creating the same steps as part of the new macro, you can include the existing Minimize macro in the new macro. To do so, you would simply press Ctrl-N (your shortcut key for the Minimize macro) at the appropriate time when recording the new macro.

What if you discover a better way to minimize a window? All you need to do is replace the Minimize macro with the improved version and make sure the new macro is called with the Ctrl-N shortcut key. Every macro that used the Minimize macro would run the improved macro.

Keeping Recorder within Reach

The greatest limitation of Recorder is that you need to load it before you start enjoying the benefits. What good is a time-saver if it takes too much time to use?

The solution is to make Recorder load automatically with each Windows session. Since Recorder occupies only 26k when it's loaded, you'll probably find that it's well worth having around. On the other hand, systems with 1 Mb or less may not have the memory to spare.

The following sections show two strategies for keeping Recorder loaded all the time.

Loading Recorder at Startup

The Startup program group in Program Manager loads programs each time Windows is run. To have a macro file available automatically every day, you need to put a copy of the Recorder icon associated with a file in the Startup group window. To do so, you can either use the Copy command on Program Manager's File menu, or hold down the Ctrl key while you click on the Recorder icon and drag it to the Startup icon or window.

Creating Unique Icons for Recorder Files

The slickest way to use a macro is to create an icon devoted to a single macro. It uses extra memory, but it's the best way to use Recorder. To do this, you need to create a program item icon in Program Manager that opens a particular Recorder file. You may want to create several new icons for different Recorder files and give each icon the name of the Recorder file in the Properties Description text box.

As you will see in the upcoming example, there is one trick to running a particular macro as soon as you load a Recorder file: You need to substitute an alias, or symbol, for the control key that is part of the macro's keyboard shortcut preceded by **-h**. The aliases for the three control keys are:

Alt	%
Ctrl	^
Shift	+

The following exercise shows you how to use an alias. The exercise creates an icon that runs the macro we just created to print a Calendar schedule.

1. In Program Manager, open the window that you use most often; it's the program group where the new icon will reside.

2. Press Alt-F-N to open the New Program Object dialog box.

3. Select Program Item and press Enter. The Program Item Properties dialog box opens.

4. In the Description text box, enter **Schedule Print** or whatever name you prefer.

5. In the Command Line text box, enter **RECORDER.EXE -h ^A SCHEDULE.REC** (see below). You don't need to select Run Minimized, because Recorder will minimize itself as soon as it runs the macro Ctrl-A.

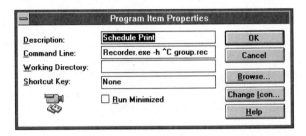

6. Press Enter. The dialog box closes and a new Recorder icon appears, labeled *Schedule Print*, or whatever name you entered in step 4.

7. Test the new icon by double-clicking on it. Immediately, the Recorder window opens, then Calendar opens, and the appointment book is sent to the printer.

After Recorder executes the macro, it remains active, although it minimizes itself.

Recorder's Menus: A Complete List

File
New
Open. . .
Save
Save As. . .
Merge. . .
Exit

Macro
Run
Record. . .
Delete
Properties

Options
Control+Break Checking
Shortcut Keys
Minimize on Use
Preferences. . .

Help
Contents
Search for Help On. . .
How to Use Help
About Recorder. . .

9

Customizing Windows with Control Panel and SysEdit

The Control Panel

Editing the INI Files

ONE OF THE GREATEST ADVANTAGES OF WINDOWS IS ITS FLEXIBILITY. Almost every aspect of its behavior can be modified. In this chapter, I'll show you how to make the most of your options. In the process, we'll explore how Windows works with hardware. During Setup, Windows installs Control Panel, a program that lets you configure your system's hardware—video board, printer, modem, and so on. Control Panel is the easy way to control basic Windows settings, since it provides dialog boxes for viewing and choosing them. Control Panel does its job by writing values into the two initialization files—WIN.INI and SYSTEM-.INI—that Windows reads every time it loads into memory. (That's one reason why you must wait several seconds every time you load Windows before you can use it.) Windows knows which printer to install, which fonts to print, and which colors to use in your menus, by reading the values defined in these two files.

Control Panel does not give you a way to directly view these initialization files, which are, in one sense, its data files. It does, however, display the values for each setting indirectly using dialog boxes. To access the initialization files directly, you can use either a word processor or a utility called SysEdit that comes with Windows. Later in the chapter I'll explain how to make SysEdit a permanent part of your Windows Desktop.

If you're a power user you may be eager to start changing Windows settings directly, but Control Panel is a much easier way to change them. Control Panel also prevents you from choosing the wrong value for any setting by limiting you to a valid range of values. After you've grown familiar with these ranges and the syntax of the initialization (INI) files, you'll probably come to favor SysEdit over Control Panel. But until you've changed the settings a few times, Control Panel will be more useful.

The Control Panel

The Control Panel is automatically installed in the Main program group when you set up Windows. It differs from other programs that come with Windows: When you run it, you see individual modules represented by icons instead of a workspace where you enter data. These modules are used to change the default settings established by the Windows Setup program or changed by you when running a program.

Control Panel's Unique Design

You open Control Panel by double-clicking on its icon in the Main program group window or by entering **control** at the Run command in the Program Manager's File menu.

Control Panel's opening window displays 11–13 icons. A Network icon appears only when a network is installed, and a 386 Enhanced icon appears only when Windows is running in 386 Enhanced mode. The Control Panel in Figure 9.1 displays all 13 icons.

Figure 9.1

Eleven icons appear in every version of Control Panel. Two more appear only when Windows runs in 386 Enhanced mode and when the PC is attached to a network.

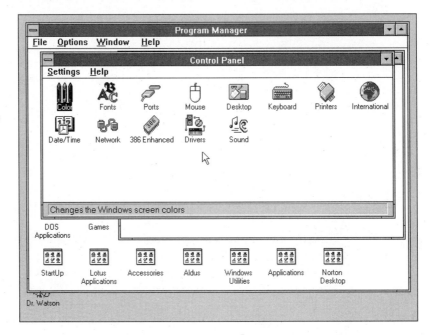

There are two ways to choose a particular module:

- Double-click on an icon. (To make your selection, either position the mouse on the icon or press the keyboard arrow keys until you've high-lighted the correct icon.)

- Choose the module by selecting its name from the Settings menu. Press Alt-S to select that menu.

With Windows 3.1, Microsoft has enabled software publishers to add new modules to Control Panel. For example, a word processing program might insert its own setup module into Control Panel. Such icons will appear only if a program that uses this new capability is properly installed on your system.

You can take only three actions from the Control Panel main menu:

- Open a module

■ Open the Control Panel help system

■ Exit from Control Panel

All changes to settings are made from within the individual modules. The following sections cover each of the modules in the order they appear in the Control Panel window.

Color

This module controls the colors used in specific screen elements throughout Windows: title bars, borders, and scroll bars (see Figure 9.2). A few Windows programs use their own *color scheme*—a carefully coordinated set of colors for the different screen elements—but most programs use the color schemes established here.

Figure 9.2

Your choices in the Color dialog box range from carefully designed schemes of coordinated colors for all screen elements to a spectrum of thousands of dithered patterns that you can blend on Windows's palette and assign to screen elements.

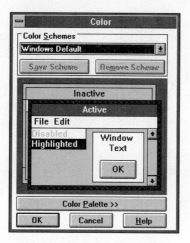

The simplest way to modify your colors is to use one of the installed color schemes. They've been professionally designed for the most judicious mixture of colors. Arizona was designed for those who like earth tones; Ocean, for people who want to tinge their work with a nautical motif; and Cinnamon, for those who like warm, soft tones. So if you're not fussy about the color scheme, you should choose one of these schemes from the Color Schemes list in the main Color window, click on the OK button, and be done with the Color module. If you do select a color scheme, you may want to skip ahead to the "Fonts" section, because the next several pages provide an in-depth discussion of color selection and the way Windows uses color.

Laptop Color Schemes

New in Windows 3.1 are four color schemes that will work best on laptops:

- LCD default screen settings

- LCD reversed (dark)

- LCD reversed (light)

- Plasma power saver

The first three are most effective on battery-powered laptops with blue, gray, and white displays; the last, on the green screens used on portables like the Compaq Portable 386 and the Toshiba T5100.

Custom Color Schemes

If you want to customize your color scheme, be forewarned: It will take a bit of time and experimentation to get it right.

Building a simple color scheme means assigning one of 48 basic colors to each of the 17 screen elements (menu bars, menu text, title bar, and so on), three of which require two colors depending on whether the element is active or inactive. And if you want to get really fancy, you can even blend your own colors, using a technique explained later in this chapter in "Selecting Custom Colors."

The Color module provides a list of the 17 screen elements to use in assigning colors. The elements with active and inactive modes require different colors for each mode. If you decide to create a custom color scheme you can use Table 9.1 for planning. For example, the colors of inactive and active screen elements should be complementary, and title bar text color must be legible when viewed against the title bar color.

The best way to create a new color scheme is to change one of the default color schemes. Here are the steps you take:

1. With the Color dialog box open, press Alt-S to highlight the Color Schemes option. The name highlighted in the text box represents the color scheme in the sample window directly below the text.

2. Press ↓ to see the next color scheme. The name in the dialog box and the colors in the sample screen will change. (To see the list of all color schemes, press Alt-↓.)

3. When you've selected the scheme closest to your taste, click on the Color Palette >> button. The dialog box doubles to include a range of color choices (see Figure 9.3).

4. Drag the mouse to the sample screen and point at the area of the screen that you want to change. Click. Note that the Screen Element list box

now displays the name of the selected screen element, and the current color for this element is highlighted in the Basic Colors grid.

Table 9.1 **The Screen Elements Controlled by the Color Module**

	One Color	Active and Inactive Colors
Desktop	x	
Application workspace	x	
Window background	x	
Window text	x	
Menu bar	x	
Menu text	x	
Title bar		x
Title bar text		x
Border		x
Window frame	x	
Scroll bars	x	
Button face	x	
Button shadow	x	
Button text	x	
Button highlight	x	
Disabled text	x	
Highlight	x	
Highlighted text	x	

5. Choose a new color from the Basic Colors grid. The sample screen will display the new color of the selected screen element. (If you've created custom colors, you can select them in the same way you that you select basic colors. See "Selecting Custom Colors" to learn how you create custom colors.)

6. Repeat steps 4 and 5 to change the colors of other screen elements.

Figure 9.3

When you click on the Color Palette >> button, the Color dialog box doubles in size to present color choices. This dialog box includes a grid of 48 basic colors and a drop-down list box to display all the screen elements that can be tinted.

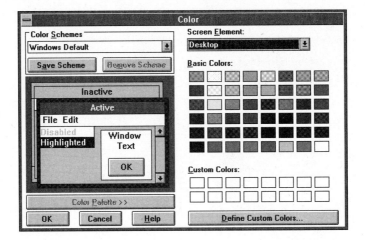

7. Press Alt-A or click on the Save Scheme button. The Save Scheme dialog box opens.

8. Enter a new name and press Enter.

How Windows Displays Color

If you look very closely at the grid of 48 basic colors displayed when the Color dialog box is expanded, you'll probably find that there aren't 48 true colors. Depending on the display adapter in your system, you'll most likely see either 16 or 20 colors. VGA and EGA adapters display 16 pure colors; Super VGA, 8514, TIGA, Targa, and other advanced video boards display 20 pure colors. (A few boards on the market display 48 different colors here, but, as of this writing, they're rare.)

The other colors in the Basic Colors grid are mixtures of colors produced by *dithering*, the process of simulating a color by creating a pattern out of two or more colors. When done well, a dithered pattern tricks the eye into seeing a true color; when done poorly, the patterns are crudely obvious.

Before you venture into mixing custom colors in the next section, we'll need to discuss how a solid color and a dithered color differ and how Windows displays colors. Two factors control the display of color on any computer screen:

■ A computer monitor uses three colors (red, green, and blue), in combination, to produce all colors.

■ The precise color displayed is a result of how brightly the monitor displays each of the three colors at each pixel.

At the resolution used by Windows, VGA and EGA adapter boards can mix red, green, and blue well enough at each pixel to generate 16 solid colors, because the video board has just enough memory to store 16 predefined blends of the three basic colors. These 16 colors appear solid because the monitor displays the exact same blend of the three colors at every pixel, so the eye perceives pure color.

Super VGA boards have more video memory and can generate 256 solid colors in Windows's 640-by-480 resolution mode. More advanced boards, such as TIGA and Targa adapters, can generate thousands more colors at even higher resolutions.

To allow you to use the most advanced hardware possible, Windows reserves space for a maximum of 16.7 million colors, which represents 256 levels for each of the three colors ($256 \times 256 \times 256$). However, Windows displays color in two distinct processes. The basic process allows for the display of only 20 different colors at any one time. To use more than 20 colors, software has to access a more advanced process called the Palette Manager, which lets the program display as many colors as the hardware allows.

Only a handful of the hundreds of Windows programs use the Palette Manager to display colors (for example, graphic design programs like Page-Maker). Most programs, including Control Panel, rely on the basic process for displaying colors, so most video boards display screen elements in only 16 or 20 colors.

To simulate more than 16 or 20 colors for displaying screen elements, Windows blends the three basic colors into dithered patterns. If you use a magnifying glass to look at the colors on your monitor, you can plainly see that some of the colors are arranged in a geometric pattern; a few of these dithered colors are so crude that the patterns are apparent to the unaided eye (see Figure 9.4).

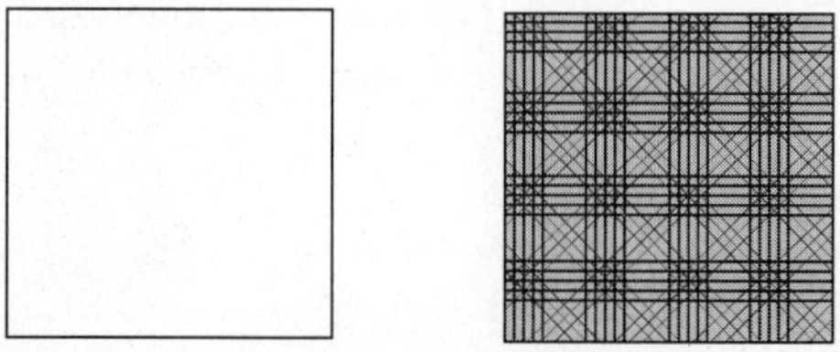

Figure 9.4

The square on the left represents a pure color: The entire square has a uniform color. The square on the right represents a dithered color, a blend of many red, green, and blue dots that simulate a color by repeating a geometric pattern.

The dithering process used by most VGA and EGA drivers defines 64 levels of saturation for each color. Since there are three colors, these boards display 262,144 colors (64 × 64 × 64), some of them pure but most of them dithered. On an EGA or VGA system, when you define custom colors in the Color dialog box, you'll be choosing among 262,144 colors (including the 16 hardware-generated solid colors).

Because Windows uses the 16 solid colors in creating the dithered patterns instead of using the pure reds, greens, and blues, the process of blending the colors is not scientific. With some settings, increasing the hue by one level causes a color change; with others, you'll need to increase the hue by seven or eight levels before you see a change.

(As of this writing, a few programmers are working on techniques for tricking Windows into using more than 20 colors in Control Panel, so it's possible that if you own a Super VGA or other high-color board, you'll eventually be able to upgrade your drivers and display all the colors your video board is capable of.)

Dithering is a compromise process with imperfect results. Many dithered colors appear grainy, but others appear so solid that most people can't see the pattern. (In fact, on EGA and VGA systems most of the 48 basic colors are dithered.) To spare you from unsavory dithered patterns, the Custom Color Selector dialog box includes both a dithered representation of the color you've blended and a sample of the closest solid color. After blending the dithered color, you may decide that you're better off using the solid color that's most similar.

The default color schemes that come with Windows for the most part use pure colors and avoid the grainy dithered colors. That's one reason why they're so aesthetically pleasing.

Selecting Custom Colors

If you want to use a dithered color that's not included in the Basic Colors grid, you can build a Custom Colors palette that will be displayed below the grid of 48 basic colors in the expanded Color dialog box. Your custom colors can then be applied to screen elements.

To select a color, click on the Define Custom Colors button in the Color dialog box. The Custom Color Selector dialog box opens, presenting three methods for selecting a color (see Figure 9.5):

- The color refiner box, the large box in the upper half of the window, where you can select a color by pointing at it.

- Red-green-blue mixing, or color mixing, which lets you specify the amount of each color in the blend on a scale of one to 256. Even though each selection box for red, green, and blue has 256 levels, with most drivers you can only select 64 different levels for each color; the indicators allow you to enter any number in the text box, but not every number changes the color.

Figure 9.5

The Custom Color Selector dialog box has three methods for blending colors: the color refiner box lets you select a color by pointing to it; the other two methods require that you select a color by entering a numeric value.

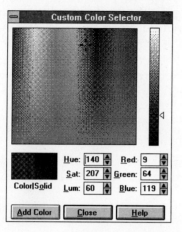

■ Luminosity control, which lets you choose a color by first selecting the level of brightness displayed at each pixel and then fine-tuning the saturation and color.

In a moment we'll take a closer look at each of these methods.

Comparing Solid and Dithered Colors

The Color/Solid box at the left side of the Custom Color Selector dialog box displays the color you've currently selected in two ways: on the left, as a dithered color; on the right, as the solid color that most closely approximates it.

After you've selected your color, click on the Add Color button to transfer it to the Custom Colors palette. The new color appears in the first unused box in the palette. To transfer it to a specific open box, click on the box before you click on the Add Color button. If you prefer to use the solid color, press Alt-O and then click to add it to the palette; otherwise, Windows will use the dithered color.

Of course, if you choose the solid color, you're duplicating a color already found in the 48 basic colors, but there may be a very good reason to do just that. You may want to create your own palette to use in customizing Windows applications throughout your company. If you distribute a copy of the WIN.INI file with these custom color choices throughout the organization, it will be easier to set a standard.

Saving Color Schemes

After you assign new colors to screen elements, you can store the settings as a unique color scheme by clicking on the Save Scheme command button. Windows stores color assignments in the file CONTROL.INI under the heading "color schemes."

Three Ways to Select a Custom Color

The following three sections explain the three distinct methods for selecting a custom color. All three involve the Custom Color Selector dialog box.

Color Refiner Box   This large colorful square right under the title bar represents the easiest method to select a color, since you can pick a color by clicking with the mouse. The box is arranged from left to right along the natural color spectrum known as ROYGBIV (red-orange-yellow-green-blue-indigo-violet).

To the right of the Color Refiner box is a vertical bar that represents *luminosity,* or brightness. You must choose a brightness level by moving the triangular indicator before you select a color, since the level of brightness controls which colors can be used. When the indicator is at the top of the bar, a color is displayed at its brightest, which means that the monitor is working at its brightest level. Drag the indicator down to darken a color.

The Color/Solid box at the bottom left shows the color that the pointer is highlighting. Once you've selected the luminosity, drag the pointer around the color refiner box and notice the changes in the Color/Solid box. When luminosity is high, you'll see many bright and near-white colors. When luminosity is low, you'll see many dark grays and near-black colors. You'll get the richest colors when the luminosity indicator is slightly more than halfway up the scale.

Color Mixing   Mixing colors is the most straightforward way to choose a new color, since it lets you determine the exact amount of red, green, and blue in the blend. However, it also requires some time to fiddle with the values for each color.

The numbers in the Red, Green, and Blue text boxes represent the *saturation* of each color—how strongly the monitor will display the individual pixels that make up the color. You choose the blend by entering a number in the Red, Green, and Blue text boxes.

- When all three are at their highest setting (256), the Color/Solid box displays white (solid color).

- When all three are at the lowest setting (0), the Color/Solid box displays black (the absence of color).

- When all three are at midpoint (128), you'll see gray.

- When one color is at its highest setting (256) and the other two are at zero, you'll see the purest example of red, green, or blue that your monitor can display.

Luminosity Control This system is closest to the way the graphic adapter and monitor work, but unless your brain is as logical as an Intel microprocessor, it's also the most difficult way to choose a color.

You use the Hue, Sat, and Lum text boxes to control color by setting the amount of light displayed at each pixel by the three color guns in the monitor (red, green, and blue). To use this method, you should first enter a value for luminosity (Lum), then a saturation level, and finally a hue. Windows gives priority to the settings in that order.

- **Luminosity** is the brightness of the color on a scale of 0 to 240, with black the lowest and white the highest. When you change the value in the Lum text box, the luminosity indicator on the Color Refiner box moves to the new position.

- **Saturation** is the purity of the hue on a scale of 0 to 240. Zero represents gray (at the bottom of the Color Refiner box); higher numbers represent purer colors (the top of the box).

- **Hue** is the position of the color on the ROYGBIV (red-orange-yellow-green-blue-indigo-violet) spectrum, represented by a number between 0 and 239.

If you set luminosity and saturation so that colors are displayed at their richest level (about 160 for each), you can progress through the color spectrum by increasing the hue value. You'll see the color change from red (at zero) to orange (about 25) and yellow (about 40), with every hue in between. When luminosity and saturation are higher than about 160, the display is overly bright and the colors appear faded.

Fonts

The main purpose of the Fonts module in Control Panel is to allow you to remove and add fonts: You can free RAM by removing Windows's built-in fonts from memory, and you can install new fonts when you obtain new software.

When you open the Fonts dialog box (see Figure 9.6), you see a list of installed typeface families and fonts. The Sample of Font display shows a sample of the characters in the highlighted font or typeface. At the bottom of the dialog box is the Size of Font on disk indicator, to help you determine whether you want to remove the highlighted font. If you're trying to save disk space, this indicator lets you know how much you'll save by deleting the font file.

Chapter 12 explains in detail the techniques that Windows uses in displaying and printing fonts. To help you make the best use of the Fonts module, however, it's worth summarizing the most important points here. First, let's clarify the distinction between a typeface and a font.

Figure 9.6

The Fonts dialog box lets you see each of the fonts installed in your system. Here, the Fonts window shows a sample of the characters in the Arial typeface family.

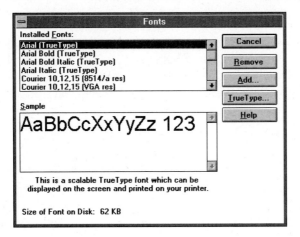

- A *typeface* is a design for characters that can be used in many sizes and styles. Courier is a typeface.

- A *font* is a set of characters of a particular typeface, in a specific size and style. Examples of styles are italic, boldface, and boldface italic. Courier 9-point bold is a font. Fonts are usually measured in points: Six-point type is very small; 9-point type is about the size most newspapers use; and 30-point type is the size of a typical newspaper headline.

Since the actual font information is stored on disk in font information files, you don't lose much by removing fonts from the Installed Fonts list. If you feel you'll rarely use the Script and Symbol fonts, for example, you can delete them from the list by highlighting them and clicking on the Remove button.

If you later decide to use a font you've removed, select Add, and specify the name of the file in the Add Font Files dialog box; if you're adding one of the Windows system fonts, it will be stored in the \WINDOWS\SYSTEM directory.

Don't expect to gain too much by removing typefaces from the list. Typefaces generally take up only about 2–3k of RAM, and about 60k of disk space, so there's rarely a compelling reason to remove them. If you're experiencing sluggish performance due to a lack of RAM, such a small amount won't be enough to help. However, if you're setting up Windows for a large group of users and want Windows to be as simple as possible to use, you may want to remove some of the typefaces to limit the choices to the best ones.

The Add Font Files dialog box is also used when you've obtained new fonts. You can buy fonts from companies like Bitstream and Adobe. These companies also sell their own font managers, which you may want to use instead of this option.

TrueType Fonts and No Other

Chapter 12 explains the difference between TrueType and other fonts. In short, these fonts produce characters that appear the same on screen and when printed. Unless you own a product like Bitstream FaceLift or Adobe Type Manager, you'll probably want to use TrueType fonts for most of your work.

You can restrict the available fonts in Windows so that only TrueType fonts are presented as options when you open a Fonts dialog box. To do this, first click on the TrueType command button in the Fonts dialog box (Figure 9.6); the TrueType dialog box opens (see below).

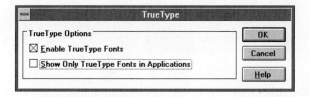

The Enable TrueType Fonts option is checked as the Windows default; by checking the Show Only TrueType Fonts in Applications check box, you'll tell Windows to display only TrueType fonts when you open any Fonts dialog box within Windows. (It will not affect the list of fonts displayed in Control Panel.)

Don't select this option if you use the Terminal communications program, since it will prevent access to the best fonts for the Terminal display. (See "Terminal Fonts" in Chapter 7.)

Windows does not remove these fonts from your disk when you check this option. You can always make non-TrueType fonts available by turning this option off.

Ports

The Ports module in Control Panel lets you set default parameters for up to four serial ports (COM1 through COM4).

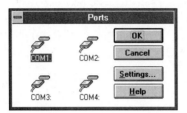

The default settings for each port are 9600 baud, 8 bits, no parity, 1 stop bit, and no flow control, parameters that are fine for most serial printer connections. If you're using a serial port for a modem, there's no need to enter the proper settings here, since your communications software, whether it's Terminal or something else, establishes its own settings for sending data through the serial ports. Set your modem using the communications program, not the Ports module. If you do need to change the settings, highlight the correct serial port and select Settings.

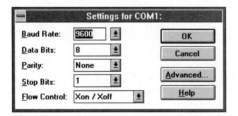

The most common use of the Ports module is to establish parameters for connecting a printer via the serial port; the default in the Ports module is set to work with most common printers. If your AUTOEXEC.BAT file has a Mode statement to set up a serial printer, you should use the Ports dialog box to set up your COM port for a printer.

Many Windows users who attempt to use more than two serial (COM) ports have difficulties. The way to troubleshoot these problems is to specify the I/O port address and interrupt request (IRQ) line by selecting Advanced from the Settings dialog box.

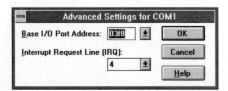

You may need to check your communication device's manual for help in choosing the right I/O port and interrupt lines. As a general rule, make sure each device has a unique setting. The advanced settings are added to the 386 Enh section of the SYSTEM.INI file. You may find that you're better off directly editing SYSTEM.INI if you need to change these settings. See "SYSTEM.INI" later in this chapter.

The best solution to serial-port conflicts may be to buy a program called TurboComm, which enhances Windows's use of multiple serial ports.

Mouse

Windows comes with default settings that Microsoft believes will suit most users; if you want to customize your computer, you'll probably want to tinker with these settings. There are three mouse settings in the Mouse dialog box, described in the following three sections. (If your mouse is not working, this is not the place to fix it. To install a mouse, use the Setup program, typing **SETUP** at the Run command of Program Manager's File menu or at the DOS command prompt.)

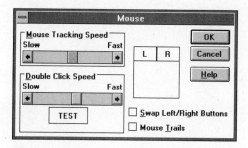

Mouse Tracking Speed

You can choose among seven mouse speeds from slow to fast, with the default setting midway between the two.

- If you feel that the mouse pointer jumps ahead of where you want it to be, reduce your mouse tracking speed.

- If your pointer feels like a ton of bricks that takes forever to move where you want it, increase the speed.

People who have very little desktop space for mousing may prefer a faster speed, which takes less hand movement; you can move the mouse pointer from one end of a VGA screen to the other by moving your hand only an inch. Moving the same distance at a low speed requires 3½ inches.

A fast speed will not prevent you from moving the mouse slowly, but it may make you feel that the mouse is out of control, since sudden hand movements will seem exaggerated. If you do a lot of design work requiring precise object placement, you'll probably want a slower speed. A paint program, for example, may be easier to use at a slow speed. To summarize:

Rate	Benefit
Slow	Precise control; easier to grab screen items
Fast	Pointer accelerates; requires shorter hand movement

Mouse Double-Click Speed

A double-click is usually the same as pressing the Enter key. A single-click is usually the same as moving the cursor with an arrow or Tab key.

When you click the mouse button, Windows determines whether you're moving the cursor or beginning an "enter" instruction. It establishes a time period that it will wait after the mouse is clicked before it interprets the click. *Double-click speed* refers to the amount of time that Windows will wait for that second click after you've clicked once.

When you set the double-click speed to slow, you may double-click at either a leisurely or a frantic pace; both work fine. If you set double-click to its fastest rate, you'd better have what runners call "fast-twitch muscles." At the highest speed, I am not able to click quickly enough to get Windows to recognize my double-clicks no matter how hard I try (and I'm a fast-walking, fast-talking New Yorker).

The TEST box beneath the Double-Click Speed indicator lets you try the current speed. The box will be highlighted when you've successfully double-clicked but won't be if you double-click too slowly for the current speed.

Most people will want the mouse speed set relatively slow. You have nothing to lose by reducing the double-click speed, and it may be a big help on days when you don't have as much energy as you'd like. The only people who'll want the mouse speed set very high are those who work very quickly with the mouse and find that Windows is losing some rapidfire clicks.

Hint. If you set your double-click speed too high and then find you can't even open the Mouse module to change it back, use the Enter key to reopen the module.

Left-Handed Relief for Mouse Clicking

Designed to make life easier for left-handed users, the Swap Left/Right Buttons check box reverses the way Windows interprets mouse button clicks. Click here to insert an X, and Windows will immediately accept right-button clicks as valid whenever a left-button click is normally required, and vice versa.

A diagram of a mouse is provided in the dialog box, so you can be sure you've made the correct selection before you leave the Mouse dialog box. To find out, move the mouse to a spot where it's not selecting anything and click; the selected L or R button is highlighted briefly.

If you insert an X in the check box and want to change back, remember to use the right button.

Mouse Trails for Laptop Users

If you're using a desktop PC with a color monitor, you'll find the Mouse Trails option is more of an amusement than a practical aid. When this option is selected, a series of mouse pointers will appear in the wake of every mouse movement. In essence, Windows dramatically increases the number of times it draws the mouse as it moves. One result of this is a slowdown in overall performance (and a big headache if you attempt to watch the mouse too closely).

This option is extremely valuable on portable PCs where it can be difficult to follow the moving cursor. Because LCD and gas-plasma screens redraw the display far less frequently than desktop PC screens, the extra number of times that the mouse is drawn with this option active can greatly enhance your ability to use Windows with a laptop.

Desktop

The Desktop module is one of the first places that beginners like to explore as soon as they find out how much fun it can provide. It controls the *wallpaper* (the image that appears behind all active windows) and the *screen saver* (the special effects display that comes up when you leave the machine unattended for a period you specify). Often overlooked, however, are some other useful controls, such as icon spacing and border widths, which can make your work in Windows easier. See Figure 9.7.

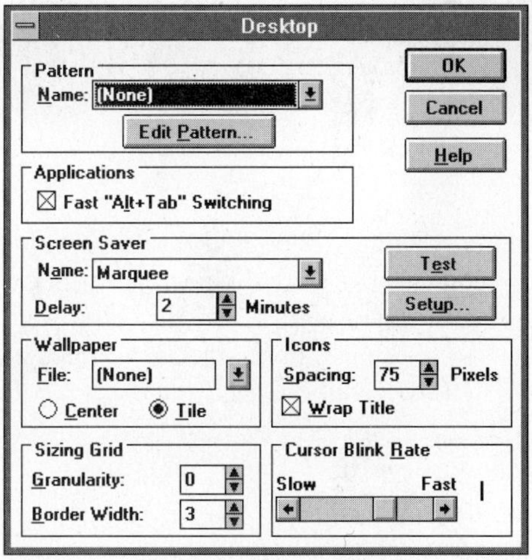

Figure 9.7
The Desktop dialog box controls a motley group of settings: Desktop background (pattern and wallpaper); screen saver; cursor blink rate; sizing grid; and icon spacing in Program Manager.

Patterns and Wallpaper

You'll recall from Chapter 1 that the *Desktop* includes everything on the screen when Windows is running. Patterns and wallpaper are two ways to decorate the Desktop. They serve as a backdrop for all windows and icons on the Desktop. Every new icon or window sits on the Desktop and obscures the pattern or wallpaper beneath it; you see the pattern or wallpaper only where there are no icons or active windows. See Figure 9.8.

Figure 9.8
Wallpaper covers the entire screen, but it can be seen only in places where there's no icon or active window. Here, the Program Manager window is open, against "chess" wallpaper.

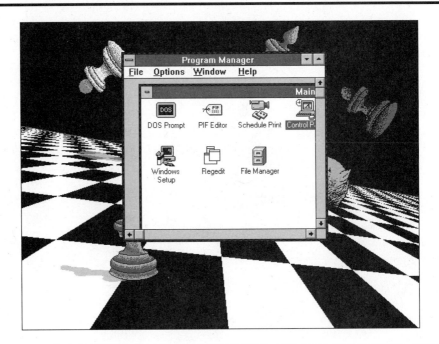

Patterns are small square images repeated thousands of times to fill the entire screen. Although you can use only the patterns that come with Windows, you can edit them to create a completely different patterns. Patterns use two colors from the active color scheme that you specify in the Control Panel's Color module: The background uses the Desktop color, and the foreground uses the Window Text color. (If you don't see your pattern, you have probably selected the same color for both elements.)

Editing a pattern is simple. When you click on the Edit Pattern button of the Desktop dialog box, an editing grid appears (see Figure 9.9). Click on any square in the larger box to change its color. Since there are only two colors, your choices are limited. The effects of your changes to the pattern appear in the smaller Sample box, to the left. To permanently replace a pattern, select Change after you've finished editing the pattern.

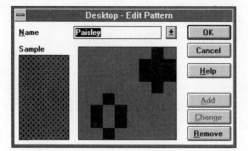

Figure 9.9
To edit a Desktop pattern, click on any rectangle within the larger box. There are only two colors in any pattern, so individual rectangles appear as either filled or empty. The technique is similar to fat-bit editing in Paintbrush, described in Chapter 6.

Wallpaper can be any graphic file stored in Windows's bit-mapped format (BMP) that you designate in the Desktop dialog box. Windows comes with several BMP files, stored in the main Windows directory.

When you select the Wallpaper list box, Windows displays every BMP file in the directory. Any BMP file that you add to this directory appears on the Wallpaper list and can be used to decorate your desktop. You can use Paintbrush to edit the images that Windows provides for wallpaper or to create your own. (See Chapter 6 for details on creating a new wallpaper BMP file.)

If the BMP file is not large enough to fill the display, you have an option of centering it so that it appears once or tiling it so that it repeats as many times as necessary to cover the entire desktop.

One way to help you choose between a pattern and wallpaper is to consider how much RAM you can afford to devote to the display of a single image. Patterns use very little memory, since the repeating bit-mapped image is very small. Wallpaper, however, can take up several hundred kilobytes of RAM, depending on the size of the BMP file. Generally, intricate BMP images with many colors and lines use lots of memory; BMP images with large areas of a single color take up less memory.

The wallpaper images that come with Windows do not use excessive amounts of memory. The largest (Winlogo) uses about 38k; the smallest (Thatch) uses less than 1k. But since you can use any BMP file, it's possible to use up several hundred kilobytes of valuable RAM for displaying a wallpaper image.

You can tell how much RAM the wallpaper image will use by looking at the file size of the BMP image (either from the DOS DIR command or with File Manager); it uses roughly the same amount of RAM as it occupies on disk.

And remember, when any window is maximized, the Desktop can't be seen at all. You don't want to run out of memory when you use a spreadsheet simply because your monitor's displaying a beautiful landscape image that can only be seen a few minutes out of the day. And since Windows uses all available memory for juggling programs and tasks, a large wallpaper image will slow down all of your Windows activity.

Wallpaper is fun, but it can be an obstacle to getting the most from your PC.

Applications

There's just one option in the Applications section: the ability to control whether Windows will let you quickly switch between open programs with the Alt-Tab key combination.

With the Fast Alt+Tab switching option on, when you hold down Alt and then press the Tab key, Windows will display a message box with the name of a program that's running in memory but is currently in the background. For example, if you were running a Windows program but had a DOS session running in the background, you could press Alt-Tab to see the message below.

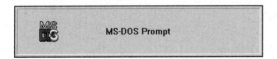

If you release the Alt key with this message displayed, Windows will switch to the DOS session.

The default for this option is on; the only reason to turn it off is if you use a program that requires the Alt-Tab combination.

Screen Saver

A screen saver has two functions: it protects your monitor from the damage that might result after the same image is displayed for many hours; it also provides you with privacy by hiding a display when you leave your machine unattended for a specified period.

Windows is installed without a screen saver. To use a screen saver, select any of the five that are listed in the Screen Saver drop-down list box in the Desktop module:

- **Blank Screen**   A completely blank screen appearing as if the monitor were turned off.

- **Flying Windows**   Starts as a black screen with increasingly large copies of the Microsoft Windows logo.

- **Marquee**   A wide banner appears in the center of the screen, with a message marching across the screen. Choose Marquee as the active screen saver, then enter your message using the Marquee Setup dialog box. (See Figure 9.10.) You can choose the font and colors used.

- **Mystify**   A constantly moving pattern of polygons. Choose Mystify as the active screen saver, then adjust the number and colors of polygons using the dialog box.

- **Starfield Simulation**   A screen full of moving dots that creates the illusion that you're in a moving starship. Choose Starfield Simulation as the active screen saver, then control the speed using the dialog box.

Figure 9.10
The choices for setting up a Marquee as your screen saver include password protection and a personal message that marches across your display.

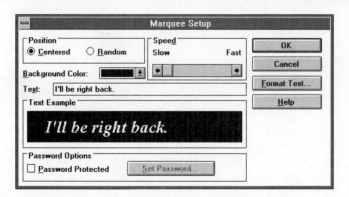

Marquee, Mystify, and Starfield Simulation let you set password protection for your display. After you select one of them as the active screen saver, you choose the password as an option in the dialog box. The default screen saver does not have a password option.

You can see what the screen saver looks like by clicking the Test button on the Desktop dialog box while a particular screen saver is the active choice. (Click again to return to the normal display.)

A screen saver goes into effect when there's no keyboard or mouse activity for a specified period. In the Delay box on the Desktop dialog box you establish the number of minutes without activity that Windows will wait before switching from the current display to the screen saver. Any key you press will stop the screen saver, but if a password has been set, you must type the correct password before you can reuse the system. If you forget your password and need to use the system, reboot (Ctrl-Alt-Del); then immediately run the Desktop module and change the Name text box in the Screen Saver box to None.

Cursor Blink Rate

If you're distracted by the blinking cursor, you may want to slow the rate at which it blinks. You can choose from 50 rates, which will take effect in common applications such as word processors and spreadsheets. At the slowest rate, the cursor appears solid for a relatively long period (about a full second) and disappears for a slightly shorter period. The cursor's blink rate does not affect mouse pointers.

Sizing Grid

Windows uses the *sizing grid* to manage the placement of windows on the screen. The idea is that the screen will be easier to read if active windows can appear only at specific points. To do this, Windows carves up the screen, horizontally and vertically, into an invisible grid. When a window or dialog box is opened, each corner rests on a grid coordinate (known as *snapping to grid* in computer-aided design and graphics software). Of the two settings in the Sizing Grid group, Granularity and Border Width, Granularity has the most effect on the sizing grid.

Granularity   Each number in the Granularity setting represents eight pixels; the highest setting is 49. A granularity of 1 lines up windows and icons at every eighth pixel; a granularity of 2, at every sixteenth pixel. The default setting for granularity is zero, which means there is no sizing grid in effect.

Since Windows must make each new window conform to a grid, if the grid has long distances between coordinates (high granularity), windows and dialog boxes will be larger. For example, with a granularity of 1, a newly opened window must snap to a smaller grid than with a granularity of 49.

The best way to appreciate the effect of the sizing grid is to compare granularity values of zero and 10. When you move an active window with no granularity, the window moves freely and you can place it anywhere on the screen. With granularity set at 10, you'll notice that you can move the window only to specific places; it snaps to a larger grid. (See Table 9.2.)

If you use granularity at all, you'll probably find that a value between one and three is best. A granularity set higher than twenty is impractical, since the objects jerk around the screen, and what you gain in appearance you lose in flexibility.

Table 9.2   **How to Choose Desktop Granularity**

Setting	Effect	Benefit
Low granularity	Windows and icons can be placed almost anywhere.	More control
High granularity	Windows and icons are restricted to fewer positions on screen.	Neater appearance

Border Width   Wider window borders are easier to control when you want to size a window, but they take up slightly more space on screen. Narrower borders can be difficult to click on the sizing pointer at just the right time. The default setting for border width is three, but I find that a setting of five works better: The extra width makes it easier to select the sizing pointer (the double arrow) as it passes over a border.

Printers

The Control Panel's Printers module, shown in Figure 9.11, offers two basic functions: selecting printers, and choosing options for printers you've selected. You need to run this module to install a printer, but you can adjust printer options from within most Windows applications by using the File menu's Printer Setup option.

Figure 9.11
Several printers can be installed for your version of Windows, although only one can be active at a time. To add a new printer, you must have a copy of its software driver either on your hard disk or on a floppy disk.

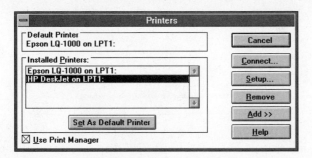

When Windows is installed, it gives you the option of installing several printers. The printer installation process copies printer drivers from the Windows installation disks to your hard disk in the \WINDOWS\SYSTEM subdirectory; it also makes a notation in the WIN.INI file that this printer driver is available. Though Windows lets you keep several printers in your stable, only one can be active; you can print only to that printer.

Adding a Printer

To install a new printer, you must first have the printer driver file. Common printer drivers are included on the Windows installation disks. If you've purchased a new printer, a disk with Windows printer drivers is probably in the box. You may also want to replace an installed printer driver with an updated version.

For any of these situations, follow the steps below, making sure you have the Windows installation disks or a disk with the correct driver at hand.

1. Open the Printer module in the Control Panel.

2. Press Alt-A or click on the Add>> printer button; the Printers dialog box doubles in size, displaying the List of Printers list box (see Figure 9.12).

Figure 9.12

When you choose the Add>> printer button, the Printers dialog box expands to present a list of all the printers that can be installed using the drivers that came with your version of Windows.

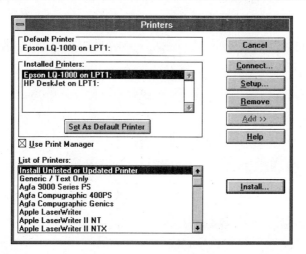

3. Use the keyboard arrow keys or scroll bars to find the name of the printer you want to add. Typing the first letter of the name of the printer's manufacturer highlights the first printer beginning with the letter. (For example, type **E** to see the first Epson printer listed.)

4. If you see your printer name on the list, highlight it and press Enter. A dialog box opens, prompting you to insert a specific Windows installation disk in a disk drive. Make sure you've typed the correct drive letter and inserted the correct disk, then select OK. If your printer is not on this list

or if you have a disk with drivers for a new printer, select Unlisted Printer at the top of the list; a dialog box opens, prompting you for the disk drive with the new file. If your printer is not listed and you do not have a new driver, choose another printer from the same manufacturer or a printer that uses the same printer emulations as yours. All printers conform to at least one standard emulation, and the printer manual will list them.

5. When the process is complete, the name of the printer appears in the Installed Printers box. If you plan to print to this printer instead of the current active one, highlight the new printer name and click on the Set As Default Printer button.

Configuring a Printer

After a printer's been installed, click on the Connect button to tell Windows how to communicate with it. When the Connections dialog box opens, you choose the port from a list of parallel (LPT) and serial (COM) ports. In the list of ports, Windows lets you know whether it has detected an active port by displaying a message, either Local Port, Local Port Not Present, or Network Port.

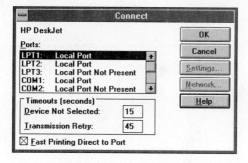

At the end of the list of ports are some special options. EPT is used for PostScript printers like the IBM Personal PagePrinter. File is used when the printer you'll be using is not connected to your system. Windows gives you the option of printing to a file whenever you choose Print in an application; you can later print the file on a system that's connected to the right printer or use the file in a document. Finally, there are two parallel port options that should be used when OS/2 is the active operating system (LPT1.OS2 and LPT2.OS2).

Below the printer list in the Connections dialog box are two special Time-out settings for dealing with printing problems. When Windows can't connect with a printer, the first setting, Device Not Selected, determines how long Windows will wait before it gives up and tells you there's a problem. This type of printer timeout can result from the printer being turned off or out of paper.

If you don't want Windows to wait 15 seconds before telling you it's having a problem with the printer, select zero. If you share a printer using an A-B box or some other printer-sharing device, you may want to set a high value (60 or 70) for Device Not Selected, so that you'll have time to walk over to the printer and check whether the print-sharing device is properly set. This way, you won't get error messages that stop your print job as you walk over to the device. The second Timeout setting, Transmission Retry, is the length of time Windows will continue to try to send the file to the printer if Windows succeeds in connecting with the printer but has some other problem in printing. As with Device Not Selected, set Transmission Retry high if you share a printer and low if you have your own printer.

The Fast Printing Direct to Port option allows Windows to bypass DOS when printing. The default is on; turn it off only if you're using software that is having trouble printing.

Printer Setup Options

After you've chosen Connections, click on the Setup button in the Printers dialog box to choose default options for your printer. The dialog box that opens next is different for every printer. The choices reflect the features available on your printer. Figure 9.13 shows the dialog box for an Epson LQ-1000.

Figure 9.13

Each printer has a unique Setup dialog box. The dialog box shown here opens for users making settings for an Epson LQ-1000.

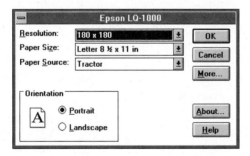

It's impossible to give you a guide to each of the hundreds of printers on the market, but the following list should help you understand the setup options for your particular printer. Your printer manual should offer the best guidance to making choices in choosing printer options.

- **Paper Source**   Refers to the paper trays on laser and inkjet printers. Common tray sizes are 8 1/2 × 11 in, 11 × 17 in, and envelope size.

- **Paper Feed**   Refers to tractor-feed devices installed on dot-matrix printers.

- **Orientation**   Refers to the portrait and landscape modes. A normal letter is considered portrait, while a page on its side is considered landscape.

- **Font Cartridges**   Plastic cases that generate specific fonts on the printer. If your printer has a font cartridge installed, you must select the name from the list for your Windows programs to print those fonts. If you purchase a new font cartridge, you can change the settings here.

- **Memory**   Refers to the RAM installed in the printer (*not* the RAM in your PC). Memory upgrades are available for most laser printers, and you'll need to change this setting after installing more memory.

- **Graphics Resolution** or just **Resolution**   The number of dots per square inch (dpi) that the printer will use when printing graphic images. Higher resolutions (300 dpi, for example) take longer to print but have much sharper definition. A laser printer with a small amount of memory (512k) may not be able to print any but the smallest graphic images at 300 dpi.

- **Text Mode**   Refers to a dot matrix printer's two options for printing text, letter (which is a higher resolution) and draft.

- **Copies**   Lets you print several copies of a single document, saving trips to the copying machine or time-consuming repetitions of the Print command. The default is 1.

- **Print Quality**   Lets you choose between fast printing (draft) and higher-quality printing (letter).

Choosing Printer Options within Programs

When you choose Printer Setup on the File menu in an application, you see a dialog box that's different from the one that opens in Control Panel. In most cases, it makes more sense to use the Setup box from within the application instead of running Control Panel. You'll decide upon orientation or resolution from task to task, and it's quicker to make the choice at print time from within the application. Some printer settings can only be made from the Control Panel's Printer Setup dialog box, but these are changes that need to be made infrequently, such as font cartridges and downloadable soft fonts.

Print Manager

The Windows Print Manager is a *spooler,* a program that uses some of the available system RAM to offload the job of printing from the main program. It works only with Windows applications and does not affect DOS programs printing while Windows is active. When the Print Manager is used, you usually don't have to wait for your document to finish printing before you can use your PC again, because Print Manager works in the background, letting you get back to work in the foreground; you'll be able to use your computer while Windows communicates with the printer. However, if you're making heavy use of the processor and hard disk while Print Manager is working, it will take longer for the print job to finish than if you had let the system concentrate on printing.

Most people will want to select the Use Print Manager box. Among the reasons *not* to use it are that your PC has very limited memory (1Mb or less) and you rarely print. Or, you may want to use a print spooler that you've bought, such as SuperPrint or PrintCache.

International

The International settings make it possible to adjust date, time, currency, and number formats for different countries and languages (see Figure 9.14). Changing the settings in the Country and Language text boxes does *not* change Windows menus into a new language: Country determines how the date, time, currency, and number formats are set, and Language affects only those programs that have language-specific versions.

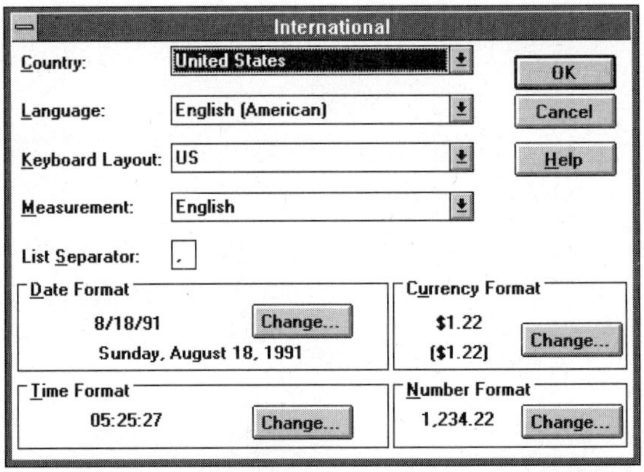

Figure 9.14

The International dialog box controls values for those features of the Windows display that vary by language and country.

Some Windows programs (Microsoft Excel, for example) offer their own commands for establishing the way dates, times, currencies, and numbers are displayed within the program. The International dialog box sets the defaults used by programs that don't have special settings.

You can customize the date, time, currency, and number format by double-clicking on the corresponding Change button in the International dialog box. The following sections explain how to set up each of the four formats.

Date Format

The Date Format dialog box gives you control over how Windows displays dates. The dialog box has two distinct parts: the top controls the short form (1-1-95); the bottom controls the long form (January 1, 1995), as seen in Figure 9.15.

You can adjust everything from the use of leading zeros (01 has a leading zero, 1 does not) to the separator used between date, month, and year. Look at the following list to get an idea of the possible formats.

Short Form
1-2-93
1/2/93
1.2.93
01-02-93
01-2-93
1-02-93
1-2-1993
01-02-1993
93-1-2
93/1/2
1993-1-2
1993/1/2

Long Form

Saturday, January 1, 1993

Sat, January 1, 1993

Sat, 01 01, 93

Sat, 1 1, 93

Saturday, Jan 1, 1993

Saturday, Jan 01, 1993

Saturday. Jan 01. 1993

Saturday- Jan 01- 1993

Time Formats

The International - Time Format dialog box lets you choose between a 12-hour and 24-hour clock, and select how time is displayed.

When the United States is selected as the country, the 12-hour clock is the default, with a colon (:) used to separate hours, minutes, and seconds. No matter which country is selected, or whether you display the time on a 12-hour or 24-hour clock, you can use any punctuation mark to separate the hours, minutes, and seconds. To change from the default value (colon), press Alt-S to select the Separator box and enter a different punctuation mark.

Currency Format

When the United States is the default country, the default currency format places the dollar sign before the value and includes two decimal digits, as in $1.22. Using the International - Currency Format dialog box you can place the dollar sign before or after the number and display negatives in parentheses or with a negative sign.

The list below shows some of the ways of formatting the dollar sign. Be aware, however, that it's possible to concoct a currency format that's not accepted by any financial institution.

Positive Amounts
$2.14
$ 2.14
2.14$
2.14 $

Negative Amounts
($2.14)
(2.14$)
–$2.14
$–2.14
$2.14–
2.14–$
2.14$–

You can also change the currency symbol, which can be useful if you're temporarily working in another currency. Simply insert a different character (Y for yen, P for peseta, and so on) in the Symbol text box. You can use the extended ANSI character set to insert currency symbols. For example, to use the Yen symbol, enter **Alt-0165**; for the British pound, enter **Alt-0163**. (You must type the numbers using the numeric keypad, rather than the numbers that appear above your keyboard's letter keys.) If you'll be doing extensive work in a different currency, change your language selection in the main International dialog box.

Finally, it's possible to extend the number of displayed digits to the right of the decimal point from two places, the default, to nine places.

Number Format

The default format for displaying numbers includes a comma marking the thousands, a period as the decimal point, and two digits to the right of the decimal point. For example: 1,000.02 uses a comma as the 1,000 separator, a period as the decimal separator, and two as the decimal digits value.

Using the International - Number Format dialog box you can use any alphanumeric character as the indicator of thousands or decimals, and you can display up to nine decimal places. You also can choose to display or omit a leading zero when fractions are used (0.7 instead of .7); the default is to display leading zeros.

Keyboard

In the Control Panel's Keyboard module, you can change the way Windows behaves when you hold down a key—how long it waits before repeating the key and then how quickly it repeats that key. Since Backspace is one of the most often repeated keys in text editing, be careful when choosing these settings, or you may wind up with a Backspace key that deletes more text than you had intended.

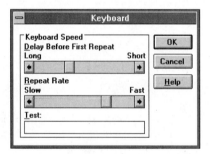

- **Delay Before First Repeat**   Establishes how long Windows waits before it begins to repeat a key that's being held down. There are four settings; the default is in the middle. If you have a "heavy hand," you'll want a long delay (set to the far left); otherwise, Windows may begin to repeat a key that you intended to press just once. If you're a fast typist, you'll want a short delay (the far right).

- **Repeat Rate**   A high setting causes characters to appear very rapidly when you press a key and keep it down. A low setting causes characters to repeat very slowly. Use a slow repeat rate if you find that you erase more than you planned when you press the Backspace key to delete characters. The default setting is 16 on a scale of one to 32.

You can test the effect of changing either of the two settings by clicking in the Test text box and then holding a single key down.

Date & Time

The Date & Time module lets you change the date used throughout Windows and by DOS. You can use this module to change the setting stored in the computer's battery-backed CMOS memory; if your system's battery goes dead, you can enter the correct date and time here after it's been replaced. You'll probably find that the Date & Time dialog box is much easier to use than your computer's setup program for changing the date and time.

When changing the date or time, note that each field—day, month, year, hour, minute, and second—must be adjusted separately, either by typing in a new value or by clicking on the up and down arrows. Use the Tab key to move from field to field. You can use this module to switch between standard and daylight savings time.

Sound

The Sound module lets you assign files that are played whenever common events happen within Windows, such as a message box opening. Chapter 13 explains sound options in detail.

Before you can use Windows sound effects, a sound driver must be properly installed. (The following section explains how to get a sound device working.) When a sound device is running, you can use the Sound module to hear a WAV (waveform) file that consists of an audio recording. Then, you can assign it to one of seven Windows events.

If you're not sure whether a sound device is running, open the Sound dialog box; if Windows does not recognize any device, all of the entries in the Events and Files lists will be grayed out. To hear a sound played, highlight one of the WAV files in the Sound dialog box's list of files (such as CHORD-.WAV). Then click on the Test command button.

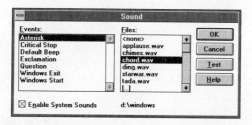

You'll hear a sound instantly. If not, the Sound device may not be installed properly. See the next section for help on installing sound drivers.

Some of the seven events listed in this dialog box are interpreted differently from one application to another. For example, either Asterisk, Exclamation, or Default Beep is played when you are trying to execute an unsupported command (like clicking outside of an open dialog box). You'll have to experiment with your most common programs if you want to make links between events and sounds that suit your taste.

If you'd like to assign sounds to events, follow this procedure:

1. You'll want to test all of the sound files so you know what to expect. You do that by highlighting a file name and then clicking on Test.

2. Now you can assign a file to each event. Highlight the first event listed.

3. Click on the sound file you'd like to hear when this event occurs.

4. Repeat steps 2 and 3 for each event.

5. Select OK. The dialog box closes, and your choices are now in effect.

Windows comes with several files in the WAV file format; you can add new WAV files to your system and use them instead. If you have a microphone connected to your sound board, you can use the Sound Recorder program to create new WAV files. (See Chapter 13 for details.)

The easiest way to use WAV files for Windows events is to copy them to your default Windows directory. Then they'll be listed in the Files dialog box. If they're stored in a different directory, you need to change from the Windows directory while in the Sound module. First, double-click on the root for your Windows directory; it's represented in the Files window by the symbol [..]. Then, move through your directory path structure by double-clicking on the directory names. When you've opened a directory that has WAV files, all of them will be listed and you can follow the steps above to assign a sound to an event.

Drivers

Windows requires many *drivers* to be installed properly; your system has drivers for a video board, printer, mouse, and even the keyboard. But the only drivers that you can install from the Control Panel's Drivers module are those that add sound to your system.

All PCs have some sound capability in the form of a very limited sound chip and a speaker that is used primarily to beep when errors happen. Sound boards, however, can add the ability to play, record and edit all types of sound. If you have one of these devices, you need to use the Drivers dialog box to make it work within Windows. You can also use the Drivers dialog box to turn your PC's speaker on or off.

You can also play WAV sound files without a sound board, using your PC's speaker. It won't sound pretty but it is more interesting than hearing only a beep. You need to obtain the driver software for your speaker from Microsoft. Either call Microsoft's technical support and inquire, or connect to one of Microsoft's forums on CompuServe, where you can download the file. Once you have the software, you can use the Driver module to add the device.

The sound devices that are already installed are listed in the Drivers dialog box.

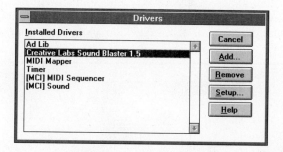

To remove a device, highlight it on the list and then click on the Remove command button. To add a device, click on the Add command button. You'll need to have a disk with the necessary driver files. Windows comes with the software for a number of devices, including boards from Ad Lib, Sound Blaster, and Roland. Even if your sound card isn't included, there's a good chance that it is compatible with one of these. (The product's manual should have this information.) If not, you'll need a software driver from the manufacturer.

When you add sound drivers, Windows makes changes to both the SYSTEM.INI and WIN.INI files so that the drivers are loaded when Windows runs and so that Windows uses the correct hardware channels.

As you install a sound card, you may need to know the port (between 210 and 260) or interrupt (2 through 7) used by your board. These settings are usually established by DIP switches or jumpers on the board. If you're not sure, check the manual that came with the board. Or, you can use a diagnostic program like Check-It to show you how your ports and interrupts are assigned. Windows comes with a program that may help; to use it, type **MSD** at the Program Manager's File Run command.

As a last resort, you can guess, and repeat the process if your guess is wrong.

386 Enhanced Mode

If your system is running in 386 Enhanced mode, a special icon appears in Control Panel for setting options specific to this operating mode. It appears only on systems that use a processor compatible with Intel's 80386 chip, including 386SX and 486 PCs.

The choices in the 386 Enhanced dialog box (see Figure 9.16) allow you to set multitasking priorities—to specify which communications ports and active tasks take priority when more than one program is running. The settings are required only in 386 Enhanced mode, because only this mode allows DOS programs to operate simultaneously with Windows programs. In 286 Standard mode you can open a DOS program and switch to a Windows program, but the DOS program remains dormant while you work in Windows.

Figure 9.16

The 386 Enhanced dialog box is available only if your system uses a 386 processor (including compatible PCs like the 386SX and 486) and has enough memory to run in 386 Enhanced mode. These options set priorities when more than one program is running.

```
┌─────────────────────── 386 Enhanced ───────────────────────┐
│  ┌─Device Contention──────────┐                            │
│  │ Com1        ▲  │ ○ Always Warn        ┌────── OK ──────┐ │
│  │ Com2           │ ○ Never Warn         ┌──── Cancel ────┐ │
│  │             ▼  │ ◉ Idle (in sec.)  [2]▲▼                │
│  └────────────────┘                      ┌ Virtual Memory...┐│
│  ┌─Scheduling─────────────────────┐      ┌───── Help ─────┐ │
│  │ Windows in Foreground:  [100]▲▼ │                        │
│  │ Windows in Background:   [50]▲▼ │                        │
│  │ ☐ Exclusive in Foreground       │                        │
│  └─────────────────────────────────┘                        │
│  Minimum Timeslice (in msec):  [20]▲▼                       │
└─────────────────────────────────────────────────────────────┘
```

Device Contention

This section of the 386 Enhanced dialog box sets the priority that Windows will observe when a DOS (non-Windows) program is competing with an active Windows program for the use of a modem, printer, fax board, or other device that uses communications ports. This setting is necessary because, while Windows programs are designed to work in a multitasking environment, DOS programs always assume they have sole access to communications ports. Windows has to mediate between a Windows program and a DOS program when they both want to use a device.

To set priorities for a device, first choose the communications port (serial or parallel), and then select one of three priorities for that device:

- **Always Warn** Generates the Device Conflict query whenever two programs attempt to use the port simultaneously.

You must then choose which task gets to use the device by clicking the appropriate button. Select Always Warn if you sometimes have rush jobs that should get priority over other tasks. In most cases, when you give priority (reassign the port) to Windows, you've essentially deactivated the DOS program. You'll have to switch back to DOS and start the task fresh, after the Windows program has finished using the port.

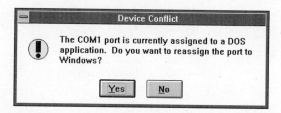

- **Never Warn**   Is planned chaos. All tasks can try to use the device at the same time and, as a result, if two tasks are sent to the port at once, it will probably produce garbage. Select this option only if you're sure two programs will never use the same port simultaneously. Even then, you can reduce Windows's overhead only slightly and make a very small performance improvement.

- **Idle (in sec.)**   Lets the task using the device finish and waits the specified number of seconds before allowing the task-in-waiting to proceed. Idle is the option that makes the most sense for typical business applications; therefore, it's the default.

The amount of time specified as the idle period is important because an application may sometimes pause while using a port. For example, a communications program may pause for several seconds after it's received a busy signal before trying to dial again. The number of seconds you'll want to establish for Idle should be based on how long you expect a task will need access to the device. For example, if you use a communications program that often fails to make a connection, give it enough time to reset the modem and try again, about five seconds, to be safe. If you don't give it enough time, the program will lose access to the port and probably not be able to reset itself. You can set idle time as high as 999 seconds, over 16 minutes.

Your preferences should be based on how you work. In general, device contention is something you want to avoid, because it adds extra overhead to the processor and slows down your system.

Scheduling

A *timeslice* is the amount of time that the processor in your system will spend on a particular task before switching to the next task. See "Minimum

Timeslice" for more information on setting the timeslice and switching between DOS and Windows. The Scheduling section of the 386 Enhanced dialog box allows you to set a ratio between the amount of processor time received by an active DOS and Windows program. Remember, DOS programs that are open but not actively performing a task—such as sorting a database or recalculating a spreadsheet—don't need much of the processor's time. If you tend to leave a DOS program open without active tasks in progress, be sure you don't waste precious processor time by giving the DOS programs too many timeslices.

Exclusive in Foreground   This check box makes scheduling very simple: When a Windows program appears in the active display, DOS programs in the background are suspended, and all processing is devoted to the Windows program. This setting makes sense for most people who switch between DOS and Windows, because they usually do not perform calculations in the DOS program after they have switched back to Windows.

The other two Scheduling options establish ratios between active Windows and DOS programs. Use these options only if you require that DOS programs perform several minutes of uninterrupted processing in the background when you switch back to Windows.

Windows in Foreground and Windows in Background   The numbers you enter at the two settings, Windows in Foreground and Windows in Background, are used to create a ratio. This ratio divides the processing time that all active programs share when a DOS program is running.

The Windows in Foreground setting establishes how to determine the ratio for an active Windows program when a Windows program occupies the active window and there's at least one DOS program running in the background. The Windows in Background setting establishes how to determine the ratio for Windows programs running in the background when either a DOS or Windows program is running in the active window (or full-screen display), and one or more Windows programs work in the background.

The values you enter here make sense only when compared to the values you enter in a DOS program's PIF. (See "PIF Settings for 386 Enhanced Mode Only" in Chapter 10.)

Here's how the ratio is created. In both cases, Windows totals the timeslices allocated for all Windows programs and for DOS programs. (The number allocated to each DOS program is established in the program's PIF.) Windows takes that total and gives each program a percentage of the processor's time.

For example, let's say there are three Windows programs running in the background, one DOS program running in the background, and a Windows program running in the foreground. Each program has a value of 200 in its respective setting. This was established by entering **200** whenever a scheduling option was available. (For both the foreground and background Windows programs, the settings are made in the 386 Enhanced dialog box; for the DOS programs, the setting is made in the PIF dialog box.) The total is 600. The three Windows programs operating in the background receive one-third, which is divided among them. The background DOS program and the foreground Windows program also get one-third.

Let's say you want your background programs to run faster and you don't care too much about slowing down the program that's displayed in the foreground. If you left the foreground and DOS values at 200 and made the background setting 1,000, you'd create a total of 1,400; the ratio given to the background tasks would be 71 percent and the foreground Windows task and the background DOS task would each get just under 15 percent.

The maximum value for each setting is 10,000.

Minimum Timeslice

The Minimum Timeslice box controls the way Windows alternates processing of Windows and DOS applications. When a DOS program and a Windows program are working simultaneously, Windows gives one timeslice to all Windows activities and then one timeslice to the DOS program. The default timeslice is 20 milliseconds. Reduce the timeslice only if you frequently switch between DOS and Windows and want to switch more quickly. If you choose a lower timeslice, Windows alternates between the two types of tasks more often, creating the illusion of more efficient operation because the switching time is shorter. But in fact, the system is working slower, because of the extra work required for constant switching.

If you do a lot of DOS multitasking and don't need to constantly look at each display, you should increase the timeslice length to 50 milliseconds or more. The increased switching time will be apparent only when the active programs are in the middle of a task; if the active programs are idle, there will be no visible slowdown when switching.

Virtual Memory

The Virtual Memory option for 386 Enhanced mode lets you establish a file that can be used to emulate memory. This file is called a *swap file,* and you can make it permanent to improve performance.

When Windows is installed, the Setup program analyzes your hard disk and makes a recommendation on how the Virtual Memory option is used. Installing the swap file improperly can make performance deteriorate and can reduce the amount of storage available on your hard disk for DOS, so if you don't have a thorough understanding of the DOS disk structure and virtual memory, don't experiment with the settings.

Windows will work faster if you have a permanent swap file, since it will know the address of the disk sectors. If the swap file is temporary, Windows needs to pass information on to DOS each time data is read or written.

However, you can only make a swap file permanent if there is enough contiguous (that is, uninterrupted) disk space free to accommodate the size you want to use. If your disk has been used heavily, you may not have enough contiguous disk space even if you have a large amount of free space, since DOS breaks up files to fit available space.

```
┌─────────────────────────────────────────────────────────┐
│ ─  │                  Virtual Memory                      │
├─────────────────────────────────────────────────────────┤
│ ┌─Current Settings──────────────────┐    ┌──────────┐    │
│ │ Drive:   C:                       │    │    OK    │    │
│ │ Size:    3,328 KB                 │    └──────────┘    │
│ │ Type:    Temporary (using MS-DOS) │    ┌──────────┐    │
│ │                                   │    │  Cancel  │    │
│ └───────────────────────────────────┘    └──────────┘    │
│                                           ┌──────────┐    │
│                                           │ Change>> │    │
│                                           └──────────┘    │
│ ┌─New Settings──────────────────────┐    ┌──────────┐    │
│ │                                   │    │   Help   │    │
│ │ Drive:   [▤ c: [gv]          ▼]   │    └──────────┘    │
│ │ Type:    [Temporary          ▼]   │                    │
│ │                                                        │
│ │ Space Available:            8,454  KB                  │
│ │ Recommended Maximum Size:   4,227  KB                  │
│ │                                                        │
│ │ New Size:                  [ 4227 ] KB                 │
│ └───────────────────────────────────┐                   │
│ ☒ Use 32-Bit Disk Access                                 │
└─────────────────────────────────────────────────────────┘
```

The Virtual Memory dialog box lists a recommended maximum size; if you want to exceed that, enter a new amount in the New Size text box. You can also choose between Temporary and Permanent from the Type list box. When you execute the changes, Windows will alert you to potential problems, providing ample opportunity to cancel significant changes to the swap file, so you may want to test your system's limits. Just remember that when you make a swap file permanent, you reduce the amount of disk space available for storing files.

The Use 32-Bit Disk Access option should be set on if you're using a 386-compatible PC and you have more than 2 megabytes of RAM. This option turns on Fastdisk, a way of accessing the hard disk. Fastdisk virtualizes the disk BIOS, meaning that a copy of the input/output table for using the disk is placed in RAM. That makes disk accesses faster than if Windows had to refer to your PC's ROM BIOS when it needed to use the disk. It also makes Windows faster because Windows does not have to switch from 386 protected mode into Real mode as often. Turn this option off only if you are extremely short of RAM and absoultely need a few more megabytes to load a file. Otherwise, keep it on, since it can make a big improvement in performance. It's only available when running in 386 Enhanced mode and does not work with some hard disks. The Setup program turns the option on if it determines that your system has a compatible hard disk and sufficient RAM.

Networks

The Network module in Control Panel is available only if Windows is able to detect an active network connection. The correct network drivers must be properly installed under DOS, the network card in the PC must be actively communicating with the server, and Windows Setup must have properly installed the correct network drivers. When all of these conditions are met, a network icon is visible in the lower-right corner of the Control Panel.

The dialog box that opens when you double-click on the network icon varies with the network operating system installed. For most types of networks, the dialog box allows you to log onto a server where you have access privileges and to connect to a network printer where you have printing privileges. Both privileges must have been previously granted at the server by a network administrator.

Editing the INI Files

If you use only the programs that came with Windows, you won't have much need to change the WIN.INI and SYSTEM.INI files, and you won't need the information in the rest of this chapter. But if you use different programs under Windows, you will want to change your WIN.INI and SYSTEM.INI files frequently by adding new settings for programs, and you'll want to learn how to directly edit these essential files. This can help you debug problems and improve overall Windows performance.

You have two ways of editing these files: with any word processor that writes files as pure text (ASCII); and with the SysEdit utility that comes with Windows.

Many applications create their own INI file for controlling program options. The Windows Clock, for example, uses the file CLOCK.INI every time it's run. The Control Panel keeps the file CONTROL.INI, which provides options for use within Control Panel; for example, the Color module stores information about which colors are assigned to screen elements. And, if you have a network installed, there's likely to be an INI file for the network (titled something like NETWARE.INI or LANMAN.INI, depending on the network operating system you're using).

You can use a word processor to edit these INI files, but you won't be able to use SysEdit, which works only on system configuration initialization files. Appendix C has some help for understanding both files.

Word Processors and INI Files

Any word processor that reads and writes ASCII text files, including Windows Notepad, can be used to make changes to the INI files. (For an explanation of

ASCII text, see Chapter 4.) When using a word processor, you should be especially careful that you save INI files as text. If you inadvertently save the file in your word processor's format, you will add non-ASCII formatting characters, and Windows will not run. The only way to get Windows running again is to remove the extraneous characters.

If you're unsure of your ability to store the INI files as ASCII text, be certain to save a backup copy of the files before you begin work. Copy the original WIN.INI to a new file (WIN.OLD, for example). If you have problems editing WIN.INI, you can delete it and rename WIN.OLD as WIN.INI by typing **RENAME WIN.OLD WIN.INI** at the DOS command prompt.

SysEdit, the System Configuration Editor

SysEdit—or, more formally, the System Configuration Editor—is a utility installed by the Windows Setup program. It doesn't appear in any of the program groups, because Microsoft considers it potentially dangerous and wants to discourage users from tinkering with INI files. But if you know enough to install SysEdit as an icon, you already know much of what you need to confidently modify either INI file; you'll learn the rest of what you need to know in the following pages.

To run SysEdit, type **sysedit** at the Run command of Program Manager's File menu. To create a new icon for SysEdit, select the New command of Program Manager's File menu. (For detailed instructions see "Adding a Program Item" in Chapter 2.)

What You Need to Know Before Using SysEdit

When SysEdit opens, four document windows appear, one window for each of the two Windows INI files (WIN.INI and SYSTEM.INI) and one window for each of DOS's two configuration files (CONFIG.SYS and AUTOEXEC-.BAT). (See Figure 9.17.)

SysEdit includes access to the two DOS configuration files because their contents can have an important impact on Windows's performance. For example, the DOS Path statement in AUTOEXEC.BAT must include a reference to the Windows directory, and many Windows programs require a TEMP path. In the CONFIG.SYS, *DEVICE=HIMEM.SYS* must appear for Windows to use extended memory.

You can begin to edit any of the four files, but go slowly: SysEdit has no mechanism for checking your work. If you've made an invalid entry by misspelling a word or if you've deleted a required statement, the only way you'll know about it is that DOS or Windows won't be installed properly. (Although DOS will always install if you've created an invalid CONFIG-.SYS or AUTOEXEC.BAT file, Windows may not install at all if one of the boot options is not correctly set in SYSTEM.INI or WIN.INI.)

Figure 9.17

SysEdit's opening screen displays the Windows and DOS configuration files in a cascaded arrangement.

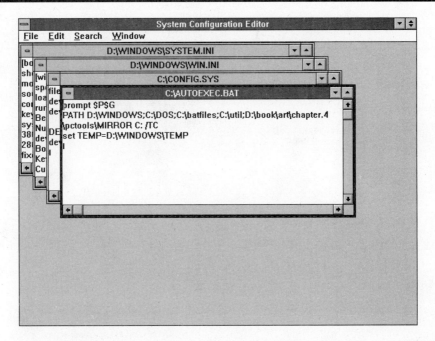

To use SysEdit properly you need knowledge of the syntax used by the INI files and a healthy respect for the power of these two files. You already have the proper respect if you've ever accidentally deleted a valuable file or inadvertently formatted a hard disk; you know how easy it can be to destroy data and ruin your day with a foolhardy move. The rest of this chapter will help you understand the syntax of these files. As long as you're careful to follow the INI file syntax and always keep a backup of the files before you begin editing, you shouldn't have any trouble accessing the INI files.

How SysEdit Works

SysEdit is a subset of the Windows Notepad with a minimal set of commands. There's no command for opening a file, because the four configuration files always open when you run SysEdit and no other files are accessible. You can save changes to these files, but you cannot rename the files. You can print any of the files, but you cannot format them in any way.

The editing commands are common to all Windows programs: You can cut, copy, and paste blocks of text, and you can undo a single delete or move action. There's also a Search command that will find text forward or backward in the file. The display itself can be cascaded (as in Figure 9.17) or tiled (as in Figure 9.18). As in all Windows programs that have more than one document window, you can use the Ctrl-Tab shortcut key to move from one window to the next.

Figure 9.18
The SysEdit display can be tiled, with all four configuration files visible at once.

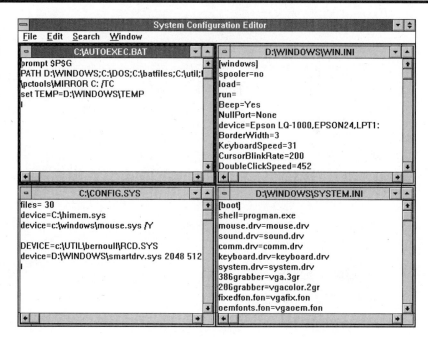

SYSTEM.INI

Every time Windows starts up on your PC, it reads the SYSTEM.INI file to determine which files Windows should use to communicate with your PC's hardware, except for the modem and printer. (The modem and printer information is set in the WIN.INI file.) If all PCs were identical, there wouldn't be any reason for the SYSTEM.INI file, but since there is a wide range of video displays, network cards, mice, keyboards, and processors, SYSTEM.INI is required for Windows to use these different components.

The original values in SYSTEM.INI are created on your PC when you run Setup to install Windows. If you run Setup again to change a component (replacing your keyboard, for example), the Setup program edits SYSTEM-.INI automatically. For a keyboard change, it changes the name of the file that follows *keyboard.drv=*.

See Table 9.3 for a guide to the most important variables in SYSTEM-.INI's boot section. Other entries you'll find in the file that are not included here are self-explanatory; *keyboard.drv,* for example, installs the keyboard driver. Some Windows programs you install may add their own entries as well.

Table 9.3   **Some of the Boot Settings in SYSTEM.INI**

Setting	Purpose
386grabber	Transfers data from DOS program screens to Windows programs when running in 386 Enhanced mode
286grabber	Transfers data from DOS programs to Windows programs when running in 286 Standard mode
shell	Installs program that manages the Windows session (either Program Manager, File Manager, or a shell program you purchase separately)
network.drv	Installs a driver for communicating with a network
language.dll	Opens communication with a dynamic link library (DLL) that has language-specific settings
fixedfon.fon	Installs the system font used by old versions of Windows for displaying text in menus and dialog boxes (used for compatibility with old Windows programs only)
comm.drv	Installs a driver for setting up communications ports
sound.drv	Installs a driver for communicating with the sound chip or a sound board
oemfonts.drv	Installs the terminal font, which allows display of the high-order ASCII characters (also called OEM fonts)
fonts.fon	Installs the system font used for displaying text in menus and dialog boxes in all Windows 3.0 and 3.1 programs
display.drv	Installs a driver that communicates with your display adapter (for example, VGA, EGA, Hercules)
scrnsave.exe	Installs the screen saver program specified in the Desktop module of Control Panel

SYSTEM.INI's syntax is simple. Words between square brackets—as in [boot]—are section headings describing the type of settings that follow. Words followed by an equal sign and the name of a file or option are specifications. The section heading [boot], for example, tells Windows which drivers (.DRV files) to read when installing essential boot-up hardware. The line *shell=progman.exe* within this section tells SYSTEM.INI that the file *progman.exe* (Program Manager) should be loaded to satisfy the shell requirement.

Files whose names appear to the right of the equal sign were copied to either the main Windows directory or the SYSTEM subdirectory automatically created below the main Windows directory when Setup installed Windows on your PC. When the SYSTEM.INI file is read, Windows looks in this subdirectory for the driver files and then uses the data in the drivers for setting up Windows in your system's RAM. Be sure that any drivers that you add to SYSTEM.INI are stored in the SYSTEM directory; if they're not, Windows will not run. It may freeze your system or simply quit the installation and return to DOS.

Some Windows programs add an entry to SYSTEM.INI as they install their data files on your PC. Adobe Type Manager, for example, adds the line *atm.systemdrv=system.drv.*

It's quite common to decide that you don't want to keep a new program on your system after you've used it for a while. Under DOS, you could simply delete the files that came with the program to remove all trace of it from your system. However, in Windows you'll need to delete entries from SYSTEM-.INI after you've erased the program's files to remove it completely.

WIN.INI

WIN.INI is read after SYSTEM.INI and exercises options on the hardware that SYSTEM.INI installs into RAM. SYSTEM.INI establishes lower-level hardware parameters, and WIN.INI finishes up the Windows installation, choosing the options that are possible now that the PC's RAM is full of instructions for using the PC's hardware. For example, SYSTEM.INI loads device drivers, and WIN.INI loads executable files that use these devices.

Table 9.4 shows the settings in WIN.INI that you may want to edit. Other statements throughout the file should be self-explanatory: ScrollBar in the [Colors] section, for example, sets the colors for the scroll bar; iDate in the [Intl] section sets the international date; sDate establishes the date separator.

The WIN.INI file uses the same syntax as SYSTEM.INI: The section headings appear within brackets, and the specifications are established as equations. Most of the Control Panel dialog box choices are stored in WIN.-INI, and it's not too difficult to figure out which WIN.INI statements are controlled by which Control Panel options.

For example, the fifth line of WIN.INI reads *Beep=yes* or *Beep=no,* corresponding to the choice made in the Control Panel's Sound dialog box. *MouseSpeed=* indicates the mouse speed you chose; the number following the equal sign reflects how many clicks the mouse speed indicator bar moved to the right of the point farthest left.

Since the statements are grouped into sections, you can usually decipher a cryptic statement by considering the context. In the [intl] section, for example, there are separate entries for iCurrency and sCurrency; the first is the international currency format you've chosen, and the second is the separator for currency.

Many of the settings are stored as 1 or 0, and these usually reflect a choice between yes (1) or no (0), and on (1) or off (0).

Table 9.4 **Some of the Boot Settings in WIN.INI**

Setting	Purpose
load	Loads a program into memory when Windows runs, and reduces it to an icon
run	Loads a program into memory when Windows runs, and keeps it running in an open window
beep	Turns the warning beep on or off
spooler	Runs the Print Manager or turns it off
device	Installs a printer
programs	The file extensions that Windows shell programs like File Manager will attempt to execute
swapdisk	A file that Windows uses in 386 Enhanced mode for storing data on disk when it does not fit into memory

WIN.INI Tips: Loading Programs

In earlier chapters, we saw how to use the load and run statements to launch programs when Windows starts up. (Load was described in "Loading Recorder at Startup" in Chapter 8; Run was covered in "Notepad Tips" in Chapter 4.) If you always use the same group of programs, by all means load and run as many as you wish by editing these two statements.

■ **Load** programs that you want to have available as icons.

■ **Run** programs that you want to have active.

The only limitation is the amount of memory in your system.

To use the Load and Run statements, enter the full name of the program (for example, CALC.EXE) after the equal sign on either line. To load or run more than one program, enter a *space* after a program name, and type the next name. For example, this is a valid load statement:

```
load=calc.exe terminal.exe pbrush.exe recorder.exe
```

You can even use names of data files in the Load or Run statements, as long as the file extensions are associated with a Windows program later in the WIN.INI file. Associations were explained in "Associating Files with Programs" in Chapter 3.

Until version 3.1 of Windows, this was the only way to automatically run or load programs when Windows was started. But Windows 3.1 added the Program Manager Startup group, which runs every program whose icon appears within it. You can still use the WIN.INI Load and Run commands, in addition to the Startup group.

WIN.INI Tips: Associating Programs with Data

If you use File Manager frequently, you'll probably want to add to the file formats listed in WIN.INI's extensions section. The statements in this section reflect the associations made in File Manager: Data files with a specified extension are associated with a program, so that if you double-click a data file, the application runs automatically.

By default, WIN.INI associates Notepad with files having the .TXT extension, so that any time you double-click on a file with that extension, Notepad runs with this file active. If you want to use a different word processor when you use text files, change the WIN.INI statement that reads

```
txt=notepad.exe ^ .txt
```

so that the executable file for a different word processor appears in place of NOTEPAD.EXE. You can do the same with any file extension. For example. if you use Lotus 1-2-3, you may want to add the statement

```
wk1=123.pif ^ .wk1
```

so that whenever you double-click on a worksheet file from File Manager, Windows launches 1-2-3, using the Windows PIF file to properly install 1-2-3 under Windows.

This is the same technique used by File Manager's Associate command to establish a connection between a program and a type of data file. By editing WIN.INI yourself, you can add associations between data files and applications more quickly and remove old associations that you don't use any more.

WIN.INI Tips: Keep It Clean

From time to time, it's a good idea to clean out unused sections of the WIN-.INI file if you experiment with new software. As in the SYSTEM.INI file, new programs install their own statements in WIN.INI. The main difference is that many more statements are added to WIN.INI.

These new statements are easy to identify, since they tend to have their own section heading. For example, if you run Windows Calculator and choose the Scientific mode just once, a new section will be added to WIN.INI with the heading [SciCalc]. Beneath it will be one line, *layout=*. If you will never use the Scientific calculator again, there's no benefit to having these two words in your WIN.INI file; they slow down Windows as it loads into memory and take up a small amount of disk space. You should delete these and any other statements that you are absolutely sure are no longer needed.

The only way you can really be sure that your WIN.INI file is not cluttered up with lots of unneeded data is to read it periodically. When you install a new Windows program, make a backup of the original and compare it to the new version. Over time, you'll get to know your system's personality very well. Understanding your WIN.INI file can help you debug problems and avoid potential problems before they occur.

Control Panel's Menus: A Complete List

Settings

Color
Fonts. . .
Ports. . .
Mouse. . .
Desktop. . .
Keyboard. . .
Printers. . .
International. . .
Date/Time. . .
Network. . .
386 Enhanced Mode. . .
Drivers. . .
Sound. . .
Exit

Help

Contents
Search for Help On. . .
How to Use Help
About Control Panel. . .

10

Running More than One Program

Making the Right Hardware Choices

Running Several Windows Programs

Running DOS Programs

Switching between DOS Programs and Windows Programs

THE EASE OF USING MENU COMMANDS AND CLICK-AND-DRAG TECHNIQUES is only part of Windows's appeal. Windows is also an excellent platform for running more than one program at the same time. If your PC has a 386-compatible chip, Windows can run several programs at the same time. You can have your database sort a long list at the same time that you edit a report with your word processor. And you can run multiple DOS programs, multiple Windows programs, or both DOS *and* Windows programs at the same time. A PC with a 286 chip lets you open several Windows and DOS programs, but only one task can take place at a time. Other programs remain suspended in memory until you reactivate them.

This chapter first explains the principles that Windows follows in running programs and then shows you how to run as many programs as possible, as efficiently as possible.

Making the Right Hardware Choices

Before you spend a lot of time trying to run several programs, it's a good idea to take stock of your system so that you can plan the best strategy for getting the most from it. There's no point in trying to push your system to run several programs if it will only get so bogged down that you can't use it effectively. Whenever you put a second program into memory, you slow down the entire system somewhat. If your system is well-suited to running multiple programs, you'll hardly notice the performance degradation; otherwise, it will slow down to the point where it's virtually unusable.

The next few pages will give you an idea of what you can accomplish; if your system doesn't have the requisite hardware, you'll be better off adding RAM before trying to use several programs at once.

Two hardware items place limitations on the ability of your system to run more than one Windows program: the processor and the amount of RAM.

■ The processor's limit is absolute; you can improve it only by buying a new system or making a very expensive upgrade.

■ RAM, on the other hand, can be added easily and at relatively low cost. Adding 2Mb to a system can cost less than $100 if your system has open sockets for memory chips; if you need to buy a memory board, it might cost as much as $200. (Prices fluctuate, but these estimates are based on average RAM prices since 1989.)

If your system has 1–2Mb of RAM, you'll probably be inclined to add more RAM after you try to run more than one program. Four megabytes is a practical amount of RAM if you're going to run several programs.

Two Modes: Standard and 386 Enhanced

To make the best use of the processor, Windows has two modes: Standard and 386 Enhanced. (In the previous version of Windows, there were three modes, one of which, the Real mode, was eliminated in version 3.1.)

Standard Mode

If you use a 286-based PC, you have no choice but to run your system in Standard mode. The number of programs you'll be able to use depends solely on how much RAM is in your system.

The Windows manuals tell you that Standard mode uses *extended memory,* or memory above the 640k that limited DOS and earlier processors. Extended memory is really a phrase of the past, referring to the way the first IBM PC ATs used memory above 640k for a RAM disk because there was no software that could make better use of it. In effect, Standard mode pools all of the memory in your PC.

Standard mode can use all of your PC's memory to run programs, because when you load Windows it switches the Intel 80286 processor from the mode that your PC runs when it boots up (known as Real mode) to 286 protected mode. When you double-click on the DOS icon or start a DOS program from Windows, the processor switches back to Real mode and you are once again limited to 640k for DOS programs; when you leave DOS and return to Windows, the processor changes modes, and once again you have access to the protected mode's larger memory space for running multiple Windows programs.

When you run a DOS program in Standard mode, Windows gets out of the way, turning over control of the PC to the DOS program and leaving only enough code in memory to let you switch back to Windows when you're done or to capture data on screen to the Windows Clipboard.

386 Enhanced Mode

If you use a PC based on a 386DX, 386SX, 386SL, 486DX, or 486SX processor, you can run Windows in either Standard or 386 Enhanced mode. (From here on, we'll refer to a machine that has any of these processors as a 386 PC.) If you have 2Mb of RAM or less, Windows automatically runs in Standard mode, but you can force it into 386 Enhanced mode by typing **WIN /3** when you load it. If you have more than 2Mb of RAM, Windows automatically runs in 386 Enhanced mode, but you can force it into Standard mode by typing **WIN /S** when you load it.

In 386 Enhanced mode, Windows takes advantage of several features of 386-compatible processors not available in 286 processors. Most important, the processor can manage memory better; it lets Windows move bits of code around, putting them on the hard disk when necessary or breaking up the greater amount of memory into blocks that it juggles so it can fit more data into memory.

To run DOS programs in 386 Enhanced mode, Windows switches the processor into a special mode called *8086 protected mode*, which lets each DOS program have its own protected memory space. It can do this several times, so you can run several DOS programs. And it can give them a *virtual address space,* which means that each program acts as though it is using the first 640k of memory, even though it may be running in memory that's much higher. Without the ability to create virtual address space, Windows wouldn't be able to make DOS programs run in a window or to run several DOS programs at once.

As a result, 386 Enhanced mode can do much more with DOS programs than Standard mode. It can run them in Windows, run several of them at once, let them use expanded memory, and keep them running while other programs are active.

When a DOS program is running at the same time as other tasks, it's said to be running in the *background;* the tasks that are visible on screen are said to be in the *foreground.* In Standard mode you can put a DOS program into the background, but the background task is suspended; no processing takes place until you switch the program back to the foreground. But in 386 Enhanced mode, the processing can continue in the background.

While any 386 PC is capable of using its processor in the 386 Enhanced mode, you need more than 2Mb to make practical use of it; after all, the point of 386 Enhanced mode is to juggle pieces of memory. If you're not sure which mode you're using, you can find out by running the About command (shown in Figure 10.1) on the Help menu in Program Manager, File Manager, or any of the Windows accessories.

Figure 10.1

You can find out which Windows mode you're using—Standard or 386 Enhanced—by using the About command in Program Manager.

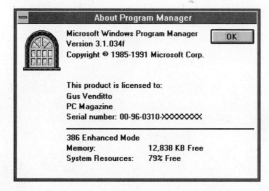

How Windows Uses RAM

Both Standard mode and 386 Enhanced mode give all of the RAM in the system to Windows applications as you start them. As long as there's plenty of RAM, Windows programs place their program code and data in RAM, and the system works quickly and efficiently. Things get more complicated when you run DOS programs and when you try to put more program code or data into RAM than your system can accommodate.

How RAM Is Used to Run DOS Programs

Each mode manages DOS programs differently. DOS programs were written as though they could use up to 640k of memory, but Windows tries to limit the DOS programs to what they need, in order to make more memory available to other programs.

In Standard mode, Windows gets out of the way, turning over the lower part of the PC's memory (the first 640k) to the DOS session, leaving only a small amount of code in memory. (It uses the file WINOLDAP.MOD for this function.) DOS programs run fine in Standard mode, with three exceptions:

- They run slightly slower than without Windows.

- You can't put them in a window, so they're completely isolated from Windows programs.

- You can't access expanded memory unless you install another memory manager, such as Quarterdeck's QEMM.

Because Standard mode has to turn over the system to the DOS program and switch to a different processor mode, virtually all of the code used by Windows (including any open Windows programs) is *swapped to disk*—stored temporarily on your hard disk—when you switch to a DOS session. When you switch back to the Windows session, the entire DOS session is stored on a disk file and the Windows session is *swapped from disk*—transferred from your hard disk into RAM. Because of this lengthy process, switching between DOS and Windows programs can be painfully slow in Standard mode.

In 386 Enhanced mode, Windows is very much in charge while DOS programs are active. It moves data around in memory, expanding and contracting the amount of memory allocated to DOS programs and adeptly sharing RAM between DOS and Windows programs. 386 Enhanced mode swaps data to disk only when it's about to run out of RAM.

Disk swapping is valuable in a pinch, since it can help you with a chore that wouldn't have been possible within DOS's 640k limit. But you don't want to be doing this all the time—it's slow. In fact, accessing RAM is literally a million times faster than accessing a hard disk.

Another drawback to disk swapping is that if you turn off your system without closing Windows, your hard disk will be cluttered with the very large files that Windows uses for swapping, with names like ~WA0000.TMP. Delete them, but only when Windows is not running. Most systems store these temporary files in a directory called \WINDOWS\TEMP; others use a directory specified by the SET TEMP= statement in the AUTOEXEC.BAT file. The SET TEMP= statement may already have been established on your system by a program that updated the AUTOEXEC.BAT file during installation.

In running multiple programs, make the use of RAM your first priority. You should have a general idea of how much RAM the programs are using and how much is free. The following sections will help you plan, based on the amount of memory in your system.

A 286 or 386 PC with 1Mb of RAM

You have limited options for running several programs efficiently. Windows begins swapping programs to disk if you run new programs beyond three or four Accessories (such as Notepad, Cardfile, and Recorder) or other relatively small Windows programs. You barely have enough memory to run a single large Windows program like Lotus 1-2-3 for Windows or Word for Windows before swapping begins. And if you attempt to run a second Windows program (even a tiny one) with a large program in memory, you'll be constantly waiting for Windows to exchange data with the swap file as you try to get your work done.

A 286 PC with 2Mb of RAM

You can run several Windows programs in Standard mode. You'll still have to wait as Windows swaps to disk when you run a DOS program, but you can run a large Windows program and a couple of smaller ones without disk swapping. You should put a high priority on closing programs when you're finished using them.

A 286 PC with More than 2Mb of RAM

You'll be able to run several DOS sessions and several Windows programs at a good speed, since disk swapping begins only after you have four or five programs active. All of the DOS sessions will run full screen, and none of the programs will be able to process in the background, but other than that, you have most of the functions of a 386 PC.

You may find that Windows is a valuable task-switcher, letting you run several DOS sessions and switch between them—if you're willing to wait for the disk swapping that takes place each time you switch between DOS and Windows. If you do run a large number of DOS programs, pay special attention to the settings in each program information file, or *PIF*, so that your DOS programs don't have conflicts using expanded memory, serial ports, and the keyboard. PIFs contain instructions that Windows uses when you run a

DOS program. PIF settings are established automatically, but they can be customized. Later in this chapter, in "Creating and Editing PIFs," these settings are explained in detail.

A 386 PC with 1-2Mb of RAM

While you can run in 386 Enhanced mode with a 386-compatible and less than 2Mb of RAM, you're much better off with Standard mode, since applications will run faster. Use 386 Enhanced mode only when you absolutely must run a DOS program in a window or run DOS programs in the background.

A 386 PC with More than 2Mb of RAM

This is the optimal system. You can run several Windows programs and several DOS programs, and you can process in the background while working in the foreground.

You'll still want to be stingy with your RAM, however, since it's so easy to become accustomed to starting many programs that you can run out of RAM quickly. You'll also find that your system's performance slows down, because DOS starts swapping to disk when you begin to use up RAM.

The old saying, "You can never be too rich or too thin," has been updated for Windows users: "You can never have enough RAM." Once you start enjoying task-swapping with many programs, you may find you'll want to have as much as 8Mb of RAM. And as you experiment with some of the new technologies planned for Windows (they're discussed in Chapter 15), it's not hard to imagine a day when you'll want 12–16Mb of RAM in your 386 PC.

Use the Task List to Stay Organized

After you start using more than one program, you have to devote some attention to keeping your bearings. The best way to know what's going on in your system is to check the Task List by pressing Ctrl-Esc. Here you'll see every program in memory—both DOS and Windows programs.

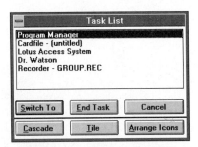

The Task List helps you manage memory. This is especially valuable because, with Windows, it is easy to load the same program twice or find yourself running a program that you finished using hours ago.

The Task List also lets you arrange Windows programs into a tiled or cascaded display, the only way you can quickly get an overview of everything going on in your Windows session. The Tile and Cascade commands don't arrange Windows as neatly as the Tile and Cascade commands in Program Manager, File Manager, and other Windows programs. Those programs deal with uniform document windows, while the Task List works with application windows more diverse in design. Furthermore, not all Windows programs use the entire display, and full-screen DOS sessions cannot be put into a window (although Task List does make sure they're visible as icons).

Figure 10.2 shows the effect of using the Task List's Tile command with the following programs loaded: Cardfile, Recorder, Notepad, Dr. Watson, a windowed DOS prompt, and Lotus 1-2-3 in a full-screen DOS session that was minimized and is represented by an icon only.

Figure 10.2

The Task List's Tile command arranged every active program in this display so that at least a part of it is visible. The Tile command makes room at the bottom of the display to show icons for minimized programs and for full-screen, inactive DOS sessions.

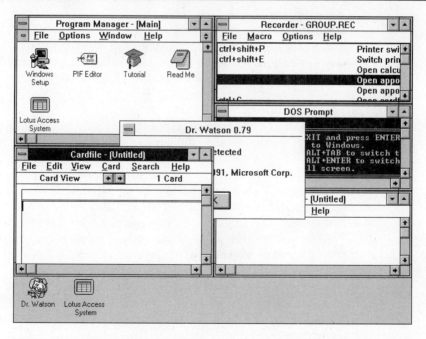

The Task List lets you close a Windows program with the End Task command. Don't be afraid to use this button because you're concerned about losing data; if there's an open data file, you will be prompted to save it before the program closes. You cannot, however, close a DOS application with the Task List; you must switch to that application and close it using its own command.

Keep an Eye on Free Memory

Just as you probably keep a close eye on the gas gauge in your car, you should get in the habit of checking available memory when you run a number of programs. You can find out the amount of free memory in your system by using the About command (see Figure 10.1) on the Help menu in Program Manager, File Manager, Notepad, and the other Windows Accessories. (The same dialog box shows you the mode you're running.)

You'll see that there's more free memory available than you have installed in your system. For example, on a 386 PC with 4Mb of RAM, Windows commonly reports that 14Mb (displayed as 14,000k) are free. That's because Windows includes the amount of memory it provides when it swaps memory to disk after you start running out of real RAM.

Don't be fooled into thinking that Windows has plenty of RAM just because the About box shows a large amount. Remember that you want to avoid disk swapping, using it only on the rare occasions when you have a very large data file. Your system is running out of RAM when it works slower or when the hard-disk light blinks on and off frequently during simple tasks that shouldn't require reading or writing a file on disk.

System Resources

It's possible that Windows will refuse to run a program and post an Out of Memory error message even though you have plenty of free memory. If this happens, you've exhausted your *system resources,* a fixed part of memory that Windows sets aside in its internal structure (the place programmers call the local heap for the Graphical Device Interface, or GDI, and User areas). Each screen item (window, dialog box, icon, and so on) requires a percentage of the system resources to be displayed on your screen.

You can keep track of system resources by noting the percentage in the System Resources indicator, just below the Memory indicator in any About box (see Figure 10.1). When Windows starts, the Systems Resources indicator is about 85%. Each new window or icon that you add to the screen consumes system resources. Most of the Windows Accessories consume about 2% each, but for some applications it can be far more. Write, for example, requires about 6%. And large applications like Microsoft Word for Windows can consume 15-20%.

It's up to a software publishing company to make sure that its applications don't take too much of this space. Still, it's common for new programs to grab too much system resources and then to scale back in revisions; even the Accessories and program items in Windows 3.0 used far more of the system resources than they do in version 3.1. If you find that you've run out of memory because system resources are low, you'll probably find that you're running an application that's hogging resources by using 30% or more. Ask the vendors if there's a newer version of the program, and they'll probably fix the problem by modifying the program.

Be concerned only when you have less than 40% available. To free up system resources, close open programs. As a general guideline, you can save the greatest amount of system resources by closing the programs with the largest number of commands.

Since system resources use a fixed part of Windows memory, reducing the percentage you use won't help overall performance. Your first concern should be to avoid using so much of the available pool that you can't run a new program when you need to.

A Strategy for Avoiding Disk Swapping

You can use the Memory indicator in the About box to help you plan your activity so that you minimize disk swapping. Start by using the Memory indicator to learn how much RAM each of your programs uses on an average day. Get accustomed to checking free RAM as soon as you start Windows. Write that number down, and then check it again every time you load a program. After you've loaded the programs you use most often, check available memory and write down the number. Now subtract that amount from the amount displayed when you first started Windows. That's how much memory you're using.

Finally, add about 500k to account for the amount of RAM that Windows itself needs, and subtract this total from the amount of RAM you know is installed in your system to find out how much RAM is actually free. Now you have an idea of how many more programs and data files you can open before you start to slow down your system with disk swapping.

For a good level of performance, your goal should be to leave several hundred kilobytes of memory free after all the programs you need to do your work are loaded. For the best possible performance, you'll want about 512k free so that Windows can use disk caching. (Disk caching is explained in Chapter 14 as part of a strategy for getting maximum performance.)

For example, if you have 2Mb of RAM, and you learn that the three applications you perform every day use a total of 1Mb, you'll be getting good performance from your system, since you'll have just enough room for Windows's overhead; you *won't* have enough RAM if you load any more programs into memory. The About dialog box will show that you have 5–10k of RAM available, but that includes the space available on disk for swapping, and you should avoid using all of the space if you can. You'll get a big performance improvement by adding more memory, since Windows will then be able to cache disk files into memory.

Running Several Windows Programs

There are several ways to run more than one Windows program. At least one program must be started by either double-clicking on its icon or using the Run command of the Program Manager's File menu. To start the next program, switch to Program Manager using one of the following techniques:

- **Task List**   Press Ctrl-Esc to open the Task List, which lists all programs that are running. Double-click on Program Manager. When Program Manager becomes the foreground task, start your second application. This is the technique I recommend, because the Task List helps you keep track of what's running, and it has tools to keep you organized, such as tiling active program windows.

- **Alt-Esc**   This key combination cycles through program windows and minimized icons, including Program Manager, in the order they were started. When you reach Program Manager, you can open the new program from there. This is probably the most common method I've seen people use. It seems quick, but I find it more time-consuming than using the Task List.

- **Alt-Tab**   This combination is similar to Alt-Esc in that it will cycle through the open programs, but instead of switching the entire display with each press of the keys, it pops up a little billboard that shows the name of program. When you find the program you want, release the Tab key; the desired window becomes active. To use this key combination, hold down Alt and then press the Tab key. With each press, you'll get a new choice. When you want to select a program, release both keys.

- **Alt-Spacebar**   This key combination opens the Control menu, which has a Switch To command. Switch To can be used to open the Task List.

- **Click on Program Manager**   This technique can be used only if some part of a Program Manager window is visible. When you click on any part of any program group window, Program Manager becomes the active window, and you can open a program.

■ **Double-Click on Program Manager's Icon**   This technique works well if
you minimize Program Manager using the Minimize on Use setting on
Program Manager's Option menu. If you don't see the icon because a window is obscuring the lower left corner of the screen, press Alt-Esc.

Running DOS Programs

The DOS Prompt icon that appears in the Main program group window is
the simplest way to run DOS programs: Double-click on it to start a DOS
session virtually identical to the PC session that opens when you boot without Windows.

You can also run DOS programs directly from Windows by creating
icons for them, bypassing the DOS prompt. The key to doing this is the program information file, or PIF, the data file that establishes settings for the
way a DOS program runs under Windows.

When you tell Windows to run a DOS program, one of the first things it
does is search the main Windows directory for a PIF with a file name that
matches the DOS program. For example, if you try to run 123.EXE, Windows looks for 123.PIF. If Windows doesn't find such a PIF, it runs 123.EXE
using the settings in the file _DEFAULT.PIF.

You need not create your own PIFs when you run popular programs like
Lotus 1-2-3, because Microsoft has made sure the default PIF will load them.
You will need to create PIFs if you want to customize the way your DOS programs run and to solve any problems requiring special attention. (Microsoft
programmers call programs with such problems "ill-behaved.") The following
sections will help you customize your DOS sessions to avoid such problems.

Program Information Files (PIFs)

PIFs (in spite of their unfortunate name) are powerful tools for controlling
the way a DOS program runs with Windows active. They tell Windows how
to interact with DOS programs. PIFs are less important if you're running in
Standard mode, because Windows turns over most of the PC's resources to
DOS programs; they have a major impact on DOS programs in 386
Enhanced mode, because Windows and DOS programs must share the PC's
hardware in that mode.

PIFs are not 100% effective. Since DOS programs were designed to use
all of the hardware, freely accessing memory and printer ports, DOS and
Windows programs can undermine each other when they're running at the
same time. When this happens, your system could freeze, or you could
receive a General Fault Protection message advising you to reboot your system because the integrity of an open program was violated.

Because there are thousands of DOS programs on the market that use a wide range of clever tricks, sometimes Windows simply can't run a particular program. If you encounter such a program, the company that sells it or Microsoft may have a solution, which they'll provide at a nominal fee. Less serious problems, such as a screen displaying garbled characters or a modem not working properly, can usually be fixed by adjusting the settings in a PIF, as you'll learn to do shortly.

Creating PIFs Automatically

The Windows Setup program can create PIF files for many of your DOS applications. If you selected the Set Up Applications option when you installed Windows, the installation program searched through every file on your hard disk and created a PIF in your main Windows directory for every DOS application that it found.

If you did not choose this option when you first installed Windows, you can do it at any time by running Setup. Double-click on the Setup icon (or type **SETUP** at the Run command of Program Manager's File menu). Then choose Set Up Applications from the Options menu.

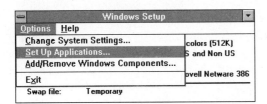

The dialog box that opens gives you the option of creating a PIF for every application or for just one application.

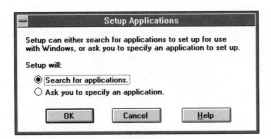

It's a good idea to have Windows create PIFs for you, because in addition to creating PIFs it creates new program item icons. If you didn't do this at the time of installation, do it now.

When you add new DOS applications to your system, you should open Setup and attempt to have Windows create a new PIF. It may not be able to do it, because Windows can only create PIFs for applications that it knows about. It will not have any information for new programs, and if you try to install one, it will tell you that it can't do it.

When you execute the Setup Applications command and select the Ask you to specify an application option in the Setup Applications dialog box, Setup opens the Setup Applications dialog box, which lets you browse through your hard disks looking for applications.

Using the drop-down list box in this dialog box, you can also choose the Program Manager group where the new icon will be stored.

After Windows has created both the PIF and the program icon, you may still need to customize them. Program Item Properties were explained in Chapter 2; the following sections will help you fine-tune your PIFs by editing them directly.

Creating and Editing PIFs

You create or edit a PIF with the PIF Editor, a program with two distinct faces: one for Standard mode and the other for 386 Enhanced mode. Standard mode uses one dialog box, and 386 Enhanced mode uses two dialog boxes. Figure 10.3 shows the Standard mode dialog box.

The procedure for creating a PIF has four steps.

1. Open PIF Editor either by double-clicking on its icon in the Main program group or entering **pifedit** at the Run command of the Program Manager's File menu.

2. Choose the mode—Standard or 386 Enhanced—from the Mode menu. If you always work in the same Windows mode, this step is not necessary.

3. Enter a value in each of the dialog box's fields. Make a selection for every field. You won't always need to change the default value, but it's a good idea to stop at each one to make certain the option is set correctly. You'll learn how to determine these values in the upcoming sections.

4. Save the file, using the Save command on the File menu. Give it a name that will remind you of the DOS program it controls. For example, use

WP or *WordPerf* for a WordPerfect PIF. (It's a good idea to use the program's file name for your PIF file name if you don't create a program item icon, because when Windows tries to execute a DOS program when no PIF is specified, it first searches for a PIF that matches the program's name in the Windows directory.)

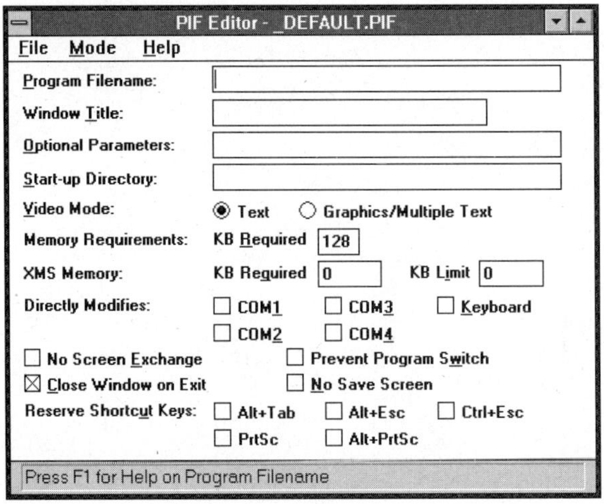

Figure 10.3

The PIF Editor dialog box appears when you run in Standard mode.

When editing an existing PIF, follow the procedures explained in the next section, with one difference. After you open the PIF Editor, open the PIF using the Open command of the File menu.

Working with the Two PIF Modes

Each PIF can have different settings for the different modes. When you run Windows in 386 Enhanced mode, the PIF runs the application using the settings for 386 Enhanced mode. If you then quit Windows and restart it in Standard mode, Windows uses the same PIF file, but with the settings for Standard mode.

In most cases, you'll want to use the same value for each setting in both modes, but if you have a distinct way of working in one or both modes, you'll probably have reason to use different values for the different PIF modes.

The following section will guide you through the PIF settings used by both modes. Then, there'll be three sections on the settings unique to one or the other mode:

Basic PIF Settings	Settings common to both Standard and 386 Enhanced modes
Standard PIF Settings	Settings for Standard mode, not including the basic (common) settings
386 Enhanced Settings	Settings in the first PIF dialog box in 386 Enhanced mode, not including the basic (common) settings
Advanced PIF Settings for 386 Enhanced Mode Only	Settings in the second PIF dialog box for 386 Enhanced mode

Basic PIF Settings

The following settings are common to PIFs in both Standard and 386 Enhanced modes. These shared settings appear in the Standard mode PIF Editor (see Figure 10.3) and in the 386 Enhanced PIF Editor discussed later, but the position varies somewhat between the two editors.

Program Filename This setting is the command you would normally enter at the DOS prompt to run the program, except that here you must also include the extension. If your DOS path includes the correct directory, you can enter just the file name and extension, but it's a good idea to enter the directory, too. For example, to create a PIF for WordPerfect on a system where the WP.EXE file, which starts the program, is in the directory C:\WP51, you'd enter C:\WP51\WP.EXE here.

Or, let's say that in the directory C:\BATFILES you have a batch file called WP.BAT that switches to a WordPerfect directory and then runs Word-Perfect. It works from the DOS command line in any directory, because your Path statement includes \BATFILES. You can enter **WP.BAT** in the PIF Editor's Program Filename text box. However, Microsoft recommends that you include the DOS directory where you store WP.BAT, in this case, **C:\BAT-FILES\WP.BAT**. Including the directory here ensures that Windows can find the program if your path changes.

Windows Title This setting is the name that appears underneath the application's icon when it has been minimized. If you're using 386 Enhanced mode, this name also appears in the title bar when the DOS program is running. (Since Standard mode cannot run a DOS application in a window, it uses the information only as the title of the minimized icon.) If you describe the PIF's program icon using the Program Manager's Properties command, that name appears in the title bar instead of the name entered here.

When the Windows Title text box is left blank, Windows inserts the name of the DOS program file without its extension (for WordPerfect, that would be WP).

Optional Parameters   These settings are needed by a few DOS programs to help them install correctly. Most programs don't use them, but if you enter a parameter when you load your DOS program, enter it here. If you want Windows to prompt you for the parameter to load, type a **?** here.

If you establish environment variables in your AUTOEXEC.BAT file with the SET command, you can insert them here; type them, enclosed by **%** (percent signs). DOS sessions inherit the environment in place before Windows was started, so you need to set DOS environment variables only if you want to use a DOS environment statement that's not in your AUTOEXEC.BAT file.

Start-up Directory   This setting establishes the default directory that the application uses once it's loaded. It's a good idea to enter the directory where your data files for this application are stored.

The Properties command in Program Manager also lets you establish the start-up directory for the program icon; if you enter different directories in the PIF Editor and in Program Manager Properties, the latter takes precedence.

Memory Requirements   This setting tells Windows how much free RAM must be available—KB Required—before it can load the application. If Windows does not find this much free RAM when it tries to run the DOS program, it displays an error message. You might want to set this amount a bit higher than the minimum needed as a way of sending yourself a warning when your system is running low in memory.

If you're having trouble running an essential DOS application, enter **-1** here. This tells Windows to give the application all available conventional memory.

In 386 Enhanced mode, you can set KB Desired (as well as KB Required), to establish the maximum amount of memory that this program will be allowed to use; the upper limit is 640k.

XMS Memory   This setting establishes the minimum (KB Required) and maximum (KB Limit) amount of XMS memory the program can use. XMS stands for *Extended Memory Specification* and was created by Microsoft to let everyone know how Windows would use memory above 1 megabyte. The Windows program HIMEM.SYS controls extended memory (according to XMS), making it possible for Windows to use all the memory on your PC. Very few other programs use XMS, so it will be rare that you'll need to establish a minimum setting.

DOS 5 uses XMS to install device drivers and small programs in extended memory; however, you do not need to allocate memory to these programs here. DOS 5 allocates memory on its own.

Reserve Shortcut Keys   This setting establishes certain keys for the exclusive use of this DOS program when it is active. Windows ignores the key combinations that are checked under this option and lets you use them to switch between the DOS program and Windows activities. This option prevents your DOS program from being undermined by Windows. Check one or more key combinations only if your DOS program uses them.

In Standard mode, any or all of the following keys can be disabled in Windows and reserved for the DOS program: Alt-Tab; Alt-Esc; Ctrl-Esc; PrtSc; and Alt-PrtSc. In addition, in 386 Enhanced mode two key combinations are used to open the Control menu (Alt-Space and Alt-Enter). Since Standard mode programs can't run in Windows, there's no need for the Control menu. Thus, in 386 Enhanced mode, any or all of the following keys can be disabled in Windows so that the DOS program can use them: Alt-Tab; Alt-Esc; Ctrl-Esc; PrtSc; Alt-PrtSc; Alt-Space; and Alt-Enter.

Close Window on Exit   This setting shuts down the program and frees up memory when you quit the DOS program. You'll probably prefer to have the window close on exit. If you leave this option blank, the DOS prompt usually appears and you'll need to type **EXIT** or use the Control menu to close the window.

Some DOS programs have difficulty if you don't select the Close Window on Exit option. They won't be able to display the DOS prompt, and you'll need to press a key before the Control menu can be opened.

PIF Settings for Standard Mode Only
The following settings appear only when the PIF Editor is running in Standard mode. (See Figure 10.3.) The settings common to Standard and 386 Enhanced modes were discussed in the previous section.

Video Mode   This setting helps Windows decide how much memory to allocate to the program. Since programs that run in graphics mode require more memory than programs that run in Text mode, you should select Graphics/-Multiple Text mode only if you know that the program uses graphics or uses more than one video page.

If the display goes blank when you're running this DOS program, it's possible you've set the Video mode incorrectly. DOS programs that use graphics mode may run out of memory and display a blank screen if you select Text mode.

Directly Modifies   This setting turns over control of the serial ports (COM1 through COM4) or the keyboard to the application. If you check boxes for any of these devices, the DOS program takes sole control of the device while it's running. A DOS communications program, for example, generally requires that you select the communications port where your modem is running.

Some programs, especially memory-resident DOS programs such as macro utilities, require complete use of the keyboard. If you check Keyboard in the PIF for such a program, you give it control of the keyboard and can return to Windows only by quitting the program.

No Screen Exchange   This setting disables Windows's ability to copy data from the DOS program screen to the Windows Clipboard. Selecting this option may save some memory.

Prevent Program Switch   This setting has the same result as disabling the shortcut keys, but it saves more memory. With this option checked, you can return to Windows only by quitting the DOS program.

No Save Screen   This setting is a way to free up memory by disabling one of Windows's safeguards. When No Save Screen is selected, Windows does not make a copy of the video memory for this DOS program. Instead, it relies on the DOS program to display memory on its own. Since most DOS programs can do this, you may be able to save some memory by turning this option on. Be aware, however, that many DOS programs behave erratically if their screens are not saved; parts of the screen may be blank after you switch to Windows.

PIF Settings for 386 Enhanced Mode Only

The following settings appear only when the PIF Editor is running in 386 Enhanced mode. (See Figure 10.4.) The settings common to Standard and 386 Enhanced modes were discussed in "Basic PIF Settings."

Video Memory   This setting helps Windows decide how much memory to allocate to the DOS program when it first loads. Text mode sets aside the least amount of memory (under 16k); Low Graphics mode sets aside enough to display CGA-resolution graphics (about 32k); High Graphics mode sets aside enough to display EGA and VGA graphics (about 128k).

If the program requires more memory after it is running, there will be no problem as long as there's still free RAM. The Video Memory setting establishes the minimum amount reserved for displaying the DOS program, but Windows in 386 Enhanced mode provides more, if it's available.

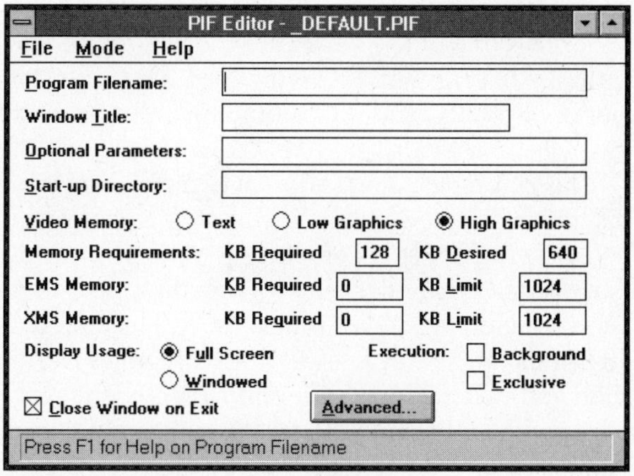

Figure 10.4

This dialog box appears when you run PIF Editor in 386 Enhanced mode. It is the first of two dialog boxes for this mode.

```
┌─────────────────────────────────────────────────────┐
│ ─        PIF Editor - _DEFAULT.PIF              ▼ ▲ │
├─────────────────────────────────────────────────────┤
│  File   Mode   Help                                  │
│                                                      │
│  Program Filename:    [                          ]   │
│  Window Title:        [                          ]   │
│  Optional Parameters: [                          ]   │
│  Start-up Directory:  [                          ]   │
│                                                      │
│  Video Memory:    ○ Text   ○ Low Graphics  ● High Graphics │
│  Memory Requirements:  KB Required [128]  KB Desired [640] │
│  EMS Memory:           KB Required [0]  KB Limit [1024]    │
│  XMS Memory:           KB Required [0]  KB Limit [1024]    │
│  Display Usage: ● Full Screen    Execution: ☐ Background │
│                 ○ Windowed                  ☐ Exclusive  │
│  ☒ Close Window on Exit    [ Advanced... ]           │
├─────────────────────────────────────────────────────┤
│  Press F1 for Help on Program Filename               │
└─────────────────────────────────────────────────────┘
```

EMS Memory   This setting works the same way as XMS Memory, setting the minimum and maximum amount of memory that this application can use as expanded memory (EMS). EMS refers to memory used according to the Lotus-Intel-Microsoft Expanded Memory Specification (LIM EMS). It's used by some programs to store data files. Lotus 1-2-3, for example, can open some large worksheets only when there is EMS memory available.

In most cases, KB Required should be set to zero, since EMS is rarely a requirement for a program. Unless you know that you'll use EMS memory, you should also set the KB Limit to zero, because some applications claim EMS memory even though they don't need it.

One way to determine the maximum amount of EMS memory you'll need is to find out the size of the largest file you'll use in that application; you'll always need fewer kilobytes of EMS than are in this file.

There's no penalty for setting a KB Limit, up to 1,024k.

Display Usage   This setting lets you choose between running the application in a window (which lets you view active Windows programs while the DOS program is running) or full screen (the way the application would appear when it's running under DOS).

The advantages of running a DOS application in a window are that you can view other programs simultaneously and copy data from the DOS window to the Windows Clipboard and share it with other programs. The advantages of running a DOS application full screen are that it will perform faster and use less memory. DOS applications always perform slower in a window than at full screen.

You'll probably find that you like to run DOS programs both ways, and you may want to save two PIFs for a single DOS program—differing only in the Display Usage setting. If you do create two PIFs, be sure to create a separate program icon for each PIF.

Display Usage is one of the few PIF settings that you can change while you're using the DOS program. To do so, open the Control menu (press Alt-Spacebar), choose Settings, and select either Window or Full Screen.

Execution   This setting lets you choose whether your DOS application runs when it's not the active window. If you do not choose an Execution option, your DOS program stops processing when you switch to a different program. That doesn't mean that the program disappears from memory, only that it remains dormant: Whatever is displayed on screen remains displayed. A spreadsheet in the middle of a recalculation taking several minutes would be halted when you switched to a different window. The recalculation would resume when you made the spreadsheet the active window or displayed it full screen again.

Choose the Background setting to let the program continue running after you switch to a different program. Running a DOS program in the background uses a percentage of the processor's time determined by the setting in the Control Panel's 386 Enhanced module (see Chapter 9).

Choose the Exclusive option to let this program take priority over every other program, suspending even those programs that are set up for background processing. The only activities that will continue are Windows housekeeping chores. You'll get the most benefit from this option if you run the DOS program full screen, because if you run it in a window, you'll increase Windows's work while this program is running.

You'll get the most out of the Background and Exclusive options by coordinating them with the settings in the 386 Enhanced module of Control Panel (see Chapter 9) and the Multitasking Options settings in the Advanced Options dialog box of the PIF Editor.

Advanced PIF Settings for 386 Enhanced Mode Only

The following settings are found in the Advanced Options dialog box, which opens when you select the Advanced command button at the bottom of the PIF Editor in 386 Enhanced mode (see Figure 10.5). These options give you additional control over multitasking, memory, display, and other aspects of your system.

Multitasking Options   This setting establishes the way the processor's time is divided when you have chosen one of the options under Execution on the first PIF Editor dialog box.

Background Priority establishes the amount of processor time devoted to a task if Background is selected under Execution on the PIF Editor. The value entered here affects performance only when the program is running in the background. Foreground Priority establishes the amount of processor time devoted to a task while other tasks are at work in the background.

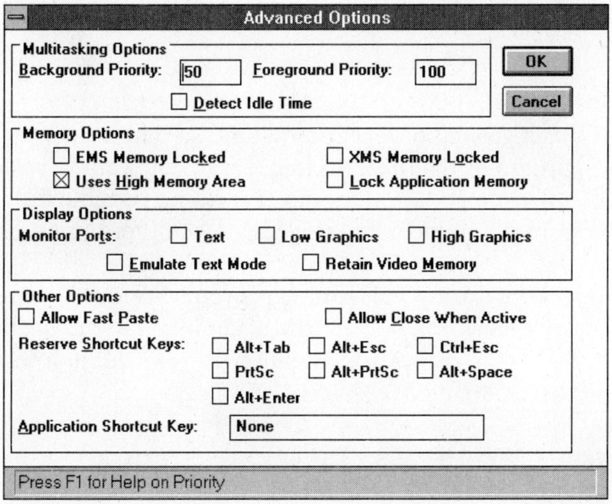

Figure 10.5

The Advanced Options dialog box opens when you click on the Advanced command button in the PIF Editor in 386 Enhanced mode.

The number you enter in either box can range from 0 to 1,000, with a default of 50 for Background and 100 for Foreground. These numbers do not measure anything concrete, like seconds. They establish a ratio among all the tasks active at any one time, according to a complex formula that you probably don't need to learn.

As a general rule: Make only large changes to the priorities (500 instead of 50), and make changes only when you want a particular program to run faster. For example, let's say you run a DOS communications program in the background, but it takes far too long to download files. You should give it a Background Priority of 500 only if your other PIF files use a relatively low Background and Foreground.

Remember that the processor can't be pushed to work faster; other programs run slower when a single program gets a higher priority. Be selective in changing Background and Foreground priorities. If you start increasing every program's priorities, you'll cancel out the effect.

In most cases you'll prefer a lower Background than Foreground priority, but there's no reason why it has to be that way. If you do not do much processing with the Foreground program (a word processor, for example) and the Background task requires a great deal of processing (a database, for example), you should give the Background task a priority higher than that of the Foreground task.

If you're still interested in the formula, here's how it works: Windows totals the Background Priorities of every program running in the background. Then it adds the Foreground Priority for the program running in the foreground. Each program gets a slice of this total depending on its percentage of the total priorities, and is assigned that percentage of the processor's time.

Detect Idle Time   This setting tells Windows to detect when nothing is happening in a background or foreground task, so that it can give more processor time to programs that need it. In general, you want to select this option. Turn it off only when you want to do everything possible to speed up this particular DOS program, including slowing down other programs.

EMS Memory Locked   This setting prevents Windows from swapping EMS memory to disk. If you lock EMS memory, this application uses data in EMS memory as fast as possible but interferes with Windows's effort to maximize RAM by swapping data to disk.

XMS Memory Locked   This setting prevents Windows from swapping XMS memory to disk. If you lock XMS memory, this application uses data in XMS memory as fast as possible but interferes with Windows's effort to maximize RAM by swapping data to disk.

Uses High Memory Area   This setting enables the DOS program to use the high memory area (HMA), the first 64k of extended memory above 1024k. Selecting this option neither requires that the DOS program use HMA nor prevents other programs from using it. It merely makes the memory available to the program. The only reason to switch this option off is if you are running another DOS program that must use HMA but is prevented from doing so by this DOS program. Very few programs require HMA, but some memory management programs do use it to free memory in DOS's 640k area.

Lock Application Memory   This setting prevents Windows from swapping this program's conventional memory to disk. If you lock the application memory, this application uses its data as fast as possible but interferes with Windows's effort to maximize RAM by swapping data to disk.

Monitor Ports   This setting helps Windows deal with DOS programs that control the video ports directly instead of using the system's ROM BIOS commands. When you select one of the three options—Text, Low Graphics, and High Graphics—you're telling Windows to devote processing time to the information the DOS program is sending to the video adapter in these modes. (Most IBM display adapters have more than a dozen video modes, and each of these options represents several modes.)

The only reason to change one of these options is if the DOS program's screen is not correctly displayed after you've switched away from it and returned. Text mode represents displays in normal text modes; Low Graphics represents low-resolution, CGA-quality graphics modes; High Graphics represents high-resolution EGA-or-better graphics modes. If the DOS program's display is missing information in any part of the display, you should turn the Monitor Ports option on for this mode. (If the DOS program's display is completely blank, you are more likely to fix the problem by setting the Video Memory option on the first dialog box for 386 Enhanced mode to High Graphics.)

Emulate Text Mode This setting tells Windows to use its built-in code for emulating the system's ROM BIOS when displaying text. Since most DOS programs use the ROM BIOS for video, selecting this option helps the program run faster, and this is the default. Deselect this option only if your DOS program's display is garbled (if, for example, your cursor disappears or appears in the wrong place).

Allow Fast Paste This setting helps Windows deal with programs that don't properly accept data pasted from the Clipboard. Most DOS programs don't have this problem. Turn this option on only if the DOS program loses information copied from the Clipboard.

Allow Close When Active This setting lets you live dangerously. Normally, if you try to close a DOS program from the Task List or to quit Windows while a DOS program is open, Windows will prevent it, advising you to switch to the DOS program and close it using a DOS command. Switching to the DOS program helps to ensure that you don't lose data by closing a program without saving your files.

If you select Allow Close When Active, Windows does not stop you when you try to close an active DOS program; it closes the DOS program even if there's an open data file. You may want to choose this option for programs that don't use data files.

Application Shortcut Key This setting lets you establish a key combination that, when pressed, switches a DOS program to the foreground. You should use the same shortcut key here that you used in the Program Manager as a shortcut key for a program icon. (You can see the program icon's shortcut key by selecting Properties from Program Manager's File menu when the icon is highlighted.) The shortcut key you assign here does not load the application; the Program Manager's icon shortcut key does that. It only works when the program is already loaded and running in the background.

The key combination must start with either Alt or Ctrl, it must be two or three characters long, and it cannot include Tab, Esc, Enter, Tab, Spacebar, PrtSc, or Backspace. If you use three keys, the second must be either Alt, Ctrl, or Shift. Examples of valid shortcut keys include Ctrl-A, Ctrl-Shift-F1, and Alt-5. If you use a shortcut key here that's used by Program Manager to launch a program, the Program Manager shortcut takes priority.

Creating an Icon for a PIF File

After you create a new PIF file, you'll want to create a new program item icon for it. To do so, use the New command from the File menu in the Program Manager, as explained in Chapter 2, under "Adding a Program Item." (If you use the Setup program to create your PIF, a program icon is created automatically.)

With the Program Item Properties dialog box open, enter the name of the PIF in the Command Line text box. In most cases, you can enter the PIF name without using the PIF extension; for example, if you saved the PIF as WP.PIF, you can enter **WP**. The PIF Editor stores PIF files in the main Windows directory, and since that directory is part of the Windows environment path, you don't need to tell Program Manager where to find them. And because Windows accepts any file name with the extension PIF (or COM, EXE, or BAT) as an executable program, you need only enter the first part of the PIF file name.

Switching between DOS Programs and Windows Programs

The Task List is the best tool for managing programs in memory. I've seen many people get confused trying to run several programs because they couldn't bring an inactive program to the foreground, but as soon as I showed them the Task List, the confusion vanished. The following sections show you how to use the Task List and other techniques to improve your control over the programs you run under Windows.

Cycling through Open Programs: Alt-Esc

You'll often want to switch between programs more quickly than the Task List allows. The Alt-Esc key combination does that very well. If it doesn't bring you to the right program, press it again and again until you highlight the icon, the window, or the full-screen DOS session that you want. This is called cycling through open programs.

Cycling through programs makes each program in memory active, one at a time, each time you press Alt-Esc. Minimized programs that are obscured by a window are highlighted and moved to the foreground; windows hidden behind larger windows are also moved to the foreground. Not all windows will be highlighted, though; you can only cycle through application windows. A document window is considered part of an application window, and even if many document windows are open in one application, all are treated as a part of the one application window.

Alt-Esc cycles through applications in the order they were started. Although it does not cycle through full-screen DOS sessions, it does highlight their icons. You must double-click on an icon to return to the DOS session when you're cycling.

If all open programs are in RAM, Alt-Esc works very quickly. But if any have been swapped to disk, you'll have to wait for the swapping to take place. This happens in Standard mode whenever you call a DOS session.

Cycling through Message Boards: Alt-Tab

When you have more than two programs open, the fastest way to switch is with the Alt-Tab key combination. You hold down the Alt key and then press Tab; each time you press Tab, a message board will pop up displaying the name and program icon for one of the programs in memory.

When you see the program you want, release Alt; that program will become active.

Changing Settings of DOS Programs in 386 Mode

When you're running a DOS program in 386 Enhanced mode, the PIF settings establish whether a DOS program starts in a window or full screen and determine the multitasking options (Background or Exclusive, as well as Background and Foreground priority). You can change these settings on the fly using the Control menu for the DOS session. Even if the DOS session is full screen, you can press Alt-Spacebar to open the Control menu. Select the Settings command to open a dialog box (see Figure 10.6) whose title matches the name of your program item icon. Change the settings here. (An even quicker way to switch a DOS program between a window and full screen is to press Alt-Enter.)

By choosing Exclusive under Tasking Options, you suspend other applications at work in the background while this program is active. By choosing Background, you allow this application to continue running after you switch to another window. If you do choose Background, you can also change the application's multitasking priority. The priorities follow the rules explained earlier in this chapter in "PIF Settings for 386 Enhanced Mode Only."

Figure 10.6
When DOS programs are running, you can use the Control menu (Alt-Spacebar) to call up a dialog box that controls settings. The title of this dialog box has the same name as the program icon. In this case Editor is the name of a word processor's program icon.

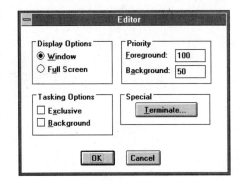

Switching Quickly from a Window to Full Screen

DOS programs are more responsive when they run full screen but you'll often want to run them in a window, especially when you want to keep an eye on a different program.

The quickest way to switch between a window and full screen for an active DOS program is with Alt-Enter. This is the same key combination that allows you to edit the properties of an icon when you're running Program Manager; with a DOS program active, it changes just one property.

Alt-Enter works very quickly, and you may want to use it to put your DOS program in a window for just a second, and use it again to return to the original display.

Closing Programs

Whenever you've saved your data and are ready to move on, it's best to get into the habit of closing the program. In real life, however, you're rarely certain that you've completely finished a task. So the next best habit is to use the Task List to switch to a program and then close it.

Use Alt-F4 as a shortcut key for closing Windows programs, and pressing these keys repeatedly is the fastest way to close several programs. You can also use the End Task command on the Task List to close Windows programs.

You must always close DOS programs using their own internal commands, but you may end up at the DOS prompt. Type **EXIT** to close the DOS session, return to Windows, and free up memory. (If you prefer to have the DOS session close the window when you quit a particular DOS program, select Close Window on Exit in the PIF Editor for this program's PIF.)

When the DOS session won't allow you to do that—if the display is frozen, for example—you can try to close it from the Control menu by selecting Close. If that fails, you have at least one more choice. In Standard mode, use the Terminate command on the Control Menu. If you're running in 386 Enhanced mode, you have two choices: the Terminate command or the Ctrl-Alt-Del key combination.

The Terminate command will attempt to shut the current DOS program and will probably result in the loss of any unsaved data. However, it may not fix the problem that caused the DOS program to freeze; it's possible that some of the information in RAM that another program needs has been corrupted. Close all other Windows programs and exit Windows—before you run into another problem.

In 386 Enhanced mode, press Ctrl-Alt-Del any time a DOS program freezes. This key combination reboots the PC when you're in DOS, but under Windows in 386 mode, it closes only the DOS session. You can then continue to work in Windows and even return to the DOS program (although you may want to use PIF Editor to adjust the DOS program's settings before you do so).

It's better to use Terminate or Ctrl-Alt-Del than to turn off the system's power, because you'll still want to store any open data files in other Windows programs, and you'll want to give Windows a chance to clear the swap file it was using.

Responding to Freeze-Ups

The problem that caused your DOS display to freeze up should be solved before your system freezes up again. When you next run Windows, open the Dr. Watson diagnostic program by typing **DRWATSON** at the Run command of Program Manager's File menu. Then try to re-create the situation that caused your display to freeze up. If the diagnostic program is able to detect the problem, it will pop up.

Speeding Up Sluggish DOS Programs

Every DOS program is slightly different, and you may need to tinker with PIF settings to get all of your programs working just right. However, you can use the following table as a general guide when you find that large programs using lots of system resources are running too slowly:

Full Screen	Checked
Exclusive	Checked
Display Options/Video Memory	High Graphics
Retain Video Memory	Checked

Making DOS Program Icons Stand Out

After creating a PIF for a DOS program, you still must create the icon using the Program Manager's File New command. You see a choice of icons when you select the Change Icons command button from the File New command's dialog box. And you can change the icon at any time by using the File menu's Properties command.

It's a good idea to try to vary your selection of icons so that they're more recognizable.

The default selection of icons is stored in a file called PROGMAN.EXE. To see more icons, change the file name in the Change Icons dialog box to MORICONS.DLL.

Customizing PIFs for a Large Group

When the Setup program adds a PIF to your system, it reads the settings from the file APPS.INF in the SYSTEM directory below your main Windows directory (usually the directory called \WINDOWS\SYSTEM). You can read, print, or edit this file with Notepad or any word processor. In fact, if you want to share new PIF settings with others, you can create new PIF defaults by changing the settings for listed applications or adding statements for new DOS programs. Then you can distribute the edited file to others. Figure 10.7 shows a typical APPS.INF displayed in Notepad.

You can make simple changes to APPS.INF like including your company or department name in a Window title. At the other end of the scale, you can customize multitasking settings to the way your company uses applications, sparing your coworkers the laborious job of deciphering the complex formula Windows uses in dividing processor time.

If you copy the new version of APPS.INF to the \WINDOWS\SYSTEM directory of other users, your settings will override Microsoft's and create the PIFs when users run Setup. The following section will help you decipher the APPS.INF file.

The Default PIF Settings Stored in APPS.INF

The APPS.INF file is a series of data statements that Setup uses to create PIFs. Setup reads the statements here, and if it finds a match for a file name on your hard disk, it uses the cryptic information here to create the new PIF.

Lines beginning with a semicolon (;) are remarks to help you understand the file. You can freely edit them if you're going to exchange the file with others. Lines following [pif] are the settings for each application. The name of the application appears first, then an equal sign, then the name of the PIF. For example,

```
ACAD.EXE = ACAD
```

means "if a file named ACAD.EXE is found, create a PIF named ACAD-.PIF." This is where you'd provide the name of a new DOS program.

Figure 10.7

Setup reads the APPS.INF file to identify the settings it uses when it creates PIFs. You can edit the file to control the way Setup creates new PIFs.

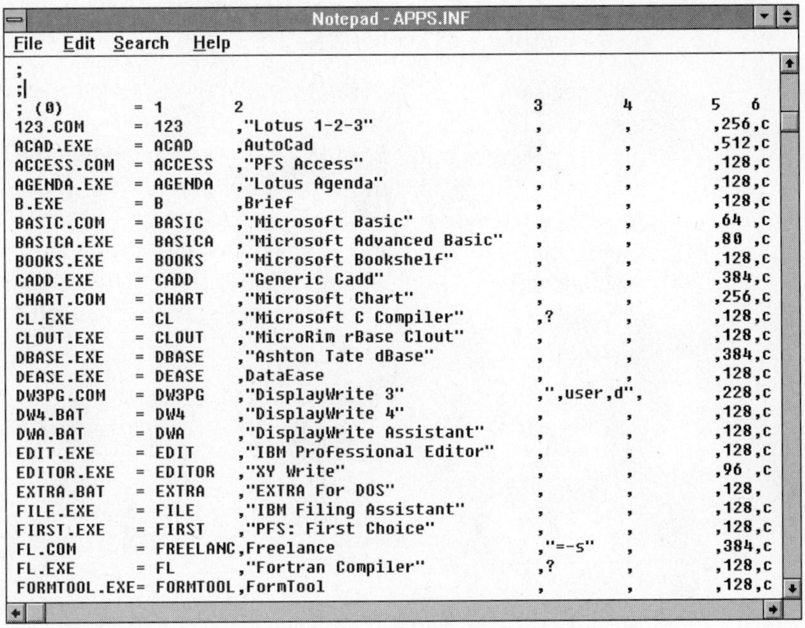

```
┌──────────────────────── Notepad - APPS.INF ──────────────────── ▼ ▲ ┐
│  File   Edit   Search   Help                                        ▲ │
│ ;                                                                     │
│ ;|                                                                    │
│ ; (0)      = 1         2                        3       4      5   6  │
│ 123.COM    = 123       ,"Lotus 1-2-3"           ,       ,      ,256,c │
│ ACAD.EXE   = ACAD      ,AutoCad                 ,       ,      ,512,c │
│ ACCESS.COM = ACCESS    ,"PFS Access"            ,       ,      ,128,c │
│ AGENDA.EXE = AGENDA    ,"Lotus Agenda"          ,       ,      ,128,c │
│ B.EXE      = B         ,Brief                   ,       ,      ,128,c │
│ BASIC.COM  = BASIC     ,"Microsoft Basic"       ,       ,      ,64 ,c │
│ BASICA.EXE = BASICA    ,"Microsoft Advanced Basic" ,    ,      ,80 ,c │
│ BOOKS.EXE  = BOOKS     ,"Microsoft Bookshelf"   ,       ,      ,128,c │
│ CADD.EXE   = CADD      ,"Generic Cadd"          ,       ,      ,384,c │
│ CHART.COM  = CHART     ,"Microsoft Chart"       ,       ,      ,256,c │
│ CL.EXE     = CL        ,"Microsoft C Compiler"  ,?      ,      ,128,c │
│ CLOUT.EXE  = CLOUT     ,"MicroRim rBase Clout"  ,       ,      ,128,c │
│ DBASE.EXE  = DBASE     ,"Ashton Tate dBase"     ,       ,      ,384,c │
│ DEASE.EXE  = DEASE     ,DataEase                ,       ,      ,128,c │
│ DW3PG.COM  = DW3PG     ,"DisplayWrite 3"        ,",user,d",    ,228,c │
│ DW4.BAT    = DW4       ,"DisplayWrite 4"        ,       ,      ,128,c │
│ DWA.BAT    = DWA       ,"DisplayWrite Assistant" ,      ,      ,128,c │
│ EDIT.EXE   = EDIT      ,"IBM Professional Editor" ,     ,      ,128,c │
│ EDITOR.EXE = EDITOR    ,"XY Write"              ,       ,      ,96 ,c │
│ EXTRA.BAT  = EXTRA     ,"EXTRA For DOS"         ,       ,      ,128, │
│ FILE.EXE   = FILE      ,"IBM Filing Assistant"  ,       ,      ,128,c │
│ FIRST.EXE  = FIRST     ,"PFS: First Choice"     ,       ,      ,128,c │
│ FL.COM     = FREELANC,Freelance                 ,"=-5"  ,      ,384,c │
│ FL.EXE     = FL        ,"Fortran Compiler"      ,?      ,      ,128,c │
│ FORMTOOL.EXE= FORMTOOL,FormTool                 ,       ,      ,128,c ▼│
│ ◄ ►                                                              ►  │
└──────────────────────────────────────────────────────────────────────┘
```

A series of data statements separated by commas supplies the following information, in this order:

■ Window title.

■ Start-up directory.

■ Close window on exit: *CWE* indicates the window is closed; a blank indicates the window is to remain open.

■ Icon file: If blank, use zero for the first icon; the PROGMAN.EXE file contains the icons to use.

■ Icon number: This number selects the icon from the icon file. If you're using Windows's default icon file, you can determine the icon number by opening the Program Manager's Properties command and browsing through the icons. For example, you'll find the DOS Prompt icon is number one, the word processing icon is number two, and the spreadsheet icon is number three.

- 286-specific settings: This section is filled with a code that refers to a section that appears later in the APPS.INF file as either [g286], [c286], or [gc286], depending on which of three classes a program falls into: a graphics program that doesn't modify the COM ports (g286); a text-mode program that does modify the COM ports (c286); or a graphics program that does modify the COM ports (gc286).

- 386-specific settings: This refers to one of the sections that appears later in the APPS.INF file as either [np386], [b386], or [npb386]. These sections put the program into one of three types, depending on whether it should not run in the background and cannot manage fast paste (np386), should run in the background and can manage fast paste (b386), or should run in the background but cannot manage fast paste (npb386). You can read through these sections and get a pretty good idea of how the program establishes the values for each of these more advanced settings.

PIF Editor's Menus: A Complete List

File
New
Open. . .
Save
Save As. . .
Exit

Mode
Standard
386 Enhanced

Help
Contents
Search for Help On . . .
Standard Options
386 Enhanced Options
Advanced Options
How to Use Help
About PIF Editor. . .

11

Sharing Data among Programs

The Clipboard

OLE: Object Linking and Embedding

Dynamic Data Exchange

THERE ARE THREE SYSTEMS FOR SHARING DATA AMONG WINDOWS programs: the Clipboard; Object Linking and Embedding (OLE); and Dynamic Data Exchange (DDE). Cutting and pasting with the Clipboard has been mentioned in many places throughout the book. In Chapter 5, for example, "Exchanging Data with Clipboard" showed how to transfer text from Notepad to Write. In this chapter, I'll explain in greater detail all the techniques and tricks you'll need to transfer data using the Clipboard. Then I'll explain the two other systems—OLE and DDE—which greatly increase the power of the concept underlying the Clipboard.

The Clipboard

The Clipboard acts like an unseen messenger who carries just one message at a time. First you give data to the messenger by copying it from a file. Then the data is available for "pasting," or inserting, into the same file or a different one whenever you want, until you send a new message.

A Clipboard utility lets you view the current content of the Clipboard before you insert it into a new location. To eliminate any confusion, I'll refer to this program as the Clipboard Viewer, even though its icon in the Main program group is labeled Clipboard.

The Basic Cut and Paste Operation

The Edit menu in most Windows programs uses the services provided by the Clipboard message system. The procedure for using it has four steps.

1. Highlight the data you want to transfer.

2. Select either Cut or Copy from the program's Edit menu.

3. Move your cursor to the place in the same file or a different one where you want to insert the data.

4. Select Paste. The data highlighted in step 1 is inserted.

Figure 11.1 shows how the process works.

Cut, Copy, and Paste

The Cut and Copy commands transfer highlighted data from Windows programs to the Clipboard for use elsewhere.

- When you use **Cut**, the highlighted data is *removed* from the original program and placed on the Clipboard.

- When you use **Copy**, the highlighted data *remains* in the original program *and* is placed on the Clipboard.

Figure 11.1

These four screens illustrate the four-step cut-and-paste operation in a Write document. In the top screen, text is highlighted. In the second screen, Cut is selected. In the third screen, the cursor is moved to a new location in the file, and Paste is selected. In the last screen, the block of data appears in the new location.

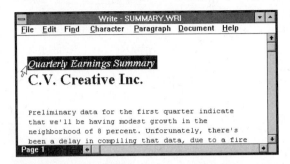

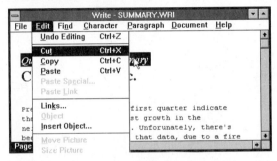

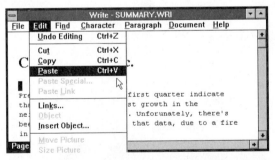

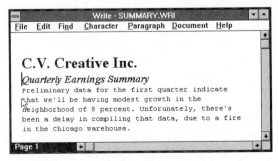

■ When you use **Paste**, a copy of the data on the Clipboard is inserted into the currently active program at the cursor. The data remains on the Clipboard until you cut or copy something else.

Another Way to Copy

The Copy command can be less than satisfying—nothing seems to happen. When you copy something, the data is silently, invisibly copied to the Clipboard, and there's no way of knowing whether you did it correctly. No dialog box opens, and the highlighted data remains unchanged.

Of course, you'll know that the Copy command worked correctly when you use Paste to insert the data into a new spot. Being human, you may not want to wait that long, especially when you're trying this technique for the first few times.

One way of seeing immediate results is to cut instead of copy. Since you can use the Paste command to insert the same data as often as you want, you can paste the data in its original location as soon as you've cut it. Then, move to the new location and paste again.

Clearly, this involves an extra step. But if you're not familiar with copying and pasting, it's a good way to start. Be sure to experiment first with non-essential data. After you've mastered the cutting and pasting, you'll gradually feel more comfortable with copying and pasting.

Clipboard Shortcut Keys

Throughout the book, I've discouraged you from memorizing all of Windows's shortcut keys, since there are so many of them. But Cut, Copy, and Paste are shortcut keys worth remembering.

One of the changes made to Windows 3.1 may make that task easier, since a second group of shortcut keys was added. Both the original and new commands work in most programs, although some programs use different shortcut keys. Table 11.1 shows both sets.

These are only general guidelines, though. Many older Windows programs do not use the new shortcut keys, but you can expect to see them added to future releases. For the time being, programs that use the new shortcut keys should also work with the original keys.

It takes most people some time to become familiar with the differences among the Cut, Copy, and Paste commands. For that reason, it's a good idea to select them from the Edit menu until you're familiar with them and only then, gradually, to begin to use their shortcut keys.

Table 11.1   **Clipboard Shortcut Keys**

Edit Menu Command	Original Shortcut	New Shortcut	Effect
Cut	Shift-Del	Ctrl-X	Moves data to Clipboard
Copy	Ctrl-Ins	Ctrl-C	Copies data to Clipboard
Paste	Shift-Ins	Ctrl-V	Copies data from Clipboard

Exchanging Data with DOS Programs

The Clipboard works with DOS programs, with some limitations, depending on the type of data and on whether you are running in Standard mode or 386 Enhanced mode.

Copying and Pasting in Standard Mode

You cannot copy parts of a screen from a DOS program when you are running in Standard mode. Instead, you must copy the entire screen to the Clipboard and paste that screen into a Windows program. Even this works only when the DOS screen is displaying text; you cannot capture screens from a DOS program displayed in *graphics* mode. Similarly, you cannot paste graphics into a DOS program while you're running in Standard mode.

To copy the entire screen of a DOS program to the Clipboard, press the PrintScreen key. (On some PCs you must use Alt-PrintScreen or Shift-Print-Screen.) After the screen is captured, switch to a Windows program and select Paste. All of the text displayed in the DOS program appears, including the menu commands. For example, Figure 11.2 shows the result of pressing PrintScreen when a Lotus 1-2-3 for DOS spreadsheet is displayed in Standard mode: The menu commands and auxiliary data, like the row and column headings, are captured along with the actual data. To trim the image, you need to edit it after you've pasted it into a Windows program.

Sometimes you must format the text captured from a DOS program using the Display menu in the Clipboard Viewer. That's because Windows uses the special OEM font when displaying DOS text; once the data is captured in Windows, standard Windows fonts are used. If you want to adjust the text so that it matches the DOS display, you may need to select OEM Text on the Clipboard's Display menu. In Figure 11.2, this command was used to make the columns align correctly; without the command, the numbers would not align in neat columns.

Figure 11.2

The Clipboard displays data captured from a spreadsheet created in Lotus 1-2-3 for DOS running in Standard mode.

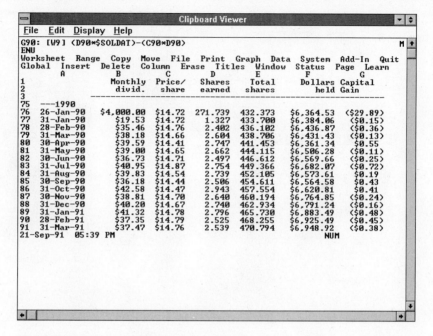

If you have problems capturing a screen, check the PIF settings for the DOS program. Make sure that you have *not* selected No Screen Exchange or checked PrintScreen in the Reserve Shortcut Keys section (the check boxes should be empty).

Copying and Pasting in 386 Enhanced Mode

When a DOS program is running in 386 Enhanced mode, you can capture either the entire screen (in text or graphics mode) or a part of it that you define with a click-and-drag operation. The Control menu for a DOS program (the dash in the upper left corner, which you open by pressing Alt-Spacebar) has an Edit command, which in turn gives you four commands for copying to and pasting from the Clipboard (see Figure 11.3).

The Mark command is used when you want to define a block of data without using the mouse. Here's how you use it:

1. With a DOS application displayed in a window, press Alt-Spacebar to open the Control menu, select Edit, and select Mark. The menus close, and a highlight cursor appears in the upper left corner of the DOS application's window.

Figure 11.3

When running DOS applications in 386 Enhanced mode, you can copy a specific block of text to the Clipboard.

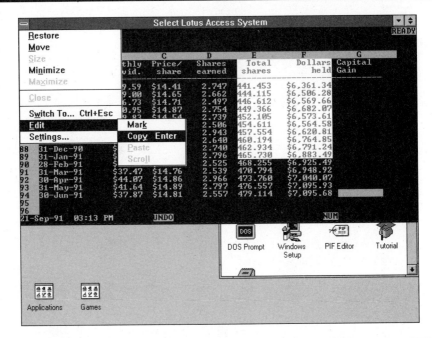

2. Hold down the Shift key while you use the Arrow keys to define the block you want to copy.

3. When you've defined the block, press Alt-Spacebar to open the Control menu, select Edit, and select Copy. The block of text is copied to the Clipboard.

These steps work whether the DOS program is displayed full screen or in a window.

The Copy command is used if you're selecting the block with the mouse. To use it, first highlight the block of text with a click-and-drag operation, then open the Control menu, select Edit, and select Copy. After you've highlighted the block, you can use the Copy shortcut key (either Ctrl-C or Ctrl-Ins) instead of the Copy command.

The Paste command is used to copy data from the Clipboard into the DOS window. You can use it to transfer text you've captured from a Windows program, from another DOS program, or from the window you're using.

The Clipboard Viewer

The Clipboard Viewer runs when you double-click on the Clipboard icon in the Main program group window. You can also run it by typing **clipbrd** at the Run command of Program Manager's File menu.

The Clipboard Viewer has two principal purposes. The first is to let you see the data that's been captured. This can be helpful when you're having problems keeping track of what you copied or cut. Because the Copy command gives you no confirmation that data was copied to the Clipboard, you may want to open the Clipboard Viewer to see whether you've really captured a block of data.

The second purpose is to change captured data from one format to another. For example, when you cut or copy text, you can use the Display menu to display it either as normal Windows text or in OEM font, which is provided to help ensure compatibility with DOS programs. Since DOS programs usually display characters using a font in the video board instead of using DOS, Windows often has problems making an accurate translation of the text. To fix inaccurate translations, you can switch the displayed font from Text to OEM. Switching to OEM is useful when working with tabular material, such as rows and columns from a spreadsheet.

You are not able to edit the Clipboard contents; you must do that either before or after the data is transferred.

Saving the Contents of Clipboard

You can save the data displayed in the Clipboard by using the Save As command on the Clipboard Viewer's File menu. The contents of the Clipboard are saved with the extension of .CLP. As we've already seen, the Clipboard can hold just one block of data at a time, so you'd want to save the current content of Clipboard if you plan to paste it again but must first copy different data onto the Clipboard.

When you use the Open command of the File menu to display an old block of data that was saved from Clipboard, Clipboard clears the current contents but warns you first, to give you a chance to save the current contents to a file.

OLE: Object Linking and Embedding

Windows 3.1 adds a new dimension to the way you share data between programs: Object Linking and Embedding (OLE). By linking programs OLE offers a more efficient way of sharing data than that used by the Clipboard, which merely transfers data. When files are *linked,* changes you make in the original data using the program in which it was created are reflected wherever the linked data has been inserted. When data is *embedded,* the data becomes part of the file into which it is pasted, but you can edit it by running the program that created it.

Not all Windows programs take advantage of OLE, and only four of the programs that come with Windows—Write, Cardfile, Sound Recorder, and Paintbrush—do so.

The following sections explain how to use OLE linking and embedding. Before we do that, it's necessary to introduce some concepts.

OLE Clients, Servers, and Objects

The concepts central to an understanding of OLE are *server application* and *client application*. An OLE server application is a program you use to create data. For example, Paintbrush is an OLE server application because you use it to create a graphic image. An OLE client application is a program in which you insert data created elsewhere. For example, Cardfile is an OLE client application because you can use it to display a graphic image created in Paintbrush. Some programs can be either a server or a client (Lotus Ami Pro, for example), but others can only perform one of these roles.

An OLE *object* is the block of data that is highlighted in a server application and used by a client, either as an embedded object or as a linked object. An object is the data you would normally copy onto the Clipboard. When the program is capable of linking and embedding, the copied data takes on additional features.

To use embedding and linking, you paste an object from an OLE server application into an OLE client application.

One way to tell whether a program is an OLE client is to look at its Edit menu, which will have the commands Links, Object, and Insert Object. Server applications don't have any telltale signs within the program, but they will be listed in the "embedding" section of the WIN.INI file.

Embedding Objects

Embedding is a natural extension of the cut-and-paste concept: With both, you transfer data from one program to another. The difference is that, after the embedded object is pasted into the client application, you can use the server program to edit the data. When you double-click on the data, the server program opens with the object already loaded. After you finish editing it, you don't save the file normally; instead, you choose Update in the server application and then return to the client program.

Say you want to embed an illustration in a word processed document. You could, for example, use Paintbrush to create a map showing clients how to find your office and embed it into a Write form letter inviting them to see you. Since you would need to change the map depending on each client's location, you'd want to embed the map. Using this method, you'll keep the original for use in Paintbrush and make customized versions for each client in Write documents.

To embed data, you use either the Paste or Paste Special command from the client application. When the originating program is an OLE server and the receiving program is an OLE client, the data is treated as an embedded object, instead of as an ordinary piece of data. An embedded object is ordinarily stored in the file where you pasted it. It is stored as a separate file by the originating program only if you explicitly save the file in that program, too.

Here's a step-by-step example of how you'd create and use an embedded object. In this example, we'll create a map in Paintbrush and embed it in a Write document. Then, we'll update the embedded map.

1. Open Paintbrush, and create the map.

2. Use the Pick tool to select an area of the map that will fit in the letter, and select Copy from the Edit menu. You should highlight an area as in Figure 11.4.

Figure 11.4

An embedded object is similar to any file or object, only you must use an OLE server application to create it.

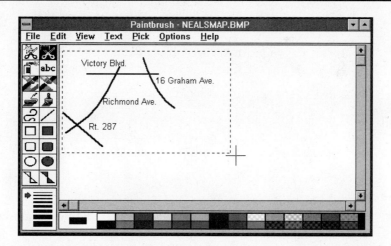

3. Save the file, and close Paintbrush.

4. Open Write, create a letter, and move the cursor to the spot where you want the map to appear.

5. Select Paste Special from the Edit menu. The Paste dialog box opens. Don't change the default for File Type, Paintbrush Picture. Click on the Paste command button. The map is inserted into the letter, as in Figure 11.5.

Figure 11.5

To insert an embedded object into an OLE client application, you paste data from an OLE server application. This Write document has an embedded Paintbrush drawing.

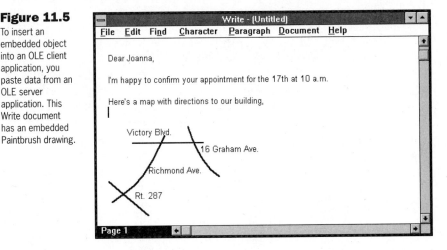

6. In Write, move the I-beam pointer to the map area to highlight it.

7. Open the Edit menu, with Paintbrush Picture Object as an option.

8. Select Paintbrush Picture Object. Paintbrush opens with the map already loaded. Edit the map using Paintbrush tools.

9. Select Update from the Paintbrush File menu.

10. Select Exit and Return to Write from the File menu. The Paintbrush window closes, and the Write window becomes active. Note that the map has been changed to reflect the changes you made in Paintbrush.

11. Save the Write file.

The letter is saved with the embedded object. The next time you open the letter, the map will appear and you'll be able to edit it in Paintbrush by double-clicking on it.

You might notice that the size of the Write file increases substantially when you embed an object, since the graphic information is being stored in this file. Save the file as a Paintbrush drawing separately only if you plan to use it in other programs; otherwise you should avoid using disk space for duplicates of the graphic image.

It's worth noting how the Edit menu in Write changes after a file is embedded (see Figure 11.6). The dimmed Object command becomes an active Paintbrush Picture Object command when the cursor highlights the map; this indicates that you can edit the object in Paintbrush. As soon as you

move the cursor to a different part of the drawing, the menu item changes
back to the dimmed Object command.

Figure 11.6

When the cursor
rests on an
embedded object,
the Edit menu
changes so that
you can activate
the OLE server
application.

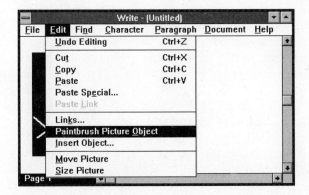

Pasting without Embedding

You may want to insert data from a server application into a client application without embedding. The copied object becomes a *static object,* since it
can't be changed after it is pasted. A static object uses less disk space than an
embedded object, so it's a good idea to make an object static if you are certain it will not be edited after it is pasted.

To make an object static, you copy and paste as if you were embedding it,
but when the Paste Special dialog box opens, you change the default so that it
does not specify the server application. In the example just completed, you
would change the default from Paintbrush Picture to either Bitmap or Picture.
In applications from which you are copying text rather than graphics, you'd
choose text instead of the name of the word processor that created the link.

Linking Objects

Like embedding, linking is an extension of Clipboard's copy-and-paste technique. With linking, when the object is inserted into an OLE client application, it doesn't become part of the new file. The linked object does appear in
the display of the file and will print with it, but the data resides in a file
stored by the OLE server application.

Linking has a significant advantage over embedding: It always presents
the latest version of a linked object. It's very useful if you want to share a file
among several programs or documents, since you can make many enhancements to the original object in the server, and you will always get the most

recent version of the object in the clients. You also use less disk space, because only one copy of the object is stored on disk.

Linking is especially useful if your data changes frequently. You can freely insert it into any document created with a program that supports object-linking, confident that you'll always have the latest version of the data when you use that document.

One disadvantage of linking is that you must keep track of your linked objects when you share files with other people. You'll need to make sure that anyone sharing one of your files has both the linked data file and the server application.

Creating and Updating Linked Objects

You create new links in the same way that you embed objects, with one difference. After you select the object in the OLE server application, you insert it into the OLE client application by choosing the Paste Special command and clicking on the Paste Link command button. Or, you can insert the link by clicking on the Paste Link command. Some programs offer both methods, and others offer only one.

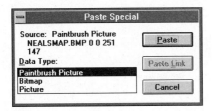

After the object is pasted into the OLE client document, you'll be able to edit the linked object by double-clicking, just as you would edit an embedded object.

Before you create a link, the original data must be stored in a file in the server application; otherwise, the link commands will not be available. As soon as the original data is saved and then placed in the Clipboard, you'll be able to create a link.

You can see a list of the linked objects in any file by selecting the Links command in the Edit menu (see Figure 11.7). You can also choose to have a link updated immediately. Normally, links are updated when a file is opened, but if you've made changes to the file since you last called it from disk, you'll want to click on the Update Now command button.

You may want to inhibit the automatic linking that Windows performs by default by selecting the Manual option button. From then on, you'll have to select the Update Now command to update the linked object in this file.

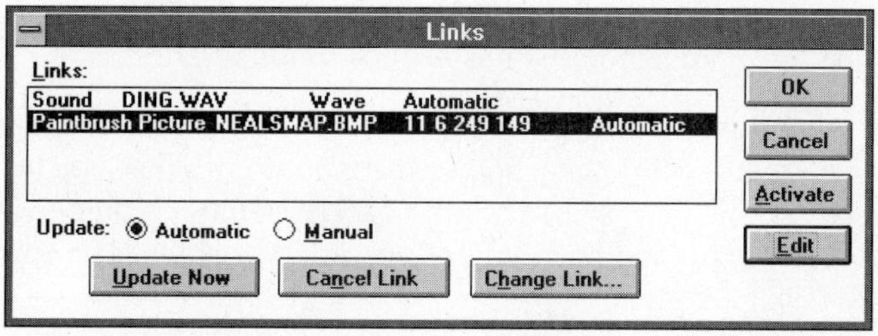

Figure 11.7
The Links dialog box lets you update or remove the link between the OLE server application and the OLE client application.

Links				
Links:				**OK**
Sound	DING.WAV	Wave	Automatic	**Cancel**
Paintbrush Picture	NEALSMAP.BMP	11 6 249 149	Automatic	**Activate**
				Edit

Update: ● Automatic ○ Manual

Update Now   **Cancel Link**   **Change Link...**

You would want to deactivate a link if you expected to continue working on the linked data in the server application before returning to the client; otherwise, the object would be constantly updated, slowing down your system. After you finished working on the linked object, you could reactivate the link.

The Change Links option in the Link dialog box lets you specify a new object when the data you want to access is not on the Clipboard. This command works a bit differently from one application to another. Some server applications let you simply change data files, while others require that you specify a location with the new data file. Sound Recorder, for example, will let you change a link by selecting a new file. On the other hand, when the link connects with a spreadsheet, you will probably be able to select a file and a range within that file.

OLE is a specification for how programs can behave, and you'll find that there are significant differences in the features that each program offers.

The Three Paste Commands

Programs that can be OLE clients have three Paste commands on their Edit menu: Paste, Paste Special, and Paste Link. Programs that have just one Paste command may be an OLE server or may have no OLE capabilities at all.

- **Paste** always inserts the data that is on the Windows Clipboard. If the data was cut or copied from an OLE server application and the program receiving the data is an OLE client, then the data is automatically embedded. Otherwise, the data is pasted like ordinary static data.

- **Paste Special** appears only in programs that are OLE clients. It lets you choose whether the object is static, embedded, or linked. When you choose Paste Special, a dialog box opens. If you want the data to be static, choose a data type that is not a program name. (For example, choose Bitmap instead of Paintbrush Picture Object.) If you want the object to be embedded, choose Paste but make sure the data type list includes the name of the server application you want to use. If you want the object to be linked, click on the Paste Link command button.

- **Paste Link** appears only in programs that are OLE clients. Choose this command when the Clipboard contains data that you want to link. It inserts the linked object immediately, without either giving you the choice between embedding and linking or letting you select a data format.

Paste Special and Paste Link are available only when data from an OLE server application is on the Clipboard; at other times, they're dimmed.

The Object Packager

The techniques for embedding and linking objects that we've explained are most useful when you're working with just two programs. The Object Packager is useful if you make extensive use of embedded or linked objects and wish to represent each object by an icon, to make it easier to paste it over and over again in as many OLE client applications as you want. An object (either linked or embedded) represented by an icon is a *package*, and the icon is called a *packaged icon*. When you paste data into the Object Packager program, you can edit the icon that will represent it.

You should become thoroughly familiar with the concepts of object linking and embedding before you attempt to use Object Packager.

You run Object Packager either by double-clicking on its icon in the Accessories program group window or by typing **PACKAGER** at the Run command of Program Manager's File menu.

Creating a Packaged Icon for an Entire File

The contents of a package can be an entire file or just the part of a file that you copy to the Clipboard. If you make a package out of an entire file, it cannot be linked, only embedded. When you make a package out of a portion of a document, it can be either linked or embedded.

Here are the steps you take to package a file. In this example, we'll create an icon for the Paintbrush map used in earlier examples.

1. Open Object Packager by typing **Packager** at the Run command of Program Manager's File menu.

2. Open the File menu, and select Import. A File Open dialog box appears.

3. Highlight a file created by an OLE server application. In this example, we'll choose a .BMP file. Click on OK. The Paintbrush icon appears in

the left Object Packager window, with the name of the file below. In the right Object Packager window the message

```
Copy of <file name>.BMP
```

appears, with <file name> replaced by the name of the file you've chosen. (See Figure 11.8.)

Figure 11.8
The Object Packager window has two displays. The left side shows an icon that represents the data, and the right side shows either the data or a description of it.

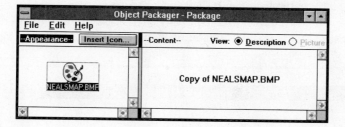

4. Open the File menu, and select Save Contents.

5. Enter a name for this file, and click on OK.

Creating a Package for a Portion of a File

When you create a package out of just a portion of a file, you use the same general techniques you'd use to transfer data to the Clipboard, except you paste the data into the Object Packager, where it is stored so that it can be used repeatedly.

Here are the steps:

1. Open Paintbrush, and use the Pick tool to highlight the portion of the drawing you want to use.

2. Select either Copy or Cut from the Edit menu.

3. Switch to the Program Manager, and open the Accessories program group window. Double-click on the Object Packager icon. The Object Packager window opens.

4. Select Paste from the Object Packager's Edit menu. The message

```
Copy of Paintbrush Picture
```

appears in the right window, and the Paintbrush icon appears in the left window.

5. Select Save Contents from the File menu, and name the package.

Inserting a Packaged Icon into a Document

Once you've created a packaged icon, you can repeatedly paste it into documents just as you would paste any kind of data. (This is the equivalent of highlighting a block of data before copying it to the Clipboard.) If you're going to use a packaged icon that you've already stored, use the Import command on Packager's File menu to make it active. You then choose Copy Package on the Edit menu. The packaged icon is transferred to the Clipboard. You can now insert the icon into any OLE client application. In Figure 11.9, a package that consists of a Paintbrush drawing is inserted into a Write letter.

Figure 11.9
This Write document includes a packaged icon, representing the map shown in Figure 11.5.

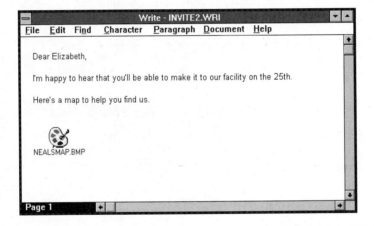

By inserting the packaged icon into the Write document, we've achieved the same result as we did earlier by embedding the Paintbrush file; the documents print the same, whether the object is packaged or embedded. One difference between "packaging" and embedding (or linking) an object is how it appears while you're working with it: With Object Packager you only see an icon. Another difference is that, because you can store a packaged icon, you can use it repeatedly without running the OLE server application, loading the file, and copying the data to the Clipboard.

Packaged Icon Options

You can change the text that appears below a packaged icon by selecting the Label command on Object Packager's Edit menu.

You can also add a command line to the packaged icon so that another program will run when you click on the icon. To do so, select the Command Line command on the Object Packager's Edit menu and fill in the Command text box as you would fill in the Run command in Program Manager.

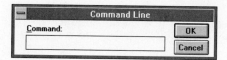

For example, if you entered **CALC.EXE** in the Command Line text box and pasted the packaged icon into a Write document, Calculator would run when you double-clicked on the packaged icon.

Finally, you can change the icon that identifies the package by double-clicking on the Change Icon command button to open the Insert Icon dialog box. You can choose a new icon by scrolling through the choices until you find one that you like.

Dynamic Data Exchange

Dynamic Data Exchange (DDE) lets files from two different programs communicate in both directions: Change the data in one program, and the linked data in the other program changes too.

Two programs that use DDE are Microsoft Excel and Lotus Ami Pro. (None of the programs that come with Windows, such as the Accessories, use DDE.) You could use DDE to create a spreadsheet in Excel that calculated prices for a product line. In Ami Pro, you could create a form letter that described the products. At the appropriate places, you'd establish a dynamic link between the two files, so that the form letter would always retrieve the latest prices from the spreadsheet. As a result, you would never have to retype the prices in the form letter and always be assured of using the most recent changes to your spreadsheet file.

There are several differences between using DDE and an OLE-linked object. DDE links two equal applications; there's no client-server relationship.

The method of updating is completely different as well. DDE is a fast and unobtrusive way for separate documents to share data; OLE is a way to help you edit one file using the services of another.

To use DDE, you have to be running two programs that use this form of communication. In addition, both programs have to be running at the same time. To use DDE you must have plenty of available memory.

Creating DDE Links

Creating a DDE link is like linking an object:

1. Open the document that has the data you want the other, DDE-compatible application to use.

2. Highlight the data.

3. Switch to the other application. If it's not running, start it. Open the document that you want to share the data.

4. Move the cursor to the place in the document where you want the linked data to appear.

5. Choose Paste Link from the Edit menu. The data will be inserted into this document while remaining in the original document.

Once the link is established, you can deactivate it. If you don't deactivate the link, every time you open a file that has a link, the other application must be run. Usually, links can be left inactive until you need to analyze the most recent version of the data or print a document with the most current data.

Clipboard Viewer's Menus: A Complete List

File
Open. . .
Save As. . .
Exit

Edit
Delete   Del

Display

Help
Contents
Search for Help On. . .
How to Use Help
About Clipboard Viewer. . .

Object Packager's Menus: A Complete List

File
New
Update
Import. . .
Save Contents. . .
Exit

Edit

Undo	Ctrl+Z
Cut	Ctrl+X
Copy	Ctrl+C
Delete	Del
Paste	Ctrl+V
Paste Link	
Copy Package	
Links. . .	
Label. . .	
Command Line. . .	
Object. . .	

Help

Contents
Search for Help On. . .
How to Use Help
About Object Packager. . .

12

Controlling the
Print Process

*Understanding How
Windows Prints*

Controlling Fonts

*Getting the Most
from Your Printer*

*Controlling Jobs
Sent to the Printer*

F OR SOME PEOPLE, PRINTING IN WINDOWS IS EASY. THE SETUP PROGRAM prepares Windows to communicate with their printer without any problem, and they merrily send print files in all of their applications without ever seeing the need to change a thing. If this describes you, you don't know how lucky you are. But if you're like most people, you'll want to improve the quality of your printer's output. You'll want to speed up print jobs. You'll want to make better use of fonts. And you'll occasionally find that the printed copy does not match your expectations. This chapter should help with all of these problems.

Understanding How Windows Prints

Windows's printing features are plagued by a paradox: Windows uses several different systems to make the best use of your printer and simplify printing, but sometimes what you print may not be what you expected, and printing can seem unnecessarily complicated. Usually, you're shielded from the different printing systems; Windows programs rarely ask you to choose between fonts, printers, or printing options. Instead, they use default settings. To get the best printed output from your system, you have to take the initiative and change those defaults.

Before you start tinkering with settings, you should understand the rules that govern them. Because there are literally thousands of different ways to set the print options to deal with the many printers on the market, it's not possible to give you a simple guide to setting up your own system. However, once you realize what's really going on between Windows and your printer, you should have no problem getting better results, whatever printer you use.

Differences between Printers

Printing can become complicated because there are many different kinds of printers. More than 100 new printers for PCs have been introduced annually for the past few years. While each new printer conforms to some established standard, each one also adds a new twist to the technology: more memory in the printer, new fonts, new paper trays, and innovations unheard of the previous year. Windows has to control all of these printers.

There is some common ground: Every printer understands at least one printer control language. Epson, Hewlett-Packard, and IBM are the leaders in maintaining these standards, and other companies' printers always make sure that each new printer meets one of these standards.

The intelligence for speaking to a printer in its language is contained in a file on your hard disk called a *printer driver*. The printer driver has default settings for options such as paper quality, letter trays, and font cartridges.

Windows comes with dozens of printer drivers, and many new printers include a disk with a Windows printer driver.

The dialog boxes called from the Control Panel's Printer module or the File menu's Printer Setup command display the options provided by the printer driver. If your printer has a feature that you cannot control from these dialog boxes, the driver is incomplete. Contact your printer's manufacturer to find out whether new drivers are available. (Updated printer drivers are usually sold by printer manufacturers at a nominal charge.)

Device Independence

One of Microsoft's loftiest goals for Windows programs is *device independence*: to give printing services to each Windows program, freeing it from communicating directly with the printer. Windows itself manages printing, and each Windows program turns the printing work over to Windows's print system.

There are several advantages to this centralized system:

- Each Windows program is smaller (both on disk and in memory) than it would be if it included the software to control the printer.

- Each Windows program prints the same way, using the same commands and dialog boxes, because there's just one driver telling Windows which options to use. And when you set printing options the way you want them, all of your Windows programs can share this setup.

- Each Windows program sends the file to be printed to the Windows Print Manager and makes itself available for working on new files that much sooner.

When you run a DOS program, Windows does not control the printer, although it can provide spooling for the DOS program's printing. Since the DOS program sends formatting commands to the printer, you must be sure you've set up your DOS program to work properly with your printer. You can't control that from Windows.

Choosing Printer Settings

When Windows is installed, the Setup program asks you to specify one or more printers. It copies the drivers of the printers you specify to the \WINDOWS\SYSTEM subdirectory and adds a statement to the WIN-.INI file telling Windows which printer drivers to use.

To add a new printer driver and attach a new printer to your system, call up the Printers dialog box by opening the Control Panel's Printer module (shown in Figure 12.1). Here, using the Setup command button, you can also change default options by choosing, for example, a legal-size paper tray or landscape orientation (printing the page sideways). (Printer options were covered at length in Chapter 9.)

Figure 12.1

You install printer drivers using the Printers dialog box, which you access by selecting the Printer module in Control Panel.

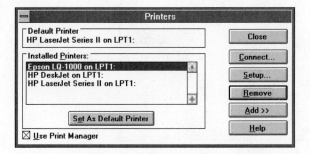

You can also change these options in most Windows programs that use printing (such as Write) by selecting the Printer Setup option on the File menu. When more than one printer is installed, the Print Setup dialog box that opens in most Windows programs gives you a choice between setting options for this printer (Default Printer) or switching to a second printer (Specific Printer), as shown in Figure 12.2. After confirming that you're selecting options for the correct printer, you can select options for: orientation (portrait or landscape), paper size, and paper source.

Figure 12.2

The Print Setup dialog box lets you set the most commonly changed options for the default printer and open a second dialog box to change other options.

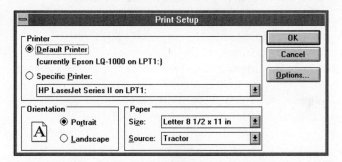

If you need to choose options that aren't covered in the dialog box, click on the Options command button. The dialog box that opens is unique for your printer, since it uses information in the printer driver file. Figures 12.3 and 12.4 show examples of two subtly different dialog boxes that might open when you choose the Printer Setup command from a File menu or the Setup command button from the Control Panel's Printer module, and then choose

Options. Some Windows programs—especially programs released before Windows 3.1—have more limited printer setup options.

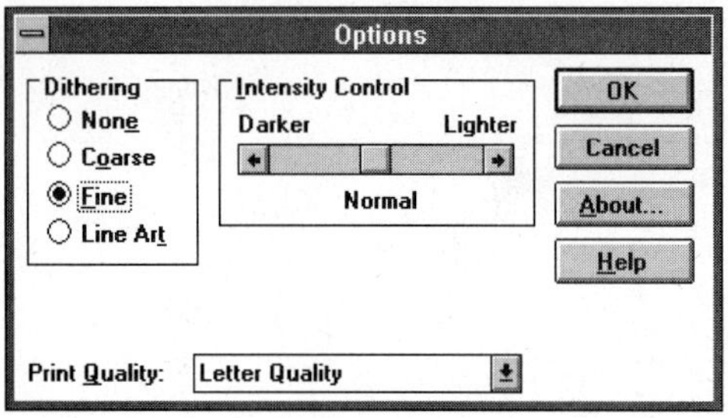

Figure 12.3

The Options dialog box that opens when an Epson LQ-1000 is installed.

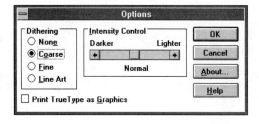

Figure 12.4

The Options dialog box that opens when an HP LaserJet II is installed.

When You Have More than One Printer

Windows makes it relatively easy to control several printers, whether or not they are attached directly to your PC. To add another printer, you open the Printers dialog box by selecting either the Printer module in Control Panel or the Printer Setup command in the Print Manager program. (See "Adding a Printer" in Chapter 9 for detailed instructions on using this dialog box.)

When several printers are installed, one is designated as the default printer, and all files will use that printer. Some Windows programs let you send files to a different printer by using the Print Setup dialog box (Figure 12.2).

Other programs don't have that option, so you must change the default printer, following these steps:

1. Open the Printers dialog box (Figure 12.1), an option available on many programs' File menu and on the Printer module in the Control Panel.

2. Highlight the new printer on the Installed Printers list.

3. Click on the Set as Default Printer command button. The name of the printer in the Default Printer box changes.

4. If you need to change a printer setting, click on the Setup command button to use that dialog box.

5. Click on the Close command button. The dialog box closes.

Now, all files sent to the printer will use the new printer. When you want to switch back to the original printer, repeat these steps, highlighting that printer in step 2.

Using Different Printer Settings for Different Files

The settings established at installation and controlled by the Control Panel's Printer module are the defaults used by all programs. However, by changing the Printer Setup options on the program's File menu, you can make different settings available for different files.

For example, let's say you print a leaflet in Write that includes a map created in Paintbrush. When you print the leaflet in Write, you want the best quality possible; when you print the map in Paintbrush, you just want to get a quick idea of what your graphic looks like. Therefore, you would want the Print Setup dialog box in Write to specify that your documents print at letter quality, which is the default, so you wouldn't have to change it. In Paintbrush you would specify draft quality in the Options dialog box before printing the file. These settings will be in effect the next time you use each of the files. New files will continue to use the default Printer Setup settings.

Controlling Fonts

Getting the most from your printer would be fairly simple if setting the options in the setup dialog boxes were the only consideration. However, there are also several systems for using fonts, and each system handles fonts differently depending on whether they're displayed on screen or printed.

Before discussing fonts, I should define font and typeface, terms dating from the invention of the printing press. Then I'll explain Windows's systems for managing digital fonts and typefaces.

Font Characteristics

A *typeface* is a family of characters of the same design. This book is printed in a typeface known as Times Ten Roman. A typeface can be thought of as a broad outline of how characters (both letters and numbers) appear on a page. A typeface in a specific size and style is called a *font*. The most common styles for fonts are regular (or Roman), bold, and italic. Sizes are measured in points; one inch is approximately 72 points. Thus a 12-point font consists of characters that are about ⅙ of an inch high, measured from the top of a capital to the baseline, the line on which characters rest.

The width of a character (also called its pitch) is determined by the design of the typeface, and you'd probably never specify it. Character width is very important in determining how many characters will fit on a line, and Windows uses it as a crucial measurement in displaying characters on screen.

Here are some examples of different fonts within the Times Ten typeface:

- This is Times Ten Roman, sometimes called regular or normal. Roman is the most commonly used font within a typeface family.

- **This is Times Ten Roman bold.** Characters are heavier, and the font is used for special emphasis in text, headings, and other places to which you want to draw attention.

- *This is Times Ten Roman italic.* Italics are delicate and fancy and are used for emphasis. Some typefaces create italics by slanting the characters to the right.

- ***This is Times Ten Roman Bold Italic.*** This font combines bold and italic, most often in a heading to emphasize a few words.

Typefaces on a PC are copyrighted; some of the most successful licensors of typefaces are CompuGraphic (CG), Linotype, Bitstream, and Adobe. So it's possible to have several versions of the same typeface, each of them licensed from a different source.

The Font Dialog Box

Most Windows applications use a Font dialog box similar to the one shown in Figure 12.5.

Figure 12.5

The Font dialog box lets you choose the font (really the typeface), the style, and the size of the characters that will be displayed. The Sample box shows four letters (in capitals and lower case) for the highlighted font.

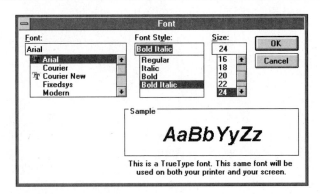

To choose a font, you would normally start from the left, choosing the typeface to which it belongs. (Note that Windows makes the common mistake of referring to a typeface family as a font in this dialog box. In earlier versions of Windows, fonts were the only option; Windows didn't have the flexibility to offer entire families of typefaces, so when you chose the style in which a character printed, you had only font choices. Microsoft has retained the old terminology to ease the transition from working with individual fonts to working with entire typeface families.)

Next to the font names are icons: TT or a printer. TT indicates that this is a TrueType font, and the printer is used for fonts stored in your printer's hardware. (The difference is explained in the next section.) After you've selected the font, choose the style and the size for that font. For each selection, the Sample box displays the characters *AaBbYyZz* in that font.

Note that Windows displays one of three messages below the Sample box. The message

```
This is a scale TrueType font which can be displayed on the
screen and printed on your printer
```

appears when you've selected a TrueType font, the built-in Windows fonts that appear the same on screen and when printed. If you selected the Show Only TrueType Fonts in Applications option in the Control Panel's Font module, this is the only message you'll see because you won't be able to display non-TrueType fonts.

The message

```
This is a bitmap or vector font
```

appears when you've selected a font that will not necessarily match the printed output. This message appears because you've chosen either a software font or a printer font that is not available in enough sizes for Windows to match the display and output. If it's a printer font, the printed output will be sharp even though the characters displayed may be fuzzy or may appear in the wrong size. If it's a software font, the appearance of characters, both on the screen and when printed, may be disappointing.

How Windows Generates Fonts

Over the years, Windows has come to support several systems for displaying and printing fonts. Windows originally offered few font choices. It has retained them for the sake of compatibility even as it has added better technologies. With version 3.1, Microsoft has added what it believes is the optimal font technology: TrueType.

The following sections discuss all the fonts that Windows can display (screen fonts) and print (printer fonts).

Screen Fonts

Windows uses several methods to display fonts on screen. Each method requires that a separate file with font information be stored in the \WINDOWS\SYSTEM subdirectory for each font to be displayed.

Bit-mapped Fonts   These fonts are the crudest. Characters are composed of graphic information that's a facsimile of the characters in every style and size. Each individual character is *bit mapped*, meaning that bits are used to map out the shape of the character. (It's as though each character had an individual PCX file.) When a character is displayed, Windows copies the bit map to screen. Bit-mapped fonts are sometimes called *raster* fonts, because rasterizing is the process of displaying or printing a bit map.

MS Sans Serif, MS Serif, Courier (in specific sizes only), and Symbol are the bit-mapped fonts that come with Windows. On systems with VGA graphics adapters, they're stored in the SSERIFE.FON, SSERIFF.FON, COURE.FON, and SYMBOLE.FON files, respectively. These files are named differently on systems with other graphics adapters; the system Windows uses to name the files is to append a letter to the description (SERIF, for example) according to the display adapter. The letters that Windows appends are A for CGA, B for EGA, C and D for printer fonts, E for VGA, and F for 8514.

System Fonts   These are provided for Windows to use in displaying dialog boxes and menus. They're bit-mapped fonts not available for printing or for use in most applications. There are three types of system fonts:

- A proportional font used in Windows 3.1 for menus

- A fixed-pitch font, which versions of Windows before 3.0 used for menus

- A terminal font (also called OEM font), which is provided only for compatibility with specific adapters' special character sets

The system fonts are installed in the SYSTEM.INI's [Boot] section, unlike other fonts, which are installed in the WIN.INI file's [Fonts] section. All of the system fonts are named to indicate the graphics adapter and the type of system font. For example, VGASYS.FON is the VGA proportional system font, VGAFIX.FON is the VGA fixed-pitch system font, and VGAOEM.FON is the VGA terminal font. Never delete these files from your hard disk, since Windows won't run without them.

Vector Fonts   These fonts are built from geometrical shapes—lines and curves—that can be scaled to different sizes. They take up less space on disk because there's much less information needed to define each character. They often look misshapen at small sizes but good at large sizes. Modern, Roman, and Script are the vector fonts that come with Windows. They're stored in the files, MODERN.FON, ROMAN.FON, and SCRIPT.FON.

TrueType Fonts   These fonts, new to Windows 3.1, were created to ensure that the printed page matches the display. They're similar to vector fonts in that Windows draws each character from mathematical information at the time the character is displayed, but TrueType uses a completely different technique than vector fonts. It does not build the characters out of lines and curves, but instead stores a description of each character's shape. This description can then be scaled to the correct size. Since TrueType fonts use the same information for displaying and printing, the screen and printed page match.

Arial, Courier, Times New Roman, Symbol and WingDings are the TrueType typefaces that come with Windows. Each is available in regular, bold, italic, and bold italic fonts, except Symbol and WingDings, which are available only in regular. They're stored in files whose names suggest the font. For example, there's ARIAL.FON for regular Arial; ARIALBD-.FON for bold; ARIALBI for bold italic; and ARIALI.FON for italic.

Printer Fonts

There are several ways of printing fonts on a printer. The most important consideration is your printer's internal options.

True Printer Fonts   These fonts are stored on the printer, either in a font cartridge (for laser printers), a font card (for advanced dot-matrix printers), or in the printer's ROM chips (all printers). Printer fonts often produce the best hard copy possible on your printer. The only way to know for sure which fonts are in your printer is to refer to the printer manual.

Unfortunately, Windows often does not display an accurate match for these fonts on screen. It uses one of its bit-mapped fonts for the display, attempting to find the font that matches the printed output; because it uses the width of the font as its criterion, the font may be completely wrong. In the next section this problem is explained in depth.

Soft Fonts   These fonts are sold on disk by companies like Bitstream and Adobe. You copy the font information into files on a hard disk, and when needed, the information is downloaded (sent) to the printer. These fonts require adequate memory in the printer and are usually used only with laser printers.

If you use a font manager such as Bitstream's FaceLift or Adobe Type Manager, the displayed font will match the printout. Otherwise, the two may differ.

TrueType Fonts   These fonts send the same information to the printer and to the screen, guaranteeing that the displayed and printed pages match. Windows comes with four TrueType families, and you can buy more.

They work in roughly the same way as soft fonts, except that they match the TrueType screen fonts and do not require that the printer have extra memory. TrueType also downloads each character to the printer at the time of printing, unlike soft fonts, which need to be downloaded to the printer before they can be used. For this reason, TrueType fonts often print faster than soft fonts.

How to Get Your Printed Page to Match Your Displayed Page

In trying to support all printers and a wide range of fonts, a Windows display can be misleading. Rather than limit Windows because some printers could not print some types of fonts, Microsoft gave Windows the flexibility to print fonts that can't be properly displayed.

When you don't use TrueType fonts, Windows finds the closest match for a specified font. Problems develop when none of your screen fonts matches a printer font. The choice that Windows makes for the display font may look nothing like the font you've chosen, because the most important criterion in choosing the font is character width. Other factors (font style, design, and height) are secondary. For example, if you select a 12-point Garamond that your printer has on a font cartridge, Windows might display 10-point Courier, because the width of the 10-point Courier matches 12-point Garamond closer than any other bit-mapped font. By displaying an incorrect bit-mapped font of similar width, Windows is able to show you where the lines will break and thus give you the best possible idea of how much text will fit on a page—even if the font mismatch is blatant.

Microsoft chose this system because you may want to use a document created on another system. Instead of refusing to display the document because you don't have the font, Windows uses a formula to look at all the installed fonts and pick the closest match. All of this happens within the internal part of Windows known as the Graphical Device Interface (GDI) every time you choose a font from a menu and send a document to the printer.

Though the system sometimes gives you the wrong screen font, you'll get the right printer font as long as you've installed the right driver for your printer. If you've installed the wrong printer driver, Windows offers you options not available on your printer; you might select a font cartridge you don't have, or you might install downloadable soft fonts incorrectly. A common mistake on laser printers is to choose the wrong amount of memory or to try to print soft fonts that were not downloaded to the printer. As long as you have the correct printer driver installed, Windows's font menus give you a selection of fonts that matches your printer—even if your displayed document indicates you've made a mistake.

The next section looks at a solution to the problem of matching screen and printer fonts.

The TrueType Solution

Microsoft couldn't find a practical way to display the printer fonts for every printer on the market, so it added TrueType to Windows, a new system that scales a font to the right size every time you display or print a character. Because it uses the same file for both screen and printer, there's a perfect match.

You can make your printing much more predictable by selecting the True-Type Only option in the Control Panel's Font dialog box. This way, the font choices in all of your programs will display only those fonts that appear on screen exactly as they do on the printed page. To do this, click on the True-Type button in the Control Panel's Fonts module. Then, select the Show Only TrueType Fonts in Applications option. The default option is Enable True-Type Fonts.

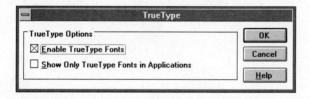

Programs That Have Their Own Fonts

Some applications, especially graphics programs like Aldus PageMaker and Corel Draw, install their own soft fonts on your system. These were made available to ensure that everyone who bought the program would have a good range of quality fonts that matched on the screen and on the printed page.

Since Windows 3.1 adds TrueType, you may find these older fonts unnecessary. You may even want to remove some of them, since TrueType fonts usually take up less disk space.

In evaluating whether you should keep fonts that come with other programs, remember that Windows will not let you use duplicates of a font. If TrueType Courier bold is installed, a second Courier font in any style or point size will be ignored; Windows will always give precedence to the TrueType font. The extra Courier font will waste disk space, and you should consider taking it off your hard disk. It's probably a good idea to copy the font file to a floppy disk before you delete it, just in case you need it later.

Creating an Alias for a Font's Name

Documents created with older versions of Windows may use fonts not available in Windows 3.1. For example, Helvetica and Times Roman were provided in Windows 3.0 as soft fonts, but they've been replaced in Windows 3.1 with MS Sans Serif and MS Serif, respectively. If you work with documents created on a system that used fonts unavailable on your current system, you should create an *alias* for the old font. The alias tells Windows what font to use instead of the font that's no longer on the system.

In the WIN.INI file, there's a section called [Font Substitutes]. During Setup on most systems, Windows automatically inserts alias entries here, such as

```
Helv=MS Sans Serif
```

and

```
TmsRmn=MS Serif
```

This prevents problems that could develop if you run an old Windows program that requires the earlier Helvetica and Times Roman typefaces.

You can add more aliases yourself to the WIN.INI file. For example, if you want documents that use Garamond to use Arial instead, add this line to the [Fonts] section:

```
Garamond=Arial
```

Whenever a document with Garamond characters is opened, TrueType Arial characters will now appear in their place, both on screen and in print. Chapter 9 provides detailed instructions for editing WIN.INI.

Adding New Fonts and Removing Old Ones

The WIN.INI file has a section titled [Fonts], where it establishes the names of each available font and specifies a file with the information Windows needs to build it. A typical entry is

```
Arial (TrueType)=arial.fot
```

When Windows loads, it reads this information into memory and uses it to display menus. Thus, for a font to be available in Windows, this line must be present in WIN.INI. If you add new fonts to the system, a new WIN.INI entry must be added, which takes place automatically during installation when you use the Control Panel's Fonts module to add a font.

Since some applications come with their own fonts, this section of WIN-.INI usually becomes cluttered with fonts that you don't use anymore. You can remove this information by using the Remove command in the Fonts module of Control Panel, or you can delete the line yourself. You may want to copy the font file to a floppy disk before removing it from your hard disk.

Unsupported Printers

You can install new drivers by using the Add command in the Control Panel's Printer module. If your printer is not listed in the Printer module, Windows does not have the driver to control it directly. Usually, the printer works fine if you choose a similar printer.

Virtually all printer manufacturers conform to one of the most popular printer standards, and the printer manual should mention the nearest emulation. If the information isn't available, here's a general rule: for a 9-pin dot matrix printer, try Epson FX-80; for a 24-pin dot matrix printer, try IBM Proprinter X24; for a laser printer, try HP LaserJet Series II.

These drivers may give you basic printing without access to some of your printer's options. You should contact your printer's manufacturer to find out whether new drivers have been made available; these are usually sold for a nominal fee.

Getting the Most from Your Printer

It's impossible to make many blanket statements about all printers, because there are so many different printer designs. In almost all cases, however, you must usually choose between speed and quality. The following sections present some of the choices you can make.

Choices for Graphics Printing

Most of this chapter has dealt with fonts, the most complicated area of printing. You have far fewer options for printing files that include graphics. When you create and print graphics, you're usually using features provided by the particular program, such as Paintbrush. There are few graphics options common to all Windows programs.

The following sections summarize your choices. In Chapter 9, the section on the Printers module gave detailed instructions on selecting these settings.

Letter or Draft Quality?

Letter quality output is higher in quality than draft, but it always takes longer to print—nearly twice as long on some printers. This choice is usually available only on ink jet and dot-matrix printers, especially the earlier models. Sometimes, options such as dithering and choice of gray-scale values are presented. As a general rule, the less dithering (coarse rather than fine, for example) and the lower the gray-scale values, the faster your jobs will print, although the quality will suffer.

Resolution

The higher the dpi (dots per inch), the longer it takes to print. This applies only to the printing of graphics, not fonts. A choice of dpi is usually available only on laser printers; 75 dpi, 150 dpi, and 300 dpi are common choices. Some laser printers may not have enough memory to print a full page at 300 dpi, but they may be able to print part of a page at that resolution. Choose 75 dpi when you're printing documents just to check the progress of a graphic you're still working on.

Displaying Special Characters

The 88 or 101 keys of a PC keyboard don't have all of the characters needed for many business situations. To display and print trademarks, copyright symbols, and foreign-language characters, you need to use the ANSI character set, consisting of 256 characters numbered from zero to 255. Half are used to display the characters on your keyboard, including upper- and lowercase letters. To display and print ANSI characters, you can use Character Map, a small utility that comes with Windows. You can also find many unique characters in the Symbol font; however, the Symbol font characters may look out of place when used next to your other font. If you can't find a special character you need by using Character Map to display your current font, then use Character Map to display the Symbol font. Chances are it will be there, and you can insert the character into your document using the same techniques described in the following section.

Character Map

You run Character Map by double-clicking on its icon in the Accessories window or typing **CHARMAP** from the Program Manager's File Run command.

Character Map (see Figure 12.6) displays the code for special characters, so that you can make a special character by learning its code and typing it directly at the keyboard. If you do use Character Map to make a special character, you use the Windows Clipboard to paste that character into your document. Most Windows fonts offer the same characters, but some, such as Symbol, offer a totally unique set of characters.

In order for the correct characters to appear in your document, you must use the same font in your document as the one you selected in Character Map. If you insert special characters and you don't see the characters you selected, try changing the font in your application and Paste the characters again.

To find a character, first make sure you've displayed the font you're working with by choosing it from the Fonts drop-down list box. You can highlight a character with either the keyboard arrow keys or your mouse. When you click on any character, it enlarges for easier reading; hold down the mouse button as you move the mouse, and you'll be able to see each of the characters under your mouse pointer more easily.

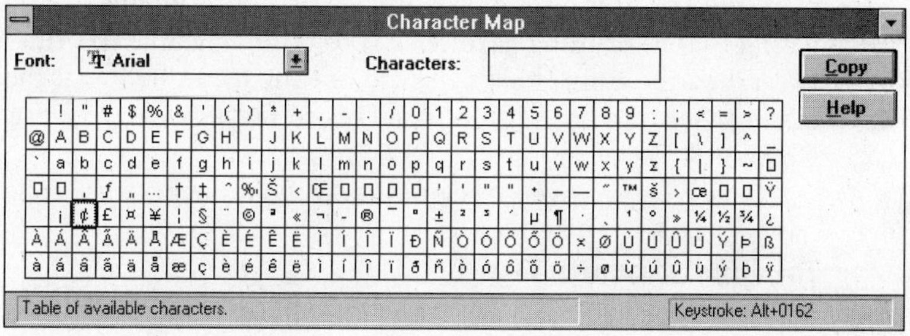

Figure 12.6

Character Map displays a diagram of all the characters available in the font displayed in the upper-left corner.

Double-click on a character to select it and insert it automatically into the Characters text box. You can add as many characters here as you wish. When you've selected the characters you want, click on the Copy button. All of the characters selected will be copied to the Clipboard. Switch back to the application you were using and select Paste (Shift-V) to insert the characters into your document.

In the lower-right corner of Character Map, the ANSI code for the character is displayed. Make a note of this code and use the following procedure to insert the character directly into a file *without* using Character Map.

Inserting ANSI Codes

To display one of the special characters directly, hold down the Alt key, type the number 0, and type the character's ANSI code. You must type the numbers on the numeric keypad.

Here's how you would insert the ¢ character into a document:

1. Check the ANSI Character Set table in the Character Map or Windows manual to find the number for the ¢ character (162).

2. Make sure your keyboard's NumLock light is on; if it's not, press the NumLock key.

3. In any Windows document that uses fonts, enter **Alt-0162**. The ¢ character appears.

The fonts that come with Windows all support the ANSI character set, but some fonts on the market do not. If you get unpredictable results in displaying and printing special characters, check the manual that came with the font. The font probably has a unique character set.

Common Mistakes

The most common mistake made by computer users is sending a job to a printer that doesn't have paper or that's not turned on. Most other problems that develop in Windows are caused by installing the wrong driver for the connected printer. This can cause all sorts of problems, from printing the wrong font to printing garbled text to not being able to print at all.

When the printer uses a serial port, text can be lost if the Control Panel's Port settings are set too high. These settings were covered in depth in Chapter 9.

Once you've covered the basics, try to remember the following guidelines.

The Right Memory Size

It's easy to set your laser printer's memory size incorrectly. If you set it lower than the amount in your printer, your jobs will take longer because Windows will take longer to send the file to the printer. If you set memory too high, you may get incomplete pages, since parts of a large print job can get lost when Windows sends it to the printer and the printer can't accept it.

Most laser printers have a built-in routine that will print the amount of memory installed; you may need to check the printer manual to find out how to run the routine. In a large corporation, you may have to request this information from the department responsible for ordering computer equipment. If you do know the amount of memory in your laser printer, it's a good idea to tape the information to the side of the printer.

If you do not have at least 512k of memory in your laser printer, you may not be able to print a full page of graphics at high resolutions. You'll get only part of the page or an error message. To remedy this problem, you can add more memory to the printer or print the document at a lower resolution.

Portrait versus Landscape

People often confuse portrait and landscape. These terms refer to a document's orientation. Portrait is the way a standard business letter is printed, vertically; landscape prints sideways, or horizontally. The terms come from the art world, where everyone knows that da Vinci's Mona Lisa is a portrait and van Gogh's Starry Night is a landscape.

Don't Expect Color from a Black-and-White Printer

When creating graphics for a black-and-white printer, remember that the use of color can be deceiving. Red and blue may look good on the screen, but your printer will convert them to dithered patterns. When creating documents with shaded areas, devote some extra time to learning how your application's colors are converted into black-and-white patterns by your printer.

Don't Fight Your Printer's Optimization

TrueType is a better way to print fonts for most people, but the most recent Hewlett-Packard laser printers run slower on many print jobs if you use True-Type fonts. The HP LaserJet III and later models have their own internal scalable fonts, using a system that attempts to do the same thing as TrueType. On these printers, you're better off avoiding TrueType if you want your documents to print faster.

On most other printers, including earlier HP LaserJets, TrueType usually provides good performance and sometimes prints faster than the internal fonts, depending on the size and type of characters in the document.

Some Ways to Get Better Performance

Better performance usually means giving up something. Your PC can send a file to the printer faster if there's less going on—no tasks working in the background. Also, simpler documents print faster.

Print Long Jobs in Standard Mode

Print jobs take slightly less time in Standard mode than in 386 Enhanced mode. The difference is hardly noticeable when you print two or three pages but becomes significant when you're printing very long documents.

If you're running in 386 Enhanced mode, one way to improve printing time is to close as many programs as possible. The fewer open programs and windows, the faster Windows will print.

Make Fewer Font Changes

Each font generally requires access to one file. When you use bold and italic fonts as well as new typefaces in a document, you're increasing the amount of work your PC has to do to send the document to the printer, especially with TrueType. If you need to print a long document quicker, use just one font to speed up the job.

Use TrueType Regular Fonts

Whenever you use a TrueType font, Windows must create the dimensions of each character. To speed this up, Windows creates a font cache file on your hard disk. This cache is essentially an index with information about how Windows will build each character; by referring to the font cache, it can generate TrueType characters more quickly.

Windows creates this font cache only for the regular font in each TrueType typeface, so the regular fonts in Arial, Times New Roman, scalable Courier, and scalable Symbol are displayed and printed faster than the bold, italic, and bold italic fonts in each of these typefaces.

Install a Disk Cache

The easiest way to improve Windows's performance in many areas is to install more RAM on your system. When part of your system's memory is devoted to a disk cache, most tasks, including printing, take less time.

The disk cache that comes with Windows, SMARTDRV.SYS, keeps parts of actively used disk files in RAM so they can be used faster; your printing jobs will get to the printer with fewer time-consuming hard-disk reads. You'll need at least 2Mb of RAM to take advantage of this disk cache, however. Procedures for setting up a disk cache can be found in Chapter 14.

Controlling Jobs Sent to the Printer

Windows has a special program for managing files sent to the printer: Print Manager. Once you've used the Print command in your program's File menu, Print Manager takes over. (Any file printed from a DOS program is not controlled by Print Manager; the DOS program maintains full control over the way the file prints.) Print Manager lets you check the status of files sent to the printer, change the order in which files print, or pause a print job. These features are valuable if you must often print under deadlines.

When a file is being prepared for printing, Print Manager opens. It closes automatically if the file is sent without problems. If problems do develop, Print Manager remains active until they are resolved. When your program is running in a window, you can see the Print Manager icon in the lower-left corner; when you're running in a full-screen window, you can see the Print Manager by using the Task List (Ctrl-Esc).

Print Manager

There are two principal roles for Print Manager, both of which you control from the Print Manager dialog box (see Figure 12.7):

- To check on the status of files sent to the printer

- To rearrange the order in which they'll print

From Print Manager, you can also access the same Print Setup dialog boxes found in the Control Panel's Printer module.

The Print Manager dialog box shows the status (Idle or Printing) of each printer on your system and the status of every file waiting to be printed or currently being prepared by Windows for printing. To show the progress already made on the file that's being printed, the Print Manager displays the percentage of the file that's already been sent to the printer. As soon as Windows is finished sending the file to the printer, the file disappears from Print Manager. For a long file, the printer may continue to work on the file after it disappears from Print Manager.

In Figure 12.7, Print Manager shows the status of three printers installed on a system. Only the HP DeskJet printer is active; the other two are idle. Two files have been sent to the active printer. The first is three percent finished, and the second is waiting to be processed. Note the printer icons to the left of the printer (HP DeskJet) and the file (D:\WINDOWS\WIN-INI.TXT) being printed, indicating that both items are active.

Figure 12.7
The Print Manager window shows the status of printers as well as of files being printed. Here, three printers are on the system, and two files have been sent to the one active printer.

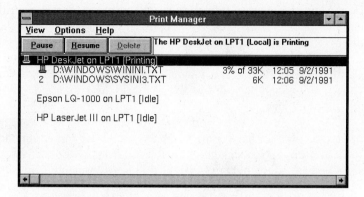

Changing the Order in Which Files Are Printed

Each file waiting to be printed appears in the Print Manager window. If a file is not here and you think it should be, it may have finished printing already, or you may not have really sent it to the printer. Most programs display a second dialog box after you select Print, prompting you for a confirmation before printing starts. If you switch to a different Windows task, you might not see this dialog box. To switch to this program, press Alt-Tab.

If you want a file at the end of the line to print sooner, you can click on the file name and drag it to a new position. Or you can select it, hold Ctrl, and use the keyboard arrow keys to move it.

Stopping Files from Printing

There are three command buttons in the Print Manager window: Pause, Resume, and Delete.

Use the Pause button if you realize the printer is low on paper. After you've paused and resolved the problem, click on Resume. Use the Delete button to remove any file from the Print Manager window that you do not want to print. "Deleting" a print job does not affect the file stored on disk, but merely stops it from printing.

Print Manager's View Menu

The View menu lets you specify whether the Print Manager window shows the time and date when the file was sent and the size of the file. This information can help you solve printing problems, since they let you know when they occurred.

If you're connected to a network printer, you can use the Refresh, Select Net Queue, and Other Net Queue buttons to check on the progress of files that you've sent to a remote printer.

Since there may have been progress in printing since you last opened the Print Manager, choose Refresh to get the most recent status. Print Manager updates the network status periodically, so you don't need to select Refresh often.

The Select Net Queue command displays the status of all of the files waiting to be printed at the network printer. Normally, Print Manager shows you the status only of your own files; choose this command to see which files are ahead of yours.

The Other Net Queue command lets you see the files waiting to be printed on another network printer. You might use this command if the network printer you're using has many files in front of yours and you want to see if you can find a network printer that is less popular. You can't use Print Manager to move your job from one printer to another, but you can use what you learn here to decide whether to select another network printer. You can then use the Network Connections command to establish connections with a different network printer.

Your ability to connect with a network printer and see the queue is controlled by the network administrator. (Just because you're on a network doesn't mean you can use all of its resources.) If you can't connect with a network printer or see the queue, you should ask the network administrator to give you access to it.

Print Manager's Options Menu

The Options menu lets you change the speed at which Print Manager sends data to the printer port. It can't make the printer work any faster once the file's there, but it can tell Windows to devote more or fewer resources to preparing the file for printing.

In most cases, you won't be able to make a significant speed improvement. By default, Print Manager gives each file the highest priority. All you can do is slow the rate at which Print Manager processes the file, by selecting Low Priority or Medium Priority. You'd do this if you wanted Windows to devote more resources to processing other activities than to preparing the file for the printer.

Three commands on the Options menu let you choose how Print Manager deals with problems:

- **Alert Always**   Print Manager, even if it's minimized, will pop up a message box to let you know there's an error (for example, the printer's out of paper and the file can't print). You may want to select this option since Print Manager appears by default as an icon rather than as a window.

- **Flash If Inactive**   If Print Manager is minimized, the icon will flash when there's an error instead of displaying a message. This is the default.

■ **Ignore If Inactive** Print Manager will not display error messages until you double-click on its icon.

Dragging Files to the Printer in File Manager

If you're using File Manager, you can print files by clicking and dragging, without opening the program that created the file. You can do this only with files for which you've established an association between the file type and the application. And you must make sure the Print Manager icon is visible as a minimized icon, as a Program Manager icon, or as an open window. File associations were explained in "Associating Files with Programs," in Chapter 3.

For example, a file with the extension TXT is associated with Notepad. If you open a File Manager directory window that displays the file WININI.TXT, as seen in Figure 12.8, you could click on the file and drag it to the Print Manager icon or window. Release it to start printing. You'll see a Notepad window message box open, which lets you know that Windows is preparing the file for the printer. To check on the progress of printing, open Program Manager.

Figure 12.8

You can drag a file to Print Manager to send it to the printer without opening the application that created it. The file name must be displayed in a File Manager window, and some part of Print Manager must be displayed.

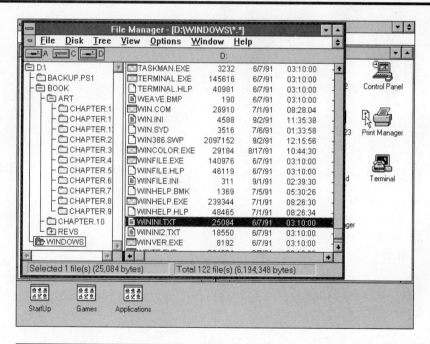

You can create additional associations between file types and programs from the File Manager's File menu.

Print Manager's Menus: A Complete List

View

Time/Date Sent
Print File Size
Refresh   F5
Select Net Queue. . .
Other Net Queue. . .
Exit

Options

Low Priority
Medium Priority
High Priority
Alert Always
Flash if Inactive
Ignore if Inactive
Network Settings. . .
Network Connections. . .
Printer Setup. . .

Help

Contents
Search For Help On. . .
How to Use Help
About Print Manager. . .

13

The Sound Tools

What You'll Need

*The Basic Techniques
of Sound Recording*

Sound Recorder

Media Player

THIS CHAPTER EXPLORES THE RICH POSSIBILITIES OF TWO PROGRAMS IN the accessories group: Sound Recorder and Media Player. First we'll learn how to use them to play, record, and edit sound files. And finally, we'll see how to embed a sound file in a word processing file. The programs described in this chapter represent the basic sound features distributed with Windows 3.1; more advanced features can be added with a product called Multimedia Windows, which is distributed with PCs and hardware kits that have an MPC (Multimedia PC) logo. Windows 3.1 is compatible with Multimedia Windows, so you'll be able to use Sound Recorder, Media Player, and any data files that you create using them if you ever upgrade to Multimedia Windows.

What You'll Need

You can play sound files in Windows with any PC, though the results will be disappointing if you don't have a sound board. Windows comes with support for the most popular sound boards, such as Sound Blaster, the Ad Lib card, and the Roland MPU-401. Newer boards should come with their own drivers. If you buy a sound board other than the ones just mentioned, make sure you'll be getting drivers for Windows.

If you don't have a sound board, Microsoft can provide you with a software driver that will let you hear sound through your PC's speaker. To obtain one, call technical support or log onto Microsoft's Windows forum on CompuServe, where you can download the file.

For help in getting a sound board running, see the "Drivers" section in Chapter 9.

The Basic Techniques of Sound Recording

Sound—whether it's music, speech, or just noise—is a vibration that our ears can understand. Windows sound files are digital encodings of those vibrations. They're stored in files that have the extension WAV and use the "pulse code modulation" technique for sampling and recording.

Pulse code modulation is based on the fact that in nature, sound appears as a series of pulses or waves. The up and down curve of the waves reflects changes in loudness (amplitude of the wave) and pitch (the frequency with which the waves occur). In order to capture these waves as data files, a sound board will "sample" incoming sound waves, taking a reading every fraction of a second and storing that reading as a number that is used to replay or alter the sound.

Sampling rates have a dramatic impact on the quality of recorded sound. Ideally, you'd want almost constant sampling to get realistic digital recording; an audio CD samples 44,000 times a second (44.1 kHz). However,

CD-quality sound requires lots of storage: about 600Mb of data to store one hour's worth of music, which works out to 10Mb per minute or 171k per second.

You can dramatically reduce the amount of disk space needed for sound files by reducing the sampling rate. Windows allows three sampling rates: 11.025 kHz, 22.05 kHz, and 44.1 kHz. You can also save disk space and use a less expensive sound board by reducing the intensity of the sound (which is measured in decibels). Sound files stored in 8-bit files have a dynamic range of 48 decibels; files stored in 16-bit files have a dynamic range of 96 decibels. Audio CDs store data in 16-bit files. Finally, you can save on disk space by choosing between stereo and mono. As you might expect, stereo sound requires exactly twice as much space as single-channel sound.

Your sound card will determine the type of sound files that will work on your system. If you attempt to play a 16-bit stereo file recorded at a sampling rate of 44.1 kHz on a PC that supports only the lowest sampling rates, the resulting sound will be distorted and scratchy.

If you're planning to buy a sound board, remember that you may need to buy a larger hard disk to get much use from it. Even at the lowest level of recording, sound files use lots of disk space. An 8-bit mono recording at an 11.025 kHz sampling rate requires 660k of storage for one minute of sound. That works out to 11k per second.

If you have a MIDI (Musical Instrument Digital Interface) device installed with Windows 3.1, you'll be able to play some of your files in Media Player but you'll need to either upgrade to Multimedia Windows or use software that comes with your hardware in order to edit or record MIDI files.

Sound Recorder

The Sound Recorder lets you play WAV files, capture audio and store it as a WAV file (if you have a properly installed sound board), and edit sound files.

To run the Sound Recorder, click on its icon in the Accessories group or type **SOUNDREC** at the Program Manager's File Run command. The program's small dialog box will open (see Figure 13.1).

Playing WAV Files

Before using Sound Recorder to play or edit sound, you need to open a sound file that conforms to the WAV format. You can use the File Open command or the Edit Insert command. Either command opens a dialog box that displays the WAV files in your Windows directory.

When the WAV file is opened, it's stored in RAM and does not play immediately. You need to use the program's commands to make the sound file begin to play.

Figure 13.1

The Sound Recorder uses command buttons that are similar to the buttons on a tape recorder. The Microphone button will be available only if a sound board with recording features is installed.

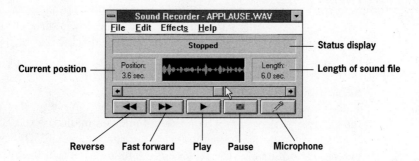

Sound Controls

The Sound Recorder dialog box displays push buttons that are based on a typical tape recorder, as well as a scroll bar.

- The scroll bar shows your current position within the open sound file. When the scroll button is at the far left, Sound Recorder is ready to play the beginning of the file; when the scroll button is at the far right, the sound file is ended. You move the current position ahead or back within the sound file by dragging the scroll button, clicking on the arrows, or clicking on the scroll bar itself.

- The Reverse button (two left-facing arrows) resets the sound file so that the beginning is ready to be played.

- The Fast-forward button (two right-facing arrows) provides an instant fast-forward through the open sound file.

- The Play button (a single right arrow) will begin to play the open sound file, starting from the point where the scroll bar is resting. If the scroll bar shows that you are at the end of the file, Play will start from the beginning.

- The Stop button (a square black box) will stop the sound file.

- If a microphone is installed on a system's sound card, the Record option will be available. Click on the microphone button, and Sound Recorder will start to capture audio.

How to Read the Display

It will take only a few minutes to get your bearings with the Sound Recorder's controls.

As soon as a WAV file is loaded, Sound Recorder shows the length of the file in the display window on the right side. On the left side, it shows your position within the file. As you move through the file, the center window shows a representation of the sound waves as they're played. You can see this most dramatically if you drag the scroll bar slowly through the file and then back to the beginning. On a short file, the display may change too quickly to notice.

Adjusting the Volume

You can increase or decrease the volume of a sound file by 25 percent with the Increase Volume and Decrease Volume commands on the Effects menu. You can use either command to bring the volume back to its original state, but you cannot change the volume more than 25 percent from the original volume.

You'll get better control over volume by adjusting the loudness control on your sound board. The commands on the Effects menu are the only way to adjust the volume if you're using your PC's built-in speaker.

Special Effects

Using commands on the Effects menu, there are four ways to alter the sound of a recording. As soon as you select one of these options, you can play the recording and hear the difference. If you then save the file, it will be stored with the special effect in place.

Increase Speed by 100%   Tells Sound Recorder to race through the sound clip; as a result, the length of the recording is made shorter. You can use this command over and over, so that a 10-second clip is reduced to 5 seconds, then 2.5, then 1.25, and so on until the sound clip plays so fast you can't even hear it.

Decrease Speed   Slows down the sound clip, increasing the length of the recording. You can use this command over and over, too. Sound Recorder has a limit of 60 seconds worth of sound, so if you make the clip too long, you'll receive an Out of Memory message, indicating that you cannot decrease the speed of the recording any further.

Add Echo   Increases the resonance of the sound, similar to the effect of an echo chamber in a recording studio. You can repeat the command for a deeper echo. The result of using the echo command once is only a mild echo; to give the sound clip a real echo, you need to execute the command several times.

Reverse   Plays the sound back in reverse.

You can remove all special effects with the Revert command in the File menu. Exiting without saving a file will also preserve the original file.

If you save a file while special effects are active, you won't be able to use Revert. The Revert command is available only when one of the commands on the Effects menu is active.

Cutting and Mixing Sound

The Edit menu has five commands that are used to shorten sound clips, mix them with other sounds, or use them in other applications.

Copy   Places the current sound on the Clipboard, with all special effects active. You can use this command to insert a sound file into a program that can receive embedded objects. See "Embedding Sound in Other Programs" later in this chapter, to learn how to do this.

Insert File...   Lets you place another WAV file into the current file. It will be inserted at the current position and will replace any sound after the current position. Before you use this command, make sure the scroll bar is resting at the spot where you want the new sound to begin.

Mix with File...   Lets you overdub another WAV file into the current file. It will be inserted at the current position, and the newer file will be heard at the same time the rest of the original file is heard.

Delete Before Current Position   Removes all sound before the current position, shortening the file. It's most useful when used after you've recorded a sound that's longer than you need it to be. Before you select the command, check to make sure that the scroll bar is resting on the desired spot within the sound file. To find the exact spot where you want to make the cut, it's useful to check the display of the sound waves as you move the scroll bar back and forth. Selecting the exact spot will take time at the beginning, but with a little practice you'll be able to coordinate the display with the sound you're hearing. When you choose the command, Windows gives you the chance to confirm or cancel the deletion by displaying a query like this:

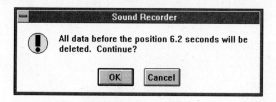

Delete After Current Position   Removes all sound after the current position, shortening the file. It works like the Delete Before Current Position command.

Recording Sound

You must have a microphone or some other input device (such as a tape recorder) plugged into your sound card in order to make a recording. Once you're properly set up, recording is simple. You click on the Record command button, wait a second until the Sound Recorder display indicates that recording has begun, and then speak or turn on the music. When you've finished, click on the Pause button.

If you begin recording again after you've selected Pause, the new sounds will begin after the current recording. You can record over the old sounds by dragging the scroll bar back.

When done recording, you can use all of the Sound Recorder commands to edit the recording. When you've got it just right, save it.

Embedding Sound in Other Programs

You can use Sound Recorder to store memos or instructions that are played back when you run other programs. For example, you could record a message and then place it inside a Write document; whenever you open that document, you can hear the message.

Sound Recorder is an OLE server application, so this technique will work with any program that is an OLE client application. (Chapter 11 explained the relationship between OLE clients and servers.)

Here are the steps you'd take to embed a sound file within a Write document:

1. Open Sound Recorder and record your message.

2. Edit the sound and save it.

3. Select Copy from the Edit menu; a copy of the sound is placed in the Clipboard.

4. Run Write (or any other OLE client application) and open the data file you'll be using.

5. Move to the spot in the file where you want the sound icon to appear.

6. Open the Edit menu and select Paste Special; a Sound Recorder icon appears (see Figure 13.2).

7. Click on the Sound Recorder icon to hear the sound.

Figure 13.2

You can embed sound clips within the documents of any Windows program that is an OLE client application. Here a sound clip was inserted into a Write file.

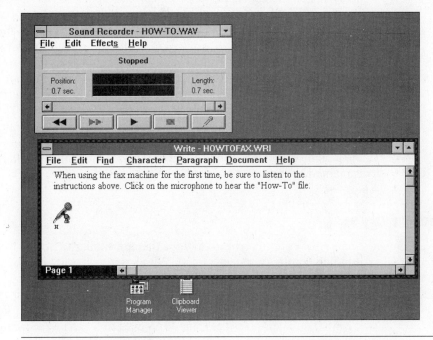

8. Save the Write document.

The next time you open the Write file, you'll see the Sound Recorder icon and you'll be able to play the sound clip, even if Sound Recorder is not loaded. If Sound Recorder or the data file is deleted from the system, you will not be able to hear the clip.

When this document is open in Write, you can change the sound file that opens by using the Links command. Position your cursor on the sound icon and select Links from the Edit menu. The following dialog box will open:

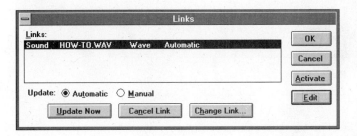

Click on the Change Link command button if you want to replace the current sound file with a new one. You can also change the status of this link to Manual so that Windows will not attempt to find the sound file whenever you open the document. If you keep the link set to Automatic (which is the default setting), every time you open the Write document, Windows will look for the sound file. By changing the link to manual, you can save a few seconds each time the file is loaded, but you have to take the extra step of opening the Links dialog box in order to run the sound file.

The steps above show the quick, simple way to embed sound files. If you want to customize the way the sound icon appears—with a special label for the icon or with a different icon—you can use the Object Packager (as explained in depth in Chapter 11) to change the properties of the linked icon.

Media Player

Media Player has playback features that are similar to Sound Recorder, but it has no editing or special effects. With a design based on a compact disc player, it is a simple way to play sound files. If you have a compact disc player installed, you can use Media Player to control it, or you can use Media Player to play sound files through a sound board or the PC speaker.

Media Player plays the same WAV files that can be recorded by Sound Recorder. It can also play MID files, which can be created only with a MIDI device such as a Roland MPU-401.

Media Player Controls

You can use the scroll bar or the four command buttons to control the way Media Player works (see Figure 13.3).

Figure 13.3
Media Player has command buttons that are based on a compact disc player.

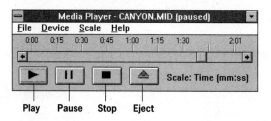

■ The scroll bar shows your current position within the open sound file. When the scroll button is at the far left, Media Player is ready to play the beginning of the file; when the scroll button is at the far right, the sound file is ended. You move the current position ahead or back within the sound file by dragging the scroll button, clicking on the arrows, or clicking on the scroll bar itself.

- The Play button (the single right arrow) will begin to play the open sound file, starting from the point where the scroll bar is resting.

- The Pause button stops playing at the current position; to begin to play from this position, click the Pause button again.

- The Stop button (a square black box) will stop the sound file. To begin to play again, you must use the Play button. When you're using a CD player, this button will return you to the beginning of the recording; when you play sound files, the current position is not changed.

- The Eject button is available only when a CD player is installed. It will stop playing and open the CD tray.

Controlling Media Player

Media Player provides two ways of opening a file. You can use the File menu's Open command or select the device from the Device menu. When you use the File Open command, you'll get a choice of files that work with the device that's currently selected. It's easier to open a file by using the Device menu; you simply choose the device you're using, and a File Open dialog box appears with a list of files that are compatible with that device.

When you choose Sound, the Open dialog box displays a list of WAV files, since these are the data files that a sound board or the PC speaker can play.

When you choose MIDI Sequencer, the Open dialog box displays a list of MID or RMI files, since these are compatible with MIDI sequencers. If your sound board has some MIDI compatibility, you will be able to play some of these files, but your system's sound capability is the limiting factor.

After you open a sound file, you can use the command buttons to play, pause, or stop the file. Once the sound file is playing, you may want to minimize the Media Player dialog box so you can use other Windows programs as you listen to the recording.

Two Scales

The Scale menu lets you see the recording divided by time or by tracks. The Tracks option, designed for CD players, gives you the ability to drag the scroll bar to a desired track.

Sounder Recorder's Menus: A Complete List

File
New
Open. . .
Save
Save As. . .
Revert. . .
Exit

Edit
Copy   Ctrl+C
Insert File. . .
Mix with File. . .
Delete Before Current Position
Delete After Current Position

Effects
Increase Volume (by 25%)
Decrease Volume
Increase Speed (by 100%)
Decrease Speed
Add Echo
Reverse

Help
Contents
Search for Help On. . .
How to Use Help
About Sound Recorder. . .

Media Player's Menus: A Complete List

File

Open. . .
Exit

Device

MIDI Sequencer. . .
Sound. . .

Scale

Time
Tracks

Help

Contents
Search for Help On. . .
How to Use Help
About Media Player. . .

14

Maximum Performance

Setting Up Your Machine

Working Smarter

Secret WIN.INI Commands to Customize Your Desktop

■ N THE FIRST THIRTEEN CHAPTERS I SHOWED YOU TECHNIQUES FOR MAKING the most of Windows's commands and options. In this chapter, I'll introduce several Windows techniques for making the best use of your PC's resources. The first part of this chapter covers techniques for configuring your system to improve Windows's performance. You may want to use the section headings as a checklist of techniques; implementing these techniques should result in considerable performance advantages. The second part of this chapter, "Working Smarter," offers tips for customizing the Windows Desktop, both what you see on it and how you interact with it.

Setting Up Your Machine

When you install Windows, the Setup program attempts to make some changes to your PC's configuration files, CONFIG.SYS and AUTOEXEC-.BAT, to improve Windows's performance. If you have more than 1Mb, Setup adds two programs to CONFIG.SYS to make better use of your system's RAM; the way these two programs are installed depends on how much RAM you have. Setup also changes the PATH statement in AUTOEXEC-.BAT, to make DOS aware of your Windows directories. Although you can choose *not* to allow Setup to change CONFIG.SYS and AUTOEXEC.BAT automatically, you should allow it to make the changes. You can always customize either configuration file by editing it later.

The Different Types of Memory

Figure 14.1 illustrates how the memory in a PC is organized. Because Windows runs from DOS, it inherits DOS's 640k limit initially. To use memory beyond 640k, Windows relies on device drivers such as HIMEM.SYS, which is installed in your CONFIG.SYS file. By using the memory management tools provided by this device driver, Windows is able to use all of the memory in your system, not just 640k.

Following is a brief description of each type of memory:

Conventional memory	Memory below 640k; where both DOS and Windows are first installed. DOS programs can run only within conventional memory, unless you've installed a memory manager or DOS 5.0.
Upper memory	Memory between 640k and 1,024k; where your system stores BIOS information about the way the hardware works. Windows does not normally use this memory, but some memory managers can store device drivers and programs here.

High memory area	A small area of memory (64k) that starts at 1,024k; used by Windows's HIMEM.SYS device driver for storing information about the memory above it.
Extended memory	Memory that begins above the high memory area and continues as far as the amount of installed RAM.
Expanded memory	On some systems, the area above 1,024k is configured according to a specification called LIMS EMS (for Lotus-Intel-Microsoft Expanded Memory Specification), developed so that DOS programs could store data. It is used by a few DOS programs, and only when they're running files too large to fit in conventional memory. For example, because Lotus 1-2-3 for DOS uses expanded memory, you can open a spreadsheet that uses more memory than is available in conventional memory.

Expanded memory is installed in many 286 PCs through an add-in board such as the Intel Above Board. When you configure some of your memory as expanded, Windows cannot use that memory for running programs or using the disk cache.

Choosing between Expanded and Extended Memory

The following sections explain how to make the best use of your system's memory. In most cases, the way you configure your memory depends on whether you're running Windows in Standard mode or 386 Enhanced mode.

Remember, if you have a 286 PC or a 386 or 486 PC with less than 2Mb of RAM, you must run in Standard mode. If you have a 386 or 486 PC with 2Mb or more, you have the choice of running in 386 Enhanced mode or Standard mode, though you'll usually want to run 386 Enhanced mode. For more information on the differences between these two modes, see Chapter 12.

The following two sections explain the options available for both modes. While setting up memory for one mode will not prevent you from running in a different mode, you may end up using memory at less than peak efficiency when you run the other mode. If you tend to run both

Standard mode and 386 Enhanced mode, you may want to keep a separate version of your CONFIG.SYS file for each mode. When you switch modes, you can replace the CONFIG.SYS file and reboot your system.

Figure 14.1

When the device driver, HIMEM.SYS, is installed, Windows is able to use all of the PC's extended memory for running programs and loading files. If the memory above 1,024k is configured as expanded memory, it's not available for Windows.

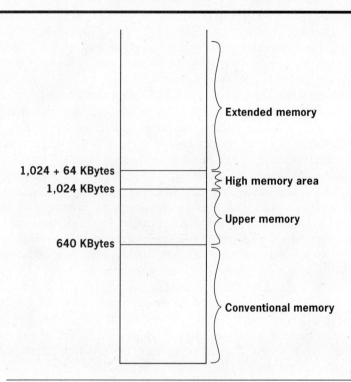

Using Expanded Memory in Standard Mode

If you don't use a program that requires expanded memory for large data files, you'll be able to improve Windows's performance in Standard mode by changing the expanded memory to extended memory. You should maintain expanded memory only for those times when you run programs in DOS that use expanded memory. If you're gradually switching from DOS programs to Windows programs, you'll eventually have no use at all for expanded memory.

As a general rule, you should set aside only as much expanded memory as the largest data file requires. A simple way to estimate how much memory the largest file requires is to estimate how much memory is available in the DOS application before any files are loaded (let's say 256k). Subtract that amount from the size of your largest data file (let's say 400k). The result is the minimum amount of expanded memory you need to load your largest file (in this case, 144k). You should leave a comfortable safety margin when you allocate expanded memory, so that this file has room to grow. In this example, 256k of expanded memory should be sufficient.

You can adjust many expanded memory boards by moving jumpers or sliding DIP switches so that some of the memory is extended and some is expanded. (You'll need to check the manual that came with the board, or call the manufacturer, for precise instructions.) If your board cannot be adjusted, consider replacing it with an extended memory board.

Using Expanded Memory in 386 Enhanced Mode

Most 386 PCs have all of their memory configured as extended. When expanded memory is needed, emulators are usually installed using the CONFIG.SYS file. For example, Compaq distributes CEMM.EXE with DeskPro 386 PCs, and many people use Quarterdeck's QEMM. These programs let you establish exactly how much available memory will be set aside as expanded, and make the rest available as extended.

Windows cannot coexist with many of the expanded-memory managers, such as Compaq's CEMM.EXE. Instead, Windows comes with EMM386.SYS to perform this same function. Commercial emulators (such as Quarterdeck's) have been upgraded to work with Windows. You'll need the most recent versions of these products to emulate expanded memory.

If you run Windows in 386 Enhanced mode, you may not need any expanded memory at all, since when you run DOS programs from Windows, expanded memory is created as needed. If you run 386 Enhanced mode and sometimes want to use expanded memory for a DOS program when Windows is not loaded, you should install the Windows expanded-memory emulator, EMM386.EXE.

When you install EMM386.EXE, you must enter the amount to be used as expanded memory. To install EMMSYS.SYS with 256k of expanded memory, add the line

```
DEVICE=EMM386.EXE 256
```

to your CONFIG.SYS file after the line

```
DEVICE=HIMEM.SYS
```

using any text editor. To make 512k of extended memory available as expanded memory, the line should read

```
DEVICE=EMM386.EXE 512
```

You can also edit CONFIG.SYS by running SysEdit within Windows. To do so, type **SYSEDIT** at the Run command of Program Manager's File menu.

Make Sure You're Using High Memory

No matter how much memory is available on your system, you'll be limited to 640k unless an extended-memory manager is installed in DOS. Conveniently, one of the programs that Setup installs on your system if you have more than 1Mb of extended memory is HIMEM.SYS, an extended-memory manager that installs itself in the first 64k above 1,024k and lets Windows use all of the memory above it. Most people will have no need to alter the way HIMEM.SYS is installed, but there are several options that you may need, especially if HIMEM.SYS does not run. These options are listed later in this section.

HIMEM.SYS can be installed only if your CONFIG.SYS file has the line

```
DEVICE=C:\<path>\HIMEM.SYS
```

and if the HIMEM.SYS file is stored in the directory specified by <path>. Even if the line correctly specifies the directory where HIMEM.SYS is installed, high memory may not be available if your system doesn't have extended memory available. If you believe that your system has more than 1Mb of RAM and that the HIMEM.SYS line in your CONFIG.SYS is accurate, the memory above 1Mb is probably configured as expanded, and you should attempt to change it following the instructions at the end of the previous section.

You can set HIMEM.SYS options by editing your CONFIG.SYS file with any word processor as long as you store the file in text (ASCII) format; you can also use the SysEdit utility that comes with Windows. To run it, type **SYSEDIT** at the Run command of Program Manager's File menu.

/shadow:on	Attempts to change the way your PC uses video memory. It works only on the relatively few systems that use "shadowing" of the video ROM. These systems copy the ROM BIOS information for the video adapter out of ROM and into faster RAM. HIMEM.SYS normally tries to prevent this, in order to use as much RAM as possible for Windows; that is, by default, HIMEM.SYS turns shadowing off. If you wish to let your system copy the video ROM BIOS into RAM, then add this option. Note that some systems that use shadowing do not let HIMEM.SYS disable the process in any circumstances.
/machine	For systems in which HIMEM.SYS has compatibility problems. The README.TXT file that Windows installs in the main Windows directory lists systems that require this option and gives you the specific entry for each system.

/numhandles=	Changes the number of extended-memory block handles that can be used in Standard mode, but has no effect in 386 Enhanced mode. You can enter a value between 1 and 128, and the default is 32. Change this value only if you run a program that is having problems with Windows because it requires a larger number of extended-memory block handles.
/hmamin=	Controls the minimum amount of high memory that a program must use to receive any high memory; required only in Standard mode. You can enter any number from 0 to 63. The default value is 0, meaning that the first program that needs high memory will be able to use it. Enter this value only if you know that a program other than Windows cannot run because it needs high memory. When that program takes high memory, however, Windows will not be able to use all of the memory in your system.

You can tell whether HIMEM.SYS is running by watching your display when the system boots up; a message should appear, telling you that the 64k High Memory Area is available.

Using DOS 5's Memory Management Programs

Microsoft DOS 5 comes with its own versions of HIMEM.SYS and an expanded-memory manager, EMM386.EXE. Both of these can make a good deal more memory available to DOS.

DOS 5's version of HIMEM.SYS stores a portion of DOS and some device drivers in the first 64k of extended memory, or high memory, and lets Windows use that memory when it runs. On a 386, you can gain even more memory for DOS by using EMM386.EXE to store device drivers in upper memory. EMM386 requires that HIMEM.SYS be running and that the CONFIG.SYS file have a statement that installs it. (Both Windows and DOS 5 come with copies of EMM386.EXE.)

For example, on a 386 PC with DOS 5 installed, the following lines of the CONFIG.SYS file install a mouse driver for DOS programs and provide about 614k of free RAM for running both DOS programs and Windows:

```
DEVICE=C:\DOS\HIMEM.SYS
DEVICE=HIGH,UMB
DOS=C:\DOS\EMM386.EXE
DEVICEHIGH=C:\DOS\MOUSE.SYS
```

In earlier versions of DOS, about 560k would be available after a mouse driver was installed.

Make Sure a Cache Is Installed

A *cache* is a program that stores an index of some of your hard disk's contents in RAM, cutting down on the amount of time that Windows has to spend searching for information on your hard disk. A "smart" cache keeps a cache of your hard disk by dynamically using RAM that's not being used by a program, with the result that Windows runs even faster when there's extra RAM.

You can install a disk cache only if you have at least 512k of extended memory or 256k of expanded memory. Installing a cache in Windows does not mean that you lose all of that RAM for running programs; the cache that comes with Windows, SMARTDRV, gives up some of the memory it's using if you run a program or open a file that requires more memory.

Setup installs SMARTDRV automatically if your system has sufficient RAM. If it's not installed and your system has sufficient memory, make sure you add it. As long as your system has enough extended memory, a line that loads SMARTDRV is installed in your AUTOEXEC.BAT file by the Windows Setup program. It is an executable program that can be loaded from the DOS prompt, and you can run it anytime from a DOS prompt in order to see how its options are set. Type **SMARTDRV** at any DOS prompt. You'll see a report of the size of the cache both in DOS and when Windows is running. And you'll see a summary of the disks in your system, and whether the cache is being used on them.

Every time SMARTDRV is loaded, it looks at your system to determine how much memory to use in the cache. Therefore, even if you add new RAM chips to your system, you won't need to change SMARTDRV's settings; it will know how to make the adjustments.

You can probably accept the settings that are automatically established for your system, but if you want to tinker with SMARTDRV, you can add switches to the command line that loads it. The upcoming sections describe the changes you might wish to make.

Avoiding Possible Data Loss Caused by SMARTDRV

One setting you may want to change is the delayed-write cache. This is considered dangerous by some because SMARTDRV does not immediately store the contents of a file to disk after you execute a save command. Instead, it delays in order to let the computer respond to your next command. As soon as SMARTDRV detects an idle period, it stores the data. It won't wait longer than 5 seconds in any case, and if a system reset command (such as Ctrl-Alt-Del) is issued, SMARTDRV will store the file before it allows the reset command to be executed.

Delayed writing makes the computer more responsive, since you probably want to begin a new task as soon as you issue the save command. By delaying the disk access, Windows will be able to keep up with you. This strategy could cause data loss if you turn off the computer less than 5 seconds after executing a store command, so it's important that you try to adjust your work habits and make sure you never shut down the computer immediately after saving a file. If you fear you won't always remember to wait those 5 seconds, you probably should turn delayed writing off.

I find that the benefits of delayed writing outweigh the risk. I rarely if ever turn off my computer so soon after I finish working—I often leave it on all night—but if I did tend to quickly shut it down every day at five o'clock, I'd make sure I turned write caching off. The following section shows how to do this.

There is a command that will force SMARTDRV to write the contents of a file to disk immediately. Type **SMARTDRV /C** at a DOS prompt. This can help you work around the problem, but you still must remember to issue the command. Try placing this command at the end of a batch file that loads a DOS program so that when you quit the program, the batch file forces SMARTDRV to write the contents to disk.

Changing SMARTDRV Options

Before you change SMARTDRV options, you should find out how it's setup already. Type **SMARTDRV** from a DOS prompt; as long as SMART-DRV.EXE is stored in a directory mentioned in the DOS PATH statement, you'll see a status report of how the options are set up. (The Setup program copies SMARTDRV.EXE to your Windows programs and will normally make sure the DOS path includes this directory.) To see a few more details, type **SMARTDRV /S**. This gives you a report card on how well the cache is working and how much of the cache has been used. For a summary of the available options, type **SMARTDRV /?**.

Here's an explanation of the settings and how to use them:

Disable/Enable   You can turn the cache completely off for a drive by entering the drive letter followed by a minus sign. You can disable the delayed-write cache while keeping the read cache on by entering the letter of the drive alone. For example, this entry would load SMARTDRV with no caching of drive A: and would allow only read caching of drive C: (no delayed write):

```
C:\WINDOWS\SMARTDRV.EXE A- C
```

Note that you do not use colons in identifying the drive letter. (This entry assumes SMARTDRV.EXE is stored in the Windows directory.)

To disable all delayed-write caching on all drives on a system with two floppy disks and one hard disk, make sure this line is entered in AUTOEXEC-.BAT:

```
C:\WINDOWS\SMARTDRV.EXE A B C
```

You can enable both read and write caching by entering the drive letter followed by a plus sign, but it's not necessary, since SMARTDRV will automatically install the cache this way if Windows determines that this is the optimal setting. For example, SMARTDRV will not enable the write-back cache on drives where the disk can be removed (included floppy disk drives). You may want to enable write-back caching on these disks by adding the drive letter, followed by a plus sign; but do this only if you're sure you will never remove the disk before SMARTDRV has a chance to write the contents of the cache to the disk.

Cache Size   In earlier versions of Windows, you needed to specify two sizes for SMARTDRV as it loaded. In the current version, it does this automatically. However you can still enter the values if you want to force a particular size. Simply type two values. The first value will represent the initial size, which SMARTDRV will use in DOS and which it will attempt to use when in Windows. The second value is the minimum size it will use when in Windows. In DOS, the cache size cannot change, but in Windows, SMARTDRV will turn over some of the memory in the cache to programs if the memory is needed. If you set too high a value for the minimum in Windows, you may cause your system to run out of memory when you try to load a program.

The default values that SMARTDRV uses are as follows:

- If you have less than 1Mb of extended memory, all extended memory will be used for the initial cache in DOS and none will be used in Windows.

- If you have between 1Mb and 2Mb, the initial cache in DOS will be 1Mb and the minimum in Windows will be 256k.

- If you have between 2Mb and 4Mb, the initial cache in DOS will be 1Mb and the minimum in Windows will be 512k.

- If you have between 4Mb and 6Mb, the initial cache in DOS will be 2Mb and the minimum in Windows will be 1Mb.

- If you have more than 6Mb, the initial cache in DOS will be 2Mb and the minimum in Windows will be 2Mb.

To change the value, write both values on the same line that installs SMARTDRV using kilobytes. For example, on a system with 6Mb, you might want a 4Mb initial DOS cache and a 3Mb minimum. You'd enter this line in AUTOEXEC.BAT:

```
C:\WINDOWS\SMARTDRV.EXE 4096 3072
```

If you want to turn on the delayed-write cache on drive C: and have the same cache size, enter this line:

```
C:\WINDOWS\SMARTDRV.EXE C 4096 3072
```

Other SMARTDRV Options   There are five other options, all of which are fairly esoteric. If you're going to customize a system in minute detail, they could be a help, but most people won't need them.

- /B (buffer size) changes the amount of disk information that is stored each time the disk is read. The default is 16k, which means that each time you use the disk, SMARTDRV looks ahead 16k on disk and copies the data to the cache. If you increase the size of the buffer, more data will be stored each time you use the disk, but the cache will fill up more quickly. You can enter any multiple of 16.

- /E (element size) changes the number of bytes that SMARTDRV moves at a time. The default is 8k and any changes must be in powers of 2 (4, 8, 16, and so on).

- /L (low) prevents SMARTDRV from loading into high memory; it's available only when you're using DOS 5.0 and have enabled upper memory blocks.

- /R (reset) empties the cache and makes SMARTDRV available to start fresh.

Make Sure SMARTDRV Doesn't Waste Memory

Some hard disks (especially those on PS/2s) require that an extra copy of the disk's contents be kept by the disk cache, so SMARTDRV creates a double buffer of the disk's addresses (physical and virtual). Disks that require this usually have bus mastering controllers, but a few SCSI controllers do, too. SMARTDRV automatically creates this buffer when it believes there's a need. On MFM, RLL, and IDE controllers, it will not create the double buffer.

On some ESDI and SCSI devices, SMARTDRV cannot accurately determine whether the double buffer is needed, so it creates it anyway. If the buffer is not needed, you can save 2k of RAM by turning it off.

To determine whether your system is using the buffer, open your CON-FIG.SYS file and look for this line:

```
device=smartdrv.exe /double_buffer
```

If it's not there, SMARTDRV has determined that your disk drive does not require double buffering, and no memory is being used for it.

If the line is there, you may not need it. To find out, you need to check the status of buffering on your disks. Enter **SMARTDRV**. (SMARTDRV should be installed when you do this.) You'll see a table that shows the disk-caching status of all your system's drivers. If all of the entries under "buffering" are "no," then you should turn this option off by removing the line in CONFIG.SYS that installs the double buffer. Do not change the line in AUTOEXEC.BAT that installs SMARTDRV.

The next time you reboot your system, SMARTDRV will run without double buffering, and you'll have about 2k more RAM.

Don't Waste Memory in DOS

Because memory is so valuable to Windows, for both loading programs and giving your disk cache as much memory as possible, it's a good idea to free memory before loading Windows. Here are a few ways to free memory.

Do You Need a Mouse Driver Installed?

If Windows is your only program that uses a mouse, don't install a mouse device driver; Windows installs the mouse for its own programs without wasting memory in DOS. To recover this memory, delete the line

```
DEVICE=MOUSE.SYS
```

from your CONFIG.SYS file, or the line MOUSE.COM on your AUTOEXEC.BAT file.

Do You Need ANSI.SYS?

This device driver adds special features to your keyboard and display. It's often used to set colors in the DOS display, by giving the DOS PROMPT statement the ability to access ANSI commands. Sometimes ANSI.SYS is needed by an application, but many applications that use ANSI.SYS are old, and you may no longer run them. If you're not sure why you have ANSI-.SYS, remove it as follows; you can always reinstall it.

To free the memory ANSI.SYS uses, eliminate the line

```
DEVICE=ANSI.SYS
```

from CONFIG.SYS. You may need to simplify the PROMPT statement in AUTOEXEC.BAT to something like:

```
PROMPT=$P$G
```

Do You Need a RAM Disk?

Years ago, a RAM disk was just about the only way to use extended memory in a PC. Many people got in the habit of creating RAM disks and copying frequently used files to speed up performance. It's still possible to have a RAM disk with Windows, using the RAMDRIVE.SYS file that the Setup program copies to your main Windows directory. But it's usually not the best use of available memory.

Install a RAM disk only if you have a specific file that you access constantly. Otherwise, you're better off letting Windows manage RAM with its own smart cache.

To install a 256k RAM disk when your main Windows directory is C:\WINDOWS, add the following line to your CONFIG.SYS file:

```
DEVICE=C:\WINDOWS\RAMDRIVE.SYS 256
```

Have You Outgrown Your TSRs?

Some of the most popular TSR (terminate-and-stay-resident) programs provide features now built into Windows. Calculators, calendars, and list files with autodialers are all available in the Accessories program group.

Even if you decide that you still want to use your old TSRs, you don't have to load them automatically every day. You can run them from Windows when needed and close them when you're done. Running them this way will take only a couple of seconds more each time you double-click their icons, and can make a dramatic improvement in Windows performance. To use them most efficiently, create a PIF that gives the program the minimum amount of RAM that it needs.

Switch to MS-DOS 5 or DR-DOS 6

It's important that you have as much conventional memory free as possible before you load Windows, and either Microsoft's DOS 5 or Digital Research's DR DOS 6 can help. They release conventional memory by installing parts of DOS and device drivers in high memory. Earlier versions of DOS provided about 550–580k of RAM; DOS 5 and DR DOS 6 can provide more than 600k.

Install a Memory Manager for Device Drivers

Certain device drivers must be loaded for some of your system's components to work; DOS and Windows won't be able to use tape drives, network connections, and other devices unless their software is installed. DOS 5 can put some of these device drivers into high memory, but memory managers like Quarterdeck's QEMM and Helix Software's NetRoom do a much better job. In fact, on some systems DOS 5 cannot load device drivers in high memory because the system's ROM BIOS prevents it, but QEMM and NetRoom can overcome that limitation.

If you install one of these memory managers, make sure it is compatible with all the software on your system. Some TSRs may have compatibility problems with memory managers.

Get More Memory

A faster processor was once considered the great salvation for any PC user who wanted better performance, but not any more. A fast processor does increase most tasks in a PC, but once you achieve a speed of 16 MHz, you get more value from your upgrade dollars by adding memory rather than megahertz.

Chapter 10 outlined the various limitations you face with less than 2Mb. But 2Mb is just the start; Windows's performance increases with more RAM. Think of 4Mb as a minimum, and if you want excellent performance, increase your RAM to 8Mb. To run programs like Lotus 1-2-3 for Windows, Aldus PageMaker, and WordPerfect for Windows at the same time, you'll want even more.

Adding memory is a simple task on most PCs. Anyone who's installed an adapter card can add RAM. Most RAM for 386SX, 386DX, and 486 systems is sold in SIMM (Single-Inline Memory Module) packs, which are inserted into sockets on the memory card. When all of the memory sockets in the system are used by 256k SIMM packs, you may want to replace each with a 1Mb SIMM pack. When all of the SIMM sockets are occupied by 1Mb SIMM packs, you can replace them with 4Mb chips if your system allows, or you can add a memory card.

Make Your Swap File Permanent in 386 Enhanced Mode

When Windows runs low on memory in 386 Enhanced mode, it uses the hard disk to store data in RAM. The file it creates is called a *swap file* or virtual memory. You can improve Windows performance when memory is low by sparing Windows the work of creating a new file each time it needs to use the hard disk.

When you make the swap file permanent, Windows creates a new file in a contiguous portion of your hard disk. Instead of scattering fragments of the file across many tracks of your hard disk, the way many files are stored, Windows keeps the entire file in one block. And because Windows stores the exact location of this file in RAM, it can write to and read from the file very quickly.

You can make the swapfile permanent by running the 386 Enhanced Mode module in Control Panel. See "386 Enhanced Mode" in Chapter 9 to learn how to do this.

When the SWAPFILE program creates the new file, it also changes the SWAPFILE= setting in your WIN.INI file, so that Windows knows to use the file each time it loads. Do not attempt to create the swap file simply by changing the WIN.INI file setting, since Windows must determine the exact location of the file on your hard disk and establish certain criteria about your disk when it creates the file. The Setup program will not do this automatically; you can create the swap file only by running SWAPFILE.

Working Smarter

The beauty of Windows is that it's so flexible. Once you've fine-tuned your configuration files so that Windows can make the best use of your hardware, you can start tailoring Windows to *your* preferences. The only right way to set it up is the way that makes you feel most comfortable. The following tips should give you some ideas about getting there, but you'll probably find yourself tinkering al the time.

Create Program Groups for the Way You Work

Treat the initial program groups in Windows as a starting point. The idea of a Main program group is good, but don't include Control Panel and the Clipboard Viewer if you never use them. If you use Notepad often, move it into the Main program group.

There's no right way to build program groups and to decide which ones should be open when you start Windows, but there is a wrong way, and that's to leave the groups the way Microsoft installed them.

At your job, you probably work on different projects, which require different programs and data files. Create a program group for each project, each with the programs you use for that project. Don't limit yourself to one copy of an icon—put your word processor in every program group if you use it for each project. If your work involves four or five clients, create a program group for each client and put a copy of required program icons in each group. (See Chapter 2 for details.)

If you acquire new Windows applications, you'll have good reason to start changing the program groups, because many new programs create their own unique program group at installation. Aldus Persuasion creates an Aldus group; Lotus Ami Pro for Windows creates a Lotus group. Don't let software vendors organize your desktop for you—put icons where you want them.

The reason why applications create their own program group is to help you find the icons for the main application and that application's setup program. You won't affect the performance of these programs by eliminating the program group, as long as you move the icon into another group. The setup information that these programs need to run is stored in the WIN.INI file and may also be stored in an INI file created for the program. Ami Pro, for example, creates an AMIRPO.INI file. Changing Ami Pro's program group and moving its program item will not affect its performance in any way.

Don't Open Program Group Windows If They're Not Needed

Try to be economical with the number of icons that you display on your Desktop. Each icon displayed uses a small amount of the system resources.

In Windows 3.0, it was common to run out of system resources, but in version 3.1 Microsoft doubled the amount of memory available for system resources. Nonetheless, it's still possible to exhaust this memory.

Your personal preferences are most important in creating the best arrangement of program groups and icons, but you'll probably be able to find the icons you need more quickly if your screen doesn't show everything available all the time.

Let Windows Install DOS Icons

Learning Windows often involves changing your habits. You're probably used to performing certain tasks in DOS programs, even though Windows comes with Accessories that let you do the same jobs within Windows. But don't force yourself to run Windows programs if you hav a perfectly good DOS program that you prefer, and don't make it too difficult to switch to DOS programs. Let the Setup program create as many icons and PIFs as it can for all of the programs on your disk. Even if Setup performed this task when you first installed Windows, it may be useful to run Setup again several months later after you've installed new DOS programs.

If you upgraded Windows from version 3.0 to 3.1, be sure you take advantage of the Setup program's option for creating PIFs and icons for all of the DOS programs on your system. Microsoft added new PIF settings and DOS program icons in version 3.1. You'll probably find that some of these new PIFs and DOS icons are a significant improvement over the older ones.

Create Icons for Often-Used Files

If you find yourself using the same data file over and over, create an icon that will load that file together with the program that created it. You can do this for data files created in either DOS or Windows programs. For example, if you run WordPerfect to work on just three files, create three separate icons. Each one should load WordPerfect and then open the right file.

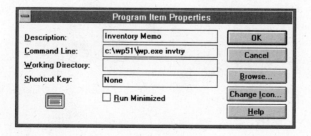

You can select an icon with the Program Manager's File menu, as explained in detail in Chapter 2. Be sure to give each icon a name that will help you quickly identify the data file.

And you may want to select a new icon for this data file to help you distinguish it from the icon that represents the main program. You can do this by executing the Change Icon command in the Properties dialog box. Also, explore other icon files. When you use the Change Icon command, the default setting uses icons in PROGMAN.EXE. Windows comes with a second icon file, called MORICON.DLL. You can use more than two dozen new icons by entering **MORICON.DLL** in the File Name box and pressing Enter.

Keep Your Opening Desktop Familiar

There's nothing worse than starting your work by having to dredge up last night's mess. Your Windows opening screen is a great opportunity to get control of Windows right from the start.

The way to do this is to spend some time arranging your program groups. Open the group windows you use most often, and give them the portion of the screen you feel most comfortable with. I keep open a program group that has the applications I use most often and give it most of the screen, but I make sure that all of the icons for my other program groups are visible and arranged in an order that makes sense (see Figure 14.2 for an example). Because I switch to DOS fairly often, I keep the DOS Prompt icon in its own program group.

When you have arranged program group windows so they occupy the right amount of space and have made sure that all group icons are visible, click on the Arrange Icons command on the Program Manager's Window menu. This command works for one group window at a time, and it works on the group icons only when one of them is selected, so you must move from window to window, executing the Arrange Icons command each time, to arrange all the icons on your screen.

Then, open the Program Manager's Options menu and check the Save Settings on Exit option and quit Windows. Restart Windows and immediately turn off the Save Settings on Exit option. The next time you run Windows, your Desktop will open the way you like it.

If you save the settings on your Desktop often, it's a nuisance to quit Windows and restart it. Here's a way to save your settings more quickly; it may seem more complicated than the way just described, but Windows can take up to 30 seconds to load, and the following way should take just about 10 seconds.

1. Change the Desktop to the way you want it to appear when you restart Windows.

2. Open any DOS session. Click on the DOS Prompt icon, for example.

Figure 14.2

Here's a way to organize the Windows Desktop that makes available the programs used most often. Note that the DOS Prompt icon has its own window, making it easier to find.

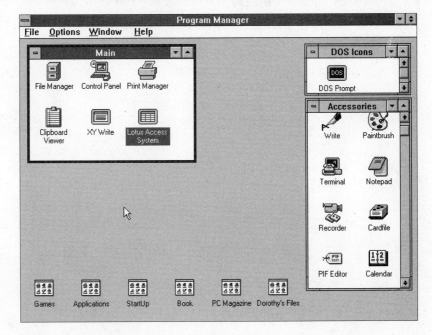

3. Press Alt-Esc or use any method to switch back to Windows.

4. Open the Options menu and make sure a check mark appears to the left of Save Settings on Exit.

5. Press Alt-F-X or use any method of quitting Windows. The Exit Windows dialog box opens, asking you to confirm that you want to end the session.

6. Click on OK. Windows now saves the settings. Before it closes, a message box appears, warning that an application is still active and that it must be closed before Windows can close.

7. Click on OK.

8. Double-click on the icon for the DOS session and close it if you wish. You may want to continue working with the DOS session active.

This technique takes advantage of the fact that when you quit Windows, the Desktop settings are saved before Windows checks whether a DOS session is open. If a DOS session is open when you decide to save the settings, it takes hardly any time.

Use File Manager for Drag-and-Drop Power

File Manager can greatly expand your use of Windows thanks to its drag-and-drop power. You can drag a data file to any icon that knows how to use it. For example, in Chapter 12 I showed how you can print a file by dragging it to the printer. When you drag a data file to a program icon, Program Manager will automatically create a new icon for the data file; when you double-click on this new icon, the program will run with the data file already open.

The key to harnessing this power is to make sure you have created associations between the data files and programs that you use most often. Then, keep a File Manager window open so that you can easily switch to it and drag files. You may want to copy the File Manager icon to the Startup group so that it loads every time you run Windows. Figure 14.3 shows one way to keep File Manager available for easy access without devoting too much of the screen to it.

Figure 14.3

When File Manager's display is visible, it's easier to drag files to other programs.

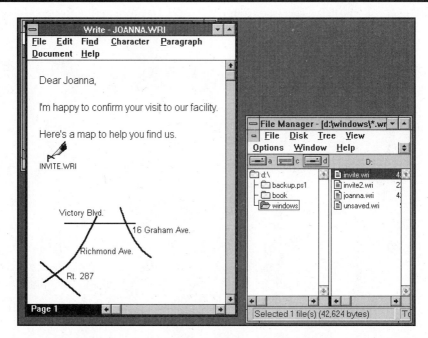

Since File Manager opens in the same sized window and displays the same directory you used when you last closed it, it's easy to become accustomed to finding the Windows files you need. To make it even easier, you may want to adjust the By File Type option on File Manager's View menu so that you see only documents that have associations or programs. See Figure 14.4.

Figure 14.4

File Manager's View By File Type option lets you limit the number of files displayed, making it easier to find files that can be dragged to other programs.

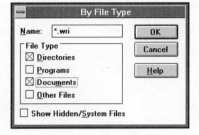

Reverting to the Original Windows Shell

Before Windows 3.0 was introduced in 1990, Windows's opening shell combined the features of Program Manager and File Manager. If you prefer that shell, you can still run it under Windows 3.1. It's stored in a program called MSDOS.EXE, which Setup copies to your main Windows directory. (See Figure 14.5.)

Figure 14.5

The MSDOS.EXE program can make Windows look like it did before Windows 3.0 was released.

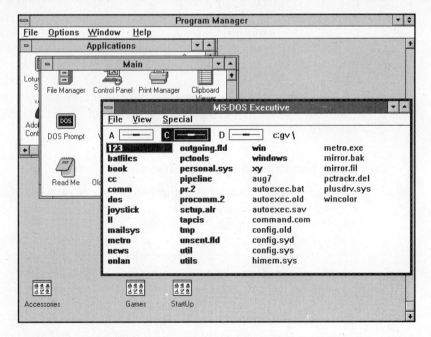

To run this shell as an application along with Program Manager or File Manager, start it from the Run command of Program Manager's File menu by typing **MSDOS**. You can also create a new icon for it, using the New command of Program Manager's File menu.

If you wish to replace Program Manager completely with MSDOS.EXE, change the third line in your SYSTEM.INI file from

```
shell=progrman.exe
```

to

```
shell=msdos.exe
```

Always Keep a Backup of WIN.INI and SYSTEM.INI

In many places throughout the book, I've shown how you can customize Windows by editing the WIN.INI and SYSTEM.INI files, which are stored in the main Windows directory.

In addition to the changes you make to the .INI files, many Windows programs automatically make changes to these files when you install them. But if you don't like a new program, you'll have no easy way of knowing what was changed. Most of the time, you can ignore the changes to the .INI files, but every additional entry adds to the time it takes for Windows to load.

It's a smart idea to keep backup copies of both WIN.INI and SYSTEM-.INI. In fact, you should probably keep them in their own subdirectory so you'll always be able to find them. (The File Manager has a Create Directory command on its File menu.) Then, any time an unwelcome change has been made to the files, you can simply copy the backup file to the main Windows directory.

Keep More than One Configuration

If you like to make extensive changes to your configuration, you may want to store multiple configurations and choose among them. Also, if you share your system with someone else, each of you will want Windows to run the way you prefer. Because there are dozens of possible configuration options—colors, fonts, mouse speed, and so on—it can be time-consuming to make all the adjustments repeatedly.

You can keep separate versions of the two configuration files—WIN.INI and SYSTEM.INI—and switch to them before you run Windows. You do this by giving all of the alternate files different names. When Windows loads, it will use the two files named WIN.INI and SYSTEM.INI to set up options. But you can keep the backups under different names, such as WIN-JIM.INI and WIN-ANN.INI. Then, when Jim wants to run Windows after Ann, he changes to WIN-JIM.INI.

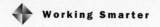

To do this, first copy your current WIN.INI and SYSTEM.INI files into new file names, such as WIN-NORM.INI and SYS-NORM.INI. From DOS you'd type

```
COPY WIN.INI WIN-MAIN.INI
COPY SYSTEM.INI SYS-MAIN.INI
```

Then, run Windows and use the Setup program to make all the changes.

Quit Windows, and from the DOS prompt, type (using personalized file names of your choice)

```
COPY WIN.INI WIN-JIM.INI
COPY SYSTEM.INI SYS-JIM.INI
```

To leave the system so that Windows will load with the original settings next time, type this at the DOS prompt:

```
COPY WIN-MAIN.INI WIN.INI
COPY SYS-MAIN.INI SYSTEM.INI
```

This technique works because DOS will replace a file when you copy a new file to it. You can make these name changes endlessly, keeping as many versions of the configuration as you like.

To make this technique easier, create a DOS batch file that will make the changes automatically when you start Windows. The following batch file will run Windows with Jim's configurations; it assumes that all of your Windows files are in a directory named WINDOWS:

```
CD \WINDOWS
COPY WIN-JIM.INI WIN.INI
COPY SYS-JIM.INI SYSTEM.INI
WIN
```

Give this file a name like JIM.BAT, and then create batch files for each user to adjust the system when they want to run Windows. Make sure there's a DOS path to the directory where you keep this file so it can be run from any directory in the system.

Choose between Super-VGA Resolutions

If you have a super-VGA or other graphics board that gives you a choice of modes, you may want to switch between two or more modes. To use a mode other than the default configuration, run the Setup program and choose the Change Hardware Settings command. There will probably be a choice of video modes, such as $640 \times 480 \times 256$ or $800 \times 600 \times 16$. (The first provides 256 colors and a standard VGA resolution, the second provides 16 colors and a higher-than-normal resolution.) You then have to restart Windows to see the effect of the change.

By keeping separate WIN.INI and SYSTEM.INI files, you can save yourself the trouble of running Setup every time you want to change modes. Use the technique explained in the previous section to make the switch easier.

Stay Current on Windows News

Users are always working on ways to improve Windows performance. Some users find tricks, and others write small Windows programs that they're willing to share with others.

Many of the new developments are printed in *PC Magazine,* but others are discussed in the Windows sections of the on-line information service, CompuServe. These on-line forums are open to the public and can be downloaded to your computer with a modem, if you're willing to pay the connect charges plus additional charges for residents of certain parts of the country. In addition, you can usually ask a question about something puzzling you and get an answer from fellow Windows users within hours.

You can log onto CompuServe with the Windows Terminal program or any other modem communications program. To find out more, contact CompuServe in Columbus, Ohio. When you're connected to CompuServe, type **GO WIN** to see a menu presenting several choices for getting more information about Windows.

Secret WIN.INI Commands to Customize Your Desktop

There are several Windows settings that you can change in WIN.INI. They don't appear in your file unless you add them. Chapter 9 explained how to edit WIN.INI using either a word processor or the SysEdit utility. Here's how you can customize Windows by adding these new settings.

Make sure you save a backup of your original WIN.INI file before you start, and make changes carefully. If you accidentally delete certain lines or add characters, you may not be able to run Windows from the edited file.

After you make these changes, you'll need to restart Windows to see them take effect.

Make Menus Align to the Right

The menus that appear in all programs align to the left of the menu name. You can have the menu align to the right (see below) by adding the Menu-DropAlignment setting to WIN.INI. To do so, add the new setting Menu-DropAlignment=1 to the [windows] section.

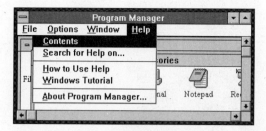

Change the Fonts in Program Icons

The font used in program icons is called MS Sans Serif. Windows uses this font automatically, but you can change it by specifying a different font and size in the [desktop] section. You can change it to MS Serif or Courier. For example, to use New Times Bold, 10 point, add these two lines to your WIN-.INI file in the [desktop] section.

```
IconTitleFaceName=MS Serif
IconTitlesSize=10
```

After you save these changes, you'll need to restart Windows to see the new fonts take effect.

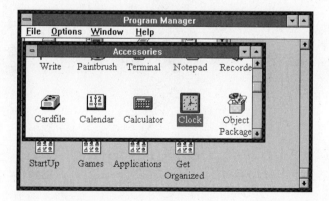

If your goal is to eliminate eye strain, change only the title size. Enter the following line in WIN.INI instead of the lines above:

```
IconTitleSize=10
```

For a very large font size, try 12. You'll see fewer program icons in your Program Manager windows, but the text will definitely be easier to read.

15

Planning for the Future

Windows Applications Coming to Market

Creating Your Own Windows Programs

Extensions Available Today

Beyond the Horizon

THE INVESTMENT YOU'VE MADE IN LEARNING WINDOWS CAN PROVIDE dividends for years to come. The philosophy that guided Microsoft in designing Windows will ensure that this happens, whether you stay with version 3.1, upgrade to the next release of Windows, or eventually switch to another operating system, like OS/2, DOS, Macintosh, or Unix.

Most important, the design of the Windows interface—including the menus, dialog boxes, and mouse-handling conventions—is very similar to that of other computing environments. The graphic interface in current versions of DOS and OS/2 was designed according to the same guidelines as Windows. These guidelines, called CUA (for Common User Access), specify rules for carrying out functions like opening a file and moving a block.

As a result you'll be comfortable using other systems with graphical interfaces if you pay attention to visual cues like control menu buttons, menu bars, and mouse pointer shapes. Not all Windows shortcut keys work on the Mac and on Unix systems, but you should be able to navigate their menu structures if you apply what you learned in Windows.

And yet, there's no reason to plan to walk away from Windows. All of the work that's gone into Windows's underlying structure was based on the concept of extensibility: features can be added to Windows by plugging new hardware devices and programs into the API (Applications Program Interface). Over the next few years, there will be an abundance of ideas for adding features that today seem like the special effects in a science fiction movie.

Windows Applications Coming to Market

Most programs that run under Windows follow the principles explained in this book, but some have a different interface. For example, command buttons in some programs can be used to access features that other programs access by menus. And icons can be used to call a command, even though the command can also be called from a menu.

Some programs, like Lotus 1-2-3 for Windows, use so many icons that they group them in a special area called a *toolbar* (see Figure 15.1). Often, you can customize the toolbar, adding or deleting icons from the group that automatically appears when you load the software.

And Norton Desktop for Windows uses icons to provide functions found in Program Manager and File Manager, so you can create a new Windows Desktop. (See Figure 15.2.)

Once you've learned the techniques explained in Chapter 1 and repeated in almost every chapter that followed, you have the skills to get started with any of these programs. The guiding rule in using Windows programs is "click away": If it looks like a button, click on it. If a dialog box opens, examine the list boxes and secondary dialog boxes to learn about the program.

Figure 15.1

Lotus 1-2-3 for Windows uses so many icons to access features that it groups them into a toolbar.

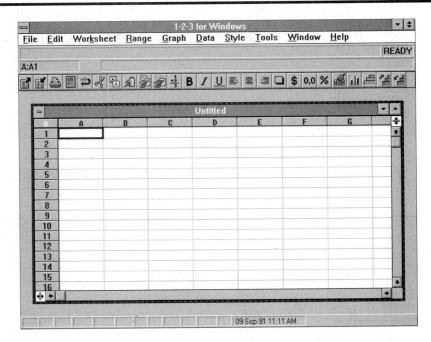

Figure 15.2

Norton Desktop for Windows replaces File Manager and Program Manager with icons that launch utilities.

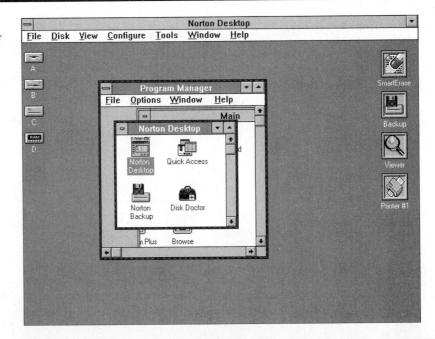

Making Applications Work Together

Chapter 11 showed the possibilities for sharing data among programs. As you look to Windows to provide new solutions, you'll want to experiment with ways of linking applications.

The Object Linking and Embedding (OLE) specification is being used by programmers to develop innovative ways of merging the powers of individual programs. You can expect future programs to have specific modules for linking with other programs. A database application, for example, may have a sorting server: If you link data to the sorter, you'll get only the database features you need for sorting.

Dynamic Link Libraries (DLLs) will be used to create active data exchange. For example, a spreadsheet could be linked to a communications program in order to download stock quotes from an on-line service and regularly update market information on the spreadsheet.

To achieve this type of interaction today, you must write your own C program. In the future, you can expect software publishers to build such functionality into their software.

What You'll Need

The programs in Windows's Accessories group give you an idea of what it's like to work in Windows. But there's a good chance that you'll soon want more powerful tools. Instead of Write, you'll consider using WordPerfect for Windows. After reaching Paintbrush's limits, you'll look at Corel Draw. And after Cardfile there's Q&A for Windows.

The first obstacle you may need to overcome in planning to use one of these programs is the size of your hard disk. New Windows programs, like those just mentioned, will need 2 to 6Mb of storage space for the programs alone. The files you create (especially if you import graphic files into your word processing documents and database records) will use up many megabytes more.

Before you buy new software, look at how much space you have available on your hard disk, remembering to keep about 10 percent of the disk free. With less free space, system performance starts to slow down considerably as new files are fragmented and stored in the few remaining spots.

In a poll of *PC Magazine* readers, we found that more than one-third of the respondents bought a larger hard disk for their system after using Windows for six months. Adding more RAM to your system is the best way to improve Windows performance today, and this will be true for years to come. Some Windows programs work with 1 to 2Mb of RAM, but if that's all you have, you won't be able to run more than one application at a time. That one application will almost certainly run sluggishly with the minimum amount of memory.

When you do add RAM, plan for tomorrow. In years to come, PCs with 8Mb of RAM will be considered average, and 16Mb will be typical among power users. So while you may be tempted to make an easy upgrade by adding one megabyte to your system, using four 256k packages of RAM, in the long run you may save money by buying four 1Mb packages and installing them in the same space. Consult your PC's manual or call the company to explore the best options for adding RAM. And don't forget that a hard-disk cache will speed up almost every program.

Creating Your Own Windows Programs

The original PC was a smash hit because the tools for creating new programs were included with the operating system at no extra charge. A BASIC interpreter was built into the IBM PC's hardware and included with every copy of DOS. This gave people with the time and inclination the ability to create their own software.

Windows does not come with such a programming tool. But you can buy software that will let you create Windows applications far more powerful than those possible with BASIC. Microsoft's Visual BASIC is probably the leading program. With this program and a minimum of programming knowledge you can build programs that have their own pull-down menus and command buttons. And if you're willing to put in the time to master the program's BASIC-like syntax, you'll be able to generate powerful Windows programs.

Experienced programmers will prefer products like Borland's Turbo Pascal for Windows, Symantec's Zortech C++, and Within Technologies's Realizer to build more sophisticated Windows programs.

If you want to create applications without learning to program, try Toolbook from Asymetrix. It's designed for creating programs that display images, such as a catalog or a training guide, and you can create these programs by choosing options from menus and dialog boxes.

Extensions Available Today

The two most ambitious capabilities being added to Windows—and the best examples of Windows's extensibility—are multimedia and pen computing. These technologies use drivers to give Windows programs the ability to control add-on devices like musical instruments and light pens.

Multimedia

The term *multimedia* means using sound and pictures in a PC program.
Applications can be as simple as a synthesizer that plays musical notation displayed on screen or as ambitious as an animated film that combines drawings
created in a paint program, live video recorded with an ordinary camcorder,
narration added with a common microphone, and music copied from your
cassette player.

These applications require a system with plenty of horsepower. You'll
need many megabytes of free hard-disk space, at least 4Mb of RAM, and
free expansion slots. And then there's the hardware, which will cost you anywhere from $200 for a barebones music card to thousands of dollars for a
complete system that can import and export video.

The MPC Standard

Because there are so many different types of products for multimedia, a
group of vendors, including Microsoft, got together to reduce the confusion
and make you feel more comfortable about buying multimedia products.
The result was *MPC* (Multimedia PC), a certification that a particular product will work with other MPC products. Products with the MPC logo have
Windows drivers that can be installed by either the Windows Setup program
or the product's own installation software.

There are a variety of sound boards that don't offer full MIDI or MPC
compatibility. These boards are supported by Windows and provide the features described in Chapter 13. Windows 3.1 has sound-processing features
that are a subset of the full capability provided in MPC. When you buy MPC
products, you get software that updates Windows to provide compatibility
with these devices and sound formats.

What You'll Need

Here's a summary of the types of products sold with MPC compatibility.

CD-ROM Players   A data CD, commonly called a CD-ROM (Compact
Disk-Read Only Memory), uses the same type of disk sold by record compa-
nies, though CD-ROM data is stored in a different way. Most PC-compatible
CD-ROM drives can read software files on a CD-ROM disk and play audio
CDs as well. (Audio CD players are not as flexible.)

CD-ROM is not required for multimedia, but it's the format in which
software publishers distribute ambitious products, like multimedia encyclopedias that can display text and reproduce the spoken word. For example,
when you look up John F. Kennedy in *Compton's Multimedia Encyclopedia,*
you can read a biography, see a photo, and hear a portion of his 1961 inaugu-
ral speech.

Not all CD-ROMs are fast enough for MPC certification; to qualify, they must be able to transfer information from disk to the PC at a rate of 150k/second or faster and have a disk access rating of 100 milliseconds or less. You need an MPC CD-ROM only if you want to run MPC software. If you're creating presentations, you may not need one.

Sound Boards   The most important standard in generating sound and music on a computer is MIDI (Musical Instrument Digital Interface). Stevie Wonder, a pioneer in this field, uses MIDI to create funky rhythms, and MIDI is built into just about every musical keyboard sold today.

MIDI components are not required to create and play MPC applications; MPC is designed primarily as a standard for playing and editing *prerecorded* sound. However, some MIDI products are MPC-compatible; many MPC sound boards are useful for playing MIDI audio, not for creating it.

Before you buy a sound board, be sure you know whether it is merely a sound board that can play and record WAV files in Windows (such as Sound Blaster, Ad Lib, and Thunder Board), or a full MPC board that can synthesize music and play back synthesized music (such as the Roland MPU-401 or the Pro Audio Spectrum). The first type of board requires no additional software to work with Windows 3.1; the second requires the additional drivers and utilities that will upgrade Windows to Multimedia Windows. This software should be provided with the board when you buy it.

Pen Computing

Pen computing is the most ambitious extension of Windows that Microsoft has made to Windows, and the uses for it are still being conceived. With pen computing you realize just how far you can go with Windows. Using a pen pointer to print words in an ordinary document window and then see the hand-printed letters transformed into characters, just as if they had been typed at the keyboard.

Most of the leading software publishers have said they will add pen functions to their applications, so the chances are good that someday you'll be using a pen to edit and draw on your PC.

What You'll Need

Digitizing tablets are plastic-encased devices about the size of a picture book. They plug into a PC adapter card and come with a pen-like pointer (see Figure 15.3). The pen sends an electric impulse to the tablet as it's dragged across the tablet surface. Since each spot on the tablet has an x and y coordinate, the computer is able to record movements and translate them into shapes on the screen.

Figure 15.3

Windows, when it's made pen-aware, will be able to translate characters printed by hand on a digitizing tablet into digital characters, just as if they had been typed in.

Professional designers have used digitizing tablets for years to create precise mechanical drawings on a PC; you can already buy a Summagraphics or Wacom tablet and use a pen as though it were a mouse. Someday, with the extensions now available for Windows, you'll also be able to use the tablet and pen to print letters into a document. For pen computing to be a reality you must have the software—DLL files and pen drivers—that knows how to use pen-generated characters. Most of your favorite Windows programs must be updated for pen computing.

Windows becomes pen-aware when you install a digitizing tablet whose setup program adds the necessary DLL files and drivers to your Windows WIN.INI and SYSTEM.INI files. The DLL files translate the shapes of hand-printed characters into text. The pen's driver gives Windows the ability to recognize these shapes and display a pen cursor right next to the mouse pointer. (The pen and the mouse can be used at the same time.)

Pen computing also requires a modification to the video driver so that Windows can display pen strokes as though they were ink. For this reason, not all video systems will work with pen computing. Drivers for VGA systems will come with most digitizing tablets, but other video systems will require special drivers.

Beyond the Horizon

Windows makes amazing things possible. Whether they become reality depends on what consumers want.

Consider this. You're sitting at your desk, working on a spreadsheet. Suddenly, an icon in the lower corner of the display beeps, much the way a Calendar alarm signals to you today. You click on the icon, and it opens a window that displays the face of a coworker. You respond to the beeping icon by picking up a nearby telephone to discuss the project with the person whose picture is in the window. Rather than telling her what you've done, you decide to show her a document you've written. You click on some icons and make some menu choices and then, as your document appears on your display, it's also sent to her PC and displayed there, all within seconds.

Far-fetched? This scenario could be a reality within three or four years. You can now transmit images over telephone lines, and by 1995 regional phone companies will enable you to send live video images over phone lines through the Integrated Services Digital Network, or ISDN.

Whether it helps you communicate with another computer user, turns your handwriting into digitized text, gives you new ways of handling images, allows you to integrate sound and music into your work, or gives you more raw computational power, a product that can do it in Windows is either on the market or on the way.

Troubleshooting

Can't Capture a DOS Screen to the Clipboard

The primary way to capture a DOS screen is with the PrintScreen key; another way is with Alt-PrintScreen. If these don't work, check the PIF settings for the DOS program. Make sure you have not either selected No Screen Exchange or made PrintScreen one of the Reserve Shortcut Keys (the check boxes should be empty).

Display on a Laptop Is Not Legible

Run the Color module in Control Panel and try other color settings, especially the LCD or plasma power-saver settings.

Mouse Is Not Working

Windows automatically recognizes the presence of a mouse. Check the manual it came with to make sure that you've installed your mouse properly. If the mouse connects to its own internal adapter card, you may need to change jumper settings on the card.

If the mouse was working and then stops, you've probably added new hardware or software that is causing a conflict. You can fix the problem by changing the settings either for the mouse or for the new device.

Mouse Is Erratic

1. If the mouse uses a roller, make sure it is rolling on a surface that provides adequate friction. The inexpensive mouse pads sold in computer stores can usually fix this problem.

2. If the mouse uses a roller, the interior may be dirty. You can usually pop open the plastic case that holds the rubber ball and clean out the interior, following the instructions in the manual.

3. Optical mice don't have rollers and work only when slid across the tablet or grid they came with. Contact the manufacturer of the mouse for assistance.

Out-of-Memory Error

1. Attempt to close programs not being used. Press Ctrl-Esc to display the Task List and see which programs are active.

2. Try to free more memory in DOS. (See Chapter 14 for help.)

3. The problem may be caused not by a lack of available RAM but by a lack of free system resources. Open the About dialog box from the Program Manager's Help menu. If the amount of system resources is less

than 30 percent, you have inadequate system resources. Close as many open windows and icons as possible. (You can close icons in a program group window by minimizing that window.)

Printer Won't Print

1. Make sure the printer is on-line; there should be a message like *Ready* or *Online*. If the printer is not ready, make sure it has paper. If that doesn't work, try turning it off and on. If it still doesn't print, consult the printer manual.

2. If the printer is on-line, check the cable connections both at the printer and at the back of the PC. The cable should be securely fastened.

3. Run the Printers module in Control Panel. The printer connected to your PC should be listed in the Default Printer text box. If it is not, click on the Add button and choose your printer from the list. (You'll probably need to use the disks that came with Windows so that the setup routine can copy the correct printer drivers.)

4. If the program that started the print job is now running in the background, switch to that program.

System-Halting Errors

When a program tries to perform a task that Windows cannot understand, you'll see an error message. It will be titled something like "General Protection Fault Error" or "Stacks," and it will include some very technical information about the location in RAM where the error happened

There's nothing you can do at the time the error occurs other than to save any open data files. In earlier versions of Windows, these system-halting problems were called "Unrecoverable Application Errors." With release 3.1, Windows provides more specific information about the type of error and where it occured to help programmers fix the problem.

You should attempt to save important data by creating new files with the Save As command on the File menu. (Do not replace files by simply saving them, since there's a chance the data in RAM was corrupted, and you may need to use the file that is stored on disk.)

In most cases the error message will give you only one option: Close the active program. Although you can then continue to work on other programs, you should do so only for the purpose of trying to save data in RAM. Do not replace files with the Save command; instead, use the Save As command to create new files.

If the error box does not let you close the application, you should attempt to salvage some of your work by pressing Ctrl-Alt-Del, which will let you close just that program. Then, close all open programs and store data in new files by using the Save As command.

When you've salvaged as much of the data in RAM as possible, quit Windows. When you reload Windows, run the Dr. Watson utility by typing **DRWATSON** at the Run command of Program Manager's File menu before loading the same programs. The Dr. Watson utility may be able to help Microsoft or the publisher of the problematic program to fix the problem that caused the error, as explained shortly. (You may want to copy the Dr. Watson icon to the Startup group window so that it will load whenever you run Windows.)

In most cases, the error reappears only when you load the same combination of programs that caused the initial error. You may be able to avoid the error by loading the program that caused the error either alone or with different programs.

When the error reappears, the Dr. Watson utility will open after you see the error message. The utility will ask you to describe the programs that were loaded and the commands you were executing when the error occurred. After you've entered the information and saved it, write or call the publisher of the program you were using and report the problem. If the company has an updated version of the program that fixes the problem, it should be available without charge.

If the company cannot solve the problem, you should write or call Microsoft, which will probably ask that you send the LOG file that the Dr. Watson utility creates. After analyzing this report, either Microsoft or the publisher of the program will be able to fix the problem.

The most important thing you can do in dealing with a system-halting error is to identify the program causing the error and to stop using the program until you get a corrected copy from the publisher.

Windows Can't Find a Program You've Tried to Run

This will happen if you've moved a program file or deleted it, or if you've deleted a file that the program needs to load itself in memory.

The error message that Windows displays will let you know whether the problem was the lack of a particular file (such as a DLL). If the problem is caused by a change in either the file's location or your subdirectory structure, you may be able to fix it by editing the section of the WIN.INI file that tells Windows where to find files for this program, as explained in Chapter 9. Or you can change the DOS Path statement in your AUTOEXEC.BAT file to include the directory where this file is now stored, reboot, and run Windows.

Windows Won't Run

1. DOS may not be able to find file WIN.COM. Try switching to the directory where Windows is stored and typing **WIN** at the DOS prompt. If this solves the problem, edit your AUTOEXEC.BAT file to include the

Windows directory in the Path statement. For example, if WIN.COM is in the directory C:\WINDOWS, your Path statement should read

```
PATH=C:\WINDOWS
```

(Make sure each directory in your Path statement is separated by a semi-colon.)

2. There may not be enough available memory. Remove memory-resident programs by rebooting your system (press Ctrl-Alt-Del). If the problem persists, check the amount of available memory; in versions of DOS through 3.3 you can do this by running CHKDSK, which is usually stored in the DOS directory. (If it's not there, it will be on one of the DOS disks.) In versions of DOS starting with 4.0, you can also type **MEM** at any DOS prompt. Either DOS command tells you how much RAM is available. If you have less than 350k of available memory, you should edit your AUTOEXEC.BAT file to remove memory-resident programs that load automatically. You can run these programs after Windows is loaded, as you need them and according to the amount of available memory.

3. You may have changed hardware. Since Windows must have the correct device drivers installed for the video adapter in the system, it will not run if the wrong video display driver is installed. Run Setup by typing **SETUP** at the DOS prompt from the main Windows directory and change the hardware settings.

4. You can try to detect where the problem is occuring by looking at the file BOOTLOG.TXT. This file is written every time you load Windows and it shows Windows all of the drivers and programs that need to be successfully installed in memory before you can use Windows.

   The BOOTLOG.TXT file has a "LoadStart" statement for each file it reads. If the file is loaded with no difficulty, "LoadSuccess" appears on the next line. When Windows is not able to load a driver or program successfully, you know this is a problem that needs to be resolved. One of the most common problems that prevents Windows from loading is a change in video drivers. If there's a failure when the vidoe driver or any other file is being loaded, you should run Setup again by typing **SETUP** at the DOS prompt in your Windows directory.

5. One of the Windows configuration files may have become corrupted. Run Setup from the main Windows directory and reinstall Windows in the directory where it was previously installed.

A P P E N D I X   B

DOS Fundamentals for Beginners

DOS, which stands for Disk Operating System, is the software that does all the file management for Windows. When a Windows program does any work on a file, such as copying, moving, or deleting, it's actually making a request that DOS perform this task.

There are three parts to the DOS file management system: drives, files, and directories.

Drives

A drive is any medium that can store data: a 5.25-inch floppy disk; a 3.5-inch disk; a hard disk; a network drive; a CD-ROM device; or one of many other kinds of storage media.

DOS identifies each drive by a letter followed by a colon. A: almost always represents the primary floppy disk drive, B: represents the second floppy disk drive, and C: and D: almost always represent a hard disk. (Your system may not have a D: drive.) These are the standard ways that DOS refers to disks, though there are special programs that can change the way the letters A:, B:, C:, and D: are assigned.

Files and File Naming

A file is any collection of data that a program stores on a disk. Files are named in two parts: the prefix and the optional extension (or suffix), which are separated by a period. The Windows manual sometimes refers to the prefix alone as the file name.

The prefix must be eight or fewer alphanumeric characters. The extension, if there is one, must be three or fewer characters. Extensions are generally used to identify a file's data type. For example, Windows Write allows you to create file names but discourages you from creating file extensions, since Write automatically attaches the extension of WRI to files.

Certain characters are off-limits for naming files, because DOS uses them for specific purposes. Since a period, for example, is used to separate the prefix from the extension, it cannot appear anywhere else in the file name. In addition, some short words or word parts that DOS uses for specific commands cannot be used in file names. A file cannot be called PRN, for example, because DOS refers to the printer as PRN. The characters that cannot be used in a file name appear in Table B.1.

Directory Structure

A directory is a collection of files. It is represented in most Windows programs by a folder icon; in DOS and in some Windows programs, a directory is indicated by <*DIR*> in a directory listing. A directory can hold hundreds of other directories, called subdirectories. And any subdirectory can have more subdirectories within it.

Table B.1   **Characters Prohibited in File Names**

Excluded Characters	Excluded Phrases
. (period)	CON
/ (slash)	AUX
\ (backslash)	COM1
[ ] (brackets)	COM2
: (colon)	COM3
; (semicolon)	COM4
, (comma)	LPT1
= (equal sign)	LPT2
" (quotation mark)	LPT3
	(vertical bar)	PRN
	NUL

In DOS notation, a backslash character (\) always separates directories and subdirectories from one another. For example, C:\WPWIN\MACROS refers to the MACROS subdirectory within the WPWIN directory of the C: drive.

The same rules apply to naming directories as to naming files. However, you can't give a new directory the same name as a file in that directory.

DOS always considers the current directory (or subdirectory) the one where the last file activity took place. When you use any Windows dialog box that shows a directory listing, you'll see the current directory. When you first run Windows, the main Windows directory is current, but after using files from other directories, you may have changed the current directory. Dialog boxes that let you use files usually indicate the name of the current directory.

Most Windows programs represent a directory with a folder icon: The current directory is represented by an open, partly darkened folder and any inactive directories by closed folders. In Figure B.1, the current directory is D:\Windows. D:\ is also open (it must be open for WINDOWS to be open), and COLLAGE.32 and SYSTEM are inactive.

Figure B.1
The Open dialog box represents the current directory as an open folder that is partly darkened.

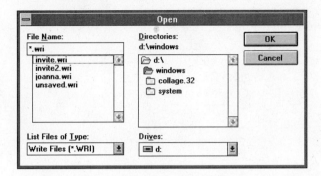

In some Windows dialog boxes, especially older Windows programs, when you look at a directory listing from within a subdirectory, the first listing is always [..] (two dots), which always represents the directory immediately above the current one (see Figure B.2). When you select [..], the directory immediately above becomes current. For example, if the current directory is D:\WINDOWS\SYSTEM, the current directory becomes D:\WINDOWS when you click on [..].

Figure B.2
This Open dialog box appears when you run Microsoft Word for Windows 1.0. Its directory listing uses [..] to represent the directory above the current one.

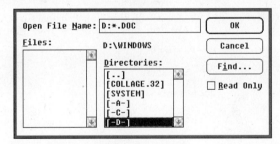

Program Files

On your PC you have some programs that can be run under DOS and other programs that can only be run under Windows. When you're in the Windows Program Manager, icons represent the Windows programs; double-clicking on an icon runs the program it represents.

DOS programs, on the other hand, can only be run when Windows has turned over the active display to the DOS command line or to a program that lets you execute DOS commands. You can automate the way you run a DOS program by using a PIF, so that you don't see the DOS command line, but in fact the PIF runs the command line so quickly before starting the DOS program that you don't see it.

A program file must have one of these file extensions:

Extension	Example
BAT	AUTOEXEC.BAT
COM	COMMAND.COM
EXE	NOTEPAD.EXE
PIF	123.PIF

Data Files

There are hundreds of different data file formats. The most common is ASCII text, which can be created and read by all word processors, including the Windows Notepad. Other data formats include WKS (spreadsheets), DBF (databases), and PCX (paint programs).

A file with a certain extension does not necessarily conform to the file type with the same letters. When you use the Open command of the File menu, you normally see only files that have the correct file extension for the application you're running. If an incompatible file has the extension of a compatible file type, it too will appear, but you get an error message if you attempt to open it.

On the other hand, you may want to use a file that is compatible with the program but that does not use the program's extension. For example, Windows Notepad stores ASCII text files as TXT files. Yet Notepad can read any text file, no matter what its extension.

To see files with names that don't conform to the conventions used by your program, you can change the List Files of Type option that appears below the File Name list to All Files.

Certain DOS and Windows programs can use the same data formats. Windows Paintbrush and Harvard Graphics both use PCX files, for example. A program's manual should list the data files that it can use.

Wildcards

There are two *wildcard* characters in DOS, the asterisk and the question mark, which you can use to see only the file names that fit a certain pattern.

The asterisk (*) is used in a search to retrieve file names whose prefix or extension varies by any number of consecutive characters. You can use the asterisk anywhere in the file name, and you can use it more than once. For example, using *.COM in an Open dialog box displays every file ending in *COM* (e.g., COMMAND.COM and WIN.COM). Using WIN.* displays WIN.COM, WIN.EXE, and any other file in that directory with the prefix of *WIN*. You can use the asterisk within a file name if you know how part of the file name is spelled; use the asterisk only for the part you don't know. For example, if you typed C*.COM, you'd find COMMAND.COM but you wouldn't find WIN.COM. And the All Files option of the Open dialog box uses two asterisks to represent all files: *.*.

The question mark (?) is a wildcard used to find files whose names vary by *one character*. For example, if you typed **?IN.COM** at the Open command, you'd retrieve WIN.COM, BIN.COM, and CIN.COM, but not SPIN.-COM. You can use ? anywhere in a file name, so it's especially useful when files are numbered 1–9. For example, you may create several REPORT files, naming them REPORT1.WRI, REPORT2.WRI, and so on. To see only files in this series, you'd enter REPORT?.WRI in an Open File Name text box.

A Guide to WIN.INI and SYSTEM.INI

This appendix is a glossary of the entries found in WIN.INI and SYSTEM-.INI, the two configuration files that control most Windows options. Chapter 9 explains in detail how to edit the entries in the file.

The entries are listed in the order in which Windows will place them in a typical installation. After the default entries in each section, there are optional settings that can be added by you or that some software may add. In addition, many programs add their own settings to WIN.INI, and the installation program that comes with some hardware adds settings to SYSTEM.INI. These additions usually appear in their own section and are easily identified. For example, Ami Pro for Windows creates a section titled [AMIPRO].

WIN.INI and SYSTEM.INI are divided into sections that are identified by a heading in brackets. The order in which the entries and sections appear is not important, except that the entries in each section must appear only beneath their respective headings.

While you can adjust optional settings in the WIN.INI file, avoid making changes to SYSTEM.INI. Most of the settings in SYSTEM.INI are dependent on the hardware in your system; if they are changed, Windows may not be able to run.

The settings that are defined here are the most commonly used settings; other settings may be needed to resolve unusual conflicts between hardware or software and Windows. The files WININI.WRI and SYSINI.WRI, which are copied by the Setup program to your main Windows directory, provide more information about other settings.

WIN.INI

[windows]   This section contains a variety of settings that are in effect throughout Windows.

Spooler   Enables Print Manager.

Load   Starts whichever Windows programs are listed here as a minimized icon every time Windows begins.

Run   Starts whichever Windows programs are listed here in a window every time Windows begins.

Beep   Enables sounds at errors and other events.

NullPort   Tells Windows where to send null characters.

BorderWidth   Sets the thickness of window borders; range is from 1 to 49.

CursorBlinkRate   Sets the number of milliseconds between cursor blinks.

DoubleClickSpeed   Sets the number of milliseconds that can elapse between two mouse clicks if they are to be considered a double-click.

Programs   File extensions that identify executable programs or batch files.

Documents   File extensions for data files. This entry is of little value; instead, use the [extensions] section to define document extensions.

DeviceNotSelectedTimeout Time   Sets the number of seconds Windows will wait for a printer to be turned on.

TransmissionRetryTimeout Time   Sets the number of seconds Windows will wait for a printer that's on to begin printing.

KeyboardDelay   Sets the number of milliseconds before a key that is held down starts to repeat.

KeyboardSpeed   Sets the number of milliseconds between repetitions of a character when a key is held down.

ScreenSaveActive   Enables the screen saver found in Control Panel's Desktop module.

ScreenSaveTimeOut   Sets the number of seconds of inactivity before screen saver is activated.

DosPrint   When on, causes Windows to use DOS interrupts for printing; when off, Windows communicates directly with the printer port.

MouseTrails   Controls the number of pointer images repeated on screen.

MouseThreshold1   Controls mouse speed according to a complex formula, when MouseSpeed is 1.

MouseThreshold2   Same as MouseThreshold1, except this value is used when MouseSpeed is 2.

MouseSpeed   Accelerates the mouse if set at 1 or 2; at zero, there is no acceleration.

NetWarn Enables network warning messages.

CoolSwitch Enables the Alt-Tab command for fast switching between applications.

Device Lists the current printer; it must also be listed below in the [devices] section.

DoubleClickWidth Sets the maximum number of pixels that the mouse can move between two clicks before it's not considered a double-click.

MenuDropAlignment Determines the direction on which menus will align. Left-aligned is 0; right-aligned is 1.

[Desktop] The settings that appear in this section control the appearance of the desktop and the positioning of windows and icons.

Pattern Sets the pattern displayed behind all active windows.

Wallpaper Lists the name of the BMP file displayed behind all active windows.

TileWallPaper Enables tiling of wallpaper. When the value is 1, wallpaper is centered.

WallPaperOriginX Sets the X-coordinate where display of tiled wallpaper begins (0, left margin, is the default).

WallPaperOriginY Sets the Y-coordinate where display of tiled wallpaper begins (0, top margin, is the default).

GridGranularity Controls how windows will align.

IconSpacing Sets the space between program icons in Program Manager group windows.

IconTitleSize Sets the size of the font used for Program Manager icon titles.

IconTitleWrap Specifies whether Program Manager icon titles will wrap.

IconTitleFaceName Specifies the font used for displaying Program Manager icon titles; default is MS Sans Serif.

IconVerticalSpacing   Sets the number of pixels that appear vertically between program icons in Program Manager.

MenuHideDelay   Sets the number of milliseconds before a cascading menu is removed (default is 0).

MenuShowDelay   Sets the number of milliseconds before a cascading menu is displayed (default is 0).

[Extensions]   Within this section, WIN.INI stores *file associations*, which are the programs that will run when a particular file extension is selected in File Manager. A default installation is the association between TXT and Notepad. If you changed Notepad to a different word processor (including a word processor that loads from a PIF), File Manager would load that word processor instead of Notepad every time you selected a file with the TXT extension. When new programs are installed in Windows, they usually add their extension here and associate it with the name of their executable file.

[colors]   This section establishes a color for the various sections of the screen, using three settings: red, green, and blue. Each color setting can range from 0 to 255, reflecting the intensity of the color; 0 is the absence of that color while 255 is the highest intensity.

Background   The area behind all active windows.

AppWorkspace   The working area for applications; this may include several document windows.

Window   The working area within a window.

WindowText   Text that appears within a document window.

Menu   The background of a menu.

MenuText   Text within a menu.

ActiveTitle   The title bar of an active window.

InactiveTitle   The title bar of an inactive window.

TitleText   Text in a title bar.

ActiveBorder   The border that surrounds an active window.

InactiveBorder   The border that surrounds an inactive window.

WindowFrame   The frame of a window.

Scrollbar   The area within a scroll bar.

ButtonFace   The area within a command button.

ButtonHilight   The accent area around the top and left edges of a command button.

ButtonShadow   The darker area behind a command button.

ButtonText   Text that appears in a command button.

GrayText   Text that is dimmed, as in an unavailable command name on a menu.

Hilight   The background of highlighted text.

HilightText   Highlighted text.

[intl]   This section defines how Windows will display dates, currency, and punctuation in languages other than United States English.

sLanguage   Identifies the language, using an abbreviation (usa for U.S. English, frn for French, etc.).

sCountry   Names the country whose standard settings will be used.

iCountry   Identifies the country, using the international dialing code (except Canada, which is 2).

iDate   (This is an obsolete setting included for compatibility with Windows 2.)

iTime   Selects a 12-hour clock (0), or a 24-hour clock (1).

iTLZero   Specifies to omit a leading zero in time (0), or to include it (1).

s1159   Establishes the letters that will appear when displaying times before noon (such as *AM*).

s2359   Establishes the letters that will appear when displaying times between noon and midnight (such as *PM*).

iCurrency   Establishes whether currency symbols appear before the value (0), or after (1).

iCurrDigits   Sets the number of digits that follow the decimal separator in currency.

iNegCurr   Specifies the format for showing negative currency amounts; 0 is ($1), 1 is –$1, and 2 is $–1.

iLzero   Generates a leading zero when displaying decimal numbers.

iDigits   Sets the number of digits displayed after the decimal point in numbers.

iMeasure   Specifies metric system (0), or English measure (1).

sCurrency   Sets the currency symbol that will be used. (If you've selected something other than the dollar sign, your word processor may not accurately display the ANSI special character that is stored here.)

sThousand   Sets the punctuation mark to be used in separating thousands in large numbers.

sDecimal   Sets the punctuation mark to be used for the decimal point.

sDate   (This is an obsolete setting provided for compatibility with Windows 2.)

sTime   Specifies the punctuation mark to be used to separate hours, minutes, and seconds.

sList   Specifies the punctuation to be used in separate items in a list.

sShortDate   Expresses abbreviations for printing dates in programs that use short dates.

sLongDate   Expresses abbreviations for printing dates in programs that use long dates.

[ports]   Establishes the communications parameters to be used when Windows sends data to the ports listed. The ports include COM, LPT, EPT (for an IBM PostScript printer), LPTx.OS2 (for OS/2 printers), and file names (for storing printer output in a file). When COM ports are specified, the values appear in this order:

```
Port  =  baud-rate,parity,word-length,stop-bits
```

[FontSubstitutes]   Creates an alias for each font listed; when the name on the left is used in a program, the font on the right will be used instead. This section is provided because with each version of Windows, older fonts are phased out and new fonts are introduced.

[TrueType]   Controls the use of TrueType fonts.

TTEnable   Enables TrueType fonts.

TTOnly   Enables the TrueType Only function; if it is negative, other fonts will be available.

[mci extensions]   Specifies the type of sound or multimedia device that Windows should use when you try to run a particular type of file.

[fonts]   Loads the fonts that you've specified during installation and tells Windows which file to use for the font information.

[embedding]   Specifies which OLE server programs are installed and the type of data files they provide.

[PrinterPorts]   Loads the driver file that Windows will use when you print to that port. Immediately after the name of the driver file, other settings may appear: port name, DeviceNotSelectedTimeout, and TransmissionRetryTimeout. The last two values will appear only if you've changed the values for this printer from the defaults. Otherwise, Windows will use the settings that appear in the [Desktop] section.

[devices]   This is the same information as in the [PrinterPorts] section, but it's provided here again because some applications written for Windows 2.0

will not work properly unless they find it. You may delete it if you're certain that you're not using any applications that were written prior to May 1990, when Windows 3.0 was released.

[network]   The settings in this section are different for every network operating system. Some network operating systems will also install their own configuration files. For example, if you're running Novell NetWare when you install Windows, the file NETWARE.INI will be created in the Windows directory.

SYSTEM.INI

[boot]   This section loads drivers and the most basic parts of Windows.

shell   Usually loads Program Manager, but other shells, such as Norton Desktop for Windows or File Manager, can be loaded.

mouse.drv   Loads the mouse driver.

network.drv   Loads the network driver.

language.dll   Loads a dynamic link library (DLL) file that contains language-specific information. If no file is listed, Windows uses the built-in United States English library.

sound.drv   Loads the sound driver, either for the PC speaker or for an add-in audio card.

comm.drv   Loads the driver that sends data to the serial and parallel ports.

keyboard.drv   Loads the keyboard driver.

system.drv   Loads the system hardware driver.

386grabber   Loads a device driver that controls DOS sessions in 386 Enhanced mode.

oemfonts.fon   Loads the font file containing characters that will work with your video card; this is needed especially for DOS programs.

286grabber   Loads a device driver that controls DOS sessions in VGA-COLOR.2GR.

fixedfon.fon   Specifies the font file containing characters that were required by older applications; it's provided only for compatibility with applications written before Windows 3.0 was released in May 1990.

fonts.fon   Loads the font file that contains characters used throughout Windows for displaying menus and dialog boxes.

display.drv   Loads the video card driver.

drivers   Loads additional hardware contained in dynamic link library (DLL) files. Drivers loaded this way are optional; sound boards are typically loaded this way.

scrnsave.exe   Loads the screen saver that was selected in Control Panel's Desktop module.

[keyboard]   This section gives Windows information that it needs to understand the keystrokes it receives. Changes made to these settings could prevent Windows from functioning properly.

subtype   Specifies a keyboard according to an internal table. It's used mostly by Olivetti and AT&T systems.

type   Specifies a keyboard according to the following system: 1 is an 83-key IBM XT or compatible; 2 is an Olivetti 102-key ICO; 3 is an 84-key IBM AT compatible; and 4 is the enhanced IBM 101- or 102-key keyboard. If the field is blank, the type is selected by the keyboard driver.

keyboard.dll   Loads a dynamic link library that defines the keyboard if your keyboard is not included among the four types listed above.

oemansi.bin   Loads OEM/ANSI code-page translation tables for systems that are not using the United States OEM character set (code page 437).

[boot.description]   This section contains a summary of how Windows is installed on your system. It is used by the Setup program. Changing these settings will not affect performance but could interfere with Setup's ability to change your settings.

[386Enh]   This section establishes settings that are needed only for 386 Enhanced mode. It is possible to solve incompatibilities and conflicts by adjusting some of these settings.

device   There will be many device entries in the [386Enh] section on a typical system. All device entries are used to specify virtual devices available in 386 Enhanced mode. Some of the entries will load files. Others—those preceded by an asterisk (*)—will load code that is stored within the Windows file WIN386.EXE.

Local   Lists the names of devices that should be handled separately in each virtual session (typically, communications devices).

EMMExclude   Specifies a range of memory that Windows will not scan to find unused address space. It's often used when a memory manager like Quarterdeck's QEMM is installed or when a video board creates a conflict with Windows. The range (two paragraph values separated by a hyphen) must be between A000 and EFFF. To exclude more than one area, enter additional EMMExclude lines.

EMMInclude   Specifies a memory range that Windows should scan when looking for unused address space. The range (two values separated by a hyphen) must be between A000 and EFFF.

EMMPageFrame   Specifies the memory address (or starting paragraph) where the 64k page frame will begin when Windows in 386 Enhanced mode cannot find a suitable page frame.

EMMSize   Specifies the total amount of memory that will be used as expanded (EMS) memory. This can be used when a DOS program grabs all the available expanded memory; by limiting it here, you can limit the amount lost to this application. The default value is 64k.

FileSysChange   Enables an automatic update system for letting File Manager know whether any file was changed. If it's on, system performance will slow down noticeably.

MinTimeslice   Sets the unit of processor time that Windows will allocate when computing its ratio for foreground and background priorities.

WinTimeslice   Lists the values for foreground and background processing established in Control Panel's 386 Enhanced module.

WinExclusive   If enabled, prevents DOS sessions from running in the background.

Com1AutoAssign   Sets the number of seconds that Windows will wait after a device stops using the communications port before it will let another device proceed. There will be an entry for each COM driver installed; these settings help Windows deal with the problem of more than one communications device attempting to work at the same time. If the value is –1, Windows will open a dialog box asking the user to decide which device gets priority whenever there's a conflict. If the setting is zero, Windows will let more than one device try to work at once. The maximum value is 1,000.

Paging   Enables the swap disk created in Control Panel's 386 Enhanced mode options. Disable paging only if you need the disk space that the swap file requires.

PagingDrive   Specifies a driver where Windows will store a temporary swap file; normally Windows uses the driver where SYSTEM.INI is installed.

Global   Overrides virtual devices that specify a device be run locally rather than globally. By default, all devices installed in CONFIG.SYS are global; if a device is installed locally only, enter it here in order to make it global in Windows. The value must exactly match the case of the device name, or this setting will not work. (Most device names are in all capital letters; therefore, this value must usually be in all capitals.)

HighFloppyReads   Enables an override of the use of DMA by Windows in the area E000:0000–EFFF:000F. This option should be used only when the system is freezing up, because this causes a conflict with the system's use of shadow RAM in this area. If this happens, disable this setting and set EMMExclude to E000–EFFF.

GLOSSARY

Active window   The window where mouse clicks and keystrokes take effect; any characters typed at the keyboard appear there. Only one window can be active at a time. It is displayed in a different color scheme from other, inactive windows. *See also* "Inactive window" and "Window."

ANSI   American National Standards Institute, an organization that publishes specifications for engineering, electronic, and related companies, ensuring the compatibility of products sold in America. *See also* "ANSI character set."

ANSI character set   A system for assigning a number to every character used on a computer, including letters and punctuation marks; created to allow computers to display foreign characters and symbols (including foreign currency symbols). Windows allows you to use these numbers to display characters. The ASCII and ANSI character sets share codes for displaying letters and numbers but differ in higher-order characters such as foreign letters.

Application   Software with many features, designed for a general task such as word processing. Applications require the services of an operating system such as DOS or Windows. Microsoft Excel, WordPerfect, and Lotus 1-2-3 are applications.

Application window   A window where all application activities take place; includes one or more document windows for displaying the application's data files. Some applications allow you to open several document windows within the application window. *See* "Document window."

Arrange   A technique for displaying windows or icons to make the best possible use of the available display space. *See also* "Tile" and "Cascade."

ASCII   American Standard Code for Information Interchange, a system for assigning a number to every character used on a computer, including letters and punctuation marks. ASCII is a standard way of storing text that enables different programs to exchange data. That's why "ASCII file" is often used synonymously with "text file," since a file that contains text without formatting codes is usually displaying only ASCII characters. ASCII was created to allow 8-bit computers to display graphic shapes (line drawings) in addition to text; DOS uses ASCII primarily for displaying characters. The ASCII and ANSI character sets share codes for displaying letters and numbers but differ in higher-order characters such as foreign letters.

Associate   Establish a connection between a Windows program and data files with one or more specific extensions. This makes it possible to open a file and launch the application that created or uses it when a file is double-clicked in programs like File Manager.

AUTOEXEC.BAT   A file that loads programs and sets certain parameters (such as a DOS path) each time you turn on your computer, immediately after the PC loads DOS.

Background   When more than one program is actively running, any program that either cannot be seen or is running in an inactive window. *See* "Inactive window."

Baud   Used to measure the speed at which data moves over a computer network or telephone line, usually (but not always) the same as bits per second.

Binary file   A term used mostly in communications to describe nontext files, which cannot be displayed on a screen in a readable form. Although every file on a computer is stored in binary form, *binary file* almost always refers just to nontext files.

Bit-mapped file   Stored as a collection of individual pixels, or picture elements. A bit-mapped data file contains a number for every pixel. Files with the extensions .BMP and .PCX contain bit-mapped graphics images. Some fonts are stored as bit maps. *See also* "Pixel" and "Vector image."

Border   The four edges of a window. To resize a window you reposition its borders with a mouse. Windows have borders, but dialog boxes and message boxes do not. *See also* "Sizing pointer."

Buffer   A block of memory used for temporarily storing data being sent to a computer device, often referring to memory reserved for holding data on its way to a printer; Print Manager, for example, maintains its own buffer. A buffer differs from a cache in that a buffer is emptied after the data moves to its destination, while a cache retains data as long as the computer is turned on. *See also* "Cache."

Cache   A block of memory used to maintain an ongoing record of often-used data; usually refers to a hard-disk cache. SMARTDRV.SYS is the cache that comes with Windows. A cache improves performance by shortening the amount of time it takes for a software program to search for data.

Cascade   A display arrangement that places one window in front of another, from the top left to the bottom right of your display, so that the title bar of each is visible. *See also* "Arrange" and "Tile."

CGA   Color Graphics Adapter, a specification for displaying graphics on a PC; introduced for the original IBM PC in the early 1980s but now superseded by the EGA and VGA specifications. *See also* "EGA" and "VGA."

Check box   Square boxes in dialog boxes in which you click with the mouse to turn an option on (with an X) or off (empty).

Click   To press and release a mouse button, usually the left one. A single click is usually used to highlight an object on screen; a double-click (two clicks in rapid succession) usually has the same effect as highlighting an object and pressing the Enter key. *See also* "Double-click."

Clipboard   A block of memory where data that is cut or copied from one file is stored until you paste, or insert, it into the same file or a different file.

COM1:   The first serial or communications port; successive serial ports are called COM2:, COM3:, etc. Note that proper spelling requires a colon immediately after the number of the port.

CONFIG.SYS   A text file read by a PC immediately after it boots and just before it reads AUTOEXEC.BAT. The file instructs DOS to install device drivers and change certain DOS default settings. The Windows memory manager, HIMEM.SYS, is installed when the CONFIG.SYS file is read. *See also* "AUTOEXEC.BAT."

Control menu   A list of commands that affect a window, including commands for minimizing, maximizing, and closing it. A Control menu's icon resembles a dash and is always located in the upper-left corner of a window. A Control menu is opened by pressing Alt-Spacebar.

Conventional memory   The first 640k of RAM in a PC; the memory that DOS controls. *See also* "Expanded memory" and "Extended memory."

Copy   (1) In File Manager or in DOS, to create a second, identical version of a file in another disk or directory. (2) On the Edit menu, to place a copy of highlighted data in the Clipboard.

Cursor   A vertical, blinking line indicating where the next keyboard input will be placed. A cursor is distinct from a pointer, which is controlled by a mouse. *See also* "Pointer."

Cut   To delete highlighted data from an active window and place it on the Clipboard.

DDE   Dynamic Data Exchange, a specification for allowing two Windows programs to share data with each other. *See also* "OLE."

Default   A setting in effect when you open a program. You can change it using a dialog box.

Desktop   The entire PC screen when Windows is running, including all windows and icons currently displayed.

Device driver   A software file that, when loaded into memory, establishes a line of communication between hardware and software. Device drivers allow Windows to issue simple instructions to the hardware device instead of elaborate commands every time the device is used. Device drivers usually have a file extension of .SYS (e.g., MOUSE.SYS) or .DRV (e.g., VGA.DRV).

Dialog box   A window that opens when a command or menu selection has options for you to set. Dialog boxes can offer one choice or many. Within a dialog box, you make choices by using text boxes, check boxes, radio buttons, and list boxes.

Directory   A way of organizing space and grouping files on a disk. Directories can have other directories within them, called subdirectories. The primary directory on a disk is called the root directory. When the Setup program installs Windows, it creates a directory for the programs needed to run Windows and a subdirectory called SYSTEM for storing drivers and other configuration files.

Dithering   A technique for simulating colors by displaying a pattern composed of pixels of two or more colors; allows Windows to display more colors than a system would normally allow. Dithering on a black-and-white system (such as a printer) is represented by different shades of gray, instead of colors.

Document window   A window that opens within an application window; displays primarily data created by or in a format compatible with the application. *See also* "Application window."

Double-click   To press and release the left mouse button twice in rapid succession. *See also* "Click."

Download   To receive a file through a modem from another computer. Windows's Terminal program has download commands. More generally, to move data or program files from one type of computer or device to another.

Draft quality   A way of printing a document in the fastest mode offered by the connected printer, usually producing hard copy of the lowest quality the printer can generate.

Drag   Moving a windows or graphic object across the screen.

Driver   *See* "Device driver."

Drop-down list box   A menu of options that can be seen only by clicking on the down-arrow icon to the right of the first option; with a keyboard, you can display the menu by pressing Alt-↓.

Drop-down menu   A list of available commands, grouped by functions, such as File and Edit. Appears when you click on its name in the menu bar or press its shortcut key (usually Alt followed by the underlined letter in the menu name).

EGA   Enhanced Graphics Adapter, a specification for displaying images on a PC. To display EGA graphic images, you must have a board that conforms to the EGA specification and either an EGA monitor or a multiscanning monitor. An EGA adapter displays fewer colors at a lower resolution than a VGA adapter. *See also* "VGA."

Expanded memory   Memory above 1024k, used by some DOS programs to load files that exceed DOS's 640k limit. Often referred to as EMS, short for LIM EMS (Lotus-Intel-Microsoft Expanded Memory Specification).

Extended memory   The memory above high memory (the first 64k above 1024k) and continuing as far as the amount of installed RAM; accessed only by a processor running in protected mode and by programs that use XMS (Extended Memory Specification). Windows uses extended memory when the extended memory device driver, HIMEM.SYS, is installed in DOS's CONFIG.SYS file. *See also* "HIMEM.SYS."

Extension   The optional characters in a file name after the period; often indicates the file's type or contents. A file called README.TXT, for example, has an extension of .TXT, indicating that it is composed of text. An extension is the same as a suffix.

Font   A typeface in a particular size and style. For example, Helvetica 10-point bold is a font within the Helvetica typeface family. *See also* "Typeface."

Graphic mode   One of several ways that a PC video adapter can display information on screen. Windows uses a graphic mode except when displaying full-screen DOS programs.

HIMEM.SYS   A file that gives Windows the ability to use more than 640k of memory. Also known as an extended-memory manager.

Hot link   A connection between two programs that allows them to share data; one program receives an update whenever data in the other changes. Hot links can conform to either the OLE (Object Linking and Embedding) or the DDE (Dynamic Data Exchange) specification. *See also* "DDE" and "OLE."

I-beam pointer   The mouse pointer assumes the shape of an I-beam when it moves into an area where text can be edited. *See also* "Pointer."

Icon   A small picture that represents a program, function, or data file. When either clicked or double-clicked, the icon performs an activity such as opening a program group window, launching a program, or opening a data file *and* launching a program.

Inactive window   A window that is no longer active. It may be either visible or hidden behind other windows. It becomes active if you click the mouse on it. *See also* "Active window" and "Background."

INI   A file with this extension provides initialization information to Windows programs. It is read while a Windows program is loading into memory and sets options for the program. For example, the WIN.INI file tells Windows which printer to use. *See also* "SYSTEM.INI" and "WIN.INI."

Macro   A series of keystrokes automatically performed in succession. A macro assigns a time-consuming series of tasks to a single keystroke, saving time and reducing errors. The Windows Recorder program lets you create and execute macros.

Maximize   To increase a window's size so that it occupies the entire screen. *See also* "Minimize."

Menu   A list of options and commands, usually displayed vertically and chosen by keyboard or mouse.

Menu bar   A horizontal listing of available menus that runs across the top of every application window. The File menu is usually first on a menu bar. *See also* "Menu."

Minimize   To reduce a window's size so that it appears only as an icon. *See also* "Maximize."

Modem   A device that enables a PC to communicate with other computers using ordinary telephone lines. Modem is short for modulation-demodulation, referring to the process of converting the computer's digital signals into an analog wave (audible tone) that can be carried over phone wires.

Moving pointer   The mouse becomes a cross with four arrow-heads when you select the Move command from a Control menu or when you place it on a Windows's title bar; allows you to drag a window to a new position. *See also* "Pointer" and "Title bar."

MSP   Microsoft Paint file format, a bit-mapped graphics format used almost exclusively by Microsoft Paint and the Windows Paintbrush program.

Multitasking   A computer's ability to run two or more programs simultaneously. During multitasking, one program operates in the foreground while the other program or programs operate in the background. *See also* "Background."

OLE   Object Linking and Embedding, a way of sharing data between Windows programs, allowing linked or embedded data to retain a connection with the program that created it. If two programs share data, OLE can simplify updates and ensure that the most recent version of the shared data is used.

Palette   A range of colors to choose from. Some programs, like Paintbrush, present a unique set of colors to choose from but also allow you to blend new colors from that set.

PCX   A bit-mapped graphics format used by Windows Paintbrush and many other graphics programs. One of the earliest and most widely used graphics formats, used principally to store color images of relatively low resolution.

PIF   Program Information File, used to store options describing how Windows should use a PC's resources when it runs a DOS program. Among other things, a PIF establishes how much memory the DOS program can use; whether the program runs inside a window or uses the full screen; and whether the program takes exclusive control of the processor. The PIF Editor, a Windows Accessory, is used to set and adjust PIF options for a DOS program.

Pixel   A contraction of *picture element*. Refers to the tiny rectangles of colored light that compose the computer display. A VGA display with a resolution of 640 × 480, for example, shows 640 rows of pixels across the screen and 480 columns of pixels down.

Pointer   A movable object, usually arrow-shaped, that indicates the place on the screen where a mouse action (such as a click) will take effect. The pointer assumes different shapes when it is carrying out different functions. *See also* "I-beam pointer," "Moving pointer," and "Sizing pointer."

Port   (1) A logical path in the computer's memory for transmitting data; for example, a program sends a file to a printer via the printer port. (2) A metal connector on the back of a computer, to which a cable is attached that connects the computer to a hardware device, such as a printer or modem.

Protected mode   Allows a processor to isolate a program's activities from other programs that are operating, making it possible for Windows to run several programs simultaneously. Protected mode is one of several modes of an Intel processor: The 80286 and 80386 processors each have a protected mode and a real mode; real mode emulates the 8088 processor. *See also* "Real mode."

RAM   Random Access Memory, implemented by PC chips that hold information; measured in bytes. Programs are stored in RAM when you load them, and current work is stored there. Although RAM stores data, it differs from a disk: When power is turned off or when the computer reboots, the contents of RAM vanish, while the contents of a disk remain available.

Real mode   A mode for running Windows that was discontinued in release 3.1. Windows programs that require real mode must be run under Windows 3.0.

Restore   To change the size of a minimized or maximized window so that it appears the same size that it did before being minimized or maximized.

Scroll   To move the screen display up or down; used for lists and document windows that can't fit in the display.

Scroll bar   A long rectangular area at the right or bottom of a window that lets you move the screen up and down, or right and left, allowing you to view data that doesn't fit in the display.

Shortcut key   A combination of two or more keystrokes that, when pressed simultaneously, perform a specific function. For example, the shortcut key that opens a File menu is Alt-F (hold down the Alt key and press F).

Sizing pointer   Used to change the size of a window. The mouse pointer becomes a two-headed arrow and can be used for sizing when it crosses a window's border. *See also* "Border."

Standard mode   One of two modes for running Windows. The other mode is called 386 Enhanced mode. *See also* "Real mode."

Subdirectory   A directory within a directory. For example, a directory used to store files relating to a particular year might contain a subdirectory for each month in the year. Each subdirectory might in turn contain a subdirectory for each day in the month. *See also* "Directory."

Suffix   *See* "Extension."

Super VGA   A specification for displaying graphics on a PC that adds several video modes to the existing VGA standard. To display images in Super VGA you must have a board that provides Super VGA modes, a monitor compatible with that particular board, and device drivers for Windows that have been installed with the Windows Setup program. Resolutions of 800 × 600 and higher conform to the Super VGA specification. *See also* "VGA."

Swap file   A file on your disk that Windows uses to store data temporarily when it runs out of RAM.

System   A PC, including all peripherals.

SYSTEM.INI   A text file that stores the parameters for several dozen hardware settings that Windows requires to perform correctly on your system. Windows reads the SYSTEM.INI file when it loads itself into memory.

System font   The font that Windows uses to display text in menus; in the current version of Windows, Helvetica 10 point.

System resource   A small amount of memory that Windows uses for each icon, open window, and every other displayed object; the memory for system resources is a special pool kept separately from the RAM available for running programs.

Task Manager   A window that pops up when you press Ctrl-Esc; a feature of Program Manager that lets you switch between open programs.

Text mode   One of the many modes that a PC display adapter can use. This mode is limited to displaying alphanumeric ASCII characters, because it displays only characters stored on a ROM (Read-only memory) chip. Windows uses text mode only when running full-screen DOS applications. At all other times, Windows uses a graphics mode. *See also* "Graphic mode."

TIFF   Tagged Image Format File, a format for storing graphics files in desktop publishing. TIFF, or TIF, is the most common file type for bit-mapped images, because of its ability to represent many levels of gray shading.

Tile   An arrangement of windows that shows a portion of each, side by side like tiles, without overlapping. *See also* "Arrange" and "Cascade."

Title bar   The band that runs across the top of any application or document window displaying either the name of the program running in the window or the data file displayed.

Typeface   A basic design for depicting letters and numbers, such as Times Roman, Helvetica, and Courier.

Upload   To send a file from one computer to another through a modem connection. The Windows Terminal program has upload commands. *See also* "Download" and "Modem."

Utility   A program with limited features. Most utilities perform a job that helps you use applications.

Vector image   An image defined mathematically by lines, angles, and curves; calculated and drawn every time the image is displayed. Some of the fonts in Windows are created this way.

VGA   Video Graphics Array, a specification that defines how a PC displays images on the screen. A board that provides this function is called a VGA adapter. A monitor capable of displaying VGA images is called an analog VGA monitor or multiscanning monitor. VGA can also display images according to the EGA specification. *See also* "EGA" and "Super VGA."

Wallpaper   An image that appears behind all open windows; a graphics file stored in the BMP (bit-mapped) format. You can switch wallpaper designs using the Control Panel's Desktop module and edit an individual wallpaper design using Paintbrush.

WIN.INI   A text file that stores the settings for Windows options and directs Windows programs to files that they need when they're loaded.

Window   A portion of the screen defined by borders, primarily used to enter or display data. The window as a whole can be changed in size, repositioned, and minimized or maximized by a mouse or by commands on the window's Control menu.

Work area   The area within an active window's borders where you can add and edit data.

Workspace   An area within an active window where you can open windows (usually data files to be used by the active application).

XGA   Extended Graphics Adapter, a graphics adapter sold by IBM and intended as a successor to VGA, since it is capable of displaying VGA modes and several other high-resolution modes. Although it provides capabilities similar to Super VGA adapters, it is not compatible with them. To run a PC or PS/2 in an XGA mode, the correct video display driver must be installed with the Windows Setup program.

INDEX

A

About command, 303, 308
About File Manager option, 91–92
active windows, 13, 443
airbrush tool, 183
Alarm menu for Calendar, 169
alarms with Calendar, 152–154
aliases for font names, 366
alignment
    in headers and footers, 106, 155
    for menus, 412–413
    with Write, 118–119, 123
Allow Close When Active option, 323
Alt-Enter keys, 326
Alt-Esc keys, 13, 38, 310, 324–325
Alt key
    for macros, 240, 245
    for shortcut keys, 16–17, 168
    for special characters, 369
Alt-Spacebar keys, 310
Alt-Tab keys, 243, 268, 310, 325
analog clock, 165–166
annotating with help text, 24–25
ANSI codes, 369, 443
ANSI.SYS file, removing, 401
Application Execution Error message box, 19
applications, 443
    client and server, 91, 340
    and Desktop, 268
    future, 415–418
application windows, 12–15, 443
appointments with Calendar, 150–155
APPS.INF file, 328–330
archive records, 76
arranging, 443
    icons, 40
    program groups, 406–407
    windows, 14–15, 36–37, 61, 87, 307
arrow keys
    with dialog boxes, 18–19
    with Directory windows, 56–57
    with Terminal, 225–226
    with Write, 112

ASCII, 443. *See also* text files
associations between files and programs, 57, 443
    creating, 90
    listing files by, 84
    for performance, 408–409
    for printing, 375
    WIN.INI for, 88–89, 295–297
asterisks (*) with file names, 70–71, 74, 430–431
attributes, file, 53, 75–76, 82
autodialing with Cardfile, 164
AUTOEXEC.BAT file, 290, 391, 444
Ave function with Calculator, 142

B

background color, 180, 197, 266
background tasks, 286–287, 303, 320–322, 444
Basic Colors grid, 253–254
baud rate, 444
    Control Panel for, 262
    for modems, 208, 210, 213
binary files, 216, 220–221, 444
binary numbers, 140, 142–143
bitmapped fonts, 362
black-and-white graphics, 179
BMP (bitmap) files, 201–202, 444
    for Paintbrush, 197–199
    for wallpaper, 267
bold fonts, 86, 360
bookmarks for help, 25–26
[boot.description] section in SYSTEM.INI, 440
BOOTLOG.TXT file, 426
[boot] section in SYSTEM.INI, 439–440
boot settings, 292–293, 295, 439–440
borders, 7–8, 271, 444
box tool, 187–188
branches, directory, 80–81
Browse dialog box, 43, 90
browsing drives, 79–80
brush tips, 185
buffers, 444
    for disk caches, 400–401
    for Terminal, 214, 222, 225

C

C++, 418
caches, 444
    disk, 309, 371–372, 397–401
    font, 371
Calculator, 135
    advanced math with, 144–146
    calculations with, 137–140
    engineer options with, 144
    memory for, 137–138, 140–141, 147
    menus for, 170
    modes for, 136–137
    with other programs, 146–147
    programmer options with, 142–143
    Statistics Box with, 141–142
    storing numbers with, 140–141
Calendar
    alarms and warnings with, 152–154
    appointments with, 150–155
    icons for, 156–157
    loading, 155–156
    menus for, 169–170
    views with, 148–150
capacity of disks, 78
Cardfile
    creating lists with, 157–158
    dialing phone numbers with, 164–165
    editing with, 161–164
    finding information with, 160–161
    menus for, 171–172
    merging with, 164
    moving in, 159–160
    printing with, 165
    views in, 159
Card menu for Cardfile, 171
carriage returns, 225, 229
carrier detect with Terminal, 211
cartridges, font, 275
cascading windows, 14, 36–37, 61, 87, 307, 444
case sensitivity in searches, 105, 113
CD-ROM players, 419–420
CEMM.EXE program, 394
CGA, 444

Character Map utility, 368–369
Character menu for Write, 132
characters
    international, 226
    special, 368–369
    Write formats for, 114–116
check boxes, 21, 445
circles, 188
clicking, 2, 8, 445
client applications, 91, 340
Clipboard, 445
    for bitmaps, 198
    with Calculator, 142, 146
    copying files to, 65–66
    for DOS screens, 423
    Edit menu with, 333–336
    exchanging data through, 127–129, 336–338
    with graphics, 162–163, 178, 191–192
    menus for, 351
    with Notepad, 104
    and PIF files, 323
    for sound, 383
    with Terminal, 221–222
    viewing data in, 339, 351
Clock, 165–166, 172
CLOCK.INI file, 289
Close Window on Exit option, 317, 329
closing
    dialog boxes, 19
    Directory windows, 62–63
    programs, 326–327
    windows, 28, 317, 329
collapsing directories, 57–58, 80–81
color
    background and foreground, 180, 197, 266
    for boxes, 187
    Control Panel for, 251–259
    for graphics, 179–181, 183
    for patterns, 266
    for printing, 370
    of selection cursor, 54–55
color eraser tool, 190

Color Refiner box, 258
color schemes, 251–254
[colors] section in WIN.INI, 435–436
columns with Terminal, 223
COM1 port, 445
combining groups of files, 75
command buttons, 20, 26–28
communications protocols, 210, 220.
    See also Terminal program
compatibility with extended memory, 395
CompuServe on-line service, 412
CONFIG.SYS file, 391, 445
   disk cache settings in, 400–401
   editing, 290
   memory settings in, 394–396
   multiple, 393, 410–411
configuring printers, 273–274
confirmations
   with dialog boxes, 19–20
   with file operations, 64, 67, 85
Connect Net Drive command, 78–79
contents, help, 26
control codes for function key shortcuts,
   228–229
CONTROL.INI file, 257, 289
control keys for macros, 240, 245–246
Control menus, 445
   for Clipboard, 337
   for closing programs and windows, 28, 327
   for Directory windows, 62–63
   for DOS programs, 325
   for moving and sizing windows, 7, 9
   for moving dialog boxes, 18
   for program groups, 31, 34
   for restoring windows, 5
   for Task List, 38
Control Panel, 249–250
   for color, 251–259
   for date and time, 281
   for Desktop, 265–271
   for fonts, 259–261
   for international settings, 276–280
   for keyboard, 280
   for menus, 298

   for mouse, 263–265
   for networks, 288–289
   for ports, 262–263
   for printers, 271–276
   for sound, 281–283
   for 386 Enhanced mode, 284–288
conventional memory, 391, 445
converting graphic files, 202
copies, printer, 275
copying, 445
   with Cardfile, 162
   to Clipboard, 333–338
   disks, 77
   files, 63–66
   graphics, 191–192
   help text, 24
   program items, 45–46
   sound, 383
   with Terminal, 221–222
Ctrl-Esc keys, 38
Ctrl key
   for copying files, 64
   for macros, 240, 245
   for selecting files, 71
   for shortcut keys, 168
   for Terminal, 225–226
Ctrl-Tab keys, 34–35, 38, 62
CUA (Common User Access), 415
currency settings, 278–279
current directory, 428–429
cursors, 445
   blink rate for, 270
   for drawing tools, 182
   in graphical word processing, 97, 102–103
   for Paintbrush, 178
   selection, 54–55
   for Terminal, 226
curved line tool, 185–187
custom colors, 180–181, 252–257
cutting, 445
   with Cardfile, 162
   graphics, 191–192
   sound, 383–384

D

daily view with Calendar, 148–150
data bits for modems, 208, 210, 213
data files, 430. *See also* associations between files and programs
date
  with Calendar, 149–150, 155
  Control Panel for, 281
  of file changes, 53, 82
  international settings for, 276–278
  in Notepad documents, 106–108
  of printer jobs, 373
DDE (Dynamic Data Exchange), 349–350, 445
decimal point indicators, 279–280
decimal tabs with Write, 121
defaults, 446
  for printers, 358–359
  for screen saver, 269
degrees with Calculator, 144
delayed-write caches, 397–399
delays
  keyboard repeat, 280
  for screen saver, 269
deleting
  Calculator entries, 139
  confirmation option for, 85
  directories, 85
  files, 66–67
  fonts, 260, 366–367
  graphics, 195–196
  icons, 40
  program items, 45
  sound, 383–384
  Write text, 113
demonstrations, macros for, 241
descriptions
  for fonts, 363
  for program groups, 31
  for program items, 44
Desktop, 3, 446
  Control Panel for, 265–271
  creating, 415
  and performance, 406–407
[Desktop] section in WIN.INI, 434–435

device contention, 284–285
device drivers, 446
  memory for, 396
  mouse, 401
  network, 288
  pen computing, 421
  printer, 355–357, 367, 370
  sound, 282–283, 379
device independence, 356
Device menu for Media Player, 389
[devices] section in WIN.INI, 438–439
diagonal lines, 187–188
dialing phone numbers. *See* Cardfile; Terminal program
dialog boxes, 15, 17–21, 70–71, 446
digital clock, 165–166
digitizing tablets, 420–421
directories, 446, 451
  collapsing, 57–48, 80–81
  creating, 69–70
  deleting, 85
  expanding and collapsing, 57–58, 80–81
  for graphic files, 199–200
  listing, 56, 84
  names of, 428
  navigating, 58
  for Notepad, 102
  for program items, 43
  searching for files in, 68–69
  selection cursor for, 54
  starting, 58–59
  structure of, 427–429
Directories list box, 43, 90
Directory Contents window, 53, 58, 61
Directory Tree window, 53, 58
Directory windows
  activating selections in, 56–57
  composition of, 81–82
  controlling, 55–56
  directories in, 57–58
  multiple, 59–63
  navigating, 52–63
  parts of, 52–54
  selection cursors for, 54–55

splitting, 82
for starting directory, 58–59
Disconnect Net Drive command, 78–79
disks and disk drives, 76, 427
    caches for, 309, 371–372, 397–401
    confirmation options for, 85
    copying, 77
    copying files between, 65
    formatting, 77–78
    icons for, 52–53
    labels for, 77–78
    listing contents of, 56
    network commands for, 78–80
    RAM, 401–402
    selection cursor for, 54
    size requirements for, 417
    swapping files to, 304–305, 308–309
    volume names for, 77–78
Display menu for Clipboard Viewer, 351
display usage option in PIF files, 319–320
dithering, 179–180, 183–184, 446
DLL (Dynamic Link Libraries), 417
document formats with Write, 120–122
Document menu for Write, 132
document windows, 12–15, 446
DOS, fundamentals of, 427–431
DOS programs, 429–430
    associating, 90
    icons for, 41–44, 311, 328, 405–406
    memory for, 304–306
    multitasking, 284, 311–324
    program items for, 41–44
    switching, 324–330
    in 386 Enhanced mode, 303
DOS screens, capturing, 423
double-clicking, 2, 264, 446
downloading and uploading files, 216–221,
    446, 452
draft quality printing, 127, 275, 367, 447
dragging, 2, 8, 447
drawings and drawing tools, 178–189
DR-DOS 6, 402
drivers. *See* device drivers
drives. *See* disks and disk drives

drop-down list boxes, 20, 447
drop-down menus, 447
Dr. Watson diagnostic program, 327, 425
Dynamic Data Exchange (DDE), 349–350, 445
Dynamic Link Libraries (DLL), 417

E

echo
    with sound, 382
    with Terminal, 224
editing
    with Cardfile, 161–164
    colors, 180–181
    INI files, 289–297
    macro properties, 239–241
    Notepad documents, 100, 102–104
    with Paintbrush, 189–197
    patterns, 266–267
    PIFs, 312–324
    text boxes, 21
    in Write, 111–114
Edit menu
    for Calculator, 170
    for Calendar, 169
    for Cardfile, 171
    for Clipboard, 333–336
    for Clipboard Viewer, 351
    for File Manager, 94
    for help, 24–25
    for Notepad, 131
    for Object Packager, 352
    for Paintbrush, 204
    for Sound Recorder, 388
    for Terminal program, 231
    for Write, 132
Effects menu for Sound Recorder, 388
EGA, 447
8086 protected mode, 303
ellipses, 188
embedded data, 339–343
    Cardfile objects, 165
    files, 91
    sound, 384–386
[embedding] section in WIN.INI, 438

EMM386.SYS driver, 394, 396

EMS memory option in PIF files, 319, 322

emulation, terminal, 211

End key, 56, 112

end marks in Write, 110

engineer options with Calculator, 144

environment variables in PIF files, 316

eraser tools for drawings, 190

erasing graphics, 195–196

error-checking protocols, 220

Esc key, 17, 19, 137

Events Horizons on-line service, 198

exchanging data, 91, 339–343

    with Cardfile, 164–165

    with Clipboard, 65–66, 127–129, 336–337

    with Dynamic Data Exchange, 349–350

    linking objects for, 343–345

    Object Packager for, 346–349

    Paste commands for, 345–346

    sound, 384–386

    with Terminal, 221–222

execution setting in PIF files, 320

expanded memory, 304, 392–394, 447

    for disk caches, 397

    in PIF files, 319, 322

expanding directories, 57–58, 80–81

extended memory, 302, 392–393, 447

    for disk caches, 397, 399

    drivers for, 395–396

    in PIF files, 316–317, 322

extensions, 447

    for associating files, 89–90, 296

    file, 427, 430

    Windows, 418–421

[Extensions] section in WIN.INI, 435

F

F1 key, 21

Fastdisk, 288

fat-bit editors, 196

File Manager, 51

    for disk operations, 76–80

    display with, 80–88

    for file management, 63–76

    navigating Directory windows with, 52–63

    and performance, 408–409

    for Program Manager, 92–93

    running programs with, 88–92

File menu

    for Calendar, 169

    for Cardfile, 171

    for Clipboard Viewer, 351

    for File Manager, 94

    for help, 23

    for Media Player, 389

    for Notepad, 131

    for Object Packager, 351

    for Paintbrush, 204

    for PIF, 331

    for Program Manager, 49

    for Recorder utility, 247

    for Sound Recorder, 388

    for Terminal program, 231

    for Write, 132

File Name list box, 43, 90

files

    activating, 56–57

    associating. *See* associations between files and programs

    binary, 216, 220–221, 444

    confirmation options for, 64, 67, 85

    copying and moving, 63–66

    data, 430

    deleting, 66–67

    embedding, 91

    finding, 68–69

    formats for, 198–199

    groups of, 70–75, 430–431

    listing, 53, 56, 58, 82–85

    names of, 67, 106, 155, 427–428

    Notepad, 99–101

    Paintbrush, 177

    printing, 66, 375

    printing to, 127

    program, 84, 429–430

    properties for, 53, 75–76, 82

    Recorder, 244

    refreshing, 88

renaming, 67

replacing, confirmation option for, 85

saving, 28

selection cursor for, 54

sorting, 83

swap, 287–288, 304–305, 308–309, 403, 451

temporary, 305

for Terminal, 230

transferring, 216–221

finding

Cardfile information, 160–161

files, 68–69

Notepad text, 104–105

programs, 38–40

Find menu for Write, 132

fixed-pitch fonts, 362

flipping graphics, 193

flow control

Control Panel for, 262

with Terminal, 211, 218

font cartridges, 275

fonts, 447

characteristics of, 359–360

Control Panel for, 259–261

deleting, 260, 366–367

dialog box for, 360–361

for directory and file listings, 86

for icons, 413

for Paintbrush, 189

for printing, 216, 359–367, 370–371

system, 117–118, 260, 362, 451

for Terminal, 224–225

Windows, 361–364

for Write, 114–118

[fonts] section in WIN.INI, 438

[FontSubstitutes] section in WIN.INI, 438

footers

for appointments, 154–155

for Notepad, 105–106

for Write, 120–121

foreground color, 180, 197, 266

foreground tasks, 286–287, 303, 320–322

formats

of dates, 149–150

of files, 198–199

international, 276–280

formatting

confirmation options for, 85

disks, 77–78

with Write, 114–116, 118–123

freehand drawing tool, 184–185

freeze-ups, 327

full screens

PIF option for, 319–320

switching, with windows, 326

function keys with Terminal, 225–229

functions with Calculator, 142, 144–145

G

General Fault Protection error message, 311

GIF files, 198–199

glossary

in help, 27–28

of Windows terms, 443–453

Go to Page command with Write, 114

gradients with Calculator, 144

granularity setting, 270–271

Graphical Device Interface (GDI), 308, 364

graphical word processing, 97–98

graphic mode, 448

graphics. *See also* Paintbrush

with Cardfile, 162–163

and Clipboard, 336

creating, 175–176

printing, 367–368, 370

resolution of, 275

in Write documents, 128–129

zooming, 196–197

grids, 270

groups

of files, 70–75, 430–431

PIFs for, 328–330

program. *See* program groups

GRP files, 48

H

handles for extended memory, 396

handshaking with Terminal, 211

hanging indents with Write, 120
hanging up with Terminal, 213–214
hard disks. *See* disks and disk drives
hardware fonts, 117
Hayes-compatible modems, 208
headers
    for appointments, 154–155
    for Notepad, 105–106
    for Write, 120–121
help, 21
    command buttons for, 26–28
    menu bar for, 22–26
help index, 23, 26
Help menu
    for Calculator, 170
    for Calendar, 170
    for Cardfile, 172
    for Clipboard Viewer, 351
    for Control Panel, 298
    for File Manager, 95
    for Media Player, 389
    for Notepad, 131
    for Object Packager, 352
    for Paintbrush, 205
    for PIF, 331
    for Print Manager, 376
    for Program Manager, 49
    for Recorder utility, 247
    for Sound Recorder, 388
    for Terminal program, 232
    for Write, 132
hexadecimal numbers, 140, 142–143
hidden files, 76, 84–85
highlighting
    with Notepad, 104, 108
    with Write, 111–112
high memory area, 322, 392
HIMEM.SYS driver, 391, 395–396, 448
HLP files, 23
Home key, 56, 112
hot links, 448
hue of colors, 259
hyperbolic functions, 144

I

I-beam pointer, 15, 21, 98, 103–104, 189, 448
icons, 448
    arranging, 40
    for Calendar, 156–157
    in Control Panel, 250
    deleting, 40
    in Directory windows, 53–54
    for disk drives, 52–53
    for DOS programs, 41–44, 311, 328,
        405–406
    fonts for, 413
    for groups, 31
    in Lotus 1-2-3, 415–416
    packaged, 346–349
    for PIF files, 324, 329
    for Recorder files, 245
    reducing windows to, 3–7
    running programs from, 37
    for 386 Enhanced mode, 284
idle time detection option in PIF files, 322
inactive windows, 13, 448
indents with Write, 120, 122–123
index, help, 23, 26
index lines in Cardfile, 157–158, 160–161
INI files, 448. *See also specific INI files*
inserting
    graphics into documents, 128–129
    packaged icons, 348–349
    Write text, 113
insertion points, 97, 103, 112
installing
    modems, 207–208
    mouse, 263
    printers and printer drivers, 272–273,
        356–357, 367
international characters with Terminal, 226
international settings, Control Panel for,
    276–280
interrupt request (IRQ) line, 262–263
intervals, appointment, 150
[intl] section in WIN.INI, 436–437
inverse functions, 144
inverse graphics, 193

IRQ (interrupt request) line, 262–263
italic fonts, 86, 360

K

Kermit protocol, 220
keyboard
    Control Panel for, 280
    copying and moving files with, 65
    for Directory windows, 55–56
    in graphical word processing, 98
    for menu options, 16–17
    moving windows with, 9–10
    with Write, 111–112
[keyboard] section in SYSTEM.INI, 440

L

labels for disks, 77–78
landscape orientation
    in printing, 275, 357, 370
    in Write, 125
LANMAN.INI file, 289
laptops
    color schemes for, 252
    displays on, 423
    mouse trails with, 265
leading zeros, 280
left-handed mouse clicking, 264
letter-quality printing, 367
levels
    directory, 80–81
    of function keys, 228
libraries for Terminal, 230
LIM EMS specification, 392
line feeds
    with file transfers, 219
    with Terminal, 225
lines, drawing, 185–188
line spacing with Write, 118, 123
line wrap with Terminal, 223
linking
    Cardfile objects, 165
    with Dynamic Data Exchange, 349–350
    future of, 417
    objects, 129, 343–345
    sound, 386

list boxes, 20
listing
    directories, 56, 84
    files, 53, 56, 58, 82–85
loading
    Calendar, 155–156
    macros, 243–244
    programs, 295–296
    Recorder, 245–246
local echo with Terminal, 224
local heap, 308
locking memory option in PIF files, 322
.LOG files, 106–108
long date form, 278
loops for macros, 241
lost files, searching for, 68–69
Lotus 1-2-3, 415–416
luminosity, 257–259

M

Macro menu for Recorder utility, 247
macros, 226–229, 448. *See also* Recorder utility
Main window, 1, 13
mapping drives, 79
margins
    in headers and footers, 106, 155
    in Write, 122–123
Mark command, 338
Marquee screen saver, 269
math. *See* Calculator
maximized windows, 3–7, 448
[mci extensions] section in WIN.INI, 438
Media Player, 386–387, 389
memory, 450
    adding, 403, 418
    error messages for, 423–424
    checking, 91–92
    for Calculator, 137–138, 140–141, 147
    for disk caches, 371–372, 397–401
    for DOS programs, 304–306
    for fonts, 259–261
    freeing up, 401–402
    for graphics, 129
    for macros, 244
    for multitasking, 301–303, 308–309

and performance, 391–396
in PIF files, 316–317, 319, 322
in printers, 275, 370
for programs, 295
for sound, 380
and task lists, 307
types of, 391–396
virtual, 287–288, 403
for wallpaper and patterns, 267–268
menu bar, 15–17, 22–26, 448
menus, 448
aligning, 412–413
for Calculator, 170
for Calendar, 169–170
for Cardfile, 171–172
for Clipboard Viewer, 351
for Clock, 172
for Control Panel, 298
for Media Player, 389
for Notepad, 131
for Object Packager, 351–352
for Paintbrush, 204–205
for PIF, 331
for Print Manager, 376
for Recorder utility, 247
for Sound Recorder, 388
for Terminal program, 231–232
for Write, 132
merging
Cardfile lists, 164
macro files, 244
message boxes, 19
MIDI (Musical Instrument Digital
Interface), 380, 386, 420
minimized windows, 3–7, 62, 449
Minimize on Use option, 40, 87
minus signs (–) in Directory windows, 58, 81
mixing
colors, 256–258
sound, 383–384
Mode menu for PIF, 331
modems, 449
installing, 207–210
ports for, 207, 210, 262

modules, Control Panel, 250
monitors
PIF setting for, 322–323
protecting, 268–270
monospaced fonts, 225
monthly view with Calendar, 148–150
MORICON.DLL file, 328, 406
mouse
confirmation options for, 85
Control Panel for, 263–265
copying and moving files with, 64
drivers for, 401
in graphical word processing, 98
in macros, 236, 241–242
for menu options, 15–16
moving windows with, 9
troubleshooting, 423
using, 1–3
with Write, 111–112
moving
in Cardfile, 159–160
dialog boxes, 18–19
between Directory windows, 61–62
files, 63–66
graphics, 129, 192
between group windows, 33–34
message boxes, 19
program items, 45
text, through Clipboard, 127–128
windows, 7–10
moving pointers, 9–10, 449
MPC (Multimedia PC) standard, 419
MPS files, 198–199
MSDOS.EXE program, 409–410
MS-DOS 5, 402
MSP (Microsoft Paint) format, 449
multimedia, 419–420
multiple appointment schedules, 152
multiple Directory windows, 59–63
multiple files, working with, 70–75, 430–431
multiple printers, 358–359
multiple program groups, managing, 34–35
multitasking, 284, 301, 449
DOS programs, 311–324

memory for, 301–303, 308–309

modes for, 302–306

PIF options for, 320–322

scheduling for, 285–287

Task Lists for, 306–308, 310, 324–330

Windows programs, 310–311

Mystify screen saver, 269

N

names

for bookmarks, 25

for directories, 428

for disks, 77–78

for files, 67, 106, 155, 427–428

for fonts, 366

for macros, 237

for Notepad files, 99–100

for PIF files, 313–315

in title bars, 12

negative numbers, currency formats for, 278–279

nesting macros, 244

NetRoom program, 402

NETWARE.INI file, 289

networks

Calendar on, 155

Control Panel for, 288–289

disk commands on, 78–80

printing on, 373–374

refreshing files on, 88

searching for files on, 69

[network] section in WIN.INI, 439

nonsequential lists of files, selecting, 71–72

Norton Desktop for Windows, 415–416

Notepad, 97–98

ASCII text with, 100–101

creating files in, 99–100

exchanging Write data with, 127–128

highlighting and word wrap with, 108–109

menus for, 131

printing in, 105–108

tools for, 101–105

numbers, formats for, 279–280. *See also* Calculator

O

Object Packager, 346–349, 351–352

octal numbers, 140, 142–143

OEM fonts, 362

OLE (object linking and embedding), 339, 449

with Cardfile objects, 165

copying files with, 65–66

embedding objects with, 340–343

future of, 417

linking objects with, 129, 343–345

Object Packager for, 346–349

Paste commands for, 345–346

with sound, 384–386

with Write, 129

opening

Directory windows, 61

graphic files, 199–201

Notepad files, 101–102

sound files, 380, 387

Write files, 110–111

optical mouse, 3

option buttons, 20

Options menu

for Calendar, 170

for File Manager, 95

for Paintbrush, 205

for Print Manager, 376

for Program Manager, 49

for Recorder utility, 247

order of print jobs, 372–373

orientation

with printing, 275, 357, 370

with Write, 125

original shell, 409–410

OS/2, printer ports for, 273

Out of Memory error message, 308

P

packaged icons, 346–349

page breaks in Write, 124

page layout

in Notepad, 105–106

in Write, 122

page numbers, 106, 155
Paintbrush, 175–176
    converting graphic files with, 202
    editing with, 189–197
    importing files with, 197–202
    menus for, 204–205
    printing with, 202–203
    saving files with, 201–202
    special effects with, 192–195
    starting drawings with, 177–181
    tools for, 181–189
paint roller tool, 183–184
Palette Manager, 255
palettes, 180–181, 252–256, 449
PAL files, 181
paper, 125, 274, 357
paragraph formatting with Write, 118–123
Paragraph menu for Write, 132
parallel ports for printers, 273
parentheses () with Calculator, 144–146
parity
    Control Panel for, 262
    for modems, 208, 210–211, 213
passwords for screen saver, 268–269
Paste command, 128, 333–338, 341, 345
Paste Link command, 344–346, 350
Paste Special command, 341, 344–346
pasting
    bitmap images, 198
    with Cardfile, 162–163
    graphics, 191–192
    with OLE, 333–338, 344–346
    and PIF files, 323
paths for program items, 43
PATH statement, 391
patterns, Desktop, 266–268
pbrush command, 175
PC Magazine, 412
PCX files, 198–199, 201–202, 449
pen computing, 420–421
performance
    and Desktop, 406–407
    disk caches for, 397–401
    and File Manager, 408–409
    freeing up memory for, 401–402
    and hard disk size, 417
    and icons, 405–406
    and memory, 391–396
    multiple configuration files for, 410–411
    and original shell, 409–410
    of printing, 371–372
    and program groups, 404–405
    and secret commands, 412–413
    and Super VGA, 411–412
    and swap files, 403
permanent swap files, 287–288, 403
personal information tools. See Calculator;
    Calendar; Cardfile; Clock
PgUp and PgDn keys, 56, 112
Phone menu for Terminal program, 231
phone numbers. See Cardfile; Terminal program
Pick menu for Paintbrush, 205
pick tool, 191–195
PIF (program information files), 305–306,
    311, 429–430, 449
    creating and editing, 312–324
    and DOS icons, 405–406
    for groups, 328–330
    menus for, 331
    and speed, 327
pitch, 360, 364
pixels, 178, 449–450
plus signs (+) in Directory windows, 57, 81
pointers, 2, 450
    I-beam, 15, 21, 98, 103–104, 189, 448
    moving, 9–10, 449
    sizing, 7–8, 451
points, 117, 359–360
polygon tool, 188–189
portrait orientation
    with printing, 275, 357, 370
    with Write, 125
ports, 450
    for Cardfile, 165
    contention for, 284–285
    Control Panel for, 262–263
    for modems, 207, 210, 262
    in PIF files, 318, 322–323

for printers, 273
for sound, 283
[ports] section in WIN.INI, 438
PostScript printers, 273
prerecorded sound, 420
printer control languages, 355
[PrinterPorts] section in WIN.INI, 438
printing, 355
    appointments, 154–155
    with Cardfile, 165
    configuring printers for, 273–274
    controlling jobs for, 372–375
    Control Panel for, 271–276
    files, 66, 375
    fonts for, 117, 359–367
    graphics, 367–368, 370
    installing printers for, 272–273, 356–357, 367
    with multiple printers, 358–359
    with Notepad, 105–108
    with Paintbrush, 202–203
    performance of, 371–372
    ports for, 262, 273
    printer setup options for, 274–275
    settings for, 356–358
    special characters, 368–369
    spooler for, 275–276
    with Terminal, 215–216
    troubleshooting, 369–371, 424
    with Write, 124–127
Print Manager, 275–276, 356, 372–376
priorities in PIF files, 321–322
PROGMAN.EXE file, 328, 406
PROGMAN.INI file, 48
program groups, 31, 404–405
    arranging, 406–407
    creating, 46–47
    moving and copying items between, 45–46
    multiple, 34–35
    running programs in, 37–40
    saving, 48
    startup, 47–48
    working with, 32–37

program items, 40
    deleting, 45
    for DOS programs, 41–44
    moving and copying, 45–46
    properties of, 32, 40–41, 44, 48
Program Manager, 1, 310–311
    File Manager for, 92–93
    menus for, 49
    minimizing, 3–5
    for program groups, 31–40, 45–48
    for program items, 40–45
    saving settings for, 48
programmer options with Calculator, 142–143
programs
    associating files with. *See* associations between files and programs
    closing, 326–327
    creating, 418
    DOS. *See* DOS programs
    finding, 38–40
    listing, 84
    loading, 295–296
    with macros, 243–244
    running, 15–21, 37–40, 88–92, 425–426
    switching, 318, 324–330
properties
    for files, 53, 75–76, 82
    for macros, 239–241
    for program items, 32, 40–41, 44, 48
proportional fonts, 225, 362
protected mode, 302, 450
protocols, communications, 210, 220. *See also* Terminal program
PrtSc key, 198
pulse code modulation, 379

Q

QEMM program, 304, 394, 402
quality of printing, 127, 275, 367, 447
question marks (?) with file names, 70–71, 74, 430–431
queues, printer, 373–374
quick formatting, 78

R

radians with Calculator, 144
RAM. *See* memory
RAM disks, 401–402
RAMDRIVE.SYS driver, 401–402
raster fonts, 362
read only files, 76, 155
Realizer program, 418
Real mode, 302, 450
Recorder utility, 235
    editing macro properties with, 239–241
    loading, 245–246
    loading macros with, 243–244
    managing files with, 244
    menus for, 247
    mouse movements with, 236, 241–242
    playing macros with, 238
    recording macros with, 237–238, 241–242
    saving and stopping macros with, 239
rectangles, 187
redialing with Terminal, 212
refreshing files, 88
renaming files, 67
repeat rate, keyboard, 280
replacing
    files, confirmation option for, 85
    Write text, 114
resolution
    of printing, 202–203, 275, 368, 370
    Super VGA, 411–412
Restore command with Cardfile, 161–162
restoring windows, 5–7, 450
reverse sound, 382
root directory, selecting, 57
ruler with Write, 122–123
Run dialog box, 15–16
running programs, 15–21, 37–40, 88–92, 425–426

S

sample files for Paintbrush, 177
sampling rates for sound, 379–380
saturation of colors, 258–259
Save Settings on Exit option, 59, 87

saving
    appointment schedules, 151
    Clipboard contents, 339
    color schemes, 257
    files, 28
    macro preferences, 242
    macros, 239
    Notepad files, 99
    Paintbrush files, 201–202
    program groups, 48
    sound files, 384
    Terminal settings, 214
    Write files, 111
scalable fonts, 118, 362–363, 370
Scale menu for Media Player, 389
schedules, appointment, 150–152
scheduling for multitasking, 285–287
Scientific mode with Calculator, 135–136
scientific notation, 139–140
scissors tool, 191
screen elements, color for, 252–253
screen exchange option in PIF files, 318
screen fonts, 362
screen saver, 265, 268–270, 318
scroll bars, 10–12, 225, 450
scroll boxes, 11–12
scrolling, 10–12, 214–215, 225, 450
searching
    for Cardfile information, 160–161
    for files, 68–69
    for help topics, 26–27
    in Notepad, 104–105
    for Write text, 113
Search menu
    for Cardfile, 172
    for Notepad, 131
secret commands, 412–413
section headings in INI files, 293–294, 296, 432–442
selecting
    in Directory windows, 56–57
    drawing tools, 181–182
    multiple files, 70–75, 430–431
    sound drivers, 283

selection cursors, 54–55

sequential lists of files, selecting, 71–72

serial ports, 262–263

    in PIF files, 318

    for printers, 273

server applications, 91, 340

Settings menu

    for Clock, 172

    for Control Panel, 298

    for Terminal program, 231

s function with Calculator, 142

shadow memory, 395

sharing data. *See* exchanging data

Shift key

    for drawings, 187–188, 194

    for file selection, 71

    for macros, 240, 245

shortcut keys, 16–17, 450

    for Clipboard, 335–336

    for macros, 237–238, 240–241

    for personal information tools, 168

    in PIF files, 317, 323–324

    for program items, 42–43

    for Terminal function keys, 226–229

short date form, 277

Show menu for Calendar, 169

Shrink & Grow option for graphics, 192,
    194–195

SIMM (Single-Inline Memory Module)
    packs, 403

size

    of disk caches, 399–400

    of drawings, 178–179

    of files, 53, 82

    of graphic files, 200–201

    of graphics, 129

    of print jobs, 373

    of sound files, 381–382

    of windows, 3–10

sizing grids, 270

sizing pointers, 7–8, 451

slanting graphics, 194

SMARTDRV.SYS file, 371–372, 397–401

smudge drawing effect, 183

snapping to grids, 270

software fonts, 117–118, 363, 365

solid colors, 257

sorting files, 83

sound, 379

    Control Panel for, 281–283

    cutting and mixing, 383–384

    embedding, 384–386

    with Media Player, 386–387

    prerecorded, 420

    recording, 384

    Sound Recorder for, 380–386, 388

    special effects for, 382–383

    with Terminal, 224

sound boards, 420

Sound Recorder, 380–386, 388

special characters, 368–369

special days with Calendar, 152–153

special effects

    for graphics, 192–195

    for sound, 382–383

Special Times with Calendar, 150–151

speed

    of macros, 241

    of mouse, 263–264

    of multitasking, 301

    and PIF settings, 327

    of printing, 374

splitting Directory windows, 82

spoolers, print, 275–276

squares, 187

standard deviation function, 142

Standard mode, 284, 302, 304–306, 451

    copying and pasting in, 336–337

    memory for, 392–394

    for PIFs, 313–315, 317–318

    printing in, 371

Standard mode (Calculator), 136

Starfield Simulation screen saver, 268

starting directory, 58–59, 316, 329

starting Windows, 1

Startup groups, 47–48, 155

static objects, 343

Statistics Box with Calculator, 136, 141–142
status
    of print jobs, 372
    of SMARTDRV, 400
status bar, 87
stop bits
    Control Panel for, 262
    for modems, 208, 210, 213
stopping macros, 239
straight line tool, 187
style, font, 86
subdirectories. *See* directories
Sum function with Calculator, 142
Super VGA, 411–412, 451
swap files, 287–288, 304–305, 308–309, 403, 451
switching
    between full screen and windows, 326
    programs, 318, 324–330
Symbol font, 189, 368
SysEdit utility, 289–292, 394–395
system clock for Calendar, 148
system disks, 78
system files, 76, 84–85
system fonts, 117, 260, 362, 451
system-halting errors, 424–425
SYSTEM.INI file, 263, 451
    backing up, 410
    [boot.description] section in, 440
    [boot] section in, 439–440
    and Control Panel, 249
    editing, 289–290, 292–294
    [keyboard] section in, 440
    multiple copies of, 411–412
    for Paintbrush, 178
    for sound drivers, 283
    system fonts in, 362
    [386Enh] section in, 441–442
system memory, checking, 91–92
System menus. *See* Control menus
system resources, 308–309, 451

T

Tab key
    in dialog boxes, 18
    in Directory windows, 56
    with help, 22
    with Notepad, 101–102
table format with file transfers, 220
tabs with Write, 121, 123
Task List, 38–40, 306–308, 310, 324–330
Task Manager, 451
telecommunications. *See* Terminal program
temporary files, 305
terminal fonts, 362
Terminal program
    dialing with, 212–214
    exchanging data with, 221–222
    function key shortcuts with, 226–229
    libraries for, 230
    menus for, 231–232
    preferences for, 222–226
    printing text with, 215–216
    scrolling text with, 214–215
    settings for, 207–212
    transferring files with, 216–221
text boxes, 21
text files, 430
    with Notepad, 100–101
    transferring, 216–220
Text menu for Paintbrush, 205
text mode, 323, 451–452
text tool, 189
thousands separators, 279–280
386 Enhanced mode, 302–306
    Control Panel for, 284–288
    copying and pasting in, 337–338
    memory for, 392–394
    for PIFs, 313–315, 318–324
    printing in, 371
    settings in, 325–326
[386Enh] section in SYSTEM.INI, 441–442
TIFF (Tagged Image Format File) format, 452
tiled windows, 14, 36–37, 61, 87, 307, 452
tilting graphics, 194
time
    Control Panel for, 281
    of file changes, 53, 82
    in headers and footers, 106, 155

international settings for, 278
in Notepad documents, 106–108
of printer jobs, 373
timeouts
with printers, 273–274
with Terminal, 212
timer mode for Terminal, 229
timeslices, 285–287, 321–322
title bars, 452
for active windows, 13
for moving windows, 9
names in, 12
titles in PIF files, 315–316, 329
to-do lists, 107
toolbar, 415–416
Toolbook program, 418
topics, help, 22–23, 26–27
tracking speed, mouse, 263–264
tracks, sound, 387
transferring files, 216–221
Transfers menu for Terminal program, 232
translating characters with Terminal, 226
Transmission Retry setting for printers, 274
Tree command, 80–81
Tree menu for File Manager, 94
trigonometric functions, 144–145
TRM files, 214
TrueType fonts, 118, 261, 361, 363–365, 370–371
[TrueType] section in WIN.INI, 438
TSRs, removing, 402
TurboComm program, 263
Turbo Pascal for Windows, 418
286 protected mode, 302
type, listing files by, 83–85
typefaces. *See* fonts

U
Undo command
for Cardfile, 161
for graphics, 195
updating linked objects, 344–345
uploading and downloading files, 216–221, 446, 452

upper memory, 391
utilities, 452

V
variables
in PIF files, 316
in SYSTEM.INI, 292–293
vector fonts, 362–363
vector images, 452
VGA, 452
video
and drawings, 178
drivers for, 426
memory for, 318, 395
PIF options for, 317, 322–323
viewing
Clipboard data, 339
files, with Terminal, 219
View menu
for Calculator, 170
for Calendar, 169
for Cardfile, 171
for File Manager, 94
for Paintbrush, 204
for Print Manager, 376
views
for Calendar, 148–150
for Cardfile, 159
for Directory windows, 81–85
for graphics, 196–197
virtual address space, 303
virtual memory, 287–288, 403
Visual BASIC, 418
volume names for disks, 77–78
volume, sound, 382

W
wallpaper, 200, 265–268, 452
warnings
with Calendar, 152–154
for device contention, 284–285
with Print Manager, 374–375
WAV files, 281–283, 379–381, 387

whole word searches with Write, 113
width
    of borders, 271
    of characters, 360, 364
wildcards, 68, 70–71, 74, 430–431
WIN command, 1
Window menu for File Manager, 95
windows, 453
    active vs. inactive, 13, 443, 448
    arranging, 14–15, 36–37, 61, 87, 307
    closing, 28, 317, 329
    document vs. application, 12–15
    with File manager, 87–88
    minimizing and maximizing, 3–7
    moving and sizing, 7–10
    restoring, 5–7, 450
Windows menu for Program Manager, 49
Windows programs
    multitasking, 310–311
    running, 425–426
    switching, 324–330
[windows] section in WIN.INI, 432–434
WINFILE command, 51–52
WINFILE.INI file, 59–60, 87, 92–93
WIN.INI file, 452
    for associations, 88–89, 295–297
    backing up, 410
    [colors] section in, 435–436
    and Control Panel, 249
    [Desktop] section in, 434–435
    [devices] section in, 438–439
    editing, 107–108, 289–290, 294–297
    [embedding] section in, 438
    [Extensions] section in, 435
    fonts in, 362, 366–367
    [fonts] section in, 438
    [FontSubstitutes] section in, 438
    [intl] section in, 436–437
    [mci extensions] section in, 438
    multiple copies of, 411–412
    [network] section in, 439
    [ports] section in, 438
    [PrinterPorts] section in, 438

    for printing, 271–272, 356–357
    for program groups, 404–405
    secret commands for, 412–413
    for sound drivers, 283
    for swap files, 403
    [TrueType] section in, 438
    [windows] section in, 432–434
WINOLDAP.MOD file, 304
word processors with INI files, 289–290. See also Notepad; Write
word wrap
    with Notepad, 108–109
    with Terminal, 218
work area, 453
workspace, 453
WRI files, 110
Write, 97
    character formats with, 114–116
    creating documents in, 110–111
    editing in, 111–114
    embedding objects with, 341–343
    embedding sound with, 384–386
    exchanging Notepad data with, 127–128
    graphics with, 128–129
    menus for, 132
    paragraph formatting with, 118–123
    printing in, 124–127

X

XGA (Extended Graphics Adapter), 453
XModem/CRC protocol, 220
XMS memory option in PIF files, 316–317, 322
Xon/Xoff flow control, 211

Z

zooming graphics, 196–197